Measurement of Stress,
Trauma, and Adaptation

Measurement of Stress, Trauma, and Adaptation

Edited by B. Hudnall Stamm, Ph.D., C.T.S.

Sidran
The Sidran Press
Lutherville, Maryland

Printed in the United States of America

Library of Congress Cataloging-in-Publication Data

Management of stress, trauma, and adaptation / edited by
B. Hudnall Stamm.
          p.   cm.
     Includes bibliographical references.
     ISBN 1-886968-02-0 (paper : alk. paper)
     1. Post-traumatic stress disorder.   2. Psychiatric
rating scales.   3. Adaptability (Psychology)   I. Stamm,
B. Hudnall
     [DNLM: 1. Stress Disorders, Post-Traumatic—
diagnosis.   2. Stress Disorders, Post-Traumatic—
psychology.   3. Psychiatric Status Rating Scales.
     4. Personality Inventory.   WM 170 M266 1996]
 RC552.P67M35   1996
616.85'21—dc20
DNLM/DLC
for Library of Congress   96-9819

Contents

Preface

I first conceived this project in 1991 and began work on it in 1992. Nothing in my previous experience would have warned me of what lay ahead. I could never have imagined the tumultuous and exciting history of this project, nor could I have guessed that there would be an explosion of instrument development. A quick review of the instrument-related information in the PILOTS database confirms what I knew, that there has been rapid and dramatic change in the measurement of PTSD and traumatic stress issues in the past 5 years.

The number of instruments listed in PILOTS that existed before 1992 (n=243) is basically equivalent to the number of instruments listed over the past five years (n=231). Limiting the search to include only the period from the beginning of "PTSD history" (1980) to the last full year before I began this book (1991) is even more revealing. Those 11 years produced one less reference than the 5 years that have passed while I have worked on this book. This rate of growth was not paralleled in the PTSD literature in general (n=2232, 1980–1991, compared to n=1867, 1992–1996).

With approximately 10,000 citations, PILOTS is arguably the most complete traumatic stress database in the world, but it tells only part of the story because it is based on published documents. From its inception, this book has focused on developing and continuing research. I have made an effort to search out instruments in process so that the knowledge that is being created can be shared. There are 98 instruments reviewed in this volume. Some of them may fade into the pages of history while others will emerge as strong contributions to our field. I wanted to make the information available, not to determine how it will be used or its potential value. I have left that task up to the reader.

The principle of this book is to promote sharing of information. From the instrument formats to the use of volunteer labor to produce it to the selection of a nonprofit press with a mission to share information, we have tried to keep the gates of science as open as possible. Thus, the reader is responsible for making decisions. With the able assistance of many colleagues, students, the National Center for PTSD, and my publisher, we have expanded the reviews to include as much information as we can imagine might be useful in making decisions about how to measure traumatic stress.

While it is exhilarating to have access to so much knowledge, the plethora of information places the reader willing to embrace this task of discernment at genuine risk of becoming lost, never to emerge from the boiling seas of expatiating science. Lest you think I jest, let me assure you I take this task seriously. In fact, this is where I have been very directive as an editor. My own research seeks understanding of underlying structures through structural analysis. In the most sincere (if a bit humorous) nod to Freud, I hope that my sublimation of my unconscious drives to organize the world are to the benefit of the reader who is at risk of being swept into the sea of information. But I would be remiss in my duties as editor if I claimed to be the reason for this book's existence. It exists for those who are in pain and ask our help.

Many people have volunteered large amounts of time and energy to this project. First, I must thank all of the contributors. I asked them to do a great deal of work, and I have returned to them many times over the years to get clarification on details, signatures, agreements, and references. Their dedication to the project and their work on their measurements are what has made this book a conceptual possibility if not reality.

The first "edition" of this book appeared at the Ninth Annual Meeting of the International Society for Traumatic Stress Studies at San Antonio, Texas, in the fall of 1993. At that time it was an elaborate handout for the ISTSS Research and Methodology Interest Group's Pre-Meeting Institute on measurement. The book was so popular that we sold 50 copies at the 1993 conference and then several hundred over the next 18 months; we released an expanded version in 1994. All of the labor to create the desktop published version was donated and the small amount of proceeds were donated to the ISTSS Research and Methodology Group, who housed the project.

In 1993, Tom Murtaugh, Director of Trauma Recovery Services at the DVA Medical Center at Perry Point, Maryland, introduced me to Esther Giller of The Sidran Foundation and Press. Sidran is a nonprofit organization dedicated to the dissemination of information about mental health, particularly in the areas of Dissociative Disorders and Traumatic Stress. While I considered other presses, it was easy to choose Sidran because it was consistent with my beliefs that the book should be produced as inexpensively as possible and that profit should not motivate the project. Over the past three years I have been thankful so many times for my decision to work with Sidran Press. Esther has been a professional publisher, a thoughtful and careful editor of the editor, a patient teacher about the ways of publishing, and most of all a friend. I could not be happier with my publisher and believe that this good relationship has improved the book because Esther has allowed me to be creative and innovative and at times, even ornery about how I wanted the final product to be. We have tried to maintain a balance between costs, quality, and the completeness of information. I am satisfied with the work that we have done.

This project has been squeezed into my spare time as a university professor. Moreover, it has been sandwiched between changes of universities, changes of student staff, and changes of computer formats. We have been working on it so long that we began with shareware on DOS-based 286 machines and ended with hypertext and Windows-based Pentiums! The paper files have expanded to fill all the available space in my office, and the computer manuscript and associated databases got so large that I carry the book around on a portable plug-and-play drive. In short, it is *big*.

Any big project has a bevy of students who have worked on it. I hope that this list is complete, for their help was invaluable. At the University of Wyoming, thanks go to the members of the Traumatic Stress Research Group in general and Ed Varra and Curtis Sandberg in particular. Ed worked as an associate editor on the early versions of the book and helped write the prospectus for this current book. With some sadness on both of our parts, we decided in 1994 that it would be best for Ed to pursue his other professional activities. Thank you, Ed; your contributions live on in this first published edition. At The State University of New York College of Oswego, the student members of the Traumatic Stress Research Group offered their input. Nichol Tuzzolo and Jessica Klusner both contributed in meaningful ways. Denise Jolly typed the bulk of the original 100 page-manuscript —mostly from handwritten forms! At The University of Alaska Anchorage, the book overtook the Traumatic Stress Research Group on more than one occasion. Those who worked on the book include Nancy Gaines, Paul Cornils, Sara Dewane, Madeline Ercolano, Heath Sandall, Joe Rudolph, and Gary Paul. Nancy and Sarah spent many hours working on the organization of the paperwork for this book. Joe, who worked with me at both SUNY-Oswego and The University of Alaska Anchorage, should be recognized for his ability to put up with me for the most years! As the senior student in the group, Joe often picked up administrative tasks in other areas, freeing me to work on this book. All of these students deserve not only my thanks for working on the book, but my thanks for covering my lapses and putting up with my distractedness while I was focused on the book.

I would also like to thank my friend and colleague, Dr. Beverly Jamison of Marymount University. Beverly, a professor of computer science, and I have learned to create "computer things" long distance. On the very last night before I mailed the final version of the manuscript to the publisher, my SQL-based computer program for indexing and I got into an argument. Ever willing and capable to solve a computer problem, Beverly sat with me— via the telephone—late into the night "training" the computer program to do what I wanted. Her closing comment to me was "Success! . . . proving once again that together we can do things that neither one of us knows how to do!" Thank you Beverly, for your confidence and your encouragement.

This book could not have existed without the help and support of my family. Multiple generations know the content all too well. My thanks go to four generations of strong women whose lives span nearly a century: to Clara, Barbara, Libbye, to Amy, and even to 3½ year old Megan who can use *Measurement of Stress, Trauma, and Adaptation* correctly in a sentence! One family member went beyond the call of family duty. Much of the detail work of tracking down publication agreements and copyrights was done by "the other Doctor Stamm," who is by training a historian. This faithful doctor spent years watching history pass by—reading every review multiple times and spending hours working with me to make the indexes and countless other tasks too numerous to list. I am glad that this edition of this book is finally out; it is high time to see if my family can hold a conversation without discussing the status of the "measurement book"!

Years ago I wrote in my master's thesis that any individual's work is actually the work of his or her community. Over the years of working on this book I have come to a new level of understanding of the truth of this statement. I am grateful to my community for their support, tolerance with my self-absorption, and their continuing love. Truly this is a work of many.

B. Hudnall Stamm, Ph.D.
St. Patrick's Day
17 March 1996
Eagle River, Alaska

How to Use This Book

This section tells you about each of the elements in the template and the underlying principles I was addressing when I designed the template. Please be aware that this information is subject to error or change. While we went through several years of painstaking editing and re-editing of the template itself and of each review, there were times when the information simply was not clear and I had to make my best guess. This is particularly true in the area of costs and copyrights; the whole area of intellectual property is changing rapidly. If you have *any* questions about information, it is best to correspond directly with the measure authors or contact persons. These people are the final word on their measurements.

The Template Elements

Title

This is the title of the instrument as it is commonly called in the literature. The measures are arranged in the book alphabetically for ease of location. The indexes list key words and then the instrument name. Thus, all citations in the book are referenced to the measure titles.

Type of Population

This section tells you what kind of population the instrument authors had in mind when they designed the measure.

Cost

This generally is blank. However, in some cases there are costs associated with the measures.

Copyright

This section gives you my best assessment of the information about the copyright. *Do not assume that this is a legal statement.* Always check with the measure authors for final confirmation. In general, you will find four categories of copyrights.

1. Copyleft

Perhaps unfamiliar to our readers is what we have called *copyleft*.

The concept of copylefting comes from computer shareware. With copylefting, you are free to make as many copies as you wish as long as (a) you do not change the product, (b) you do not sell it for profit, and (c) you do give credit to the author and the publication from which you took the material. You will find a *copylefting* statement on the reviews in this book and where complete instruments are included. This allows you to make copies legally for your work without having to track down the authors for their permission. This is what many people think of as public domain, although, as we understand it, copylefting is the more technically correct term under the current international understanding of copyright law.

2. United States Government Domain

Work produced while in the employ of the United States government cannot be copyrighted by an individual. The work is assumed to belong to the United States Government and as such belongs to the public. In the spirit of recognizing intellectual property, we have extended the copylefting concept to the US Government Domain measures. While you do not have to have permission from the authors to use the measures, we do ask that you use the modified copylefting statement with reference to the authors and this book.

3. Copyright remains with the author

In some cases authors have not *copylefted* their measures. In these cases, the measures are copyrighted by the authors and you must obtain the written permission of the authors to use and/or make copies of their instruments. It is always important to contact an author if you have any doubts about the legalities of using their work. It is also always correct to reference the author when using their instrument, talking about their instrument, or modifying their instruments.

4. Commercial Copyright

Some of the instruments in this book are commercially copyrighted. In these cases, the authors have signed over their copyright to a for-profit or non-profit publisher or to a journal or book. In order to use such measures, you must obtain permission from the publisher of the instrument. Again, if in doubt, check with the author of the measure; they will be able to direct you to the holder of the copyright.

Languages

This line tells you if any instrument has been developed or translated into languages other than English.

What it Measures

This section tells you what the measure authors believe their instrument measures. It is not necessarily a statement of content validity, but it is at least a statement of *content intent*. You will find that some reviews give a great deal of information here while others provide very little.

Measure Content Survey, Procedure, or Process

This section tells you how the measure works. It is similar to the procedure section of an APA style paper, although it is often less formal.

Theoretical Orientation

This section contains information about the theoretical underpinnings of the measure. You will find a variety of information here, from "no theoretical perspective" or "a-theoretical" (e.g. *DSM*), to long descriptions of the theory from which the measure flows. Some reviewers do not include this material: theory varies in importance to people who develop measures.

Time Estimate

This section gives you an estimate of the time it takes to administer and score the measure. In many cases we did not have access to exact information and had to estimate these figures. Consequently, you will find a rather broad time range. We have also tried to err on the side of being overly long. All figures are reported in minutes.

Administration	Scoring

Equipment Needed

This section gives you information at a glance concerning the type of equipment you will need to administer the measure. In most cases paper and pencil or pen is all you need. In other cases you may find that you need multimillion dollar laboratories! Please note that "specialized equipment" can refer to anything from a VCR to colored pencils. In the case where a computer is required to administer the measure, information about the operating system and the minimum system requirements necessary to complete the task is included.

Paper & Pencil	Computer	Basic Psycho-physiological	Specialized Equipment

Psychometric Maturity

This is one of the few sections where I exercised editorial discretion. I asked the reviewer/authors to place their instruments but I reserved final judgment to me. I determined the classification based on the following:

1. Under Construction

This indicates that little psychometric information exists for an instrument or that the review suggests psychometric evaluation is underway. In a few cases when the basic information is available but for a very limited sample, I classified the measure as under construction.

2. Basic Properties Intact

Most instruments are classified here. At the minimum, instruments in this section generally have at least one study of their psychometric properties, and have at least one journal article or several conference papers on the scale or use of the scale. At the other end of the scale, these instruments may have many studies and scores of journal articles by the same basic research team.

3. Mature

Instruments in this section have passed the test of converging lines of evidence regarding their psychometric properties. In order to be classified as mature, a measure must have basic information about its psychometric properties available. Moreover, it must have multiple peer-reviewed articles by different people. In sum, these instruments demonstrate construct validity. Because our field is so young, very few instruments have had time to be used sufficiently often to have the ability to demonstrate construct validity.

Under Construction	Basic Properties Intact	Psychometrically Mature

Psychometric Properties Summary

This section contains a summary of the basic psychometric information about the measure. You will find a variety of information here, from "to be established" through elaborate data regarding reliability, stability, validity, specificity, longitudinal applications, structural analysis (factor or principle components), as well as convergent and discriminant validity. In some cases, there are references to available norms.

Particular Sensitivity

This section is in part an outgrowth of combining work between this book and the National Center for PTSD at White River Junction, Vermont. You will notice that most of these questions generally do not get asked regarding instruments. However, we all decided that we *should* be asking these questions. Thus, we have flagged them as important. In nearly all cases, the boxes have question marks, indicating the fact that we just do not know what the effect of using the instrument in these settings might be. However, in some cases, instruments are actually designed to accommodate these areas. For example, you will find at least two instruments that ask about rural life, farming, geography, and climate. It is my desire that future editions of this book will contain more information about these and other areas to which we should pay particular attention.

Age	Change across time	Culture/ Ethnicity	Gender	Geography/ Climate	Sexual Orientation	Socio-economic Status	Urban Rural

Estimate of Number of In-Process Studies

Because this book was an outgrowth of my frustration with locating the instruments that were becoming the standards in our fields *while they were emerging*, I asked people to clue us in on how many studies were in process. In some cases, the author/reviewer did not have access to this information. In others, they knew quite well how many studies were in process. The measures with larger numbers of studies are more likely to emerge in the literature in the next several years. Although this is not a statistically tried method, it is a good indicator of the number of articles which might be published in the near future.

Unpublished References

Many of the most important papers about new measures and theories are presented at conferences or are unpublished manuscripts which are circulated via mail and e-mail. This section can assist the reader to track down the unpublished references. It is also another opportunity to prognosticate how many journal articles might appear in the near future.

Published References

This section refers to peer-reviewed journal articles, book chapters, books, and, in some cases, test manuals. It is generally an exhaustive (current to spring 1996) list of the articles that the reviewer or author believes are related to the measure.

General Comments

This section may be blank or contain a variety of information. It often tells of the author's special requests for participants in studies, of computer programs that may be available for scoring, or of important caveats regarding use of the measures.

Key Words

These words are cross-referenced to the index tables in this book as well as to the PILOTS database. I also included the list of terms that the International Society for Traumatic Stress Studies uses in its membership database. While reviewers suggested terms, in many cases I assigned the terms based on my knowledge of the field and of the instrument. I cannot say that I feel completely happy with the list. It is not exhaustive. It is not, perhaps, even very complete. However, I do hope that you find it helpful in your searching for the right instrument. Any errors here should be attributed to me, not to the reviewers or measure authors.

Population	Stressor	Topic

Reference Citation for This Review

This book is intended to serve as a common source reference for measurement in the traumatic stress field. It is my hope that people will be able to use this book as a guide for completing method sections in scientific papers. To that end, here is a suggested form for the reference in a scientific paper.

Author, A. N. (1996). Psychometric review of an instrument. In B. H. Stamm (Ed.), *Measurement of Stress, Trauma, and Adaptation*. Lutherville, MD: Sidran Press.

Measure Author Name

This section contains information about the measure authors. In some cases you will find no information. This generally means that the reviewer/contact person is the author. You may also find a list of names. This may mean credit is being given to the authors but they are not the main contact person(s). In other cases, authors have indicated to us that they wish to have their addresses included so that they can be contacted.

Measure Contact Name

This section contains information about whom to contact regarding the instrument. These people have indicated that they wish to serve as a contact person and to have their addresses and e-mails listed. In my experience, e-mail is often the easiest and the least frustrating means of obtaining information.

A Process Approach to the Scientific Method[1]

B. Hudnall Stamm, Ph.D.
Traumatic Stress Research Group
Psychology Department,
University of Alaska Anchorage

Stephen L. Bieber, Ph.D.
Department of Statistics
University of Wyoming

Introduction

For even the most experienced researchers, remembering why you started a research project and what you intended to find in the process can become blurred in the flurry of the details of doing research. This underscores the importance of the development of a well-delineated plan for the entire project *before* the data are collected. In fact, we believe that the main body of work on any project should be completed before the data collection. This means that the questions, the variables, and the analyses should be clearly in mind, as should the expected outcome and the theoretical reasons for that outcome, before any data are collected.

Because it is not common to find *the* answer to your questions in a single research project, we advocate a process approach to the scientific method: (a) delineate a research plan, (b) collect the data, and (c) use the plan as a project touchstone to be followed and modified throughout the research process.

This chapter has been developed from our consulting work with beginning to postgraduate students and with professionals in fields as diverse as traumatology, psychology, medicine, education, botany, history, economics, ecology, exercise physiology, biomechanics, marketing, geology, sociology, physics, and more. We are including it here, in this book of measures, to assist you in thinking about your research planning as you search for instruments. While it was originally designed as a research model, it can easily be adapted to a clinical model when systematic inquiry in individual assessment is the goal. In this situation, the patient becomes the identified subject and the questions of interest are the assessment referral questions. We routinely use it in our own research and in our teaching and find it successful and helpful. We hope that you will find it similarly helpful. You will also notice that it is not completely unique but flows naturally from the most basic principles of the scientific method.

A Process Approach to the Scientific Method

Interesting questions present themselves to us nearly every day. In the sciences, when we choose to take up a systematic inquiry of one of these questions, gathering our theoretical thoughts and then testing them in the context of a collection of data, we are following the scientific method. The scientific method is simply the systematic inquiry of a question using a collection of data to assess the support for one's ideas. In its basic form, it is a simple method of thinking, not a magic bullet nor a panacea. However, when approached iteratively, as a process of inquiry and not as the producer of Truth with a capital T, it is a valuable tool for the scientist.

[1] An earlier version of this chapter was presented at the Eighth Annual Meeting of the International Society for Traumatic Stress Studies, Los Angeles, CA, 21–25 October, 1992.

Fig. 1   **A Process Approach to the Scientific Method**

1. Consider what is known
    a. theory
    b. previous research
2. Formulate Question of Interest based on theory
    a. identify a priori assumptions
    b. identify a priori expectations
3. Design method to test a priori expectations
    a. expectation stated in terms of the variables
    b. operationalize variables
    c. select tests or methods
    c. identify population(s)
    d. sampling plan

4. Collect data
5. Analyze data
    a. a priori tests: planned tests
        1. generalize beyond data
    b. a posteriori tests: unplanned tests
        1. data dependent
6. Interpret Results
    a. reconnect numbers to word meanings
7. Questions of interest for future research
    a. cycles back to beginning
    b. ideas from a posteriori tests

Step One: Consider What Is Known

For a researcher, even before you realize that you are beginning the research process, a question begins to percolate to the surface of your mind. This leads you to the first step of the scientific method as presented here: *Consider what is known.* This search into what is known usually passes through the printed and electronic literature and conversations with others in the field, but ultimately it must pass through some type of explanatory theory. It is the theory that brings your thoughts together and incorporates the information from previous research and with your speculation. While it is important to consider well what others have found in similar and cognate research, in the end, it is your own understanding of your field and the processes of inquiry you use that provides the context for making meaning from your research.

Step Two: Formulate the Question of Interest

As you gain clarity in your understanding of the issues, and you begin to speculate on what should happen in a given situation, the *Question of Interest* begins to take shape. In order to be most useful, the Question of Interest should be compact and directly stated. In many complex research applications, however, the Question of Interest may be quite broad and is often not testable in its stated from. But, as the theoretical process continues, it becomes clear that the Question of Interest usually contains within it several smaller and more manageable questions. These smaller questions, which are often stated as propositions, become your *a priori expectations*. You will also probably become aware that you have a set of *a priori assumptions* that are entwined with your a priori expectations.

At this point, it is important that your articulate clearly these a priori assumptions and a priori expectations—they are the guiding principles and the limitations of your research. You can try to answer those questions that you ask, but, you must also remember that you bring with the questions their boundaries of applicability.

The importance of the questions of interest, the sub-questions, and their a priori expectations cannot be over stated. It is from this set of statements that the statistically testable questions will grow and from which the project—and by implication, the analysis—will take shape.

Step Three: Design a Method with Which to Test

Once the a priori assumptions and expectations are articulated, the next step is to design or select a method of measurement with which to test these small questions in the context of the assumptions being made. Five elements are necessary here, although the order of addressing them shifts as the process continues. More often than not, a sort of pentatic tinkering occurs among the five as changes in one necessitate changes in the others.

The five elements that make up the Design part of the process are (a) restatement of the a priori expectations[2] in terms of the variables, (b) operationalization of the variables, (c) selection of the tests or methods of measurements, (d) identification of the population of interest, and (e) the sampling plan. At times it is easier to begin with the refinement of the a priori expectation, as it may lead

---

[2] The reader will note that we avoide the use of the term hypothesis in this paper. Because of its broader applicability, we have chosen the term *a priori expectation,* of which hypothesis is one form.

directly to the identification of the variables that then obviate the choice of tests or measurement methods. For example, if our a priori expectation is:

PTSD depends on *child sexual abuse* and *poverty,*

it is immediately obvious that *child abuse, poverty,* and *PTSD* are all variables. The task at this point is to define, or operationalize, each variable. A variable is an observable manifestation of the theoretical construct which we cannot observe directly. Variables are used to help give us information about the constructs we are trying to measure. Sometimes the simplest way to operationalize a variable is to define it by a particular method of measurement. For example, PTSD could be defined by a person's score on the Impact of Events Scale—Revised (see page 186) or it might be defined as a score on the PK Scale (see page 238). In either case, the definition would differ somewhat but would reflect a convergent concept.

At other times, it is appropriate to define the variable and then seek a method to measure the researcher's definition. For example, perhaps a research team is working with a subsistence culture that has no substantial cash economy, such as can be found among some Alaska Native communities. While there are well-established income-based measures of socioeconomic status that could be appropriate for an urban culture, these measures would not reflect accurately the status of the people in this study.

A third commonly encountered problem in defining variables in trauma research is in the ambiguity of the definitions of terms used throughout the field. For example, addressing the final variable above, child sexual abuse, what does "child" mean? It is clear that there is no universally accepted definition of this term. However, it is important that you understand your chosen definition and what implications it might have in the analysis process. A good example of this can be seen in the prevalence rate of child sexual abuse. As the age of inclusion in the definition of "child" increases, so too do the prevalence rates of sexual abuse. This is logically intuitive, since there are there more years of a person's life covered, which increases the probability of the occurrence of any experience. Thus, the population of interest and the sampling plan become part of the definition of the variable. While there is no right or wrong in setting the definition, it does affect the statistical outcome of the project and, perhaps more importantly, the interpretation

of the meaning of the data. As this example illustrates, the definition of the variable, the population of interest, and the sampling method may be part of a whole.

It is important to return here to the first facet of this step of the process. The restatement of the Question of Interest or its subset, the a priori expectation, cannot be overemphasized. It is important to keep these statements simple and made in terms of the variables, because the analyses proceed from these relatively innocuous statements. In fact, these simple statements contain the vital information necessary to direct the researcher to a particular type of analysis (Stamm & Bieber, 1996).

Step Four: Collect Data

We believe that data collection should proceed only after one has defined the variables and the questions and expectations. The questions and expectations, of course, should be stated in the terms of the variables (in the context of the population of interest and the sampling plan). As this is a brief paper focused on the overall process, we will not discuss the data collection process, but assume that this is done appropriately in the context of the plan that has been set forth.

Step Five: Analyze Data

This step is simply following through on what has already been planned long before the data are collected. It is perhaps the most mechanical of the steps. All of the planning that was done in Steps 1–3 is played out here. The refinement of the a priori expectation or Question of Interest will lead the researcher to a particular class of analyses. Granted, there may be difficulties in several areas. For example, potential problems sometimes occur in encoding data without losing qualitative meaning, or even in writing computer code to accomplish the actual analysis. However, if you understand the questions you have asked and the type of variables you are using, then you will be able to articulate your needs to a team member who has computer programming skills.

A key aspect to understanding the scientific method as a process is knowing the difference between theory-driven analyses and data-driven analyses. If a researcher has well-planned, theory-driven a priori expectations, the analysis will provide a clear answer to the Question of Interest. This is most recognizable as the yes/no aspect of simple hypothesis testing. For example, let us take up again our previously posed question, does PTSD depend on child sexual abuse and poverty? If the data support the statement at a statistically significant level, the researcher concludes, yes, there is evidence to suggest that the development of PTSD depends on child sexual abuse and poverty. If the data do not return a significant statistic, the researcher concludes that there is insufficient evidence to suggest that sexual abuse and poverty cause PTSD. In theory-driven research, the researcher develops their expectations as part of the theory-driven thought process. This is done before seeing any of the data collected, so that there is no attachment to any particular set of data. Because the expectation originated outside of the data, it is generalizable outside of the data.

On the other hand, there are times when the data themselves tell the researcher information and suggest questions. In this case, the expectation is driven by the data themselves and as such is not generalizable beyond these data in the current form, no matter how theoretically appealing the idea may be. But, this is not to say that these are not valuable bits of information. It is these bits of data-dependent information that become the fuel for future research, as will be discussed below in Step 7.

Step Six: Interpret Results of Data Analysis

Regardless of whether the information gleaned from the research is theory- or data-driven, it is necessary to return it to its original metric, that is, to return the numbers to word meanings. This is perhaps the most critical step of the research process and, like everything else, is set into place in Steps 1–3. After you have given particular care and attention to understanding previous research and establish this in the context of explanatory theory, and you have carefully translated your theory to a measurable design, when the results appear, your response should be "yes, I can explain that result." Hopefully, there is evidence to support your a priori expectations and your response is an affirmation of the theoretical assumptions made at the beginning of your research. After all, this was the intent of your systematic inquiry: to provide evidence to support or refute the theoretical idea you proposed in your Question of Interest.

As mentioned earlier, at times the data themselves suggest questions. In the best of these situations, your response is one of interested bemuse-

ment—wondering to yourself why you did not think to pose the question a priori since it is so obvious to you now. If this is the case, the interpretation is relatively easy since the theory you proposed prior to your data collection would suggest such a result. On the other hand, there are times when the data suggest something entirely new or contradictory to the researcher's expectations. In this latter case, most likely either you have found something new to you or you have made a mistake. Regardless of the type of your data-driven a posteriori question, you are now poised for Step 7 and for truly making research a process.

Step Seven: Hypotheses for Future Research

Your a posteriori questions can now be used to spawn a new project. From these a posteriori questions come the seeds for the next iteration of the research process. In practice, it is rare that one research project does not produce new questions. In fact, the far more common outcome of research is the production of a plethora of new and interesting questions. When research is addressed as an iterative process rather than as a series of independent projects, the body of work that builds over time provides ongoing adaptation to changing knowledge and technologies and supports necessary paradigm shifts. At the same time, such research stands secure in the development of its own construct validity.

Conclusion

In sum, considering the scientific method as a process, good research has an identifiable thread in the questions and in the variables, which runs through it from beginning to end. The earlier the thread is identified, the sturdier the research has a chance to become. Make a plan, follow it, adjust it where needed, but do not lose sight of the plan.

In order to avoid losing one's way, we advocate writing an analysis plan long before the data collection. This plan contains each of the study's questions in simple word forms, along with their variables, and the anticipated analysis. After the data have been collected and encoded you simply go down the list, accomplishing the proscribed analysis and recording the answer. In most cases, some additional analyses will present themselves a posteriori. Indeed, being clear-minded about your a priori ideas will likely enhance your ability to spot important bits of information that are apparent a posterior.

The critical step from the analysis back to the Research Question is the interpretation. Using this method, the interpretation is the combination of the statistical results within the theoretical support and limitations set by your assumptions made in Step 2 of the process. All of the difficult work that was done in formulating your questions and identifying your variables in a theoretical framework will make this task relatively simple. Moreover, the advantage of a priori expectations will be played out in the enhanced external generalizability of the research.

It is our belief that good planning and a knowledge of one's field leads to good decisions about research and the interpretation of your results. The process that we propose here—organized and grounded in theory as well as previous research—has value in that it can keep the actual research project on course. Moreover, the plan can serve as the proposal for a dissertation, grant application, or an Institutional Review Board's ethics review.

While we acknowledge the burden of theoretical work that is necessary to do research in this manner as opposed to simply collecting data, analyzing it, and looking for interesting results, we hope the promise of reduced research-induced stress makes it a viable option.

References

Stamm, B. H. & Bieber, S. L. (1996). Data analysis: Matching your question of interest to your analysis. In E. B. Carlson (Ed.), *Trauma research methodology*. Lutherville, MD: Sidran Press.

Weathers, F. W. (1996). Review of PK Scale of the MMPI and MMPI-2 Embedded and Stand Alone Versions. In B. H. Stamm (Ed.). *Measurement of Stress, trauma, and adaptation*. Lutherville, MD: Sidran Press.

Weiss, D. (1996). Review of the Impact of Events Scale, Revised. In B. H. Stamm (Ed.), *Measurement of stress, trauma, and adaptation*. Lutherville, MD: Sidran Press.

Using the PILOTS Database to Find Information on Assessment Instruments for Traumatic Stress

Fred Lerner, D.L.S.
National Center for PTSD
White River Junction, Vermont

The PILOTS database is an electronic index to the *Published International Literature on Traumatic Stress*. It includes references to several thousand publications on:

- post-traumatic stress disorder;
- other psychiatric disorders—especially dissociative identity disorder (formerly called multiple personality disorder), other dissociative disorders, or borderline personality disorder—associated etiologically or epidemiologically with exposure to a traumatic event, or to an event experienced as traumatic by the population under discussion;
- other mental health sequelae of such exposure.

The database contains over 10,000 bibliographical records and represents the world's largest bibliographic resource for traumatic stress studies. It is available to users worldwide and may be searched free of charge, with no account or password required. As part of the Dartmouth College Library Online System, the PILOTS database combines a user-friendly search interface with a powerful range of search commands, offering researchers, clinicians, and students—as well as librarians and other professional literature searchers—a shortcut to the traumatic stress literature.

Like most bibliographic databases, PILOTS provides a bibliographic citation of each paper it indexes, an abstract of its content, and a list of descriptors indicating its subject matter. In addition —and so far as we know this feature is unique to PILOTS—each record includes an "Instruments" field listing the psychological and medical assessment instruments used in the research or clinical work reported in the document.

This feature enables PILOTS database users to:

- determine which instruments were used in the work described in a particular paper;
- determine which published papers have used a particular instrument;
- locate papers whose focus is the description, validation, or use of a particular instrument.

The "PILOTS Database Quick Reference" below explains how to access and search the database.

To make searching for specific assessment instruments possible, we have established a standard form of the name of each instrument. This form represents, to the best of our knowledge, the official name of the instrument as given by its author or publisher. We attempt to use that form consistently, regardless of the form of name used by the author of a particular paper.

These standardized names are assembled in the *PILOTS Database Instruments Authority List*. This list includes all projective tests, self-report questionnaires, structured interviews, and other instruments that have been used in papers indexed in the PILOTS Database. Each entry includes:

- the name of the instrument;
- the surnames of its creators (this information is intended primarily to indicate which instrument is meant—there are several with similar names —and should not be taken as a definitive ascription of authorship);

- a bibliographic reference to one or more publications cited as the source of information on the instrument by those reporting use of it;
- a bracketed reference to the 5-digit PILOTS ID number of the document referenced or of the document citing it.

In addition, many entries also include a brief description of the nature of the instrument or its relationship to other instruments. There are also many cross-references, linking alternate names for instruments with the form used in the PILOTS database.

It should be understood that the *Authority List* does not purport to be a complete bibliography of psychological and medical assessment instruments used in traumatic stress work. We have not attempted to maintain the standards of accuracy and completeness that we hope characterize the PILOTS database itself. The bibliographic citations in the *Authority List* are taken without revision from a wide range of publications in the traumatic stress literature, and several years of experience has shown us that many writers give deplorably incomplete information about the instruments they use in their work. The *PILOTS Database Instruments Authority List* represents our best efforts at bringing consistency to a chaotic bibliographical environment without diverting our attention substantially from our primary mission: the indexing of the worldwide traumatic stress literature.

We would encourage anyone publishing an assessment instrument, a paper about the assessment of trauma or the effects of traumatic stress, or any other literature within the scope of the PILOTS database to send us a copy to ensure that it is indexed in the database. We also welcome corrections, suggestions, or comments from database users. Please address these to:

Dr. Fred Lerner, Information Scientist
National Center for PTSD (116D)
VA Medical Center
White River Junction, VT 05009
Telephone 802.296.5132
Fax 802.296.5135
FTS 700.829.5386 or 700.829.5135
Internet ptsd@dartmouth.edu

PILOTS Database Quick Reference

For more information on each topic, see the pages indicated by numbers in [brackets] in the *PILOTS Database User's Guide*. (See below to learn how to get a copy.)

Logging On by Modem [6]   Dial (603) 643-6310 for access at 2400 baud or less, or (603) 643-6300 for access at or above 9600 baud. When you see an prompt, type `c lib` and at the -> prompt, type SELECT FILE PILOTS

Via the Internet [7] Telnet to lib.dartmouth.edu and at the -> prompt, type SELECT FILE PILOTS

Searching the Database [11–13]   The PILOTS Database may be searched by any of the following indexes:

GENERAL	searches the entire article citation
AUTHOR	searches for author names
TITLE	searches for words in article titles
DESCRIPTOR	searches for descriptor words from the PILOTS Thesaurus
TOPIC	searches for words from the title, abstract, and descriptor fields
ABSTRACT	searches for words in the abstracts of articles indexed
AFFILIATION	searches for the author's institutional affiliation
FORM	searches for the form of publication
ID	searches for the article's unique PILOTS identification number
SOURCE	searches for book or journal title or for ISBN or ISSN
INSTRUMENTS	searches for names of test or measurement instruments used in the work reported in articles indexed

Use the FIND command along with the name or abbreviation of the index, and the word(s) you are looking for:

```
FIND AUTHOR FRIEDMAN, MATTHEW or
F AU SCHNURR, PAULA

FIND TITLE EYE MOVEMENT or
F TI RATIONAL PHARMACOTHERAPY
```

```
FIND DESC RECREATION THERAPY or
F DE EPIDEMIOLOGY

FIND TOPIC ENCOUNTER GROUP or
F TOP REHABILITATION
```

To find papers in which a specific instrument is used in the work reported, type FIND INST [NAME OF INSTRUMENT] using the name as listed in the *PILOTS Database Instruments Authority List,* or significant words from the instrument name.

To find papers on a topic connected with assessment, use one or more of the following descriptors, as appropriate:

Assessment
    Assessment Instruments
    Interview Schedules
    Projective Techniques
    PTSD Assessment Instruments
    Self Report Instruments
    Trauma Assessment Instruments
Biologic Markers
    Biochemical Markers
    Brain Imaging
    Neuroendocrine Testing
    Provocative Tests
Diagnosis
    Differential Diagnosis
    Medical Diagnosis
Nosology
    Diagnostic Validity
    History
Patient History

The levels of indentation indicate hierarchical relationships among these terms, as explained in *the PILOTS Database User's Guide* [25–29].

To find papers that discuss the use of a specific instrument (as opposed to those in which the instrument is merely noted as having been used), combine a search of the INSTRUMENTS index for the name of the instrument with a search of the DESCRIPTOR index for the descriptor(s) that describe the type of instrument. For example, to look for papers that discuss the use of the Mississippi Scale for Combat-Related PTSD, type

```
F INST MISSISSIPPI SCALE AND DE PTSD
ASSESSMENT INSTRUMENTS
```

The simple search command

```
FIND INST IMPACT OF EVENT SCALE
```

will retrieve citations to 330 papers in which that scale was used. A slightly more complex command

```
FIND INST IMPACT OF EVENT SCALE AND
DE ASSESSMENT INSTRUMENTS
```

will retrieve citations to 37 papers that discuss the use of that instrument. Those who prefer projective techniques to questionnaires will find 26 papers on that approach to assessment with the command

```
FIND DE PROJECTIVE TECHNIQUES
```

(These counts are taken from the January 1995 version of the database; the numbers will increase with each quarterly update.)

Use $ for truncation and ? for wildcard searching [17].

Displaying Your Search Results [20] Use the DISPLAY command to see what your search has retrieved:

> Type DISPLAY SHORT for the condensed single-line default display.
> Type DISPLAY MEDIUM for a concise bibliographical citation.
> Type DISPLAY LONG for an extended representation of the document, including abstract.

You may also type DISPLAY followed by the names or abbreviations of one or more fields.

Results are displayed in PILOTS ID number order. To see an alphabetical display, type SORT AUTHOR or SORT SOURCE and for a chronological display by year of publication, with the most recent material appearing first, type SORT YEAR (DESC).

If You Have Problems [22] If you are ever unsure about what you have just done, or what you can do next, simply type HELP and you will see a screen that explains your situation and may teach you some new ways of using the system.

Type EXPLAIN followed by a word or phrase (such as a command name) that you want explained. Or type EXPLAIN alone to see a list of terms for which explanations are available.

If your screen becomes cluttered with "garbage characters" or is otherwise unreadable, type CLEAN and it will be "painted" again so that you can read it.

Use the Break key to back out of what you are doing, or to stop the system from completing a command. (If you haven't got a Break key on your keyboard, read your communications software manual to see how to transmit a Break command. Many programs use control-C for this purpose.)

For Further Help or Information, call us at (802) 296-5132 during business hours (weekdays 08.00–16.30 Eastern time), or send email to ptsd@dartmouth.edu.

The PILOTS Database User's Guide

The PILOTS Database User's Guide is published by the U.S. Government Printing Office. Its 252 pages cover

- access to the database;
- developing your search strategy;
- the mechanics of searching;
- what's in a PILOTS record;
- modifying your search strategy;
- displaying your search results;
- how to obtain copies of materials found in PILOTS.

Sample searches are provided to help explain these points.

The bulk of the *User's Guide* is devoted to the PILOTS Thesaurus, the controlled vocabulary that we use to indicate the subject matter of the publications indexed in the database. This vocabulary is presented in two forms. A hierarchical table shows the eight general categories of descriptors (stressors, affected persons, effects, assessment, treatment, scientific research, policy issues, and literary formats). An alphabetical index includes not only the 800-odd PILOTS descriptors but also a large number of other words and phrases that database users might have in mind. The PILOTS Thesaurus makes searching more effective by taking advantage of the intellectual effort of the National Center's indexing staff.

We have sent a copy of the *User's Guide* to each medical library, Vietnam veterans' center, and specialized impatient treatment unit in the VA system. Copies are available for purchase from:

Superintendent of Documents,
U.S. Government Printing Office
P.O. Box 371954
Pittsburgh PA 15250-7954.

You may order by telephone (202-512-1800) or fax (202-512-2250) using a credit card (Visa or Master-Card). The stock number of the PILOTS Database User's Guide is 051-000-00204-1; the price is $19.00 including postage to U.S. addresses and $23–75 to foreign addresses.

The *User's Guide* is also available free of charge in electronic form, as either a Postscript document or an ASCII text file. Other National Center publications, including the *PILOTS Database Instruments Authority List* and back issues of the *PTSD Research Quarterly,* are also available electronically. To obtain these documents either

ftp to ftp.dartmouth.edu
    log in as anonymous
    go to directory /pub/PTSD

gopher to gopher.dartmouth.edu
    go to "Research Resources/
      Biological Sciences"
    find the PTSD directory.

In either case, be sure to look at the README file first.

(Note: during peak hours, currently 10.00–18.00 ET, Dartmouth places a limit on the number of simultaneous off-campus connections to these servers. If you cannot connect during these times, try again during off-peak hours. This limitation does *not* apply to the PILOTS database itself.)

The PILOTS Database Instruments Authority List

The *PILOTS Database Instruments Authority List* is available in paper or microfiche form from:

National Technical Information Service
Springfield VA 22161

Order using the NTIS Accession Number PB95-14222816. The price code is A06 for a paper copy and A02 for a microfiche copy; the current domestic prices are $27.00 and $12.50 respectively. Telephone orders are accepted at (703) 487-4650, fax orders at (703) 321-8547.

It is also available free of charge in electronic form, as either a PostScript document or an ASCII text file, from the same source as the *PILOTS Database User's Guide* (see above). In addition to the latest version of the *PILOTS Database Instruments Authority List*, an Addendum cumulates all additions, changes, and corrections since the *Authority List* was last revised. The Addendum is available in electronic form only.

World Wide Web Access

For World Wide Web access to the *PILOTS Database User's Guide,* the *PILOTS Database Instruments Authority List,* and other National Center publications, visit the Traumatic Stress Home Page at <http://www.long-beach.va.gov/ptsd/stress.html> or the National Center for PTSD website <http://www.dartmouth.edu/dms/ptsd/index.html>.

Measurement-Related Online Information: Expanding Your Information Access

Online access offers several ways by which you can gain more information about the materials in this book. The publisher, Sidran Press, maintains a website which contains information about the measures that are reviewed in this book. The website also includes information on making submissions for future editions of the book. Two other online resources are services of the National Center for PTSD: PILOTS (at White River Junction, Vermont) and The Library of PTSD Assessment Instruments (at Menlo Park, California). PILOTS is a searchable database of 10,000 references to traumatic stress. The Library of PTSD Assessment Instruments archives all of the templates and many of the instruments reviewed in this book. Both of these services are explained in more detail below. Using these three services, you will be able to find much about the past and future of measurement in the field.

Sidran Press

Sidran Foundation and Press is a publicly-supported, nonprofit organization devoted to advocacy, education, and research in support of people with psychiatric disabilities, particularly psychological trauma. Sidran Press publishes a number of books, instruments, and informative brochures on psychological trauma. Sidran also maintains an extensive database of trauma support and treatment resources Their website <http://www.access.digex.net/~sidran/index.html> includes updates on instruments available from the Library of PTSD Assessment Instruments. Furthermore, if you are interested in contributing reviews for future editions of this book, the website describes the submission requirements.

PILOTS

PILOTS is a searchable traumatic stress database maintained at The National Center for PTSD at The VA Medical Center, 116D, White River Junction, Vermont, 05001 <http://www.dartmouth.edu/dms/ptsd/index.html>. Among the 10,000 plus abstracts on PILOTS are articles on over 400 different instruments, many of which are reviewed in this book. The indexes in this book are keyed to the PILOTS database to help you cross-reference your search. For complete information on how to use the PILOTS database, please refer to the PILOTS chapter (page 10).

Library of PTSD Assessment Instruments

The National Center for PTSD at Menlo Park, California, maintains a Library of PTSD Assessment Instruments. This library archives all of the reviews contained in this book as well as many of the instruments. As a public service, the Library will send you up to three templates from this book as well as copies of instruments that the library archives. You can check the National Center for PTSD website <http://wwww.dartmouth.edu/dms/

ptsd/index.html> or the Sidran Foundation and Press website <http://www.access.digex.net/~sidran/index.html> for updated information on the status of available measures. You may also contact Joe Ruzek, Ph.D, at the National Center for PTSD, VA Medical Center, 3801 Miranda Ave., Palo Alto, CA 94394, <jir@iserver.icon.palo-alto.med.va.gov>.

Suggestions for Applications

Search Criteria: Copyleft or Government Domain, Any Traumatic Stressor

Good Candidates for Clinical Assessment and Diagnosis

Measure Name	*Qualitative Data*	*Quantitative Data*	*Assessment Instruments*	*Diagnostic Tools*
Child's Reaction to Traumatic Events Scale (CRTS)			X	
Civilian Version of the Mississippi PTSD Scale		X		X
Clinician Administered Dissociative States Scale		X		
Clinician Administered PTSD Scale (CAPS)			X	X
Clinician Administered PTSD Scale for Children (CAPS-C)			X	X
Compassion Fatigue Self Test		X		
Dimensions of Stressful Experiences (DOSE)	X	X	X	
Evaluation of Lifetime Stressors Questionnaire & Interview	X	X	X	X
IES Cognitive & Affective Scales		X		
Impact of Events Scale Revised		X		
Life Satisfaction Scale		X		
Life Stressor Checklist Revised			X	
Los Angeles Symptom Checklist		X	X	X
Penn Inventory for Post Traumatic Stress Disorder		X		X
PK Scale of MMPI & MMPI-2		X	X	X
PTSD Checklist		X		X
Stanford Acute Stress Reaction Questionnaire		X	X	X
Stress Response Rating Scale		X	X	
Stressful Events Content Analysis Coding Scheme	X			
Stressful Life Experiences Screening		X		
Structural Assessment of Stressful Experiences	X	X	X	
Structural Assessment of Telemedical Systems	X	X	X	
Trauma Symptom Checklist 33 & 40		X	X	
Traumatic Event Screening Instrument for Children		X		
Traumatic Event Screening Instrument for Parents		X		
World Assumption Scale		X	X	

Structured Interviews

Measure Name	Structured Interview	Qualitative Data	Quantitative Data
Clinician Administered Dissociative States Scale	X		X
Clinician Administered PTSD Scale (CAPS)	X		
Clinician Administered PTSD Scale for Children (CAPS-C)	X		
Dimensions of Stressful Experiences (DOSE)	X	X	X
Evaluation of Lifetime Stressors Questionnaire & Interview	X	X	X
Stressful Events Content Analysis Coding Scheme	X	X	
Structural Assessment of Stressful Experiences	X	X	X

Good Candidates for Research

Measure Name	Self-Report	Quantitative Data	Topic Research
Civilian Version of the Mississippi PTSD Scale	X	X	X
Compassion Fatigue Self Test	X	X	X
Evaluation of Lifetime Stressors Questionnaire & Interview	X	X	X
IES Cognitive & Affective Scales	X	X	X
Impact of Events Scale Revised	X	X	X
Life Satisfaction Scale	X	X	X
Los Angeles Symptom Checklist	X	X	X
Penn Inventory for Post Traumatic Stress Disorder	X	X	X
PK Scale of MMPI & MMPI-2	X	X	X
PTSD Checklist	X	X	X
Stanford Acute Stress Reaction Questionnaire	X	X	X
Stressful Life ExperiencesScreening	X	X	X
Structural Assessment of Stressful Experiences	X	X	X
Structural Assessment of Telemedical Systems	X	X	X
Trauma Symptom Checklist 33 & 40	X	X	X
Traumatic Event Screening Instrument for Children	X	X	X
Traumatic Event Screening Instrument for Parents	X	X	X
World Assumption Scale	X	X	X

Measures with Contact Names

Measure Name	Contact Last	Contact First
Adolescent Dissociative Experiences Scale	Armstrong	Judith
Angie/Andy Child Rating Scales	Praver & Pelcovitz	Frances & David
Assessing Environments III	Ford	Julian
Assessment of Psystress Via Salivary Ions	Hinton	John
Brief War Zone Stress Inventories	Ford	Julian
Child's Reaction to Traumatic Events Scale (CRTS)	Jones	Russell
Childhood Incest Questionnaire	Ford	Julian
Childhood PTS Reaction Index	Nader	Kathleen
Childhood PTSD Interview	Fletcher	Kenneth E.
Childhood PTSD Interview—Parent F	Fletcher	Kenneth E.
Childhood Trauma Questionnaire	Ford	Julian
Childhood Traumatic Events Survey	Ford	Julian
Children's Exposure to Community Violence	Ford	Julian
Civilian Version of the Mississippi PTSD Scale	King	Lynda & David
Clinician Administered Dissociative States Scale	Bremner	J. Douglas
Clinician Administered PTSD Scale (CAPS)	Weathers	Frank
Clinician Administered PTSD Scale for Children (CAPS-C)	Newman	Elana
Combat Stress Barometer	Shay	Jonathan
Common Grief Response Questionnaire	McNeill	Fran
Compassion Fatigue Self Test	Figley	Charles
Complex PTSD Interview	Ouimette	Paige
Computerized 16-Item Visual Analog Scale of Menstruation	Tseng	Hsu-Min
Concerns & Coping With HIV Scales	Jenkins	Sharon Rae
Cultural Messages Scale	Lebowitz	Leslie
Dimensions of Stressful Experiences (DOSE)	Fletcher	Kenneth E.
Dissociative Experiences Scale (DES)	Carlson	Eve Bernstein
Early Trauma Inventory	Bremner	J. Douglas
Evaluation of Lifetime Stressors Questionnaire & Interview	Krinsley	Karen E.
Family Disruption from Illness Scale	Ide	Bette
Family Experiences Survey	Ford	Julian
Farm Stressor Inventory	Heaney	Cathy
Farming/Ranching Stress Scale II	Ide	Bette
IES Cognitive & Affective Scales	Stamm	B. Hudnall
Impact of Events Scale Revised	Weiss	Daniel
Incest History Questionnaire	Courtois	Christine
Life Orientation Inventory	Neumann	Debra
Life Satisfaction Scale	Kopina	O.S.
Life Stressor Checklist Revised	Wolfe & Chrestman	Jessica & Kelly
Los Angeles Symptom Checklist	King	Linda

Measure Name	Contact Last	Contact First
Mississippi Scale for Combat-Related PTSD—Short Form	Fontana	Alan
Multidimensional Trauma Recovery & Resiliency Measures (MTRR—I&Q)	Harvey & Westen	Mary & Drew
My Worst (School) Experiences	Hyman	Irwin A.
National Women's Study Event History—PTSD Module (NWS)	Resnick	Heidi
NCVC Brief Screening for Assault	Resnick	Heidi
Nursing Perception of Distress	Montopoli	Delia
Parent Report of Child's Reaction to Stress	Fletcher	Kenneth E.
Parent Report of Post Traumatic Symptoms (PROPS)	Greenwald	Ricky
Penn Inventory for Post Traumatic Stress Disorder	Hammarberg	Melvyn
Peritraumatic Dissociative Experience Scale	Weiss	Daniel
PK Scale of MMPI & MMPI-2	Weathers	Frank
Potential Stressful Events Interview	Ford	Julian
Problem Rating Scale	Greenwald	Ricky
Psychobiological Assessment of PTSD	Friedman	Matthew J.
Psychological & Physical Maltreatment Scales	Ford	Julian
PTSD Checklist	Weathers & Ford	Frank & Julian
PTSD Inventory	Solomon	Zahava
Purdue PTSD Scale	Hartsough	Don M.
Quality of Life Barometer	Shay	Jonathan
Retrospective Assessment of Traumatic Experiences	Ford	Julian
Schillace Loss Scale	Schillace	Ralph
Schillace Post-Traumatic Vulnerability Scale	Schillace	Ralph
Schillace Trauma Scale	Schillace	Ralph
Secondary Traumatic Stress Disorder Scale	Figley	Charles
Sexual Abuse Exposure Questionnaire	Ford	Julian
Somatic Inkblot Series Test	Cassell	Wilfred
Spiritual Assessment Structured Interview	McNeill	Fran
Standards of Practice & Ethical Issues Questionnaire	Williams	Mary Beth
Stanford Acute Stress Reaction Questionnaire	Cardena	Etzel
Stanford Loss of Personal Autonomy	Ford	Julian
Stress Response Rating Scale	Weiss	Daniel
Stressful Events Content Analysis Coding Scheme	Stamm	B. Hudnall
Stressful Life Experiences Screening	Stamm	B. Hudnall
Structural Assessment of Stressful Experiences	Stamm	B. Hudnall
Structural Assessment of Telemedical Systems	Stamm	B. Hudnall
Structured Clinical Interview for DSM-IV Dissociative Disorders—Revised	Steinberg	Marlene
Structured Interview for Measurement of Disorders of Extreme Stress	Pelcovitz & van der Kolk	David & Bessel
Structured Interview(s) of Post-Disaster Adjustment	Freedy	John R.
Tough Times Checklists	Fletcher	Kenneth E.

Measure Name	Contact Last	Contact First
Trauma Assessment for Adults	Resnick	Heidi
Trauma History Questionnaire	Green	Bonnie L.
Trauma Reaction Indicators Child Questionnaire	Greenwald	Ricky
Trauma Symptom Checklist 33 & 40	Briere	John
Trauma Symptom Checklist for Children	Briere	John
Trauma Symptom Inventory	Briere	John
Traumagram	Figley	Charles
Traumatic Event Screening Instrument for Children	Ribbe	David P.
Traumatic Event Screening Instrument for Parents	Ribbe	David P.
Traumatic Memory Inventory	van der Kolk & Fisler	Bessel & Rita
Traumatic Stress Schedule	Ford	Julian
TSI Autonomy & Connection Scales	Stamm & Pearlman	B. Hudnall & Laurie
TSI Belief Scale Revision L	Pearlman	Laurie
TSI Life Events Questionnaire	Pearlman	Laurie
War-Zone Related PTSD Scale of the SCL-90-R	Weathers	Frank
Westhaven Secondary Trauma Scale	Ford	Julian
When Bad Things Happen Scale	Fletcher	Kenneth E.
Women's War-Time Stressors Scale	Wolfe	Jessica
World Assumption Scale	Janoff-Bulman	Ronnie
World View Survey	Fletcher	Kenneth E.

Estimated Copyright Status

Measure Name	Copyleft or Government Domain	Copyright Commercial	Copyright from Authors
Adolescent Dissociative Experiences Scale			X
Angie/Andy Child Rating Scales			X
Assessing Environments III			X
Assessment of Psystress Via Salivary Ions			X
Brief War Zone Stress Inventories	X		
Child's Reaction to Traumatic Events Scale (CRTS)	X		
Childhood Incest Questionnaire			X
Childhood PTS Reaction Index			X
Childhood PTSD Interview			X
Childhood PTSD Interview—Parent F			X
Childhood Trauma Questionnaire			X
Childhood Traumatic Events Survey			X
Children's Exposure to Community Violence			X
Civilian Version of the Mississippi PTSD Scale	X		
Clinician Administered Dissociative States Scale	X		
Clinician Administered PTSD Scale (CAPS)	X		
Clinician Administered PTSD Scale for Children (CAPS-C)	X		
Combat Stress Barometer	X		
Common Grief Response Questionnaire	X		
Compassion Fatigue Self Test	X		
Complex PTSD Interview	X		
Computerized 16-Item Visual Analog Scale of Menstruation		X	
Concerns & Coping With HIV Scales			X
Cultural Messages Scale			X
Dimensions of Stressful Experiences (DOSE)	X		
Dissociative Experiences Scale (DES)		X	
Early Trauma Inventory	X		
Evaluation of Lifetime Stressors Questionnaire & Interview	X		
Family Disruption from Illness Scale	X		
Family Experiences Survey			X
Farm Stressor Inventory	X		
Farming/Ranching Stress Scale II	X		
IES Cognitive & Affective Scales	X		
Impact of Events Scale Revised	X		
Incest History Questionnaire		X	
Life Orientation Inventory			X

Measure Name	Copyleft or Government Domain	Copyright Commercial	Copyright from Authors
Life Satisfaction Scale	X		
Life Stressor Checklist Revised	X		
Los Angeles Symptom Checklist	X		
Mississippi Scale for Combat-Related PTSD—Short Form	X		
Multidimensional Trauma Recovery & Resiliency Measures (MTRR—I&Q)			X
My Worst (School) Experiences			X
National Women's Study Event History—PTSD Module (NWS)			X
NCVC Brief Screening for Assault			X
Nursing Perception of Distress	X		
Parent Report of Child's Reaction to Stress			X
Parent Report of Post Traumatic Symptoms (PROPS)			X
Penn Inventory for Post Traumatic Stress Disorder	X		
Peritraumatic Dissociative Experience Scale			X
PK Scale of MMPI & MMPI-2	X		
Potential Stressful Events Interview			X
Problem Rating Scale			X
Psychobiological Assessment of PTSD			
Psychological & Physical Maltreatment Scales			X
PTSD Checklist	X		
PTSD Inventory			X
Purdue PTSD Scale			X
Quality of Life Barometer	X		
Retrospective Assessment of Traumatic Experiences		X	
Schillace Loss Scale			X
Schillace Post-Traumatic Vulnerability Scale			X
Schillace Trauma Scale			X
Secondary Traumatic Stress Disorder Scale			X
Sexual Abuse Exposure Questionnaire			X
Somatic Inkblot Series Test		X	
Spiritual Assessment Structured Interview	X		
Standards of Practice & Ethical Issues Questionnaire	X		
Stanford Acute Stress Reaction Questionnaire	X		
Stanford Loss of Personal Autonomy			X
Stress Response Rating Scale	X		
Stressful Events Content Analysis Coding Scheme	X		

Measure Name	Copyleft or Government Domain	Copyright Commercial	Copyright from Authors
Stressful Life Experiences Screening	X		
Structural Assessment of Stressful Experiences	X		
Structural Assessment of Telemedical Systems	X		
Structured Clinical Interview for DSM-IV Dissociative Disorders-Revised		X	
Structured Interview for Measurement of Disorders of Extreme Stress			X
Structured Interview(s) of Post-Disaster Adjustment			X
Tough Times Checklists			X
Trauma Assessment for Adults			X
Trauma History Questionnaire			X
Trauma Reaction Indicators Child Questionnaire			X
Trauma Symptom Checklist 33 & 40	X		
Trauma Symptom Checklist for Children		X	
Trauma Symptom Inventory		X	
Traumagram		X	
Traumatic Event Screening Instrument for Children	X		
Traumatic Event Screening Instrument for Parents	X		
Traumatic Memory Inventory			X
Traumatic Stress Schedule			X
TSI Autonomy & Connection Scales			X
TSI Belief Scale Revision L			X
TSI Life Events Questionnaire			X
War-Zone Related PTSD Scale of the SCL-90-R	X		
Westhaven Secondary Trauma Scale	X		
When Bad Things Happen Scale			
Women's War-Time Stressors Scale	X		
World Assumption Scale	X		
World View Survey			X

Measures by Types of Data

Search Terms: Qualitative Data, Quantitative Data, Discrete Data, Continuous Data, Longitudinal Data, Likert Data

Qualitative Data, also shows other data that may be available from instrument

Measure Name	Qualitative Data	Discrete	Continuous	Likert	Longitudinal
Combat Stress Barometer	X			X	
Dimensions of Stressful Experiences (DOSE)	X	X	X		
Evaluation of Lifetime Stressors Questionnaire & Interview	X	X	X		
Family Disruption from Illness Scale	X	X			
Farm Stressor Inventory	X				
Incest History Questionnaire	X				
Multidimensional Trauma Recovery & Resiliency Measures (MTRR—I&Q)	X				
My Worst (School) Experiences	X			X	
National Women's Study Event History-PTSD Module (NWS)	X	X		X	
Parent Report of Child's Reaction to Stress	X	X		X	
Potential Stressful Events Interview	X	X			
Somatic Inkblot Series Test	X				
Spiritual Assessment Structured Interview	X				
Standards of Practice & Ethical Issues Questionnaire	X			X	
Stressful Events Content Analysis Coding Scheme	X	X			
Structural Assessment of Stressful Experiences	X	X	X		X
Structural Assessment of Telemedical Systems	X	X	X	X	
Structured Clinical Interview for DSM-IV Dissociative Disorders—Revised	X	X			
Structured Interview for Measurement of Disorders of Extreme Stress	X	X			
Structured Interview(s) of Post-Disaster Adjustment	X				
Traumagram	X				
Traumatic Memory Inventory	X				
Traumatic Stress Schedule	X				
TSI Life Events Questionnaire	X				

Quantitative Data, also shows approximate type of data available

Measure Name	Quantitative Data	Discrete	Continuous	Likert	Longitudinal
Adolescent Dissociative Experiences Scale	X			X	
Angie/Andy Child Rating Scales	X			X	
Assessment of Psystress Via Salivary Ions	X		X		
Brief War Zone Stress Inventories	X			X	
Childhood PTS Reaction Index	X			X	
Childhood PTSD Interview	X	X			
Childhood PTSD Interview—Parent F	X	X			
Childhood Trauma Questionnaire	X			X	
Childhood Traumatic Events Survey	X				
Civilian Version of the Mississippi PTSD Scale	X			X	
Clinician Administered Dissociative States Scale	X		X	X	
Combat Stress Barometer	X			X	
Common Grief Response Questionnaire	X			X	
Compassion Fatigue Self Test	X			X	
Complex PTSD Interview	X	X	X		
Computerized 16-Item Visual Analog Scale of Menstruation	X		X		
Concerns & Coping With HIV Scales	X			X	
Cultural Messages Scale	X			X	
Dimensions of Stressful Experiences (DOSE)	X	X	X		
Dissociative Experiences Scale (DES)	X			X	
Early Trauma Inventory	X			X	
Evaluation of Lifetime Stressors Questionnaire & Interview	X	X	X		
Family Disruption from Illness Scale	X	X			
Family Experiences Survey	X				
Farm Stressor Inventory	X				
Farming/Ranching Stress Scale II	X			X	
IES Cognitive & Affective Scales	X			X	X
Impact of Events Scale Revised	X			X	
Life Orientation Inventory	X			X	
Life Satisfaction Scale	X			X	
Los Angeles Symptom Checklist	X			X	
Mississippi Scale for Combat-Related PTSD—Short Form	X			X	
Multidimensional Trauma Recovery & Resiliency Measures (MTRR—I&Q)	X				
My Worst (School) Experiences	X			X	
National Women's Study Event History-PTSD Module (NWS)	X	X		X	
NCVC Brief Screening for Assault	X			X	
Nursing Perception of Distress	X			X	

Measure Name	Quantitative Data	Discrete	Continuous	Likert	Longitudinal
Parent Report of Child's Reaction to Stress	X	X		X	
Penn Inventory for Post Traumatic Stress Disorder	X	X-Summed			
Peritraumatic Dissociative Experience Scale	X				
PK Scale of MMPI & MMPI-2	X	X-Summed			
Potential Stressful Events Interview	X	X			
Problem Rating Scale	X			X	
Psychobiological Assessment of PTSD	X				
Psychological & Physical Maltreatment Scales	X			X	
PTSD Checklist	X			X	
PTSD Inventory	X	X			
Purdue PTSD Scale	X			X	
Quality of Life Barometer	X			X	
Retrospective Assessment of Traumatic Experiences	X			X	
Schillace Loss Scale	X	X-Summed			
Schillace Post-Traumatic Vulnerability Scale	X	X-Summed			
Schillace Trauma Scale	X	X-Summed			
Secondary Traumatic Stress Disorder Scale	X	X			
Somatic Inkblot Series Test	X				
Standards of Practice & Ethical Issues Questionnaire	X			X	
Stanford Acute Stress Reaction Questionnaire	X			X	
Stanford Loss of Personal Autonomy	X			X	
Stress Response Rating Scale	X			X	
Stressful Life Experiences Screening	X	X	X		
Structural Assessment of Stressful Experiences	X	X	X		X
Structural Assessment of Telemedical Systems	X	X	X	X	
Structured Clinical Interview for DSM-IV Dissociative Disorders—Revised	X	X			
Structured Interview for Measurement of Disorders of Extreme Stress	X	X			
Structured Interview(s) of Post-Disaster Adjustment	X				
Tough Times Checklists	X			X	
Trauma Assessment for Adults	X				
Trauma History Questionnaire	X	X			
Trauma Reaction Indicators Child Questionnaire	X			X	
Trauma Symptom Checklist 33 & 40	X			X	
Trauma Symptom Checklist for Children	X			X	
Trauma Symptom Inventory	X			X	
Traumatic Event Screening Instrument for Children	X	X			
Traumatic Event Screening Instrument for Parents	X	X			

Quantitative Data, also shows approximate type of data available *(continuted)*

Measure Name	Quantitative Data	Discrete	Continuous	Likert	Longitudinal
Traumatic Memory Inventory	X				
Traumatic Stress Schedule	X				
TSI Autonomy & Connection Scales	X			X	X
TSI Belief Scale Revision L	X			X	
War-Zone Related PTSD Scale of the SCL-90-R	X			X	
When Bad Things Happen Scale	X			X	
Women's War-Time Stressors Scale	X			X	
World Assumption Scale	X			X	
World View Survey	X			X	

Any Stressor crossed with type of data

Measure Name	Quantitative	Discrete	Continuous	Likert	Longitudinal
Adolescent Dissociative Experiences Scale	X			X	
Angie/Andy Child Rating Scales	X			X	
Assessment of Psystress Via Salivary Ions	X		X		
Brief War Zone Stress Inventories	X			X	
Childhood PTS Reaction Index	X			X	
Childhood PTSD Interview	X	X			
Childhood PTSD Interview—Parent F	X	X			
Childhood Trauma Questionnaire	X			X	
Childhood Traumatic Events Survey	X				
Civilian Version of the Mississippi PTSD Scale	X			X	
Clinician Administered Dissociative States Scale	X			X	X
Combat Stress Barometer	X			X	
Common Grief Response Questionnaire	X			X	
Compassion Fatigue Self Test	X			X	
Complex PTSD Interview	X	X	X		
Computerized 16-Item Visual Analog Scale of Menstruation	X		X		
Concerns & Coping With HIV Scales	X			X	
Cultural Messages Scale	X			X	
Dimensions of Stressful Experiences (DOSE)	X	X	X		
Dissociative Experiences Scale (DES)	X			X	
Early Trauma Inventory	X			X	
Evaluation of Lifetime Stressors Questionnaire & Interview	X	X	X		

Measure Name	Quantitative	Discrete	Continuous	Likert	Longitudinal
Family Disruption from Illness Scale	X	X			
Family Experiences Survey	X				
Farm Stressor Inventory	X				
Farming/Ranching Stress Scale II	X			X	
IES Cognitive & Affective Scales	X			X	X
Impact of Events Scale Revised	X			X	
Life Orientation Inventory	X			X	
Life Satisfaction Scale	X			X	
Los Angeles Symptom Checklist	X			X	
Mississippi Scale for Combat-Related PTSD—Short Form	X			X	
Multidimensional Trauma Recovery & Resiliency Measures (MTRR—I&Q)	X				
My Worst (School) Experiences	X			X	
National Women's Study Event History— PTSD Module (NWS)	X	X		X	
NCVC Brief Screening for Assault	X			X	
Nursing Perception of Distress	X			X	
Parent Report of Child's Reaction to Stress	X	X		X	
Penn Inventory for Post Traumatic Stress Disorder	X	X-Summed			
Peritraumatic Dissociative Experience Scale	X				
PK Scale of MMPI & MMPI-2	X	X-Summed			
Potential Stressful Events Interview	X	X			
Problem Rating Scale	X			X	
Psychobiological Assessment of PTSD	X				
Psychological & Physical Maltreatment Scales	X			X	
PTSD Checklist	X			X	
PTSD Inventory	X	X			
Purdue PTSD Scale	X			X	
Quality of Life Barometer	X			X	
Retrospective Assessment of Traumatic Experiences	X			X	
Schillace Loss Scale	X	X-Summed			
Schillace Post-Traumatic Vulnerability Scale	X	X-Summed			
Schillace Trauma Scale	X	X-Summed			
Secondary Traumatic Stress Disorder Scale	X	X			
Somatic Inkblot Series Test	X				
Standards of Practice & Ethical Issues Questionnaire	X			X	
Stanford Acute Stress Reaction Questionnaire	X			X	
Stanford Loss of Personal Autonomy	X			X	
Stress Response Rating Scale	X			X	
Stressful Life Experiences Screening	X	X	X		

Measure Name	Quantitative	Discrete	Continuous	Likert	Longitudinal
Structural Assessment of Stressful Experiences	X	X	X		X
Structural Assessment of Telemedical Systems	X	X	X	X	
Structured Clinical Interview for DSM-IV Dissociative Disorders—Revised	X	X			
Structured Interview for Measurement of Disorders of Extreme Stress	X	X			
Structured Interview(s) of Post-Disaster Adjustment	X				
Tough Times Checklists	X			X	
Trauma Assessment for Adults	X				
Trauma History Questionnaire	X	X			
Trauma Reaction Indicators Child Questionnaire	X			X	
Trauma Symptom Checklist 33 & 40	X			X	
Trauma Symptom Checklist for Children	X			X	
Trauma Symptom Inventory	X			X	
Traumatic Event Screening Instrument for Children	X	X			
Traumatic Event Screening Instrument for Parents	X	X			
Traumatic Memory Inventory	X				
Traumatic Stress Schedule	X				
TSI Autonomy & Connection Scales	X			X	X
TSI Belief Scale Revision L	X			X	
War-Zone Related PTSD Scale of the SCL-90-R	X			X	
When Bad Things Happen Scale	X			X	
Women's War-Time Stressors Scale	X			X	
World Assumption Scale	X			X	
World View Survey	X			X	

Continuous Data (not Likert type)

Measure Name	Continuous
Assessment of Psystress Via Salivary Ions	X
Clinician Administered PTSD Scale (CAPS)	X
Clinician Administered PTSD Scale for Children (CAPS-C)	X
Complex PTSD Interview	X
Computerized 16-Item Visual Analog Scale of Menstruation	X
Dimensions of Stressful Experiences (DOSE)	X
Evaluation of Lifetime Stressors Questionnaire & Interview	X
Sexual Abuse Exposure Questionnaire	X
Stressful Life Experiences Screening	X
Structural Assessment of Stressful Experiences	X
Structural Assessment of Telemedical Systems	X

Discrete Data

Measure Name	Discrete
Childhood PTSD Interview	X
Childhood PTSD Interview—Parent F	X
Clinician Administered PTSD Scale (CAPS)	X
Clinician Administered PTSD Scale for Children (CAPS-C)	X
Complex PTSD Interview	X
Dimensions of Stressful Experiences (DOSE)	X
Evaluation of Lifetime Stressors Questionnaire & Interview	X
Family Disruption from Illness Scale	X
Life Stressor Checklist Revised	X
National Women's Study Event History—PTSD Module (NWS)	X
Parent Report of Child's Reaction to Stress	X
Parent Report of Post Traumatic Symptoms (PROPS)	X
Potential Stressful Events Interview	X
PTSD Inventory	X
Secondary Traumatic Stress Disorder Scale	X
Stressful Events Content Analysis Coding Scheme	X
Stressful Life Experiences Screening	X
Structural Assessment of Stressful Experiences	X
Structural Assessment of Telemedical Systems	X
Structured Clinical Interview for DSM-IV Dissociative Disorders—Revised	X
Structured Interview for Measurement of Disorders of Extreme Stress	X
Trauma History Questionnaire	X
Traumatic Event Screening Instrument for Children	X
Traumatic Event Screening Instrument for Parents	X

Likert Data

Measure Name	Likert
Adolescent Dissociative Experiences Scale	X
Angie/Andy Child Rating Scales	X
Assessing Environments III	X
Brief War Zone Stress Inventories	X
Child's Reaction to Traumatic Events Scale (CRTS)	X
Childhood Incest Questionnaire	X
Childhood PTS Reaction Index	X
Childhood Trauma Questionnaire	X
Civilian Version of the Mississippi PTSD Scale	X
Clinician Administered Dissociative States Scale	X

Likert Data *(continued)*

Measure Name	*Likert*
Combat Stress Barometer	X
Common Grief Response Questionnaire	X
Compassion Fatigue Self Test	X
Concerns & Coping With HIV Scales	X
Cultural Messages Scale	X
Dissociative Experiences Scale (DES)	X
Early Trauma Inventory	X
Farming/Ranching Stress Scale II	X
IES Cognitive & Affective Scales	X
Impact of Events Scale Revised	X
Life Orientation Inventory	X
Life Satisfaction Scale	X
Life Stressor Checklist Revised	X
Los Angeles Symptom Checklist	X
Mississippi Scale for Combat-Related PTSD—Short Form	X
My Worst (School) Experiences	X
National Women's Study Event History—PTSD Module (NWS)	X
NCVC Brief Screening for Assault	X
Nursing Perception of Distress	X
Parent Report of Child's Reaction to Stress	X
Parent Report of Post Traumatic Symptoms (PROPS)	X
Problem Rating Scale	X
Psychological & Physical Maltreatment Scales	X
PTSD Checklist	X
Purdue PTSD Scale	X
Quality of Life Barometer	X
Retrospective Assessment of Traumatic Experiences	X
Standards of Practice & Ethical Issues Questionnaire	X
Stanford Acute Stress Reaction Questionnaire	X
Stanford Loss of Personal Autonomy	X
Stress Response Rating Scale	X
Structural Assessment of Telemedical Systems	X
Tough Times Checklists	X
Trauma Reaction Indicators Child Questionnaire	X
Trauma Symptom Checklist 33 & 40	X
Trauma Symptom Checklist for Children	X
Trauma Symptom Inventory	X
TSI Autonomy & Connection Scales	X
TSI Belief Scale Revision L	X
War-Zone Related PTSD Scale of the SCL-90-R	X

Measure Name	Likert
When Bad Things Happen Scale	X
Women's War-Time Stressors Scale	X
World Assumption Scale	X
World View Survey	X

Qualitative Data

Measure Name	Qualitative
Combat Stress Barometer	X
Dimensions of Stressful Experiences (DOSE)	X
Evaluation of Lifetime Stressors Questionnaire & Interview	X
Family Disruption from Illness Scale	X
Farm Stressor Inventory	X
Incest History Questionnaire	X
Multidimensional Trauma Recovery & Resiliency Measures (MTRR—I&Q)	X
My Worst (School) Experiences	X
National Women's Study Event History—PTSD Module (NWS)	X
Parent Report of Child's Reaction to Stress	X
Potential Stressful Events Interview	X
Somatic Inkblot Series Test	X
Spiritual Assessment Structured Interview	X
Standards of Practice & Ethical Issues Questionnaire	X
Stressful Events Content Analysis Coding Scheme	X
Structural Assessment of Stressful Experiences	X
Structural Assessment of Telemedical Systems	X
Structured Clinical Interview for DSM-IV Dissociative Disorders—Revised	X
Structured Interview for Measurement of Disorders of Extreme Stress	X
Structured Interview(s) of Post-Disaster Adjustment	X
Traumagram	X
Traumatic Memory Inventory	X
Traumatic Stress Schedule	X
TSI Life Events Questionnaire	X

Quantitative Data

Measure Name	Quantitative
Adolescent Dissociative Experiences Scale	X
Angie/Andy Child Rating Scales	X
Assessment of Psystress Via Salivary Ions	X
Brief War Zone Stress Inventories	X
Childhood PTS Reaction Index	X
Childhood PTSD Interview	X
Childhood PTSD Interview—Parent F	X
Childhood Trauma Questionnaire	X
Childhood Traumatic Events Survey	X
Civilian Version of the Mississippi PTSD Scale	X
Clinician Administered Dissociative States Scale	X
Combat Stress Barometer	X
Common Grief Response Questionnaire	X
Compassion Fatigue Self Test	X
Complex PTSD Interview	X
Computerized 16-Item Visual Analog Scale of Menstruation	X
Concerns & Coping With HIV Scales	X
Cultural Messages Scale	X
Dimensions of Stressful Experiences (DOSE)	X
Dissociative Experiences Scale (DES)	X
Early Trauma Inventory	X
Evaluation of Lifetime Stressors Questionnaire & Interview	X
Family Disruption from Illness Scale	X
Family Experiences Survey	X
Farm Stressor Inventory	X
Farming/Ranching Stress Scale II	X
IES Cognitive & Affective Scales	X
Impact of Events Scale Revised	X
Life Orientation Inventory	X
Life Satisfaction Scale	X
Los Angeles Symptom Checklist	X
Mississippi Scale for Combat-Related PTSD—Short Form	X
Multidimensional Trauma Recovery & Resiliency Measures (MTRR—I&Q)	X
My Worst (School) Experiences	X
National Women's Study Event History—PTSD Module (NWS)	X
NCVC Brief Screening for Assault	X
Nursing Perception of Distress	X
Parent Report of Child's Reaction to Stress	X
Penn Inventory for Post Traumatic Stress Disorder	X
Peritraumatic Dissociative Experience Scale	X

Measure Name	Quantitative
PK Scale of MMPI & MMPI-2	X
Potential Stressful Events Interview	X
Problem Rating Scale	X
Psychobiological Assessment of PTSD	X
Psychological & Physical Maltreatment Scales	X
PTSD Checklist	X
PTSD Inventory	X
Purdue PTSD Scale	X
Quality of Life Barometer	X
Retrospective Assessment of Traumatic Experiences	X
Schillace Loss Scale	X
Schillace Post-Traumatic Vulnerability Scale	X
Schillace Trauma Scale	X
Secondary Traumatic Stress Disorder Scale	X
Somatic Inkblot Series Test	X
Standards of Practice & Ethical Issues Questionnaire	X
Stanford Acute Stress Reaction Questionnaire	X
Stanford Loss of Personal Autonomy	X
Stress Response Rating Scale	X
Stressful Life Experiences Screening	X
Structural Assessment of Stressful Experiences	X
Structural Assessment of Telemedical Systems	X
Structured Clinical Interview for DSM-IV Dissociative Disorders—Revised	X
Structured Interview for Measurement of Disorders of Extreme Stress	X
Structured Interview(s) of Post-Disaster Adjustment	X
Tough Times Checklists	X
Trauma Assessment for Adults	X
Trauma History Questionnaire	X
Trauma Reaction Indicators Child Questionnaire	X
Trauma Symptom Checklist 33 & 40	X
Trauma Symptom Checklist for Children	X
Trauma Symptom Inventory	X
Traumatic Event Screening Instrument for Children	X
Traumatic Event Screening Instrument for Parents	X
Traumatic Memory Inventory	X
Traumatic Stress Schedule	X
TSI Autonomy & Connection Scales	X
TSI Belief Scale Revision L	X
War-Zone Related PTSD Scale of the SCL-90-R	X
When Bad Things Happen Scale	X
Women's War-Time Stressors Scale	X
World Assumption Scale	X
World View Survey	X

General Use Areas

Measure Name	Dissociation	PTSD	DESNOS	General Clinical	General Non-clinical
Adolescent Dissociative Experiences Scale	X				
Angie/Andy Child Rating Scales		X		X	
Assessing Environments III				X	X
Assessment of Psystress Via Salivary Ions				X	X
Brief War Zone Stress Inventories				X	X
Child's Reaction to Traumatic Events Scale (CRTS)		X		X	
Childhood Incest Questionnaire				X	X
Childhood PTS Reaction Index		X		X	
Childhood PTSD Interview		X		X	
Childhood PTSD Interview—Parent F		X		X	
Childhood Trauma Questionnaire				X	
Childhood Traumatic Events Survey				X	
Children's Exposure to Community Violence					X
Civilian Version of the Mississippi PTSD Scale		X		X	X
Clinician Administered Dissociative States Scale	X				
Clinician Administered PTSD Scale (CAPS)		X			
Clinician Administered PTSD Scale for Children (CAPS-C)		X			
Combat Stress Barometer		X			
Common Grief Response Questionnaire					X
Compassion Fatigue Self Test					X
Complex PTSD Interview			X		
Computerized 16-Item Visual Analog Scale of Menstruation				X	X
Concerns & Coping With HIV Scales					X
Cultural Messages Scale					X
Dimensions of Stressful Experiences (DOSE)		X		X	
Dissociative Experiences Scale (DES)	X				
Early Trauma Inventory		X			
Evaluation of Lifetime Stressors Questionnaire & Interview		X		X	
Family Disruption from Illness Scale					X
Family Experiences Survey				X	
Farm Stressor Inventory					X
Farming/Ranching Stress Scale II					X
IES Cognitive & Affective Scales		X			
Impact of Events Scale Revised		X			
Incest History Questionnaire	X	X	X	X	
Life Orientation Inventory					X

Measure Name	Dissociation	PTSD	DESNOS	General Clinical	General Non-clinical
Life Satisfaction Scale					X
Life Stressor Checklist Revised		X		X	X
Los Angeles Symptom Checklist		X			
Mississippi Scale for Combat-Related PTSD—Short Form		X			
Multidimensional Trauma Recovery & Resiliency Measures (MTRR—I&Q)		X	X	X	X
My Worst (School) Experiences		X		X	X
National Women's Study Event History—PTSD Module (NWS)		X		X	X
NCVC Brief Screening for Assault		X		X	X
Nursing Perception of Distress					X
Parent Report of Child's Reaction to Stress		X		X	X
Parent Report of Post Traumatic Symptoms (PROPS)		X			
Penn Inventory for Post Traumatic Stress Disorder		X			
Peritraumatic Dissociative Experience Scale	X				
PK Scale of MMPI & MMPI-2		X			
Potential Stressful Events Interview		X	X	X	X
Problem Rating Scale		X			
Psychobiological Assessment of PTSD		X		X	
Psychological & Physical Maltreatment Scales		X		X	X
PTSD Checklist		X		X	X
PTSD Inventory		X			
Purdue PTSD Scale		X			
Quality of Life Barometer		X			
Retrospective Assessment of Traumatic Experiences		X		X	
Schillace Loss Scale				X	X
Schillace Post-Traumatic Vulnerability Scale		X		X	X
Schillace Trauma Scale		X		X	X
Secondary Traumatic Stress Disorder Scale		X		X	
Sexual Abuse Exposure Questionnaire		X		X	
Somatic Inkblot Series Test	X	X		X	
Spiritual Assessment Structured Interview					X
Standards of Practice & Ethical Issues Questionnaire					X
Stanford Acute Stress Reaction Questionnaire		X-Acute			
Stanford Loss of Personal Autonomy					X
Stress Response Rating Scale		X		X	
Stressful Events Content Analysis Coding Scheme		X	X	X	X
Stressful Life Experiences Screening		X		X	X

General Use Areas *(continued)*

Measure Name	Dissociation	PTSD	DESNOS	General Clinical	General Non-clinical
Structural Assessment of Stressful Experiences				X	X
Structural Assessment of Telemedical Systems		X		X	X
Structured Clinical Interview for DSM-IV Dissociative Disorders—Revised		X			
Structured Interview for Measurement of Disorders of Extreme Stress			X		
Structured Interview(s) of Post-Disaster Adjustment		X		X	X
Tough Times Checklists		X		X	X
Trauma Assessment for					
Adults		X		X	X
Trauma History Questionnaire		X		X	X
Trauma Reaction Indicators Child Questionnaire		X		X	X
Trauma Symptom Checklist 33 & 40		X		X	
Trauma Symptom Checklist for Children		X		X	
Trauma Symptom Inventory		X		X	
Traumagram		X		X	
Traumatic Event Screening Instrument for Children		X		X	
Traumatic Event Screening Instrument for Parents		X		X	
Traumatic Memory Inventory			X	X	
Traumatic Stress Schedule		X		X	
TSI Autonomy & Connection Scales		X	X	X	X
TSI Belief Scale Revision L		X	X	X	X
TSI Life Events Questionnaire	X	X	X	X	X
War-Zone Related PTSD Scale of the SCL-90-R		X			
Westhaven Secondary Trauma Scale		X			
When Bad Things Happen Scale		X			
Women's War-Time Stressors Scale		X		X	
World Assumption Scale		X	X	X	X
World View Survey		X		X	X

Instruments by Topic

Measure Name	Diagnosis	Assessment	Clinical	Debriefing	Dissociation	Epidemiology	Ethics	Family Treatment	Forensic	General Psychopathology	General Treatment	Group Treatment	Individual Treatment	Measure Development	Memory
Adolescent Dissociative Experiences Scale	X		X		X						X			X	
Angie/Andy Child Rating Scales	X	X	X						X	X	X		X		
Assessing Environments III			X								X				
Assessment of Psystress Via Salivary Ions	X													X	
Brief War Zone Stress Inventories						X									
Child's Reaction to Traumatic Events Scale (CRTS)		X												X	
Childhood Incest Questionnaire			X											X	
Childhood PTS Reaction Index	X	X	X												
Childhood PTSD Interview			X								X			X	
Childhood PTSD Interview—Parent F	X		X								X			X	
Childhood Trauma Questionnaire			X							X				X	
Childhood Traumatic Events Survey															
Children's Exposure to Community Violence															
Civilian Version of the Mississippi PTSD Scale	X		X			X									
Clinician Administered Dissociative States Scale					X										
Clinician Administered PTSD Scale (CAPS)	X	X	X												
Clinician Administered PTSD Scale for Children (CAPS-C)	X	X	X											X	
Combat Stress Barometer														X	
Common Grief Response Questionnaire														X	
Compassion Fatigue Self Test				X			X							X	
Complex PTSD Interview	X													X	
Computerized 16-Item Visual Analog Scale of Menstruation	X														
Concerns & Coping With HIV Scales														X	
Cultural Messages Scale														X	
Dimensions of Stressful Experiences (DOSE)		X												X	
Dissociative Experiences Scale (DES)	X	X	X		X						X				
Early Trauma Inventory			X											X	
Evaluation of Lifetime Stressors Questionnaire & Interview	X	X	X								X			X	
Family Disruption from Illness Scale								X						X	
Family Experiences Survey															
Farm Stressor Inventory														X	
Farming/Ranching Stress Scale II														X	
IES Cognitive & Affective Scales											X				

Measure Name	Diagnosis	Assessment	Clinical	Debriefing	Dissociation	Epidemiology	Ethics	Family Treatment	Forensic	General Psychopathology	General Treatment	Group Treatment	Individual Treatment	Measure Development	Memory
Impact of Events Scale Revised											X				
Incest History Questionnaire			X								X			X	
Life Orientation Inventory														X	
Life Satisfaction Scale						X								X	
Life Stressor Checklist Revised		X												X	
Los Angeles Symptom Checklist	X	X									X				
Mississippi Scale for Combat-Related PTSD—Short Form	X	X													
Multidimensional Trauma Recovery & Resiliency Measures (MTRR—I&Q)	X	X									X			X	
My Worst (School) Experiences									X					X	
National Women's Study Event History—PTSD Module (NWS)	X					X			X					X	
NCVC Brief Screening for Assault		X				X			X		X			X	
Nursing Perception of Distress														X	
Parent Report of Child's Reaction to Stress	X	X									X			X	
Parent Report of Post Traumatic Symptoms (PROPS)	X												X	X	
Penn Inventory for Post Traumatic Stress Disorder	X														
Peritraumatic Dissociative Experience Scale		X			X										
PK Scale of MMPI & MMPI-2	X	X									X				
Potential Stressful Events Interview	X	X													
Problem Rating Scale	X												X	X	
Psychobiological Assessment of PTSD		X													
Psychological & Physical Maltreatment Scales															
PTSD Checklist	X														
PTSD Inventory	X	X													
Purdue PTSD Scale														X	
Quality of Life															
Barometer											X			X	
Retrospective Assessment of Traumatic Experiences															
Schillace Loss Scale															
Schillace Post-Traumatic Vulnerability Scale															
Schillace Trauma Scale															
Secondary Traumatic Stress Disorder Scale														X	
Sexual Abuse Exposure Questionnaire	X														
Somatic Inkblot Series Test	X										X				

Measure Name	Diagnosis	Assessment	Clinical	Debriefing	Dissociation	Epidemiology	Ethics	Family Treatment	Forensic	General Psychopathology	General Treatment	Group Treatment	Individual Treatment	Measure Development	Memory
Spiritual Assessment Structured Interview															
Standards of Practice & Ethical Issues Questionnaire							X								
Stanford Acute Stress Reaction Questionnaire	X	X				X									
Stanford Loss of Personal Autonomy															
Stress Response Rating Scale		X									X				
Stressful Events Content Analysis Coding Scheme															
Stressful Life Experiences Screening			X												
Structural Assessment of Stressful Experiences		X				X									
Structural Assessment of Telemedical Systems		X												X	
Structured Clinical Interview for DSM-IV Dissociative Disorders—Revised	X	X													
Structured Interview for Measurement of Disorders of Extreme Stress	X	X													
Structured Interview(s) of Post-Disaster Adjustment		X													
Tough Times Checklists		X													
Trauma Assessment for Adults	X					X								X	
Trauma History Questionnaire		X									X			X	
Trauma Reaction Indicators Child Questionnaire		X											X	X	
Trauma Symptom Checklist 33 & 40		X													
Trauma Symptom Checklist for Children		X													
Trauma Symptom Inventory		X													
Traumagram		X													
Traumatic Event Screening Instrument for Children														X	
Traumatic Event Screening Instrument for Parents														X	
Traumatic Memory Inventory	X				X						X			X	X
Traumatic Stress Schedule														X	
TSI Autonomy & Connection Scales		X													
TSI Belief Scale Revision L		X													
TSI Life Events Questionnaire		X	X												
War-Zone Related PTSD Scale of the SCL-90-R	X	X													
Westhaven Secondary Trauma Scale											X				
When Bad Things Happen Scale	X	X													
Women's War-Time Stressors Scale	X	X									X				
World Assumption Scale		X									X				
World View Survey														X	

Measure Name	Neurobiology	Psychophysiology	Research	Rural Care	Screening	Secondary Traumatic Stress	Self Care	Service Delivery	Substance Abuse	Other
Adolescent Dissociative Experiences Scale			X							
Angie/Andy Child Rating Scales						X				
Assessing Environments III			X							
Assessment of Psystress Via Salivary Ions	X	X	X	X						
Brief War Zone Stress Inventories			X							X[1]
Child's Reaction to Traumatic Events Scale (CRTS)			X							
Childhood Incest Questionnaire			X							
Childhood PTS Reaction Index			X							
Childhood PTSD Interview			X							
Childhood PTSD Interview—Parent F			X							
Childhood Trauma Questionnaire			X							
Childhood Traumatic Events Survey			X							X[2]
Children's Exposure to Community Violence			X							
Civilian Version of the Mississippi PTSD Scale			X					X		
Clinician Administered Dissociative States Scale			X							
Clinician Administered PTSD Scale (CAPS)			X							
Clinician Administered PTSD Scale for Children (CAPS-C)			X							
Combat Stress Barometer			X							
Common Grief Response Questionnaire			X					X		
Compassion Fatigue Self Test			X		X	X	X			
Complex PTSD Interview			X							
Computerized 16-Item Visual Analog Scale of Menstruation			X							X[3]
Medicine										
Concerns & Coping With HIV Scales			X							X[4]
Cultural Messages Scale			X							X[5]
Dimensions of Stressful Experiences (DOSE)			X							
Dissociative Experiences Scale (DES)			X							
Early Trauma Inventory			X							
Evaluation of Lifetime Stressors Questionnaire & Interview			X							
Family Disruption from Illness Scale			X							
Family Experiences Survey			X							
Farm Stressor Inventory			X	X				X		

1. War Zone Exposure
2. Psychosomatic
3. PMS, Gynecological Medicine
4. Appraisal, Coping, & Social Support
5. Social Roles & Trauma

Measure Name	Neurobiology	Psychophysiology	Research	Rural Care	Screening	Secondary Traumatic Stress	Self Care	Service Delivery	Substance Abuse	Other
Farming/Ranching Stress Scale II			X	X						
IES Cognitive & Affective Scales			X							
Impact of Events Scale Revised			X							
Incest History Questionnaire			X							
Life Orientation Inventory			X							X[1]
Life Satisfaction Scale			X							
Life Stressor Checklist Revised			X							
Los Angeles Symptom Checklist			X							
Mississippi Scale for Combat-Related PTSD— Short Form			X							
Multidimensional Trauma Recovery & Resiliency Measures (MTRR—I&Q)			X							
My Worst (School) Experiences			X							
National Women's Study Event History—PTSD Module (NWS)			X							
NCVC Brief Screening for Assault			X							
Nursing Perception of Distress			X			X	X	X		
Parent Report of Child's Reaction to Stress			X							
Parent Report of Post Traumatic Symptoms (PROPS)										
Penn Inventory for Post Traumatic Stress Disorder			X							
Peritraumatic Dissociative Experience Scale			X							
PK Scale of MMPI & MMPI-2			X							
Potential Stressful Events Interview			X							
Problem Rating Scale										
Psychobiological Assessment of PTSD	X	X	X							
Psychological & Physical Maltreatment Scales			X							
PTSD Checklist			X							
PTSD Inventory			X							
Purdue PTSD Scale			X							
Quality of Life Barometer			X							
Retrospective Assessment of Traumatic Experiences			X							
Schillace Loss Scale			X							
Schillace Post-Traumatic Vulnerability Scale			X							
Schillace Trauma Scale			X							
Secondary Traumatic Stress Disorder Scale			X			X				
Sexual Abuse Exposure Questionnaire			X							
Somatic Inkblot Series Test									X	
Spiritual Assessment Structured Interview						X		X		
Standards of Practice & Ethical Issues Questionnaire			X							

1. Spirituality

Measure Name	Neurobiology	Psychophysiology	Research	Rural Care	Screening	Secondary Traumatic Stress	Self Care	Service Delivery	Substance Abuse	Other
Stanford Acute Stress Reaction Questionnaire			X							
Stanford Loss of Personal Autonomy			X							
Stress Response Rating Scale										
Stressful Events Content Analysis Coding Scheme			X							
Stressful Life Experiences Screening			X		X					
Structural Assessment of Stressful Experiences			X	X		X		X		X[1]
Structural Assessment of Telemedical Systems			X			X				X[2]
Structured Clinical Interview for DSM-IV Dissociative Disorders—Revised			X							
Structured Interview for Measurement of Disorders of Extreme Stress			X							
Structured Interview(s) of Post-Disaster Adjustment			X							
Tough Times Checklists			X							
Trauma Assessment for Adults										
Trauma History Questionnaire			X							
Trauma Reaction Indicators Child Questionnaire										
Trauma Symptom Checklist 33 & 40			X							
Trauma Symptom Checklist for Children			X							
Trauma Symptom Inventory			X							
Traumagram										
Traumatic Event Screening Instrument for Children			X							
Traumatic Event Screening Instrument for Parents			X							
Traumatic Memory Inventory										
Traumatic Stress Schedule			X							
TSI Autonomy & Connection Scales			X							
TSI Belief Scale										
Revision L			X							
TSI Life Events Questionnaire										
War-Zone Related PTSD Scale of the SCL-90-R										
Westhaven Secondary Trauma Scale			X			X				
When Bad Things Happen Scale			X							
Women's War-Time Stressors Scale			X							
World Assumption Scale			X							
World View Survey			X							

1. Telemedicine
2. Spirituality

Stressor Applications

Measure Name	Any Stressor	Combat	Community Violence	Criminal Victimization	Domestic Violence	Genocide	Holocaust	Industrial Disaster	Other	Physical Abuse / Neglect	Political Ethnic Persecution	Sexual Assault / Abuse	Terrorism	Torture	Traumatic Grief
Adolescent Dissociative Experiences Scale	X														
Angie/Andy Child Rating Scales			X		X					X		X			
Assessing Environments III					X				X[1]	X					
Assessment of Psystress Via Salivary Ions	X														
Brief War Zone Stress Inventories		X													
Child's Reaction to Traumatic Events Scale (CRTS)	X														
Childhood Incest Questionnaire					X							X			
Childhood PTS Reaction Index	X														
Childhood PTSD Interview	X														
Childhood PTSD Interview—Parent F	X														
Childhood Trauma Questionnaire					X					X		X			
Childhood Traumatic Events Survey	X														
Children's Exposure to Community Violence			X												
Civilian Version of the Mississippi PTSD Scale	X														
Clinician Administered Dissociative States Scale	X														
Clinician															
Administered PTSD Scale (CAPS)	X														
Clinician Administered PTSD Scale for Children (CAPS-C)	X														
Combat Stress Barometer		X													
Common Grief Response Questionnaire									X[2]						X
Compassion Fatigue Self Test	X								X[3]						
Complex PTSD Interview									X[4]			X			
Computerized 16-Item Visual Analog Scale of Menstruation									X[5]						
Concerns & Coping With HIV Scales									X[6]						
Cultural Messages Scale				X	X				X[7]	X		X			
Dimensions of Stressful Experiences (DOSE)	X														
Dissociative Experiences Scale (DES)	X														
Early Trauma Inventory					X					X		X			
Evaluation of Lifetime Stressors Questionnaire & Interview	X														

1. Discipline, Family Dynamics, Parenting
2. Death
3. Secondary
4. Chronic Interpersonal Violence
5. Menstrual
6. HIV
6. Gender Crimes

Measure Name	Any Stressor	Combat	Community Violence	Criminal Victimization	Domestic Violence	Genocide	Holocaust	Industrial Disaster	Other	Physical Abuse/Neglect	Political Ethnic Persecution	Sexual Assault/Abuse	Terrorism	Torture	Traumatic Grief
Family Disruption from Illness Scale									X[1]						
Family Experiences Survey			X		X					X		X			
Farm Stressor Inventory									X[2]						
Farming/Ranching Stress Scale II									X[2]						
IES Cognitive & Affective Scales	X														
Impact of Events Scale Revised	X														
Incest History Questionnaire												X			
Life Orientation Inventory															
Life Satisfaction Scale	X														
Life Stressor Checklist Revised	X														
Los Angeles Symptom Checklist	X														
Mississippi Scale for Combat-Related PTSD—Short Form		X													
Multidimensional Trauma Recovery & Resiliency Measures (MTRR—I&Q)	X														
My Worst (School) Experiences	X								X[3]						
National Women's Study Event History—PTSD Module (NWS)			X	X	X					X		X	X	X	
NCVC Brief Screening for Assault				X	X					X		X	X	X	
Nursing Perception of Distress									X[4]						
Parent Report of Child's Reaction to Stress	X														
Parent Report of Post Traumatic Symptoms (PROPS)	X														
Penn Inventory for Post Traumatic Stress Disorder	X														
Peritraumatic Dissociative Experience Scale	X														
PK Scale of MMPI & MMPI-2	X														
Potential Stressful Events Interview					X					X		X			
Problem Rating Scale	X														
Psychobiological Assessment of PTSD	X														
Psychological & Physical Maltreatment Scales					X					X					
PTSD Checklist	X	X													

1. Illness
2. Farming
3. School
4. Health Care Worker

Measure Name	Any Stressor	Combat	Community Violence	Criminal Victimization	Domestic Violence	Genocide	Holocaust	Industrial Disaster	Other	Physical Abuse/Neglect	Political Ethnic Persecution	Sexual Assault/Abuse	Terrorism	Torture	Traumatic Grief
PTSD Inventory	X	X	X								X		X		
Purdue PTSD Scale	X														
Quality of Life Barometer		X													
Retrospective Assessment of Traumatic Experiences					X					X		X			
Schillace Loss Scale															X
Schillace Post-Traumatic Vulnerability Scale									X[1]						
Schillace Trauma Scale	X														
Secondary Traumatic Stress Disorder Scale									X[2]						
Sexual Abuse Exposure Questionnaire												X			
Somatic Inkblot Series Test	X	X			X					X		X			X
Spiritual Assessment Structured Interview									X[3]						X
Standards of Practice & Ethical Issues Questionnaire															
Stanford Acute Stress Reaction Questionnaire	X														
Stanford Loss of Personal Autonomy	X								X[4]						
Stress Response Rating Scale	X														
Stressful Events Content Analysis Coding Scheme	X														
Stressful Life Experiences Screening	X														
Structural Assessment of Stressful Experiences	X	X							X[5]						
Structural Assessment of Telemedical Systems	X														
Structured Clinical Interview for DSM-IV Dissociative Disorders—Revised	X														
Structured Interview for Measurement of Disorders of Extreme Stress	X														
Structured Interview(s) of Post-Disaster Adjustment									X[6]						
Tough Times Checklists	X														
Trauma Assessment for Adults				X	X					X		X			
Trauma History Questionnaire	X														

1. Vulnerability
2. Secondary Exposure
3. Terminal Illness
4. Other
5. Isolation
6. Natural Disaster

Measure Name	Any Stressor	Combat	Community Violence	Criminal Victimization	Domestic Violence	Genocide	Holocaust	Industrial Disaster	Other	Physical Abuse / Neglect	Political Ethnic Persecution	Sexual Assault / Abuse	Terrorism	Torture	Traumatic Grief
Trauma Reaction															
Indicators Child Questionnaire	X														
Trauma Symptom Checklist 33 & 40	X														
Trauma Symptom Checklist for Children	X														
Trauma Symptom Inventory	X														
Traumagram	X														
Traumatic Event Screening Instrument for Children	X														
Traumatic Event Screening Instrument for Parents	X														
Traumatic Memory Inventory		X		X	X	X	X	X		X	X	X	X	X	X
Traumatic Stress															
Schedule	X														
TSI Autonomy & Connection Scales	X														
TSI Belief Scale Revision L	X														
TSI Life Events Questionnaire	X														
War-Zone Related PTSD Scale of the SCL-90-R		X													
Westhaven Secondary Trauma Scale		X[1]													
When Bad Things Happen Scale	X														
Women's War-Time Stressors Scale		X													
World Assumption Scale	X														
World View Survey	X														

1. Civilian

Table of Particular Sensitivities

Measure Name	Age	Change across Time	Culture/Ethnicity	Gender	Geography/Climate	Sexual Orientation	Socioeconomic Status	Urban/Rural
Adolescent Dissociative Experiences Scale	X							
Angie/Andy Child Rating Scales	X		X	X				X-URBAN
Assessing Environments III				X			X	
Assessment of Psystress Via Salivary Ions	X	X	X		X		FREE	FREE
Brief War Zone Stress Inventories				X				
Child's Reaction to Traumatic Events Scale (CRTS)	X	X	X	X			X	X
Childhood Incest Questionnaire	X							
Childhood PTS Reaction Index	X		X	X	X		X	X
Childhood PTSD Interview	X							
Childhood PTSD Interview—Parent F	X							
Childhood Trauma Questionnaire	X		X	X				
Childhood Traumatic Events Survey	X							
Children's Exposure to Community Violence	X		X					X
Civilian Version of the Mississippi PTSD Scale			X					
Clinician Administered Dissociative States Scale		X						
Clinician Administered PTSD Scale (CAPS)								
Clinician Administered PTSD Scale for Children (CAPS-C)	X	X						
Combat Stress Barometer								
Common Grief Response Questionnaire								
Compassion Fatigue Self Test		X						
Complex PTSD Interview								
Computerized 16-Item Visual Analog Scale of Menstruation	X			X				
Concerns & Coping With HIV Scales			X	X		X	X	
Cultural Messages Scale		X	X	X		X	X	
Dimensions of Stressful Experiences (DOSE)	X							
Dissociative Experiences Scale (DES)								
Early Trauma Inventory								
Evaluation of Lifetime Stressors Questionnaire & Interview			X				X	
Family Disruption from Illness Scale	X				X			X
Family Experiences Survey				X				
Farm Stressor Inventory		X			X		X	X
Farming/Ranching Stress Scale II					X		X	X
IES Cognitive & Affective Scales		X						
Impact of Events Scale Revised								
Incest History Questionnaire				X				

Measure Name	Age	Change across Time	Culture / Ethnicity	Gender	Geography / Climate	Sexual Orientation	Socioeconomic Status	Urban / Rural
Life Orientation Inventory								
Life Satisfaction Scale			X		X		X	X
Life Stressor Checklist Revised	X			X				
Los Angeles Symptom Checklist	X			X				
Mississippi Scale for Combat-Related PTSD—Short Form		X						
Multidimensional Trauma Recovery & Resiliency Measures (MTRR—I&Q)	X	X		X				
My Worst (School) Experiences	X				X			
National Women's Study Event History—PTSD Module (NWS)			X	X		X		X
NCVC Brief Screening for Assault	X	X	X	X		X		X
Nursing Perception of Distress								
Parent Report of Child's Reaction to Stress	X							
Parent Report of Post Traumatic Symptoms (PROPS)	X							
Penn Inventory for Post Traumatic Stress Disorder								
Peritraumatic Dissociative Experience Scale								
PK Scale of MMPI & MMPI-2								
Potential Stressful Events Interview				X				
Problem Rating Scale	X	X						
Psychobiological Assessment of PTSD		X	X	X	X	X	X	X
Psychological & Physical Maltreatment Scales								
PTSD Checklist	X							
PTSD Inventory	X		X					
Purdue PTSD Scale								
Quality of Life Barometer								
Retrospective Assessment of Traumatic Experiences				X				
Schillace Loss Scale	X							
Schillace Post-Traumatic Vulnerability Scale	X	X		X				
Schillace Trauma Scale	X							
Secondary Traumatic Stress Disorder Scale								
Sexual Abuse Exposure Questionnaire	X		X	X			X	
Somatic Inkblot Series Test	X		X	X				
Spiritual Assessment Structured Interview			X					
Standards of Practice & Ethical Issues Questionnaire								
Stanford Acute Stress Reaction Questionnaire		X	X					
Stanford Loss of Personal Autonomy								

Measure Name	Age	Change across Time	Culture / Ethnicity	Gender	Geography / Climate	Sexual Orientation	Socioeconomic Status	Urban / Rural
Stress Response Rating Scale		X						
Stressful Events Content Analysis Coding Scheme	X	X	X	X	X	X	X	X
Stressful Life Experiences Screening		X						
Structural Assessment of Stressful Experiences		X	X		X		X	X
Structural Assessment of Telemedical Systems		X		X				
Structured Clinical Interview for DSM-IV Dissociative Disorders—Revised								
Structured Interview for Measurement of Disorders of Extreme Stress								
Structured Interview(s) of Post-Disaster Adjustment	X	X	X		X		X	X
Tough Times Checklists	X							
Trauma Assessment for Adults		X	X	X			X	X
Trauma History Questionnaire				X				
Trauma Reaction Indicators Child Questionnaire	X	X						
Trauma Symptom Checklist 33 & 40								
Trauma Symptom Checklist for Children	X							
Trauma Symptom Inventory	X		X	X				
Traumagram	X							
Traumatic Event Screening Instrument for Children	X							
Traumatic Event Screening Instrument for Parents	X							
Traumatic Memory Inventory								
Traumatic Stress Schedule								
TSI Autonomy & Connection Scales		X						
TSI Belief Scale Revision L								
TSI Life Events Questionnaire								
War-Zone Related PTSD Scale of the SCL-90-R								
Westhaven Secondary Trauma Scale								
When Bad Things Happen Scale	X							
Women's War-Time Stressors Scale				X				
World Assumption Scale			X	X				
World View Survey								

Related Instruments

Measure Name	SCL	BSI	SCID	CAPS	IES	MMPI
Clinician Administered PTSD Scale (CAPS)				X		
Clinician Administered PTSD Scale for Children (CAPS-C)				X		
Combat Stress Barometer				X		
Complex PTSD Interview				X		
IES Cognitive & Affective Scales					X	
Impact of Events Scale Revised					X	
PK Scale of MMPI & MMPI-2						X
Structured Clinical Interview for DSM-IV Dissociative Disorders—Revised			X			
War-Zone Related PTSD Scale of the SCL-90-R	X	X				

Intended Population Tables

Measure Name	Adolescents	Adults	Children	Elderly	Emergency Service Workers	Men	Perpetrators	Refugees	Veterans	Women	Other	Minorities
Adolescent Dissociative Experiences Scale	X		X							X		
Angie/Andy Child Rating Scales			X									
Assessing Environments III		X										
Assessment of Psystress Via Salivary Ions	X	X	X	X								
Brief War Zone Stress Inventories									X[1]			
Child's Reaction to Traumatic Events Scale (CRTS)	X		X									
Childhood Incest Questionnaire		X								X		
Childhood PTS Reaction Index	X		X				X					
Childhood PTSD Interview	X		X								X	
Childhood PTSD Interview—Parent F											X[2]	
Childhood Trauma Questionnaire	X	X										
Childhood Traumatic Events Survey		X										
Children's Exposure to Community Violence	X		X									
Civilian Version of the Mississippi PTSD Scale		X										
Clinician Administered Dissociative States Scale		X							X			
Clinician Administered PTSD Scale (CAPS)		X										
Clinician Administered PTSD Scale for Children (CAPS-C)	X		X									
Combat Stress Barometer									X			
Common Grief Response Questionnaire		X										
Compassion Fatigue Self Test		X										
Complex PTSD Interview		X										
Computerized 16-Item Visual Analog Scale of Menstruation	X	X								X		
Concerns & Coping With HIV Scales		X		X	X	X				X		X
Cultural Messages Scale	X	X					X			X		
Dimensions of Stressful Experiences (DOSE)			X									
Dissociative Experiences Scale (DES)		X										
Early Trauma Inventory		X										
Evaluation of Lifetime Stressors Questionnaire & Interview		X							X			
Family Disruption from Illness Scale		X										
Family Experiences Survey		X									X[3]	
Farm Stressor Inventory		X										
Farming/Ranching Stress Scale II		X										
IES Cognitive & Affective Scales		X										
Impact of Events Scale Revised		X										
Incest History Questionnaire		X										

1. Men & Women
2. Parents
3. Psychiatric Patients

Measure Name	Adolescents	Adults	Children	Elderly	Emergency Service Workers	Men	Perpetrators	Refugees	Veterans	Women	Other	Minorities
Life Orientation Inventory		X										
Life Satisfaction Scale		X										
Life Stressor Checklist Revised		X								X		
Los Angeles Symptom Checklist	X	X										
Mississippi Scale for Combat-Related PTSD—Short Form						X			X			
Multidimensional Trauma Recovery & Resiliency Measures (MTRR-I&Q)		X										
My Worst (School) Experiences	X		X									
National Women's Study Event History—PTSD Module (NWS)		X								X		
NCVC Brief Screening for Assault	X	X										
Nursing Perception of Distress		X									X[1]	
Parent Report of Child's Reaction to Stress											X[2]	
Parent Report of Post Traumatic Symptoms (PROPS)											X[2]	
Penn Inventory for Post Traumatic Stress Disorder		X										
Peritraumatic Dissociative Experience Scale	X	X										
PK Scale of MMPI & MMPI-2		X							X			
Potential Stressful Events Interview		X								X		
Problem Rating Scale	X		X								X[2]	
Psychobiological Assessment of PTSD		X				X			X	X		
Psychological & Physical Maltreatment Scales		X										
PTSD Checklist		X									X[2]	
PTSD Inventory	X	X		X								
Purdue PTSD Scale		X										
Quality of Life Barometer		X							X[3]			
Retrospective Assessment of Traumatic Experiences		X									X[4]	
Schillace Loss Scale	X	X										
Schillace Post-Traumatic Vulnerability Scale	X	X										
Schillace Trauma Scale	X	X										
Secondary Traumatic Stress Disorder Scale		X									X[5]	
Sexual Abuse Exposure Questionnaire	X		X									
Somatic Inkblot Series Test	X	X	X		X				X			
Spiritual Assessment Structured Interview		X									X[6]	

1. Health Care Workers
2. Parents
3. Combat
4. Psychiatric Patients
5. Caregivers
6. Families

Measure Name	Adolescents	Adults	Children	Elderly	Emergency Service Workers	Men	Perpetrators	Refugees	Veterans	Women	Other	Minorities
Standards of Practice & Ethical Issues Questionnaire		X									X[1]	
Stanford Acute Stress Reaction Questionnaire		X										X
Stanford Loss of Personal Autonomy		X			X							
Stress Response Rating Scale	X	X		X								
Stressful Events Content Analysis Coding Scheme	X	X	X	X								X
Stressful Life Experiences Screening	X	X										
Structural Assessment of Stressful Experiences	X	X	X	X								
Structural Assessment of Telemedical Systems		X										
Structured Clinical Interview for DSM-IV Dissociative Disorders—Revised		X										
Structured Interview for Measurement of Disorders of Extreme Stress		X										
Structured Interview(s) of Post-Disaster Adjustment	X	X										
Tough Times Checklists	X	X	X									
Trauma Assessment for Adults		X								X		
Trauma History Questionnaire		X										
Trauma Reaction Indicators Child Questionnaire			X									
Trauma Symptom Checklist 33 & 40		X										
Trauma Symptom Checklist for Children	X		X									
Trauma Symptom Inventory		X										
Traumagram		X										
Traumatic Event Screening Instrument for Children	X		X									
Traumatic Event Screening Instrument for Parents											X[2]	
Traumatic Memory Inventory		X										
Traumatic Stress Schedule		X										
TSI Autonomy & Connection Scales		X										
TSI Belief Scale Revision L		X										
TSI Life Events Questionnaire		X										
War-Zone Related PTSD Scale of the SCL-90-R		X							X			
Westhaven Secondary Trauma Scale		X						X				
When Bad Things Happen Scale	X		X									
Women's War-Time Stressors Scale		X								X		
World Assumption Scale		X										
World View Survey	X	X										

1. Caregivers
2. Parents

Elder, Any Stressor

Measure Name	Elders	Any Stressor
Assessment of Psystress Via Salivary Ions	X	X
PTSD Inventory	X	X
Structural Assessment of Stressful Experiences	X	X
Stressful Events Content Analysis Coding Scheme	X	X
Stress Response Rating Scale	X	X

Adult, Any Stressor

Measure Name	Adulls	Any Stressor
Assessment of Psystress Via Salivary Ions	X	X
Childhood Traumatic Events Survey	X	X
Civilian Version of the Mississippi PTSD Scale	X	X
Clinician Administered Dissociative States Scale	X	X
Clinician Administered PTSD Scale (CAPS)	X	X
Compassion Fatigue Self Test	X	X
Dissociative Experiences Scale (DES)	X	X
Evaluation of Lifetime Stressors Questionnaire & Interview	X	X
IES Cognitive & Affective Scales	X	X
Impact of Events Scale Revised	X	X
Life Satisfaction Scale	X	X
Life Stressor Checklist Revised	X	X
Los Angeles Symptom Checklist	X	X
Multidimensional Trauma Recovery & Resiliency Measures (MTRR—I&Q)	X	X
Penn Inventory for Post Traumatic Stress Disorder	X	X
Peritraumatic Dissociative Experience Scale	X	X
PK Scale of MMPI & MMPI-2	X	X
Psychobiological Assessment of PTSD	X	X
PTSD Checklist	X	X
PTSD Inventory	X	X
Purdue PTSD Scale	X	X
Schillace Trauma Scale	X	X
Somatic Inkblot Series Test	X	X
Stanford Acute Stress Reaction Questionnaire	X	X
Stanford Loss of Personal Autonomy	X	X
Stress Response Rating Scale	X	X
Stressful Events Content Analysis Coding Scheme	X	X
Stressful Life Experiences Screening	X	X
Structural Assessment of Stressful Experiences	X	X
Structural Assessment of Telemedical Systems	X	X
Structured Clinical Interview for DSM-IV Dissociative Disorders—Revised	X	X

Measure Name	Elders	Any Stressor
Structured Interview for Measurement of Disorders of Extreme Stress	X	X
Tough Times Checklists	X	X
Trauma History Questionnaire	X	X
Trauma Symptom Checklist 33 & 40	X	X
Trauma Symptom Inventory	X	X
Traumagram	X	X
Traumatic Stress Schedule	X	X
TSI Autonomy & Connection Scales	X	X
TSI Belief Scale Revision L	X	X
TSI Life Events Questionnaire	X	X
World Assumption Scale	X	X
World View Survey	X	X

Adolescents, Any Stressor

Measure Name	Adolescents	Any Stressor
Adolescent Dissociative Experiences Scale	X	X
Assessment of Psystress Via Salivary Ions	X	X
Child's Reaction to Traumatic Events Scale (CRTS)	X	X
Childhood PTS Reaction Index	X	X
Childhood PTSD Interview	X	X
Clinician Administered PTSD Scale for Children (CAPS-C)	X	X
Los Angeles Symptom Checklist	X	X
My Worst (School) Experiences	X	X
Peritraumatic Dissociative Experience Scale	X	X
Problem Rating Scale	X	X
PTSD Inventory	X	X
Schillace Trauma Scale	X	X
Somatic Inkblot Series Test	X	X
Stress Response Rating Scale	X	X
Stressful Events Content Analysis Coding Scheme	X	X
Stressful Life Experiences Screening	X	X
Structural Assessment of Stressful Experiences	X	X
Tough Times Checklists	X	X
Trauma Symptom Checklist for Children	X	X
Traumatic Event Screening Instrument for Children	X	X
When Bad Things Happen Scale	X	X
World View Survey	X	X

Children, Any Stressor

Measure Name	Children	Any Stressor
Adolescent Dissociative Experiences Scale	X	X
Assessment of Psystress Via Salivary Ions	X	X
Child's Reaction to Traumatic Events Scale (CRTS)	X	X
Childhood PTS Reaction Index	X	X
Childhood PTSD Interview	X	X
Clinician Administered PTSD Scale for Children (CAPS-C)	X	X
Dimensions of Stressful Experiences (DOSE)	X	X
My Worst (School) Experiences	X	X
Problem Rating Scale	X	X
Somatic Inkblot Series Test	X	X
Stressful Events Content Analysis Coding Scheme	X	X
Structural Assessment of Stressful Experiences	X	X
Tough Times Checklists	X	X
Trauma Reaction Indicators Child Questionnaire	X	X
Trauma Symptom Checklist for Children	X	X
Traumatic Event Screening Instrument for Children	X	X
When Bad Things Happen Scale	X	X

Measures Available in Languages other than English

Measure Name	Languages
Childhood PTS Reaction Index	English, Arabic, Armenian, Cambodian, Croatian, Norwegian
Civilian Version of the Mississippi PTSD Scale	English, Dutch, Spanish
Concerns & Coping With HIV Scales	English, Mexican Spanish
IES Cognitive & Affective Scales	English, German
Impact of Events Scale Revised	English, German
Life Satisfaction Scale	Russian, English
National Women's Study Event History— PTSD Module (NWS)	English, Spanish
Parent Report of Child's Reaction to Stress	English, Hebrew
PTSD Inventory	English, Hebrew
Somatic Inkblot Series Test	English, Italian, German, Hindi, Spanish
Stanford Acute Stress Reaction Questionnaire	English, Spanish
TSI Autonomy & Connection Scales	English, Chinese, Russian, Spanish
TSI Belief Scale Revision L	English, Chinese, Russian, Spanish

Equipment Needed to Administer Test

Measure Name	Paper & Pencil	Computer	Physiological	Special
Adolescent Dissociative Experiences Scale	X			
Angie/Andy Child Rating Scales		X		X
Assessing Environments III	X			
Assessment of Psystress Via Salivary Ions				X
Brief War Zone Stress Inventories	X			
Child's Reaction to Traumatic Events Scale (CRTS)	X			
Childhood Incest Questionnaire	X			
Childhood PTS Reaction Index				X
Childhood PTSD Interview	X			
Childhood PTSD Interview—Parent F	X			
Childhood Trauma Questionnaire	X			
Childhood Traumatic Events Survey	X			
Children's Exposure to Community Violence	X			
Civilian Version of the Mississippi PTSD Scale	X			
Clinician Administered Dissociative States Scale	X			
Clinician Administered PTSD Scale (CAPS)	X			
Clinician Administered PTSD Scale for Children (CAPS-C)	X			
Combat Stress Barometer	X			
Common Grief Response Questionnaire	X			
Compassion Fatigue Self Test	X			
Complex PTSD Interview	X			
Computerized 16-Item Visual Analog Scale of Menstruation		X		
Concerns & Coping With HIV Scales	X			
Cultural Messages Scale	X			
Dimensions of Stressful Experiences (DOSE)	X			
Dissociative Experiences Scale (DES)	X			
Early Trauma Inventory	X			
Evaluation of Lifetime Stressors Questionnaire & Interview	X			
Family Disruption from Illness Scale	X			
Family Experiences Survey	X			
Farm Stressor Inventory	X			
Farming/Ranching Stress Scale II	X			
IES Cognitive & Affective Scales	X			
Impact of Events Scale Revised	X			
Incest History Questionnaire	X			
Life Orientation Inventory	X			
Life Satisfaction Scale	X			
Life Stressor Checklist Revised	X			

Measure Name	Paper & Pencil	Computer	Physiological	Special
Los Angeles Symptom Checklist	X			
Mississippi Scale for Combat-Related PTSD— Short Form	X			
Multidimensional Trauma Recovery & Resiliency Measures (MTRR—I&Q)				X
My Worst (School) Experiences	X			
National Women's Study Event History— PTSD Module (NWS)	X			
NCVC Brief Screening for Assault	X			
Nursing Perception of Distress	X			
Parent Report of Child's Reaction to Stress	X			
Parent Report of Post Traumatic Symptoms (PROPS)	X			
Penn Inventory for Post Traumatic Stress Disorder	X			
Peritraumatic Dissociative Experience Scale	X			
PK Scale of MMPI & MMPI-2	X			
Potential Stressful Events Interview	X			
Problem Rating Scale	X			
Psychobiological Assessment of PTSD			X	
Psychological & Physical Maltreatment Scales	X			
PTSD Checklist	X			
PTSD Inventory	X			
Purdue PTSD Scale	X			
Quality of Life Barometer	X			
Retrospective Assessment of Traumatic Experiences	X			
Schillace Loss Scale	X			
Schillace Post-Traumatic Vulnerability Scale	X			
Schillace Trauma Scale	X			
Secondary Traumatic Stress Disorder Scale	X			
Sexual Abuse Exposure Questionnaire	X			
Somatic Inkblot Series Test	X			X
Spiritual Assessment Structured Interview	X			
Standards of Practice & Ethical Issues Questionnaire	X			
Stanford Acute Stress Reaction Questionnaire	X			
Stanford Loss of Personal Autonomy	X			
Stress Response Rating Scale	X			
Stressful Events Content Analysis Coding Scheme	X			
Stressful Life Experiences Screening	X			
Structural Assessment of Stressful Experiences	X	X		X
Structural Assessment of Telemedical Systems	X			
Structured Clinical Interview for DSM-IV Dissociative Disorders—Revised	X			

Measure Name	Paper & Pencil	Computer	Physiological	Special
Structured Interview for Measurement of Disorders of Extreme Stress	X			
Structured Interview(s) of Post-Disaster Adjustment	X			X
Tough Times Checklists	X			
Trauma Assessment for Adults	X			
Trauma History Questionnaire	X			
Trauma Reaction Indicators Child Questionnaire	X			
Trauma Symptom Checklist 33 & 40	X			
Trauma Symptom Checklist for Children	X			
Trauma Symptom Inventory	X	X (Optional)		
Traumagram	X			
Traumatic Event Screening Instrument for Children	X	X (Optional)		
Traumatic Event Screening Instrument for Parents	X	X (Optional)		
Traumatic Memory Inventory	X			
Traumatic Stress Schedule	X			
TSI Autonomy & Connection Scales	X			
TSI Belief Scale Revision L	X			
TSI Life Events Questionnaire	X			
War-Zone Related PTSD Scale of the SCL-90-R	X			
Westhaven Secondary Trauma Scale	X			
When Bad Things Happen Scale	X			
Women's War-Time Stressors Scale	X			
World Assumption Scale	X			
World View Survey	X			

Adolescent Dissociative Experiences Scale (A-DES)

Type of Population
Adolescents (clinical and non-clinical populations)

Cost
$3.00 to cover printing and mailing

Copyright

Languages
English

What It Measures
Frequency of dissociative experiences in adolescents

Measure Content Survey, Procedure, or Process
30 item self-report measure of frequency of a variety of dissociative experiences including amnesias, absorption and imaginative involvement, depersonalization, derealization, dissociative identity, and dissociative relatedness experiences. Has no theoretical orientation.

Time Estimate

Administration	Scoring
15–30 minutes	5–15 minutes

Equipment Needed

Paper & Pencil	Computer	Basic Psychophysiological	Specialized Equipment
X			

Psychometric Maturity

Under Construction	Basic Properties Intact	Mature
X		

Psychometric Properties Summary
No data available to date. Reliability and validity data now being collected.

Particular Sensitivity

Age	Change over Time	Culture / Ethnicity	Gender	Geography / Climate	Sexual Orientation	Socioeconomic Status	Urban / Rural
X	?	?	?	?	?	?	?

Estimate of Number of In-Process Studies
Unknown

Unpublished References
Unknown

Published References

Unknown

General Comments

Available for research or clinical use, but clinical use will be difficult before norms are developed.

Key Words

Population	Stressor	Topic
latency adolescents	any	clinical diagnosis dissociation measure development research treatment

Reference Citation for This Review

Armstrong, J. (1996). Psychometric review of Adolescent Dissociative Experiences Scale (A-DES). In B. H. Stamm (Ed.). *Measurement of stress, trauma, and adaptation*. Lutherville, MD: Sidran Press.

Measure Contact Name

Judith G. Armstrong, Ph.D.

Address: 501 Santa Monica Blvd.
                Suite 402
                Santa Monica, CA 90401 USA
Phone: 310.458.4443
E-mail: jarmstro@mizar.usc.edu

Angie/Andy Child Rating Scales
A Cartoon-Based Measure for Post Traumatic
Stress Responses To Chronic Interpersonal Abuse

Type of Population

Children, ages 6–11, who have been exposed to ongoing, chronic interpersonal abuse and violence

Cost

To be determined

Copyright

What It Measures

A constellation of symptoms manifested in six domains of functioning and post-traumatic stress responses as follows: regulation of affect and impulses, attention or consciousness, self perception, relations with others, somatization, systems of meaning, and PTSD.

Measure Content Survey, Procedure, or Process

Angie/Andy Child Rating Scales (A/A CRS) utilizes a cartoon based pictorial methodology with a thermometer response format. This instrument objectively evaluates symptoms in 7 categories with 23 subcategories that children often manifest in response to chronic abuse and violence.

Theoretical Orientation Summary

The 23 subcategories were generated based on: (a) a systematic review of the literature on children's emotional and behavioral responses to prolonged, repeated abuse and violence; (b) the structured interview of Disorders of Extreme Stress (Pelcovitz, van der Kolk, Roth, et al., 1993); (c) previous research of Herman (1992) and Terr (1991). The subcategories are synonymous with DSM-IV PTSD-associated features that describe a constellation of symptoms associated with interpersonal stressors (e.g., physical abuse, sexual abuse).

Time Estimate

Administration	Scoring
30–45 minutes	self-scoring/computer in process

Equipment Needed

Paper & Pencil	Computer	Basic Psychophysiological	Specialized Equipment
	in process		X (illustration cards)

Psychometric Maturity

Under Construction	Basic Properties Intact	Mature
	X	

Psychometric Properties Summary

(1) *Internal consistency* using coefficient alphas ranged from 0.70 to 0.95.

(2) *Construct validity* was supported by the following findings: Used the ANCOVA and Tukey lsd for 6 pairwise comparisons (alpha set at 0.0068). Children (N=208) in three trauma groups—Intrafamilial Violence (IV), Extra-

familial Violence (EV), and Combined Violence (CV)—each scored significantly higher than in the Non-Trauma group (NT) on the six scales, the composite scale, and the PTSD scale. The IV group comprises sexual abuse, physical abuse, witnessing family violence, community violence, and co-occurences of these events. The EV group comprises community violence and/or extrafamilial sexual abuse. The CV group comprises both IV and EV. The NT group comprises no exposure to traumatic events.

Children in the CV group scored significantly higher than the IV group on 4/6 scales and the composite scale and showed a trend on the PTSD scale. The CV group scored significantly higher than the EV on 5/6 scales, the composite scale, and the PTSD scale.

Using discriminant function analysis, the six scales and the composite and PTSD scales each significantly predicted membership in trauma and non-trauma. The scales correctly classified between 76% to 90% of trauma and non-trauma groups.

(3) *Concurrent validity* was supported by the following findings: The number of types of violence exposures correlated with A/A CRS from 0.55 to 0.74. The extent of exposure to violence and abuse correlated with A/A CRS from 0.44 to 0.57.

(4) *Convergent validity* was supported by correlations ranging from 0.71 to 0.81 of the A/A parent rating scales (an analogue to the A/A child measure) with Behavior Assessment System for Children (BASC). The BASC is a gold standard parent measure of children's emotional and behavioral symptoms.

Particular Sensitivity

Age	Change over Time	Culture/ Ethnicity	Gender	Geography/ Climate	Sexual Orientation	Socioeconomic Status	Urban/ Rural
X	?	X	X	?	?	?	X (urban)

References

Validation of a child measure for post traumatic stress responses to interpersonal abuse; submitted manuscript: Praver, Pelcovits, and DiGiuseppe (1995).

General Comments

The measure uses original artwork created by Francis Praver. Until now there were no valid child measures that evaluated responses to the insidious nature of ongoing, repeated traumatic abuse and violence. Previous PTSD measures evaluated responses to circumscribed events with discrete beginnings and endings.

See attached A/A CRS sample cartoons and questions.

Key Words

Population	Stressor	Topic
children	community violence domestic violence physical abuse/neglect sexual assault/abuse	diagnosis forensic general psychopathology individual treatment secondary traumatic stress

Reference Citation for This Review

Praver, F. & Pelcovitz, D. (1996). Psychometric review of Angie/Andy Child Rating Scales: A Cartoon-Based Measure for Post Traumatic Stress Responses to Chronic Interpersonal Abuse. In B. H. Stamm (Ed.). *Measurement of stress, trauma, and adaptation*. Lutherville, MD: Sidran Press.

Measure Contact Name

Frances Praver, Ph.D.

Address: 5 Marseilles Drive
                Locust Valley, NY 11560 USA
Phone: 516.676.1594
Fax: 516.671.3269

David Pelcovits, Ph.D.

Address: Department of Psychiatry
                400 Community Drive
                Manhasset, NY 11030 USA
Phone: 516.562.3176
Fax: 516.562.3997

54. Here Angie keeps thinking about upsetting things that happened, even though she doesn't want to. Pictures or sounds about what happened just pop into her head. How often do you keep thinking about upsetting things that happened?

42. Here Andy is scared that there is no one out there to take care of kids, like adults, parents, or God. How often are you scared that there is no one out there to protect kids?

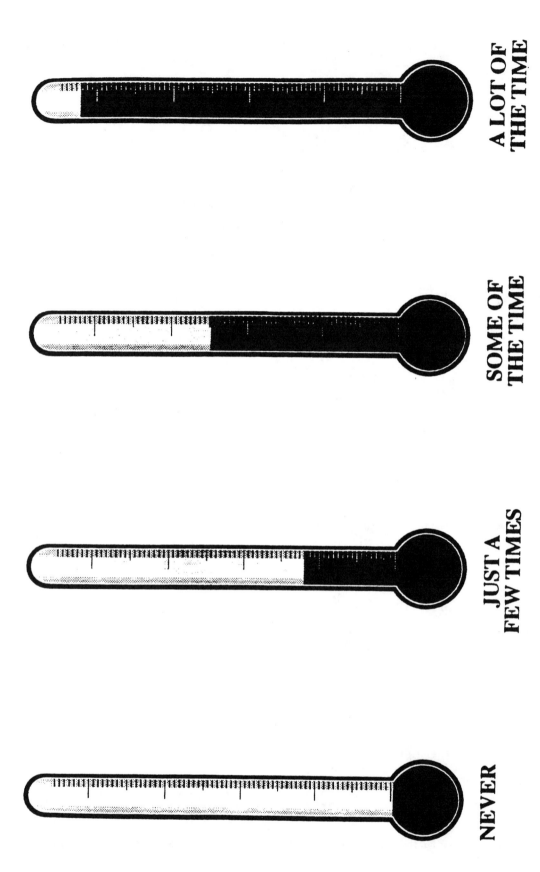

A LOT OF
THE TIME

SOME OF
THE TIME

JUST A
FEW TIMES

NEVER

Copyright (c) 1995 by Praver, Pelcovitz and DiGiuseppe

Assessing Environments—III
National Center for PTSD Review

Type of Population

Adults, Adolescents

Cost

Available from author at no charge

Copyright

J. Knutson and A. Berger

Languages

English

What It Measures

Assesses retrospectively perceived family environment and potential abuse.

Measure Content Survey, Procedure, or Process

Questionnaire consisting of 164 T-F items. Sum "T" items after reversing designated items. Interpretation of cut points is at 5+ on Physical Punishment subscale=childhood abuse.

Theoretical Orientation Summary

Empirical approaches to family relations.

Time Estimate

Administration	Scoring
10–15 minutes	5–15 minutes

Equipment Needed

Paper & Pencil	Computer	Basic Psychophysiological	Specialized Equipment
X			

Psychometric Maturity

Under Construction	Basic Properties Intact	Mature
	X	

Psychometric Properties Summary

Reliability Retest (2 months, college students): Mdn .83 (.61–.89) for subscale scores. Internal Consistency: KR20 (college students) .48–.79.

Validity Concurrent (M=5.7 for abused adolescents vs. 1.5 for nonabused controls).

Normative Data: College students, Low-income pregnant women, Parents of child psychiatric patients, Incarcerated felons, Pelvic pain patients.

Particular Sensitivity

Age	Change over Time	Culture/ Ethnicity	Gender	Geography/ Climate	Sexual Orientation	Socioeconomic Status	Urban/ Rural
?	?	?	X	?	?	X	?

Estimate of Number of In-Process Studies

25+

Unpublished References

Knutson, J., & Berger, A. (1984). Manual for the Assessing Environments III. Iowa City, IA: University of Iowa.

Published References

Knutson, J., & Selner, M. (1994). Punitive childhood experiences reported by young adults over a 10-year period. *Child Abuse & Neglect, 18*, 155–166.

General Comments

Key Words

Population	Stressor	Topic
adult	domestic violence discipline family dynamics parenting physical punishment/abuse	clinical general treatment research

Reference Citation for This Review

Ford, J. (1996). Psychometric Review of Assessing Environments—III. In B. H. Stamm (Ed.). *Measurement of stress, trauma, and adaptation*. Lutherville, MD: Sidran Press.

Reviewer Contact Name

Julian Ford, Ph.D.
Address: National Center for PTSD (116-D)
                VA Medical Center
                White River Junction, VT 05009
Phone: 802.296.5132
Fax: 802.296.5135
E-mail: Julian.Ford@Dartmouth.Edu

Measure Contact Name

John Knutson
Address: Department of Psychology
                University of Iowa
                Iowa City, IA 52242 USA
Phone:
Fax:
E-mail:

Assessment of Psystress via Salivary Ions

Type of Population
Any

Cost
Free

Copyright

Languages
English

What It Measures
Acute and chronic psychological stress (PSYSTRESS).

Measure Content Survey, Procedure, or Process
Sampling of unstimulated saliva.

No internationally agreed comprehensive test battery exists for the assessment of work-load, work-stress, and well-being. Objective physiological "anchor" variables are needed (Hinton and Burton, 1992b). Strong physiological evidence supports the use of concentration of indicants/salivary potassium $[K^+]$ and sodium $[Na^+]$ as indicants of neuro and endocrine function relating to phasic and tonic psychological stress ("psystress," Hinton and Burton, 1992a). A series of studies conducted at the Stress Research Unit of Glasgow University, in collaboration with the Department of Occupational Psychology of Dresden University, have shown that in *unstimulated* saliva, the concentration of sodium $[Na^+]$ and that of potassium $[K^+]$ indicate respectively tonic level of work-stress and phasic change with challenging task performance (Hinton, et al., 1992a, b, and c; Neilson, et al., 1993; Burton, et al., 1995, in press; Richter, et al., 1995). More recent studies have shown that simulations of real-life stressors can produce dramatic reductions in $[Na^+]$ in nurses recalling death and dying of patients (Hogg, et al., 1994), unprepared students faced with exam paper just before a critical exam (Hardman, unpublished), and people struggling to succeed with much negative feedback on a highly engaging computer task (Richter, et al., in press). Using Hinton and Burton's development of the transactional model of Cox and MacKay (Hinton & Burton, 1993), the research of our Stress Research Unit shows that perceived coping incapacity (PCI) relates significantly to reduced salivary $[Na^+]$ and that increases in $[K^+]$ relate to autonomic activation caused by both emotional disturbance and positive motivation by a perceived challenging task.

Theoretical Orientation Summary
Psychophysiological model of stress (development of transactional model; Hinton & Burton, 1992a).

Time Estimate

Administration	Scoring
10–15 minutes	depends on lab

Equipment Needed

Paper & Pencil	Computer	Basic Psychophysiological	Specialized Equipment
			Saliva sampling tubes, centrifuge, flame photometer

Psychometric Maturity

Under Construction	Basic Properties Intact	Mature	
	X		

Psychometric Properties Summary

N/A

Particular Sensitivity

Age	Change over Time	Culture / Ethnicity	Gender	Geography / Climate	Sexual Orientation	Socioeconomic Status	Urban / Rural
any age	X	appears culture free	?	appears bias free	?	appears bias free	appears bias free

Estimate of Number of In-Process Studies

Tested so far on students, schoolchildren, factory workers, nurses, aircraft pilots.

Unpublished References

Hinton, J. W. (1991). Psychological stress and salivary [K+], [Na+]. Presented at the First European Congress of Psychophysiology, University of Tilberg. The Netherlands.

Hinton, J. W. (September 1992a). Monitoring psychological stress by salivary ions. Presented at the International Congress of Psychophysiology. Berlin, Germany.

Hinton, J. W. (September 1992b). Psychophysiological monitoring of acute and chronic psychological stress and coping orientation at work. Work with Display Units, Technische Universitat, Berlin.

Hinton, J. W., & Burton, R. F. (April 1994). Application of a biopsychological model to work-stress: Relevance of salivary [Na+] to perceived coping incapacity and salivary [K+] to mental effort. European Congress of Psychophysiology. Barcelona, Spain.

Hinton, J. W., & Burton, R. F. (in press 1996). A psychophysiological model of psystress causation and response applied to the workplace. *Journal of Psychophysiology*.

Hinton, J. W., Burton, R. F., Hogg, K., & Neilson, E. (September 1994). Psychophysiology of salivary ions & the assessment of work-stress. International Symposium of Work-Psychology. Dresden University. Dresden, Germany.

Neilson, E., Hinton, J. W., Burton, R. F., & Beastall, G. (September 1992). Relationships between the concentrations of Na+, K+, and cortisol in saliva and self reported chronic psychological stress factors in a computer-component factory. Presented at the Joint Conference of the Health Section of the British Psychological Society and the British Psychophysiological Society. St. Andrews, Scotland.

Published References

Burton, R. F., Hinton, J. W., Neilson, E., & Beastall, G. (in press). Concentrations of sodium, potassium and cortisol in saliva, and self-reported chronic work stress factors. *Biological Psychology*.

Hinton, J. W. (1992c). Salivary [K+], [Na+] and psychological stress. *Journal of Psychophysiology, 6* (3), 277.

Hinton, J. W., & Burton, R. F. (1992a). Clarification of the concept of psychological stress. *International Journal of Psychosomatics, 39* (1–4), 42-43.

Hinton, J. W., & Burton, R. F. (1992b). How can stress be taken seriously? A reply to Richard Graveling. *Work and Stress, 6* (2), 103–106.

Hinton, J. W., Burton, R. F., Farmer, J. G., Rotheiler, E., Shewan, D., Gemmell, M., Berry, J., & Gibson, R. (1992). Relative changes in salivary Na+ and K+ relating to stress induction. *Biological Psychology, 33*(1), 63–71.

Hogg, K. J., Hinton, J. W., & Burton, R. F. (1995). Changes in salivary potassium and sodium in auxiliary, student and staff nurses when recalling the deaths of patients. *Journal of Psychophysiology 9,* 178.

Kaiser, J., Hinton, J. W., Krohne, H. W., Stewart, R., & Burton, R. (1995). Coping dispositions and physiological recovery from a speech preparation stressor. *Personality and Individual Differences 19,* 1–11.

Neilson, E., Hinton, J. W., Burton, R. F., & Beastall, G. (1993). Relationships between the concentrations of Na+, K+, and cortisol in saliva, and self-reported chronic stress factors in the workplace. *Journal of Psychophysiology*, 7, 263-264.

Stewart, R., Kaiser, J., Hinton, J. W., Burton, R., & Krohne, H. W. Tonic EMG and autonomic activity after release from unexpected-speech stressor: Related to emotional inhibition and introversion. *Journal of Psychophysiology* 9, 178.

General Comments

Without care in sampling, unstimulated saliva will not be obtained and results will be invalid. Anyone can learn to do the flame photometry easily and it is quick, cheap, and accurate. Saliva sampling seems to be the easiest way of obtaining psychophysiological information on the state of psychological stress.

Key Words

Population	Stressor	Topic
any children adolescents adults elderly	any	diagnosis measure development neurobiology psychophysiology research rural-care

Reference Citation for This Review

Hinton, J. W. (1996). Psychometric review of Assessment of Psystress via Salivary Ions. In B. H. Stamm (Ed.). *Measurement of stress, trauma, and adaptation*. Lutherville, MD: Sidran Press.

Measure Contact Name

John W. Hinton and Richard R. Burton

Address:	Stress-Research Unit
	Psychology Department
	University of Glasgow
	Adam Smith Building
	Glasgow G12 8RT Scotland, UK
Phone:	+141.330.5484
	+141.330.5089
Fax:	+141.339.8889
E-mail:	BERNICE@psy.gla.ac.uk (indicate F.A.O. Dr. J. W. Hinton)

Brief War Zone Stress Inventories
National Center for PTSD Review

Type of Population
Adults

Cost
Available from author at no charge

Copyright

Languages
English

What It Measures
Questionnaire, selected items from the 100-item multidimensional trauma exposure interview developed by the National Vietnam Veterans Readjustment Survey, separate scales for men and women veterans.

Measure Content Survey, Procedure, or Process
Abbreviated assessment of warzone trauma exposure in men and women veterans, with sum scores on designated items.

Theoretical Orientation Summary

Time Estimate

Administration	Scoring
5 minutes	5 minutes

Equipment Needed

Paper & Pencil	Computer	Basic Psychophysiological	Specialized Equipment
X			

Psychometric Maturity

Under Construction	Basic Properties Intact	Mature
	X	

Psychometric Properties Summary
Reliability (Coefficient alpha .96 for men, .90 for women)
Predictive Validity (correlation with full scale .95 for men, .90 for women)

Particular Sensitivity

Age	Change over Time	Culture / Ethnicity	Gender	Geography / Climate	Sexual Orientation	Socioeconomic Status	Urban / Rural
?	?	?	X	?	?	?	?

Estimate of Number of In-Process Studies

Unknown

Unpublished References

Woods, M. G., Schlenger, W., Fairbank, J., Caddell, J., & Jordan, B. K. (October 1992). Development and validation of Brief Warzone Stress Inventories for men and women veterans. Paper presented at the annual convention of the International Society for Traumatic Stress Studies. Los Angeles, CA.

Published References

Unknown

General Comments

Key Words

Population	Stressor	Topic
men veterans women veterans	combat	epidemiology research war zone exposure

Reference Citation for This Review

Ford., J. (1996). Psychometric review of Brief War Zone Stress Inventories. In B. H. Stamm (Ed.). *Measurement of stress, trauma, and adaptation.* Lutherville, MD: Sidran Press.

Reviewer Contact Name

Julian Ford, Ph.D.

Address: National Center for PTSD (116-D)
               VA Medical Center
               White River Junction, VT 05009 USA
Phone: 802.296.5132
Fax: 802.296.5135
E-mail: Julian.Ford@Dartmouth.Edu

Measure Contact Name

M. Gail Woods, Ph.D.

Address: Research Triangle Institute
               P.O. Box 12194
               Research Triangle Park, NC 27709 USA
Phone:
Fax:
E-mail:

Child's Reaction to Traumatic Events Scale (CRTES)

Type of Population
Children, Adolescents

Cost

Copyright

Languages
English

What It Measures
Intrusive thoughts and affects and avoidance behaviors

Measure Content Survey, Procedure, or Process
This is a 15-item self-report questionnaire to measure intrusive thoughts and affects and avoidance behaviors in children and adolescents. Respondents are asked to use the most recent and significant stressful life event as a referent to complete all scale items. Symptom intensity and duration are assessed by asking respondents to indicate on a 4-point scale the frequency of occurrence for each positively endorsed symptom with 0=not at all, 1=rarely, 3=sometimes, and 5=often.

Theoretical Orientation Summary

Time Estimate

Administration	Scoring
5–10 minutes	5 minutes

Equipment Needed

Paper & Pencil	Computer	Basic Psychophysiological	Specialized Equipment
X			

Psychometric Maturity

Under Construction	Basic Properties Intact	Mature
X		

Psychometric Properties Summary
Across several efforts since 1991 moderate to high Cronbach alphas. Most recently, in an investigation assessing the impact of Hurricane Andrew on children and adolescents, the following alphas were obtained: intrusion=.84, avoidance=.72, and total scale=.85. Data from both clinical and non-clinical samples are being obtained.

Particular Sensitivity

Age	Change over Time	Culture / Ethnicity	Gender	Geography / Climate	Sexual Orientation	Socioeconomic Status	Urban / Rural
X	X	X	X	?	?	X	X

Estimate of Number of In-Process Studies

Several

Unpublished References

Unknown

Published References

Unknown

General Comments

This scale includes six items derived from the original Impact of Events Scale.

Key Words

Population	Stressor	Topic
children adolescents	any	assessment measure development research

Reference Citation for This Review

Jones, R. T. (1996). Psychometric review of Child's Reaction to Traumatic Events Scale (CRTES). In B. H. Stamm (Ed.). *Measurement of stress, trauma, and adaptation*. Lutherville, MD: Sidran Press.

Measure Contact Name

Russell T. Jones, Ph.D.

Address: Department of Clinical Psychology
               Virginia Polytechnic Institute & State University
               Stress & Coping Lab
               4102 Derring Hall
               Blacksburg, VA 24061-0436 USA

Phone: (540) 231-5934

Fax: (540) 231-3652

E-mail: ptl@vt.edu

Child's Reaction to Traumatic Events Scale (CRTES)

Name _____   Date _____

Recently you experienced _____

Below is a list of comments made by people after stressful life events. Please check each item, indicating how often these comments were true for you DURING THE PAST SEVEN DAYS. If they did not occur during that time, please mark the "not at all" column.

Comment	Not at all	Rarely	Sometimes	Often
1 I thought about it when I didn't mean to.				
2 I stopped letting myself get upset when I thought about it or was reminded of it.				
3 I tried not to remember.				
4 I had trouble falling asleep or staying asleep because pictures or thoughts about it came into my mind.				
5 I had strong feelings about it.				
6 I had dreams about it.				
7 I stayed away from things that reminded me of it.				
8 I felt that it did not happen or that it was make-believe.				
9 I tried not to talk about it.				
10 I kept seeing it over and over in my mind.				
11 Other things kept making me think about it.				
12 I had lots of feelings about it, but I didn't pay attention to them.				
13 I tried not to think about it.				
14 Any reminder brought back feelings about it.				
15 I don't have feelings about it anymore.				

Childhood Incest Questionnaire
National Center for PTSD Review

Type of Population

Adult women incest survivors

Cost

Order form available from author

Copyright

M. A. Donaldson

Languages

English

What It Measures

Assesses *DSM* PTSD symptoms and stress symptoms (e.g., anger, guilt, fear, sadness)

Measure Content Survey, Procedure, or Process

Questionnaire, 52 six-point frequency of symptom items including Vulnerability/Isolation, Fear/Anxiety, Guilt/Shame, Anger/Betrayal, Reaction to Abuser, Sadness/Loss, Powerlessness, Intrusive Symptoms, Avoidance Symptoms, Detachment, Emotional Numbness. Sum scores on designated items.

Theoretical Orientation Summary

Horowitz's (1986) stress response syndromes.

Time Estimate

Administration	Scoring
10–20 minutes	10–15 minutes

Equipment Needed

Paper & Pencil	Computer	Basic Psychophysiological	Specialized Equipment
X			

Psychometric Maturity

Under Construction	Basic Properties Intact	Mature
X		

Psychometric Properties Summary

Retest reliability (one month): rp=.66–.85 for all subscales except powerlessness (rp=.29) and emotional control/numbness (rp=58)

Convergent/Discriminant Validity: Vulnerability, Fear, Sadness, Loss, Powerlessness correlate significantly with Beck DI and STAI; Guilt/Shame correlates significantly with Beck DI and STAI; Anger and Reaction to Perpetrator have zero-order correlations with Beck DI and STAI.

Particular Sensitivity

Age	Change over Time	Culture / Ethnicity	Gender	Geography / Climate	Sexual Orientation	Socioeconomic Status	Urban / Rural
X	?	?	?	?	?	?	?

Estimate of Number of In-Process Studies
Unknown

Unpublished References
Edwards, P., & Donaldson, M. (1989). Reliability and validity of the Response to Childhood Incest Questionnaire.

Published References
Edwards, P., & Donaldson, M. (1989). Assessment of symptoms in adult survivors of incest. *Child Abuse & Neglect, 13*, 101-110.

General Comments

Key Words

Population	Stressor	Topic
adult women incest survivors	childhood sexual abuse/incest	clinical measure development research

Reference Citation for This Review
Ford, J. (1996). Psychometric review of Childhood Incest Questionnaire. In B. H. Stamm (Ed.). *Measurement of stress, trauma, and adaptation*. Lutherville, MD: Sidran Press.

Reviewer Contact Name
Julian Ford, Ph.D.

National Center for PTSD (116-D)

VA Medical Center

White River Junction, VT 05009 USA

Phone:	802.296.5132
Fax:	802.296.5135
E-mail:	Julian.Ford@Dartmouth.Edu

Measure Contact Name
MaryAnn Donaldson

Address:	700 First Ave. South
	Fargo, ND 58103 USA
Phone:	
Fax:	
E-mail:	

Childhood PTS Reaction Index (CPTS-RI)

Type of Population

Children and Adolescents

Cost

Cost of copies and mailing

Copyright

Frederick, C., Pynoos, R., & Nader, K., 1992

Languages

English, Arabic (2: ages 7–10 & ages 11–17), Armenian, Cambodian, Croatian, Norwegian

What It Measures

children's reactions to traumatic experiences

Measure Content Survey, Procedure, or Process

The revised CPTS-RI is a 20-item scale used in direct semi-structured interview with children and adolescents. There is an associated training manual (copyright: Nader, 1993) which gives detailed instructions for its usage. The interview is generally preceded by a draw-a-picture/tell-a-story sequence. An associated parent interview scale (Nader, 1984; 1994) may be administered to parents.

CPTS-RI items include some of the DSM-IV PTSD symptoms from each of three main subscales and an associated feature. Each child is interviewed about his or her individual response to the event. Only direct self-report of symptoms still present are recorded. The revised CPTS-RI includes a 5-point Likert frequency rating scale ranging from "none" (rated 0) to "most of the time" (rated 4). Although the index does not provide a DSM PTSD diagnosis, there is a scoring system which establishes a level of "PTSD." Previous unpublished empirical comparisons of CPTS-RI scores with clinical assessments for severity levels of PTSD have resulted in the following guidelines: a total score of 12–24 indicates a mild level of PTS reaction; 25–39, a moderate level; 40–59, a severe level; >60, a very severe reaction (see Psychometric Properties Summary below).

Two parent questionnaires have been used with the CPTS-RI. One of them is a more extensive clinical questionnaire used in semi-structured interview with parents, permitting simultaneous education of parents and extracting of information regarding their children (Nader, 1984; 1995). The others have been adapted to specific situations to match the CPTS-RI. Exposure questionnaires have been adapted to the specific traumatic situation for the English and other versions of the instrument. A war exposure questionnaire accompanies the training manual (Nader, 1993) and is available in Arabic; a revised version of it (available in Croatian) with additional coping measures is also available (Nader).

Theoretical Orientation Summary

Time Estimate

Administration	Scoring
20–45 minutes for scale plus time exposure questions	5–15 minutes

Equipment Needed

Paper & Pencil	Computer	Basic Psychophysiological	Specialized Equipment
			Pencil, Instrument and Interviewers Blank paper, colored pens (if using draw-a-picture/tell-a-story)

Psychometric Maturity

Under Construction	Basic Properties Intact	Mature	
	X		

Psychometric Properties Summary

The scale's co-authors and their colleagues performed a study of children exposed to a sniper attack. Interrater reliability for this instrument was measured at .94, and inter-item agreement by Cohen's kappa at .878 (Nader, et al., 1990). In the unpublished study of children exposed to a tornado, interrater reliability was established at .97. In a study of Kuwaiti children following the Gulf Crisis, internal consistency for this scale was established (Cronbach's alpha=.78) and 16 of the 20 items were significantly correlated with the total score at $p<.01$ (Nader and Fairbanks, 1994).

The validity of the instrument has been demonstrated in its ability to detect differences between children exposed to violence and a comparable group of unexposed children (Pynoos, et al., 1987; Nader, et al., 1990). Previous unpublished empirical comparisons of CPTS-RI scores with clinical assessments for severity levels of PTSD have resulted in the following guidelines: a total score of 12–24 indicates a mild level of PTSD reaction; 25–39, a moderate level; 40–59, a severe level; >60, a very severe reaction. Using DSM III-R criteria, these guidelines were empirically validated in a subsample of children from a study of the 1988 Spitak earthquake in Armenia (Pynoos, Goenjian, Karakashian, Tashjian, Manjikian, Setrakian, Steinberg, & Fairbanks, 1993) in which 43.6% of those with moderate reactions on the CPTS-RI, 89.3% rated severe, and 91.7% of those rated very severe on the CPTS-RI met the DSM III-R criteria for PTSD. In an as yet unpublished study of children exposed to a tornado, in which clinicians underwent a week of thorough training (by Nader) in the instrument's use prior to administration, all of the children who entered treatment following the tornado were independently diagnosed under the review of a New York State Mental Health psychiatrist. All of them met the criteria for PTSD. Yule, Bolton, and Udwin (1992) found a correlation between CPTS-RI and clinician diagnosis and IES scores.

Particular Sensitivity
(additional exposure questions adapted to specific situations)

Age	Change over Time	Culture/ Ethnicity	Gender	Geography/ Climate	Sexual Orientation	Socioeconomic Status	Urban/ Rural
Developmentally Adapted	?	X	X	X	?	X	X

Estimate of Number of In-Process Studies

Numerous

Unpublished References

Nader, K., & Pynoos, R. (1989). Child Post-traumatic Stress Disorder Inventory: Parent Interview. Unpublished manuscript.

Nader, K., Pynoos, R., & Fairbanks, L. (1993). The therapeutic use of screening instruments.

Pynoos, R., Nader, K., et al. (1993) Differential diagnosis one year after a sniper attack.

Stuber, M., Nader, K., & Pynoos, R. (1992). The violence of despair: Responses of Head Start teachers to the Los Angeles uprising.

Yule, W., Bolton, D., & Udwin, O. (1992). Objective and subjective predictors of PTSD in adolescence.

Published References

Nader, K. (in press). Assessing traumatic experiences in children. In Wilson, J. and Keane, T. (Eds.), *Assessing psychological trauma and PTSD*. New York: Guilford Press.

Nader, K., & Fairbanks, L. (1994). The Suppression of reexperiencing: Impulse control and somatic symptoms in children following traumatic exposure. *Anxiety, Stress and Coping: An International Journal, 7,* 229–239.

Nader, K., Pynoos, R., Fairbanks, L., Al-Ajeel, M., & Al-Asfour, A. (1993). Acute post-traumatic stress reactions among Kuwait children following the Gulf Crisis. *British Journal of Clinical Psychology, 32,* 407–416.

Nader, K., Pynoos, R. S., Fairbanks, L., & Frederick, C. (1990). Children's PTSD reactions one year after a sniper attack at their school. *American Journal of Psychiatry, 147,* 1526–1530.

Pynoos, R. S., Frederick, C., Nader, K., Arroyo, W., Eth, S., Nunez, W., Steinberg, A., & Fairbanks, L. (1987). Life threat and posttraumatic stress in school age children. *Archives of General Psychiatry, 44,* 1057–1063.

Pynoos, R. S., Goenjian, A., Karakashian, M., Tashjian, M., Manjikian, R., Manoukian, G., Steinberg, A. M., & Fairbanks, L. A. (1993). Posttraumatic stress reactions in children after the 1988 Armenian earthquake. *British Journal of Psychiatry, 163,* 239–247.

Pynoos, R. S., & Nader, K. (1988). Children who witness the sexual assaults of their mothers. *Journal of the American Academy of Child and Adolescent Psychiatry, 27* (5), 567–572.

Pynoos, R. S., Nader, K., Frederick, C., Gonda, L., & Stuber, M. (1988). Grief reactions in school age children following a sniper attack at school. In E. Chigier (Ed.). *Grief and Bereavement in Contemporary Society* (pp. 29–41). London: Freund Publishing House, Ltd.

Realmuto, G. M., Masten, A., Carole, L. F., Hubbard, J., Groteluschen, A., & Chhun, B. (1992). Adolescent survivors of massive childhood trauma in Cambodia: Life events and current symptoms. *Journal of Traumatic Stress, 5* (4), 589–599.

Schwarz, E. D., & Kowalski, J. M. (1991). PTSD in children and adults after a school shooting. *Journal of the American Academy of Child and Adolescent Psychiatry, 30* (6), 936–944.

Schwarz, E. D., Kowalski, J. M., & Hanus, S. (1992). Malignant memories: Signatures of violence. In S. Feinstein, et al. (Eds.). *Adolescent Psychiatry* (pp. 280–300). Chicago: University of Chicago Press.

Stuber, M., & Nader, K. (1995). Psychiatric sequelae in adolescent bone marrow transplant survivors: Implications for psychotherapy. *Journal of Psychotherapy Practice and Research, 4* (1), 30–41.

Stuber, M. L., Nader, K., Houskamp, B., & Pynoos, R. (in press). Perceived life threat and post traumatic stress in pediatric bone marrow transplant patients. *Journal of Traumatic Stress.*

Stuber, M., Nader, K., Yasuda, P. Pynoos, R. S., & Cohen, S. (1991). Stress responses after pediatric bone marrow transplantation: Preliminary results of a prospective, longitudinal study. *Journal of the American Academy of Child and Adolescent Psychiatry* (November), 952–957.

General Comments

Children interviewed using the CPTS-RI at 1 and 14 months following a sniper attack (Pynoos, et al., 1987; Nader, et al., 1990) had significantly fewer symptoms than those with comparable exposures who were interviewed only at 14 months after the event. Thus early screening not only identifies the level of traumatic response, but may be therapeutically beneficial as well.

Key Words

Population	Stressor	Topic
children adolescents	any	assessment clinical diagnosis research

Reference Citation for This Review

Nader, K. (1996). Psychometric review of Childhood PTS Reaction Index (CPTS-RI). In B. H. Stamm (Ed). *Measurement of stress, trauma, and adaptation*. Lutherville, MD: Sidran Press.

Measure Contact Name

any of the authors
Dr. Kathleen Nader

Address:	P.O. Box 2251
	Laguna Hills, CA 92654 USA
Phone:	714.454.0628
Fax:	714.454.0249
E-mail:	knader@twosuns.org

Childhood PTSD Interview

Type of Population

Children and adolescents. It has also been used with success with retarded adults.

Cost

Free to all of those who agree to share the raw data they collect in order to help establish the scale's psychometric properties.

Copyright

K. E. Fletcher

Languages

English

What It Measures

All *DSM-IV* symptoms of PTSD, additional PTSD symptoms as manifested in children, and associated symptoms (anxiety, sadness, omen formation, survivor guilt, guilt/self-blame, fantasy denial, self-destructive behavior, dissociative responses, antisocial behavior, risk-taking behavior, and changed eating habits). Each symptom is assessed by two or more questions. The interview allows diagnoses to be made, and it allows an overall severity score to be computed.

Measure Content Survey

93 yes/no questions about presence of symptomatology, and a few additional ratings by the interviewer. With instructions to the interviewer in the right hand margin, the interview is self-scoring for diagnoses.

Theoretical Orientation Summary

Time Estimate

Administration	Scoring
30–45 minutes	self-scoring

Equipment Needed

Paper & Pencil	Computer	Basic Psychophysiological	Specialized Equipment
X			

Psychometric Maturity

Under Construction	Basic Properties	Mature
	X	

Psychometric Properties Summary

Yet to be established (but see the review of a related self-report measure, the When Bad Things Happen scale elsewhere in this publication).

Particular Sensitivity

Age	Change over Time	Culture / Ethnicity	Gender	Geography / Climate	Sexual Orientation	Socioeconomic Status	Urban / Rural
X	?	?	?	?	?	?	?

Estimate of Number of In-Process Studies

4. One of these is a national effort to gather data for validation for the interview and other related interviews and scales. If you are interested in joining this effort, please contact Ken Fletcher at the addresses and telephones below.

Unpublished References

Unknown

Published References

None.

General Comments

This scale is intended for both clinical and research use. The intent is to eventually pare down the items during the norming process. The interview can be conducted with child victims of chronic abuse or multiple stressors as well as victims of single-occurrence events such as natural disasters or fires. The interview can be conducted with non-traumatized comparison groups as well, as long as a stressor is provided (either the same stressor as the exposed group or the most stressful event that the nontraumatized child has been exposed to). This scale is one of a set. See also "Childhood PTSD Interview—Parent Form," "The When Bad Things Happen Scale," and the "Parent Report of the Child's Reaction to Stress." IBM-compatible data entry programs are available from the author for all of these scales. The data entry programs run in EPI INFO, a data entry creation program distributed (for free from other users or academic computer departments or for $50 from the Center for Disease Control or the World Health Organization). EPI INFO programs allow data bases to be created which can be analyzed on a basic level within EPI INFO itself and by other statistical programs (such as SPSS, SAS, and Systat) or by databases and spreadsheets that will read dBase file formats.

Key Words

Population	Stressor	Topic
children adolescents developmentally delayed adults	any	clinical diagnosis general treatment measure development research

Reference Citation for This Review

Fletcher, K. E. (1996). Psychometric review of Childhood PTSD Interview. In B. H. Stamm (Ed.). *Measurement of Stress, Trauma And Adaptation*. Lutherville, MD: Sidran Press.

Measure Contact Name

Kenneth E. Fletcher, Ph.D.
Address: University of Massachusetts Medical Center
             Psychiatry Dept.
             55 Lake Avenue North
             Worcester, MA 01655-0001 USA
Phone: 508.856.3329
Fax: 508.856.6426
E-Mail: fletcher@umassmed.ummed.edu

• Childhood PTSD Interview Sample Items

- Was _____ REAL scary sometimes?

- Do you sometimes think about _____ when you don't want to?

- Do you ever find yourself daydreaming about _____?

- Is it easy for you to be around people who make you think of _____?

- Since _____ does it sometimes seem like you can't feel anything, like you are a robot or you are made out of stone?

- Are you always on the look out for something bad to happen these days?

- Are you ever afraid that _____ will happen again?

- Since _____ happened, did you start to think you can tell the future?

- Do you like doing unsafe or dangerous things since _____ happened? Do you like doing crazy things that might get you or someone else hurt?

Childhood PTSD Interview—Parent Form

Type of Population

Parent or guardian interview regarding stress responses of children and adolescents.

Cost

Free to all of those who agree to share the raw data they collect in order to help establish the scale's psychometric properties.

Copyright

K. E. Fletcher.

Languages

English

What It Measures

Same as the Childhood PTSD Interview, which this interview exactly parallels, except the parent or guardian is asked about the child's responses rather than the child (or, in addition to the child). All *DSM-IV* symptoms of PTSD, additional PTSD symptoms as manifested in children, and associated symptoms (anxiety, sadness, omen formation, survivor guilt, guilt/self-blame, fantasy denial, self-destructive behavior, dissociative responses, antisocial behavior, risk-taking behavior, and changed eating habits). Each symptom is assessed by two or more questions. The interview allows diagnoses to be made, and it allows an overall severity score to be computed.

Measure Content Survey

93 yes/no questions about presence of symptomatology and a few additional ratings by the interviewer.

Theoretical Orientation Summary

Time Estimate

Administration	Scoring
30–60 minutes	10–30 minutes

Equipment Needed

Paper & Pencil	Computer	Basic Psychopsychological	Specialized Equipment
X			

Psychometric Maturity

Under Construction	Basic Properties Intact	Mature
X		

Psychometric Properties Summary

Yet to be established (but see the review of a related self-report measure, the When Bad Things Happen scale, elsewhere in this publication).

Particular Sensitivity

Age	Change over Time	Culture / Ethnicity	Gender	Geography / Climate	Sexual Orientation	Socioeconomic Status	Urban / Rural
X	?	?	?	?	?	?	?

Estimate of Number of In-Process Studies

Two. One of these is a national effort to gather data for validation for the interview and other related interviews and scales. If you are interested in joining this effort, please contact Ken Fletcher at the address and telephone below.

Unpublished References

Unknown

Published References

None.

General Comments

This scale is intended for both clinical and research use. The intent is to eventually pare down the items during the norming process. The interview can be conducted with nontraumatized comparison groups as well, as long as a stressor is provided (either the same stressor as the exposed group or the most stressful event that the nontraumatized child has been exposed to). This scale is one of a set. See also "Childhood PTSD Interview," "The When Bad Things Happen Scale," and the "Parent Report of the Child's Reaction to Stress." IBM-compatible data entry programs are available from the author for all of these scales. The data entry programs run in EPI INFO, a data entry creation program distributed (for free from other users or academic computer departments or for $50 from the Center for Disease Control or the World Health Organization). EPI INFO programs allow data bases to be created which can be analyzed on a basic level within EPI INFO itself and by other statistical programs (such as SPSS, SAS, and Systat) or by databases and spreadsheets that will read dBase file formats.

Key Words

Population	Stressor	Topic
parents	any	clinical diagnosis general treatment measure development research

Reference Citation for This Review

Fletcher, K. E. (1996). Psychometric review of Childhood PTSD Interview—Parent Form. In B. H. Stamm (Ed.). *Measurement of stress, trauma, and adaptation*. Lutherville, MD: Sidran Press.

Measure Contact Name

Kenneth E. Fletcher, Ph.D.
Address: University of Massachusetts Medical Center
               Psychiatry Dept.
               55 Lake Avenue North
               Worcester, MA 01655-0001 USA
Phone: 508.856.3329
Fax: 508.856.6426
E-Mail: fletcher@umassmed.ummed.edu

Childhood PTSD Interview—Parent Form Sample Items

- Was your child frightened by _____?

- Does your child think about _____ even when he/she doesn't want to?

- Does your child tend to daydream or stare off into space more than before _____?

- Does it bother your child when he/she sees someone or goes someplace that reminds him/her of _____?

- Does your child ever say he/she wishes he/she didn't have any feelings that remind him or her of _____?

- Since _____ does it seem like your child shows less feelings (except maybe anger) than he/she did before _____?

- Is your child always on the look out for something bad to happen nowadays?

- Does your child ever seem to be afraid that _____ will happen again?

- Since _____ happened, does your child sometimes think he/she can predict or tell the future?

- Has your child started doing more risky things since _____ happened? Like doing crazy things he/she knows are dangerous?

Childhood Trauma Questionnaire
National Center for PTSD Review

Type of Population

Adults, Adolescents in a clinical setting

Cost

Order form available from author

Copyright

David P. Bernstein and Laura Fink

Languages

English

What It Measures

Assesses retrospectively perceived childhood abuse and neglect.

Measure Content Survey, Procedure, or Process

Questionnaire, 70 five-point Likert frequency of occurrence items including physical and emotional abuse, emotional neglect, sexual abuse, physical neglect. Sum scores after reversing designated items. Interpretation of cut point is 6–9+ on Sexual Abuse Scale (Note: based on limited clinical sample [see Normative Data below] with intensive interview [Childhood Trauma Interview] as criterion, with sensitivity/specificity as low as 73–88%/76% at cut point=6, and 97%/35% at cut point=9.)

Theoretical Orientation Summary

Finklehor's traumatization model

Time Estimate

Administration	Scoring
10–15 minutes	5–10 minutes

Equipment Needed

Paper & Pencil	Computer	Basic Psychophysiological	Specialized Equipment
X			

Psychometric Maturity

Under Construction	Basic Properties Intact	Mature
	X	

Psychometric Properties Summary

Internal Consistency: Alpha=.66–.97 for five empirically derived (from 2 samples of adult or adolescent psychiatric patients) factor scores (Emotional Abuse, Physical Abuse, Sexual Abuse, Emotional Neglect, Physical Neglect) with adult substance abusers, psychiatric patients, and chronic pain patients; undergraduates; adolescent psychiatric inpatients.

Reliability Retest (3.6 months, chemical dependency outpatients): r=.80–.83. Internal Consistency: Alpha (CD outpatients)=.79–.94.

Validity: Concurrent (rp=.32 for CTQ physical abuse score and Childhood Trauma Interview); Concurrent (rp=.61 for CTQ sexual abuse score and Childhood Trauma Interview); Discriminant (rp=−.36−.08 for CTQ neglect score and Childhood Trauma Interview); Discriminant (r < .10 for CTQ scores and vocabulary, social desirability measures).

Validity, Predictive: Physical Abuse, Sexual Abuse, Physical Neglect differentiated psychiatric and chronic pain patients from undergraduates. Emotional Abuse and Emotional Neglect also differentiated psychiatric/pain patients from substance abusers.

Normative Data: Chemical Dependency outpatients Urban, Afro-American (51%), Latino (31%) populations. Gender Sensitivity: Women > Men on CTQ factor and total scores.

Particular Sensitivity

Age	Change over Time	Culture / Ethnicity	Gender	Geography / Climate	Sexual Orientation	Socioeconomic Status	Urban / Rural
X	?	X	X	?	?	?	?

Estimate of Number of In-Process Studies
Unknown

Unpublished References
Bernstein, D., Pogge, D., & Ahluvalia, T. (June 1995). A new scale for the assessment of maltreatment in adolescents. Paper presented at the annual meeting of the American Psychiatric Association. Miami, FL.

Published References
Bernstein, D., et al. (1994). Initial reliability and validity of a new retrospective measure of child abuse and neglect. *American Journal of Psychiatry, 151*, 1132–1136

General Comments

Key Words

Population	Stressor	Topic
adolescents adults	childhood abuse childhood neglect domestic violence	clinical general psychopathology measure development research

Reference Citation for This Review
Ford, J. (1996). Psychometric review of Childhood Trauma Questionnaire. In B. H. Stamm (Ed.). *Measurement of stress, trauma, and adaptation*. Lutherville, MD: Sidran Press.

Reviewer Contact Name
Julian Ford, Ph.D.

Address: National Center for PTSD (116-D)
                VA Medical Center
                White River Junction, VT 05009
Phone: 802.296.5132
Fax: 802.296.5135
E-mail: Julian.Ford@Dartmouth.Edu

Measure Contact Name

David Bernstein, Ph.D.

Address: Psychiatry Service
                 VA Medical Center
                 130 W. Kingsbridge Rd
                 Bronx, NY 10468 USA

Phone:

Fax:

E-mail:

Childhood Traumatic Events Survey
National Center for PTSD Review

Type of Population

Adults

Cost

Available from the author

Copyright

James Pennebaker

Languages

English

What It Measures

Assesses retrospectively trauma, age of occurrence, distress, and confidence in others.

Measure Content Survey, Procedure, or Process

Questionnaire scoring items including death of family or close friend, parental divorce or separation, sexual trauma, violence, or other trauma.

Theoretical Orientation Summary

Pennebaker's biopsychosocial model of affect suppression

Time Estimate

Administration	Scoring
5 minutes	5 minutes

Equipment Needed

Paper & Pencil	Computer	Basic Psychophysiological	Specialized Equipment
X			

Psychometric Maturity

Under Construction	Basic Properties Intact	Mature
	X	

Psychometric Properties Summary

Predictive validity supported by finding that, controlling for gender, age, education, social support, and adult trauma, both childhood trauma and failure to confide about childhood trauma predict self-reported illness.

Particular Sensitivity

Age	Change over Time	Culture / Ethnicity	Gender	Geography / Climate	Sexual Orientation	Socioeconomic Status	Urban / Rural
X	?	?	?	?	?	?	?

Estimate of Number of In-Process Studies

Unknown

Unpublished References

Unknown

Published References

Pennebaker, J., & Susman, J. (1988). Disclosure of traumas and psychosomatic processes. *Social Science and Medicine, 26*, 327-332.

General Comments

Key Words

Population	Stressor	Topic
adults adult incest survivors	any	research psychosomatic

Reference Citation for This Review

Ford, J. (1996). Psychometric review of Childhood Traumatic Events Survey. In B. H. Stamm (Ed.). *Measurement of stress, trauma, and adaptation*. Lutherville, MD: Sidran Press.

Reviewer Contact Name

Julian Ford, Ph.D.
National Center for PTSD (116-D)
VA Medical Center
White River Junction, VT 05009 USA

Phone: 802.296.5132
Fax: 802.296.5135
E-mail: Julian.Ford@Dartmouth.Edu

Measure Contact Name

James Pennebaker
Address: Department of Psychology
Southern Methodist University
Dallas, TX 75275 USA

Phone:
Fax:
E-mail:

Children's Exposure to Community Violence
National Center for PTSD Review

Type of Population
Children and adults

Cost
Available from author at no charge

Copyright
John Richter

Languages
English

What It Measures
Assesses current exposure to community violence

Measure Content Survey, Procedure, or Process
19-item questionnaire to assess current exposure to community violence. Scores for exposure to 18 different violent events.

Theoretical Orientation Summary
empirical

Time Estimate

Administration	Scoring
5–15 minutes	5–15 minutes

Equipment Needed

Paper & Pencil	Computer	Basic Psychophysiological	Specialized Equipment
X			

Psychometric Maturity

Under Construction	Basic Properties Intact	Mature
X		

Psychometric Properties Summary
Preliminary information is available on Children/Adolescents in support groups.

Particular Sensitivity

Age	Change over Time	Culture/ Ethnicity	Gender	Geography/ Climate	Sexual Orientation	Socioeconomic Status	Urban/ Rural
X	?	X	?	?	?	?	X

Estimate of Number of In-Process Studies

unknown

Unpublished References

Foy, D. (1994). Trauma assessment. Colloquium presented at the Dartmouth Medical School Psychiatric Research Center, November 4, 1994.

Published References

Unknown

General Comments

Key Words

Population	Stressor	Topic
children adolescents	civil unrest community violence	research

Reference Citation for This Review

Ford, J. (1996). Psychometric review of Survey of Children's Exposure to Community Violence. In B. H. Stamm (Ed.). *Measurement of stress, trauma, and adaptation*. Lutherville, MD: Sidran Press.

Reviewer Contact Name

Julian Ford, Ph.D.

Address	National Center for PTSD (116-D)
	VA Medical Center
	White River Junction, VT 05009 USA
Phone:	802.296.5132
Fax:	802.296.5135
E-mail:	Julian.Ford@Dartmouth.Edu

Measure Contact Name

John Richter, Ph.D.

Address:	National Institute of Mental Health
	Bethesda, MD USA
Phone:	301.443.5944
Fax:	
E-mail:	

Civilian Version of the Mississippi PTSD Scale

Type of Population

Any, Adults

Cost

Free

Copyright

Languages

English, Dutch (Hovens & Van der Ploeg, 1993), Spanish (Kulka et al., 1990)

What It Measures

The Civilian Mississippi Scale measures the hallmark DSM symptoms of PTSD and associated features.

Measure Content Summary

The Civilian Mississippi Scale contains 35 items, consisting of full-sentence, first-person statements depicting PTSD or PTSD-related symptoms. Each statement is accompanied by a 5-point Likert response scale (e.g., " never" to "very frequently"; "not at all true" to "extremely true"). Item scores may range from 1 to 5, with higher values indicating more symptomatology. Like its military counterpart (see below), a total score is obtained by summing across all item scores (possible range: 35–175). A lengthier version of the scale is also available, containing an additional 4 items to expand content breadth.

Theoretical Orientation Summary

The parent instrument for the Civilian Mississippi Scale is the popular Mississippi Scale for Combat-Related Posttraumatic Stress Disorder. Like the military version, the Civilian Mississippi Scale is intended to assess the PTSD symptom categories of reexperiencing, avoidance and numbing, and hyperarousal, as well as aspects of depression, suicidality, and guilt. The content was derived in a rational manner by a team of clinical psychologists with experience in PTSD research, diagnosis, and treatment. Each Civilian Mississippi Scale item was written so as to closely parallel the content of the items in the original military version. For 24 of the 35 items, the wording is identical across the two versions; for 8 items in the civilian instrument, references to "in the military" or "in the service" are changed to "in the past," and for 3 items, phrases that refer to the military are simply dropped and not replaced.

Time Estimate

Administration	Scoring
10–20 minutes	5–10 minutes

Equipment Needed

Paper & Pencil	Computer	Basic Psychophysiological	Specialized Equipment
X			

Psychometric Maturity

Under Construction	Basic Properties Intact	Mature
		X

Psychometric Properties Summary

Relatively high internal consistency reliability coefficients have been reported. Vreven, Gudanowski, King, and King (1995) obtained a coefficient alpha of .86 for the community-based sample of 668 nonveterans who participated in the National Vietnam Veterans Readjustment Study (Kulka, et al., 1990). Ouimette, Weathers, Litz, Krinsley, Brief, and Keane (1995) obtained a value of .91 for a sample of 110 male veterans seeking inpatient services for substance abuse, all of whom had no history of war zone exposure. And Love, Tolsma, and Ghosh (1995) obtained a coefficient alpha of .89 using a sample of 404 law enforcement officers, about 66% of whom were current or former undercover police officers. With regard to validity, Ouimette et al. demonstrated fairly strong convergence with scores on a number of other available self-report PTSD measures (correlations all in the .70s), as well as significant correlations with self-reported history of childhood physical abuse (.37) and sexual abuse (.34). Hovens and Van der Ploeg (993), using a Dutch translation with a sample of 200 psychiatric inpatients, judged the instrument to have satisfactory sensitivity (87%) but too low specificity (63%). Finally, Vreven et al. found expected relationships between measures of prior stressful or traumatic events and PTSD as measured by the Civilian Mississippi Scale, but they expressed some concerns and cautions regarding convergent and discriminant validity vis-a-vis its relationships with other PTSD measures versus its relationships with measures of general distress.

Particular Sensitivity

Age	Change over Time	Culture / Ethnicity	Gender	Geography / Climate	Sexual Orientation	Socioeconomic Status	Urban / Rural
?	?	X	?	?	?	?	?

Estimate of Number of In-Process Studies

Conservatively, 20.

Unpublished References

Inkeles, M., Loux, L. A., & Bourque, L. B. (submitted for publication). Dimensionality and reliability of the civilian version of the Mississippi Scale for Combat-Related Posttraumatic Stress Disorder.

Lauterbach, D., Vrana, S., King, D. W., & King, L. A. (May 1995). Psychometric properties of the civilian version of the Mississippi PTSD Scale. Paper presented at the annual meeting of the Midwestern Psychological Association. Chicago, IL.

Love, K. G., Tolsma, J. L., & Ghosh, P. (November 1994). Antecedents and correlates of PTSD in policing: Undercover assignment. Poster presented at the International Society for Traumatic Stress Studies. Chicago, IL.

Ouimette, P. C., Weathers, F. W., Litz, B. L., Krinsley, K. E., Brief, D. J., & Keane, T. M. (November 1994). Psychometric evaluation of the Mississippi Scale for Civilian PTSD in an inpatient sample of substance abusers. Poster presented at the International Society for Traumatic Stress Studies. Chicago, IL.

Triffleman, E., & Ball, S. (November 1994). Screening cocaine abusers for PTSD. Poster presented at the annual meeting of the International Society for Traumatic Stress Studies. Chicago, IL.

Published References

Brown, P. J., Recupio, T. R., & Stout, R. (in press). PTSD—substance abuse comorbidity and treatment utilization. *Addictive Behaviors*.

Hovens, J. E., & Van der Ploeg, H. M. (1993). Post-traumatic stress disorder in Dutch psychiatric inpatients. *Journal of Traumatic Stress, 6*, 91–101.

Koopman, C., Classen, C., & Spiegel, D. (1994). Predictors of posttraumatic stress symptoms among survivors of the Oakland/Berkeley, Calif., firestorm. *American. Journal. of Psychiatry, 151*, 888–894.

Kulka, R. A., Schlenger, W. E., Fairbank, J. A., Hough, R. L., Jordan, B. K., Marmar, C. R., & Weiss, D. S. (1990). *Trauma and the Vietnam War generation: Report on the findings from the National Vietnam Veterans Readjustment Study*. New York: Brunner/Mazel.

Vrana, S., & Lauterbach, D. (1994). Prevalence of traumatic events and post-traumatic psychological symptoms in a nonclinical sample of college students. *Journal of Traumatic Stress, 7*, 289–302.

Vreven, D. L., Gudanowski, D. M., King, L. A., & King, D.W. (1995). The civilian version of the Mississippi PTSD Scale: A psychometric evaluation. *Journal of Traumatic Stress, 8*, 91-109.

General Comments

The Civilian Mississippi Scale appears to be widely distributed and available from a variety of researchers.

Key Words

Population	Stressor	Topic
adults	any	clinical diagnosis epidemiology research service delivery

Reference Citation for This Review

King, L. A., & King, D. W. (1996). Psychometric review of the Civilian Version of the Mississippi PTSD Scale. In B. H. Stamm (Ed.). *Measurement of stress, trauma, and adaptation*. Lutherville, MD: Sidran Press.

Measure Authors

The instrument was developed as a part of the National Vietnam Veterans Readjustment Study conducted at Research Triangle Institute, North Carolina (researchers R. A. Kulka, W. E. Schlenger, J. A. Fairbank, R. L. Hough, B. K. Jordan, C. R. Marmar, and D. S. Weiss).

Reviewer Contact Name

L. A. King and D. W. King

Address:	National Center for PTSD
	Boston VAMC
	150 S. Huntington Avenue
	Boston, MA 02130
Phone:	617.232.9500, ext. 4938
Fax:	617.248.4515
E-Mail:	king.lynda@boston.va.gov

Civilian Version of the Mississippi PTSD Scale Sample Items

- I am able to get emotionally close to others.

- I have nightmares of experiences in my past that really happened.

- I have trouble concentrating on tasks.

Clinician Administered Dissociative States Scale

Type of Population

Adults, Psychiatric/Dissociative Disorders, PTSD

Cost

Minimal

Copyright

Languages

English

What It Measures

Dissociative States

Measure Content Survey, Procedure, or Process

The Clinician Administered Dissociative States Scale is a 28-item scale for use as a repeated measures of dissociative states. Each item has a 0-to-4 Likert rating of severity. The instrument is divided into subjective and objective components. Anchors used are specific to each item to help the individual report on severity.

Theoretical Orientation Summary

The Clinician Administered Dissociative States Scale was designed to provide objective and subjective measurement of the phenomena of dissociative states. It was designed to assess change, takes ten minutes to administer, and is intended for use in biological, descriptive, and treatment research.

Time Estimate

Administration	Scoring
10–15 minutes	5–10 minutes

Equipment Needed

Paper & Pencil	Computer	Basic Psychophysiological	Specialized Equipment
X			

Psychometric Maturity

Under Construction	Basic Properties Intact	Mature
	X	

Psychometric Properties Summary

The Clinician Administered Dissociative States Scale was developed over four years in a process of administration and revision based on experience. The Clinician Administered Dissociative States Scale has been shown to have acceptable reliability and validity and to differentiate patients with Post Traumatic Stress Disorder from other patient groups, including schizophrenia, affective disorders, healthy subjects, and Vietnam veterans without Post Traumatic Stress Disorder.

Particular Sensitivity

Age	Change over Time	Culture / Ethnicity	Gender	Geography / Climate	Sexual Orientation	Socioeconomic Status	Urban / Rural
?	X	?	?	?	?	?	?

Estimate of Number of In-Process Studies
    Unknown

Unpublished References
    Unknown

Published References
    Bremner, J. D., Southwick, S. M., Brett, E., Fontana, A., Yehuda, R., & Charney, D. S. (1992). Dissociation and Posttraumatic Stress Disorder in Vietnam combat veterans. *American Journal of Psychiatry, 149* (3), 328–332.

Key Words

Population	Stressor	Topic
adult	any	research

Reference Citation for This Review
    Bremner, J. D. (1996). Psychometric review of The Clinician Administered Dissociative States Scale. In B. H. Stamm (Ed.). *Measurement of stress, trauma, and adaptation.* Lutherville, MD: Sidran Press.

Measure Contact Name
    J. Douglas Bremner, M.D.
    Address: 116a West Haven VAMC
                    50 Campbell Ave.
                    West Haven, CT 06516 USA
    Phone: 203.932.5711 x3957
    Fax: 203.937.3886
    E-mail:

Clinician-Administered PTSD Scale (CAPS)

Type of Population

Any type of trauma

Cost

Free

Copyright

Languages

English

What It Measures

Structured clinical interview measuring the frequency and intensity of the 17 *DSM-III-R/IV* symptoms of PTSD and 8 associated symptoms. This instrument also contains five global rating questions regarding the impact of symptoms on social and occupational functioning, improvement since a previous assessment, and overall validity and severity of reported symptoms.

Measure Content Survey, Procedure, or Process

Consists of initial prompt questions, followup questions, and behaviorally-anchored 5-point rating scales corresponding to the frequency and intensity of each symptom assessed. Two versions of the CAPS are available: current and lifetime diagnostic version (CAPS-DX) and a weekly symptom rating version (CAPS-DX). A manual for the CAPS is also available.

Theoretical Orientation Summary

Descriptive psychopathology based on *DSM-IV.*

Time Estimate

Administration	Scoring
30–90 minutes	10–15 minutes

Equipment Needed

Paper & Pencil	Computer	Basic Psychophysiological	Specialized Equipment
X			

Psychometric Maturity

Under Construction	Basic Properties	Mature
		X

Psychometric Properties Summary

Test-retest reliability was assessed in 60 combat veterans given the CAPS twice, 2–3 days apart, by two independent clinicians. Test-retest correlations for three different theater pairs ranged from .90 to .98. In a sample of 123 combat veterans, internal consistency for the 17 *DSM-III-R/IV* PTSD symptoms was .94 and item-total correlations ranged from .49 to .82. In this sample the total severity score on the CAPS was strongly correlated with other measures of PTSD, including the Mississippi Scale (.91) and the PK scale of the MMPI-2 (.77). A CAPS total severity score (frequency plus intensity across all 17 symptoms) of 65 or greater had sensitivity (.84), specificity (.95), and efficiency (.89) against a PTSD diagnosis based on the Structured Clinical Interview for *DSM-III-R/IV* (SCID). Various scoring rules have been devised for translating CAPS frequency and intensity scores into a dichotomous diagnosis. The best of these rules yielded a kappa of .77 against a SCID diagnosis.

Particular Sensitivity

Age	Change over Time	Culture / Ethnicity	Gender	Geography / Climate	Sexual Orientation	Socioeconomic Status	Urban / Rural
?	?	?	?	?	?	?	?

Estimate of Number of In-Process Studies
Unknown

Unpublished References
Weathers, F. W., Blake, D. D., Krinsley, K. E., Haddad, W., Huska, J. A., & Keane, T. M. (1993). The Clinican-Administered PTSD Scale: Reliability and construct validity. Paper presented at the annual meeting of the Association for Advancement of Behavior.

Published References
Blake, D. D., Weathers, F. W., Nagy, L. M., Kaloupek, D. G., Klauminzer, G., Charney, D. S., & Keane, T. M. (1990). A clinician rating scale for assessing current and lifetime PTSD: The CAPS-1. *Behavior Therapist, 18*, 187-188.

Key Words

Population	Stressor	Topic
adults	any	assessment clinical diagnosis research

Reference Citation for This Review
Weathers, F. W. (1996). Psychometric review of Clinican-Administered PTSD Scale (CAPS). In B. H. Stamm (Ed.). *Measurement of stress, trauma, and adaptation*. Lutherville, MD: Sidran Press.

Measure Contact Name
Frank W. Weathers, Ph.D.

Address: National Center for PTSD (116B-2)
            Boston DVA Medical Center
            150 S. Huntington Avenue
            Boston, MA 02130 USA
Phone: 617.232.9500 ex. 4130/4136
Fax: 617.278.4501
E-mail   Weathers.Frank_W@Boston.VA.Gov

Clinician-Administered PTSD Scale for Children (CAPS-C)

Type of Population
Inpatient and outpatient children and adolescents, ages 7 to 18; collateral form for adult informant is available.

Cost
Free

Copyright
U. S. Government Domain

Languages
English

What It Measures
The CAPS-C was developed to measure cardinal and hypothesized signs and symptoms of PTSD in children. It is a structured clinical interview that assesses the 17 symptoms for Post-Traumatic Stress Disorder (PTSD) outlined in the *DSM-IV* draft criteria, along with eight associated features (a final *DSM-IV* version is currently being constructed). The CAPS-C provides means to evaluate: (a) self-reports of exposure to potential Criterion A events; (b) current and/or lifetime diagnosis of PTSD; (c) the frequency and intensity dimensions of each symptom; (d) the impact of the symptoms on the child's or adolescent's social and scholastic functioning; (e) the overall severity of the symptom complex.

Measure Content Survey, Procedure, or Process
The CAPS-C is a structured clinical interview for use by trained mental health professionals. The CAPS-C consists of standardized prompt questions; supplementary followup (probe) questions; and behaviorally-anchored 5-point rating scales corresponding to the frequency and intensity of each symptom assessed. Additional features to increase utility with children include: (a) iconic representations of positive symptoms; (b) opportunities to practice with the format for questioning; and (c) a standard procedure for identification of the critical one-month timeframe for current symptoms.

Theoretical Orientation Summary
Descriptive psychopathology based on *DSM* PTSD criteria, developmental psychopathology, and the extant empirical literature. The CAPS-C, designed specifically to be developmentally appropriate for children, uses a structured interview format similar to the CAPS (Blake, Weathers, Nagy, Kaloupek, et al., 1990), which has well-established psychometric properties.

Time Estimate

Administration	Scoring
30–120 minutes	5–10 minutes

Equipment Needed

Paper & Pencil	Computer	Basic Psychophysiological	Specialized Equipment
X			

Psychometric Maturity

Under Construction	Basic Properties Intact	Mature
X		

Psychometric Properties Summary

To date, no psychometric properties have been examined.

Particular Sensitivity

Age	Change over Time	Culture / Ethnicity	Gender	Geography / Climate	Sexual Orientation	Socioeconomic Status	Urban / Rural
X	Form 2	?	?	?	?	?	?

Estimate of Number of In-Process Studies

Unknown

Unpublished References

Published References

Blake, D. D., Weathers, F. W., Nagy, L. M., Kaloupek, D. G., Charney, D. S., & Keane, T. M. (1993). The development of a clinician-administered PTSD scale. *Journal of Traumatic Stress, 8,* 75–90.

Blake, D.D., Weathers, F. W., Nagy, L. M., Kaloupek, D. G., Klauminzer, G., Charney, D. S., & Keane, T. M. (1990). A clinician rating scale for assessing current and lifetime PTSD: The CAPS-1. *Behavior Therapist, 18,* 187–188.

Nader, K. (in press). Assessing traumatic experiences in children. In J. Wilson & T. Keane (Eds.). *Assessing Psychological Trauma and PTSD.* New York: Guilford Press.

Weathers, F. W., & Litz, B. T. (1994). Psychometric properties of the Clinician-Administered PTSD Scale—Form 1 (CAPS-1). *PTSD Research Quarterly, 5,* 2–6.

General Comments

The instrument is a product of the National Center for PTSD. A comprehensive manual, adult collateral format, and one-week symptom status format are available. The CAPS-C is available for clinical and research use, but normative data are not yet available. We ask that users provide us with feedback about the clinical and research utility of this instrument and invite collaboration on further psychometric development.

Key Words

Population	Stressor	Topic
children adolescents	any	assessment clinical diagnosis measure development research

Reference Citation for This Review

Newman, E., & Ribbe, D. (1996). Psychometric review of The Clinician Administered PTSD Scale for Children. In B. H. Stamm (Ed.). *Measurement of stress, trauma, and adaptation.* Lutherville, MD: Sidran Press.

Measure Authors

Kathleen Nader, Julie Kriegler, Dudley Blake, Robert Pynoos, Elana Newman, and Frank W. Weathers with The National Center for PTSD

Kathleen Nader
Address: P.O. Box 2251
               Laguna Hills, CA 92654
Phone: 714.454.0628
Fax: 714.454.0429
E-mail: knader@twosuns.org

Elana Newman, Ph.D.
Address: University of Tulsa
             Department of Psychology, Lorton Hall
             600 South College Avenue
             Tulsa, OK 74104-3189 USA
Phone: 918.631.2833
Fax:
E-mail: elana-newman@utulsa.edu

Measure Contact Names

Elana Newman (see above)

CAPS Sample Items

Criterion B. The traumatic event is persistently reexperienced in one (or more) of the following ways:
1a. (B-1) recurrent and intrusive distressing recollections of the event, including images, thoughts or perceptions.

Frequency
B-1af.

Did you think about (EVENT) even when you didn't want to? Did you see pictures in your head (mind) or hear the sounds in your head (mind) from (EVENT)?

What were they like? (Did you cover your eyes or ears to block out things you saw or heard in your head? What were you trying to block out?)

FOR YOUNGER CHILDREN: (You know how when you think about something you can see it in your mind or hear the sounds in your mind? Did you ever see in your mind the things from [EVENT]? Did you hear in your mind the sounds from [EVENT]?)

IF NEEDED: (If I say think about [A GREEN LOLLIPOP/ YOUR MOTHER], can you see [A GREEN LOLLIPOP/ YOUR MOTHER] in your mind? [AND THEN:] Did you ever see in you mind things from [EVENT]? What did you see?)

How many times did that happen in the past month /(LIFETIME WORST MONTH)?

0. None of the time
1. Little of the time, once or twice
2. Some of the time, once or twice a week
3. Much of the time, several times a week
4. Most of the time, daily or almost every day

Description/Examples
Intensity
B-1ai.

In the past month / (LIFETIME WORST MONTH), what have you done when those pictures, sounds, or thoughts came (popped) into your mind?

How did you feel?

What did you do? (Did they bother you, scare you, or make you feel bad?)

Did you stop what you were doing or were you able to keep doing what you were doing?

Could you turn the pictures off or make them go away if you wanted to?

0. Not a problem, None
1. A little bit of a problem, mild, minimal distress or disruption of activities, get a little upset
2. Some, moderate, distress clearly present but still manageable, some disruption of activities
3. A lot, severe, considerable distress, difficulty dismissing memories, marked disruption of activities
4. A whole lot, extreme, incapacitating distress, cannot dismiss memories, unable to continue activities

QV (SPECIFY) _____

B-1a. Current   Lifetime

F____   F____

I ___   I____

Sx: Y N   Sx: Y N

1b. (B-1) Note: In young children, repetitive play may occur in which themes or aspects of the trauma are expressed.

<u>Frequency</u>
B-1bf.
Did you ever play any games that were like something that went on during (EVENT)? (Did you play games where someone gets hurt? where someone gets rescued? where someone who gets hurt gets better? where someone escapes?

Can you tell me (describe) about the play?

How about drawing pictures of (EVENT)? What did you draw?

Did you play, draw, or do things like this before (EVENT)? [IF YES:] How much did you play these games before (EVENT)?

In this past month / (LIFETIME WORST MONTH), how many times did you act out things or repeat things that happened? (Did you do this more or less now than before [EVENT])?
0. None of the time
1. Little of the time, once or twice
2. Some of the time, once or twice a week
3. Much of the time, several times a week
4. Most of the time, daily or almost every day

Description/Examples: No Intensity Rating.
1) How did you feel when you did this [PLAY/ GAME]? (e.g., nothing, better, upset)
2) Could you make yourself stop? (Did you play other games? Did you want to play other games? Did you like to play other games?)
3) How long did you spend playing these games or drawing things like you went through? (Did you spend a long time or short time doing this [PLAY/ GAME]?)
4) Did you even know that you were playing or drawing things that went on during [EVENT]?

QV (SPECIFY) _____

Trauma Related?

_____   _____   _____
unlikely   definite   probable

B-1b.
Current   Lifetime

F____   F____

Sx: Y N   Sx: Y N

_ _ _ _ _
B-1a or 1b.
[HIGHEST]
B-1a. Current   Lifetime

F____   F____

II ___   II ___

Sx: Y N   Sx: Y N

7. (C-2) efforts to avoid activities, places, or people that arouse recollections of the trauma

Frequency
C-2af.
Did you try to stay away from people, things or activities that make you think about (remember) what happened? (Did you want to stay away from people or things that remind you about what happened during [EVENT]?)

Did you feel like staying away from things, people or places that make you think of (remember) what happened during (EVENT)?(If you had to go near places or people or do things that made you think about what happened, could you do that?)

What sorts of things did you try to stay away from? [IF CHILD SAYS NO, ASK:] Did you want to stay away from [NAME SOME COMMON REMINDERS TO THE EVENT] because they remind you of [EVENT]?)

How many times did you try to stay away from these people or things in the past month / (LIFETIME WORST MONTH)?

0. None of the time
1. Little of the time, once or twice
2. Some of the time, once or twice a week
3. Much of the time, several times a week
4. Most of the time, daily or almost every day

Description/Examples
Intensity
C-2ai.
In this past month / (LIFETIME WORST MONTH), how much did you want to stay away or go away from people or things that make you (remember) think about (EVENT)?

(Did staying away from people or things get in the way of (interfere, mess up) things you needed to do?

Did staying away from people or things cause you problems?)

How bad was it this past month /(LIFETIME WORST MONTH)?

0. Not at all, None
1. A little, mild, minimal difficulty, little or no disruption of activities
2. Some, moderate, some effort, avoidance definitely present, some disruption of activities
3. A lot, want to or try really hard to stay away from things that make me remember, marked disruption of activities or involvement in certain activities as avoidant strategy
4. A whole lot, want to do or do try almost anything to stay away from things that make me remember, unable to continue activities, or excessive involvement in certain activities as avoidant strategies

QV (SPECIFY) _____

Trauma Related?

_____   _____   _____
unlikely   definite   probable

Current   Lifetime

F____   F____

Ii ___   II___

Sx: Y N   Sx: Y N

6. (D-4) hypervigilance

Frequency

D-4af.

Have you felt like something bad was going to happen and you needed to be ready for it, sort of like watching out for danger or things that you're afraid of? [DEMONSTRATE BY HOLDING SHOULDERS UP AND LOOKING LEFT AND RIGHT]? (Were you kind of jumpy and worried like something bad might happen?)

Has this changed or were you always like that? [IF CHANGE:] When did you first start being watchful (worried)? (Did you ever feel this way before [EVENT]?)

In the past month/ (LIFETIME WORST MONTH), how much of the time did you feel this way?

0. None of the time
1. Very little of the time
2. Some of the time
3. Much of the time
4. Most or all of the time

Description/Examples:

Intensity

D-4ai.

In the past month / (LIFETIME WORST MONTH), how much did you watch out for something bad that might happen? Did you do anything special to make yourself feel better (safer)? [IN RATING THIS ITEM INCLUDE OBSERVATIONS OF HYPERVIGILANCE DURING THE INTERVIEW]

0. Not at all watching for danger, no hypervigilance
1. Little, mild, minimal hypervigilance, slight heightening of awareness
2. Some, moderate, hypervigilance clearly present, watchful in public (e.g. sits away from windows)
3. A lot, severe, marked hypervigilance, very alert, scans environment for danger, exaggerated concern for safety of self/family/home
4. A whole lot, extreme, excessive hypervigilance, efforts to ensure safety consume significant time and energy and may involve extensive safety/checking behaviors, marked watchful behavior during interview

QV (SPECIFY) _____

Trauma Related?

_____   _____   _____
unlikely   definite   probable

Current   Lifetime

F____   F____

I ___   I____

Sx: Y N   Sx: Y N

Combat Stress Barometer

Type of Population
Combat veterans

Cost
Minimal

Copyright

Languages
English

What It Measures
PTSD and associated symptoms

Measure Content Survey, Procedure, or Process
This is an attempt to put together a self-administered self-report version of the CAPS, which is capable of yielding severity and frequency.

Time Estimate

Administration	Scoring
20–60 minutes	15–30 minutes

Equipment Needed

Paper & Pencil	Computer	Basic Psychophysiological	Specialized Equipment
X			

Psychometric Maturity

Under Construction	Basic Properties Intact	Mature
X		

Psychometric Properties Summary
Has only been piloted for understandability of instructions and items. No psychometric data.

Particular Sensitivity

Age	Change over Time	Culture / Ethnicity	Gender	Geography / Climate	Sexual Orientation	Socioeconomic Status	Urban / Rural
?	?	?	?	?	?	?	?

Estimate of Number of In-Process Studies
Unknown

Unpublished References
Unknown

Published References

See CAPS publications

Key Words

Population	Stressor	Topic
veterans	combat	measure development research

Reference Citation for This Review

Shay, J. (1996). Psychometric review of Combat Stress Barometer. In B. H. Stamm (Ed.). *Measurement of stress, trauma, and adaptation*. Lutherville, MD: Sidran Press.

Measure Contact Name

Jonathan Shay, M.D., Ph.D.

Address: Boston VA OPC
           251 Causeway St.
           Boston, MA 02114 USA
Phone: 617.24.1067
E-mail: Shay.Jonathan@Boston.VA.Gov

Combat Stress Barometer—Recording How Bad and How Often
[Filled in examples are on the next page]

To give you the best possible advice on medications, we need to know what you have been going through. The Combat Stress Barometer is a monthly monitor of things that often cause suffering to Vietnam combat veterans. Please read each item carefully, and then tag each one with the following code for *how bad* each was for you *at its worst* in the last month, and *how often* in the last month it has been a problem for you at all. Make two passes through each item.

The **first pass** is for how bad each problem was at its worst. use these letters—N, M, I, S, E—to code how bad each item was at its worst:

N = Never In the last month this never bothered you at all. If you mark "Never" in the first box go on to the next item, skipping the second pass. Leave "Never" items blank on the second pass.

M = Mild, it was there, but it didn't cause much distress or get in the way of whatever you were doing or wanted to do. This is something you feel you can live with and maybe are even used to it, but you know your life would be better if it were gone.

I = Intermediate, it caused definite distress or got in the way of what you were doing or wanted to do, but you could deal with it. When this has happened you were able to manage, using your *regular* resources of strength, self-respect, nerve, self-control, sense of reality, endurance, control of your own mental functions, or ability to relax and sleep.

S = Severe, it caused great distress or badly upset what you were doing or wanted to do. Overcoming it called on all your resources just to stay even with where you were in your life this last month.

E = Extreme, it caused overwhelming distress and for a time totally crippled what you were doing or wanted to do. Your ability to deal with rage, fear, guilt, and to be sure of what was real was overwhelmed. You did real harm to your relationships, to yourself or your own best interests, or to someone else—or avoided these purely by luck. You don't know if you can get through it again without hurting yourself or someone else.

Here is a filled-in example for *how bad* the following item was *at its worst* for a veteran.

		How Bad Bad (or Never)	1–2 Per Month	Weekly	1–2 Per Week	Daily or Almost Daily
A.	"Superalert," or watchful or on guard?	I				

Example A: Pretty much every day in the last month you were careful about your surroundings, walking your perimeter every night before you lock up and noticing every person on the street with you in front and behind on both sides of the street, even on your own block, which you think is quite safe. This is what you're used to, but you'd like to be able to let down when it's safe. One night this month was pretty bad, getting no sleep at all because you felt you had to keep yourself awake in a corner of your room where you can scan the door and windows at a glance. You were wired for days after that.

This instrument, by Jonathan Shay, may be reproduced without charge and freely distributed, as long as no funds are exchanged.

The **second pass** through each item is for how often you have suffered from that sort of thing in the last month. "How often" means how often that happened to you *at all*, without looking at whether it was mild, intermediate, severe, or extreme — the second pass is just for how often it happened in any intensity or severity. If you marked "Never" on the first pass, leave this item blank.

Here is Example A again, with *both* how bad and how often filled in:

		How Bad Bad (or Never)	1–2 Per Month	Weekly	1–2 Per Week	Daily or Almost Daily
A.	"Superalert," or watchful or on guard?	I				X

The Combat Stress Barometer is important for your treatment. It helps us keep track of how you are doing over time. You will help us to help you if you complete it thoughtfully and honestly every month. It will take less time as you get more familiar with it. Don't hesitate to ask for help from a group leader or another veteran in the group.
More filled in illustrations of the use of the Combat Stress Barometer:

B.	Thought about people who died when you didn't, and *feeling that you should have died instead?*	E				X

Example B: Not a day goes by that you don't think of your friend who had a fever and asked you to switch his ambush duty for your bunker watch. Out on the ambush you could see the flashes of rockets hitting the firebase. When you got back in you learned he had been killed in the bunker. Every day you think, "It should have been me." You've thought this every day for the last 23 years, and the ache is so much a part of every day that you hardly notice it.

C.	Suddenly acting, feeling, or perceiving (sights, sounds, smells) as if your military experiences *were happening again?*	E				X

Example C: About once a week last month, people all began to look like Vietnamese to you on the bus going home from work. Each time, you broke into a sweat and held it together until your stop by looking closely at each face and realizing that (except for some real Orientals once) this was not so. One time last month it suddenly got so bad that you bolted off the bus past another passenger getting out, and decided to walk home, because you didn't want to get back on a bus just then. The next day was OK.

Be sure to put your name and the date at the top of each page.
Complete your Barometer for this month on the pages that follow.

name: date:	How Bad Bad (or Never)	1–2 Per Month	Weekly	1–2 Per Week	Daily or Almost Daily
1. Felt anxious if someone *got to know you well*?					
2. Trouble remembering important parts of your experiences in the Service?					
3. Avoided situations or activities *because you thought you would not be able to control* angry words or actions?					
4. Felt jumpy or easily startled?					
5. *Involuntary and disturbing* memories of your military Service? (Do not count if you *chose* to recall the memories, or if *not* disturbing.)					
6. *Wanted to off yourself* or set someone up to take you out, or looked for danger in the hope of getting lucky?					
7. Thought about people who died when you didn't, and *feeling that you should have died instead?*					
8. Avoided activities or situations *because they reminded you of Vietnam*? (Include preparing yourself ahead of time with alcohol, etc.)					
9. Felt emotionally numb, or unable to have loving feelings for those close to you?					
10. Felt like you no longer had the strength to keep it all together?					
11. Avoided *people who pressure you.* (Include zoning out by replaying combat memories, preparing yourself with alcohol, etc.)					
12. Repetitive *dreams that replay the same way* every time, just like a film?					
13. Avoided *thinking about* military experiences, *or having feelings about* them? (Include using alcohol, etc., or staying too busy to think or feel.)					
14. Felt overwhelmed by all the pressures on you?					
15. Avoided people, situations, or activities *because you were afraid you would begin crying*?					

name: date:	How Bad Bad (or Never)	1–2 Per Month	Weekly	1–2 Per Week	Daily or Almost Daily
16. Felt *emotionally upset* when something happened that reminded you of your military experiences? (Include combat anniversaries.)					
17. Felt anxious if someone got to *matter too much* to you, or you mattered too much to the other person?					
18. Loss of interest in activities *that you used to enjoy?*					
19. Avoided situations or activities *because you were afraid you'd "lose it" and go berserk?*					
20. Felt two inches tall or like a piece of shit?					
21. Felt irritable, had angry outbursts, went off on people?					
22. *Wanted to cry*, but were not able to?					
23. Had *bodily reactions* when something reminded you of your military experiences?					
24. *Drove away someone who was getting too close* by scaring, hurting, or picking a fight with the other person?					
25. Disturbing *dreams* of your military experiences?					
26. Felt like you wanted to hurt someone badly or kill that person?					
27. "Superalert," or watchful or on guard?					
28. Felt so tired of struggling in a hopeless situation that you thought you'd be better off dead?					
29. Trouble falling or staying asleep?					
30. Avoided pleasures, injured yourself or things you valued *because you didn't deserve them?*					
31. Felt hopeless and despaired that anything can improve or succeed for you?					
32. Felt like nothing meant anything any more, that *nothing mattered enough even to want to do it?*					

name: date:	How Bad Bad (or Never)	1–2 Per Month	Weekly	1–2 Per Week	Daily or Almost Daily
33. Had trouble with forgetfulness, couldn't remember things you wanted to do?					
34. Avoided situations or activities *because you knew you wouldn't be able to watch your back*?					
35. Thought about joining the dead, had dreams or visions of the dead beckoning to you?					
36. Suddenly acted, felt, or perceived (sights, sounds, smells) as if your military experiences *were happening again*?					
37. Did things to other people *before you even had a chance to think*, like automatic reactions?					
38. Thought about, reproached yourself, or felt *like you deserved to be punished* for things you did or failed to do during your military service?					
39. Avoided going to sleep *to avoid dreams, feelings, or actions that happen while you are asleep*? (Include knocking yourself out w/ alcohol, etc.)					
40. Had difficulty concentrating?					
41. *Felt betrayed* by a person, group, or institution you used to trust and respect?					
42. Felt distant or cut off from other people?					
43. Avoided situations or activities because you thought you or someone else *would do something that would leave you feeling like a piece of shit*?					
44. Felt sad, blue, down in the dumps?					
45. Felt as if *your future will be cut short*, that you will die prematurely, perhaps soon?					
46. *Pumped up with adrenalin*, just like in a firefight.					

Feedback on the Combat Stress Barometer (Use backs if you need more space):

Are these items close enough to your experience that you feel that you've given a good picture of things that have caused you suffering in the last month?

Which items are off-target (use item numbers if you like) and you think should be *dropped?*

What items would you *add* to get closer to the experience of Vietnam combat Veterans?

No printed questions, no matter how good, can get at the heart of an individual's experience, which is always unique. What do we need to know about your experience in this last month that you feel is totally missed in the Barometer?

Common Grief Response Questionnaire (CGR)

Type of Population

Adults who are grieving the death of a significant person; orginally designed for surviving family members of deceased hospice patients

Cost

Free

Copyright

Languages

English

What It Measures

The Common Grief Response Questionnaire index identifies occurrence and intensity of thoughts and feelings commonly experienced by bereaved people.

Measure Content Survey, Procedure, or Process

Subjects use a 7-point Likert Scale to indicate agreement and frequency of feelings for each statement. The 86 questions cover 11 components of grief responses.

Theoretical Orientation Summary

Time Estimate

Administration	Scoring
15–45 minutes	5–15 minutes

Equipment Needed

Paper & Pencil	Computer	Basic Psychophysiological	Specialized Equipment
X			

Psychometric Maturity

Under Construction	Basic Properties Intact	Mature
X		

Psychometric Properties Summary

Particular Sensitivity

Age	Change over Time	Culture / Ethnicity	Gender	Geography / Climate	Sexual Orientation	Socioeconomic Status	Urban / Rural
?	?	?	?	?	?	?	?

Estimate of Number of In-Process Studies

Unknown

Unpublished References

Unknown

Published References

None

Key Words

Population	Stressor	Topic
adults	life threatening illness death traumatic grief terminal diagnosis	measure development research service delivery

Reference Citation for This Review

McNeill, F. (1996). Psychometric review of Common Grief Response Questionaire. In B. H. Stamm (Ed.). *Measurement of Stress, Trauma, and Adaptation*. Lutherville, MD: Sidran Press.

Measure Contact Name

Fran McNeill

Address: Fran McNeill
               12021 Portage Dr
               Anchorage, AK 99515 USA

Phone: 907.786.4817

Fax:

E-mail: asfrm@uaa.alaska.edu

Common Grief Responses Scale

Following are thoughts and feelings that are very common when grieving. Please circle the number that best describes your feelings about each statement.

0=Not at all; 1=Strongly Disagree: I rarely feel this way; 7=Strongly Agree: I often feel this way

1. I can't seem to keep my thoughts on a single subject.	0	1	2	3	4	5	6	7
2. My mind races in different directions.	0	1	2	3	4	5	6	7
3. I feel hopeless.	0	1	2	3	4	5	6	7
4. I think that life is meaningless.	0	1	2	3	4	5	6	7
5. I think that I have fully grieved my loss(es).	0	1	2	3	4	5	6	7
6. I wish someone would just hold me.	0	1	2	3	4	5	6	7
7. I wish I could *continue* to talk to my family and friends about my loved one.	0	1	2	3	4	5	6	7
8. I am frightened much of the time.	0	1	2	3	4	5	6	7
9. Nothing makes sense to me anymore.	0	1	2	3	4	5	6	7
10. No one understands what I am going through or feeling.	0	1	2	3	4	5	6	7
11. I should be back to normal by now.	0	1	2	3	4	5	6	7
12. I need to be understood.	0	1	2	3	4	5	6	7
13. I don't want to be fixed or cheered up.	0	1	2	3	4	5	6	7
14. I want to be allowed to be where I am in my grief.	0	1	2	3	4	5	6	7
15. I don't want to be told how I should be feeling.	0	1	2	3	4	5	6	7
16. I can't seem to get things finished.	0	1	2	3	4	5	6	7
17. I am so lonely.	0	1	2	3	4	5	6	7
18. I am so tired all the time.	0	1	2	3	4	5	6	7
19. Nothing interests me.	0	1	2	3	4	5	6	7
20. I wonder if I am being punished for something.	0	1	2	3	4	5	6	7
21. I feel guilty because I can't pull myself out of this.	0	1	2	3	4	5	6	7
22. I wish I could join my loved one now.	0	1	2	3	4	5	6	7
23. All I can think about is myself.	0	1	2	3	4	5	6	7
24. I don't feel anything at all.	0	1	2	3	4	5	6	7
25. I am angry! (at something, at someone, or just generally angry)	0	1	2	3	4	5	6	7
26. I feel guilty because I can't feel happy for others.	0	1	2	3	4	5	6	7
27. I'm afraid to be by myself.	0	1	2	3	4	5	6	7
28. I don't want to see people or do things with them.	0	1	2	3	4	5	6	7
29. I am not sure who I am anymore.	0	1	2	3	4	5	6	7
30. Events in my life don't seem real to me.	0	1	2	3	4	5	6	7
31. I don't enjoy being around other people.	0	1	2	3	4	5	6	7
32. Things don't seem real to me.	0	1	2	3	4	5	6	7
33. I hear or see my loved one sometimes.	0	1	2	3	4	5	6	7
34. I am saying and doing things that aren't like me at all.	0	1	2	3	4	5	6	7
35. I may have the same illness as my loved one.	0	1	2	3	4	5	6	7
36. I have great difficulty talking about the person who has died.	0	1	2	3	4	5	6	7
37. I know that my loved one is beside me frequently.	0	1	2	3	4	5	6	7
38. I do not sleep well.	0	1	2	3	4	5	6	7
39. I am enjoying my life and activities.	0	1	2	3	4	5	6	7
40. I don't understand how the rest of the world and the people in it can just go on about their business as if nothing has happened.	0	1	2	3	4	5	6	7
41. My loved one is not really dead.	0	1	2	3	4	5	6	7
42. I feel nauseous.	0	1	2	3	4	5	6	7

This instrument, by Fran McNeill, may be reproduced without charge and freely distributed, as long as no funds are exchanged.

43. I can't eat.	0	1	2	3	4	5	6	7
44. I have lost weight.	0	1	2	3	4	5	6	7
45. I have a choking feeling.	0	1	2	3	4	5	6	7
46. I feel like there is a heavy weight on my chest.	0	1	2	3	4	5	6	7
47. I feel frantic.	0	1	2	3	4	5	6	7
48. I seem to talk all the time.	0	1	2	3	4	5	6	7
49. I am not the person I thought I was.	0	1	2	3	4	5	6	7
50. I race around all the time.	0	1	2	3	4	5	6	7
51. I sometimes feel like I am outside of my body watching myself.	0	1	2	3	4	5	6	7
52. If I keep very busy all the time, I am fine.	0	1	2	3	4	5	6	7
53. Sometimes I can't get out of bed at all.	0	1	2	3	4	5	6	7
54. I feel like I have died.	0	1	2	3	4	5	6	7
55. The person I was before doesn't exist anymore.	0	1	2	3	4	5	6	7
56. I have been sick a lot.	0	1	2	3	4	5	6	7
57. I feel like I am in a fog.	0	1	2	3	4	5	6	7
58. I can't seem to pay attention to what is going on around me.	0	1	2	3	4	5	6	7
59. This didn't really happen; it's a mistake.	0	1	2	3	4	5	6	7
60. I need to know someone really cares how much I hurt.	0	1	2	3	4	5	6	7
61. Living is too painful.	0	1	2	3	4	5	6	7
62. I wonder if I will die the same way my loved one did.	0	1	2	3	4	5	6	7
63. I keep thinking about all the things I wish I had done and/or the things I should have done.	0	1	2	3	4	5	6	7
64. I feel like everyone is irritable and angry with me.	0	1	2	3	4	5	6	7
65. Nobody likes me.	0	1	2	3	4	5	6	7
66. My friends are not supportive in the way that I need them to be.	0	1	2	3	4	5	6	7
67. I miss being touched and touching.	0	1	2	3	4	5	6	7
68. I will never make it through this.	0	1	2	3	4	5	6	7
69. I enjoy my friends.	0	1	2	3	4	5	6	7
70. Being with other people makes me more lonely.	0	1	2	3	4	5	6	7
71. I must deserve what has happened.	0	1	2	3	4	5	6	7
72. I am questioning my beliefs about life.	0	1	2	3	4	5	6	7
73. I need to talk about this more.	0	1	2	3	4	5	6	7
74. I don't want to talk to anyone.	0	1	2	3	4	5	6	7
75. I am having fun in my life.	0	1	2	3	4	5	6	7
76. My family do not give me the understanding I want.	0	1	2	3	4	5	6	7
77. I sometimes think I am losing my mind.	0	1	2	3	4	5	6	7
78. I sometimes still have difficulty believing this really happened.	0	1	2	3	4	5	6	7
79. I believe I have adjusted well to my loss.	0	1	2	3	4	5	6	7
80. My faith has let me down.	0	1	2	3	4	5	6	7
81. My church doesn't really understand.	0	1	2	3	4	5	6	7
82. I am important.	0	1	2	3	4	5	6	7
83. I have many things to do with my life.	0	1	2	3	4	5	6	7
84. People are there when I need them.	0	1	2	3	4	5	6	7
85. I rely on others to get through this.	0	1	2	3	4	5	6	7
86. I look forward to each day.	0	1	2	3	4	5	6	7

Demographic Information:

Age of person completing assessment: _____

Relationship to deceased: _____ (daughter, son, wife, husband, etc.)

Gender: Circle One   F   M

Diagnosis of Deceased: Please check one.   Cancer___   COPD___   ALS ___   AIDS___   Other___

When was the diagnosis first made: Number of months _____

Number of months since death:_____

Age of deceased: _____

Compassion Fatigue Self Test

Type of Population
Adult. Human service field, generalizable to nearly any group including psychotherapists, teachers, public safety personnel, etc.

Cost
Free

Copyright

Languages
English.

What It Measures
Addresses both trauma and burnout symptoms.

Measure Content Survey, Procedure, or Process
Burnout items taken from Pines (1993), trauma items gleaned from the trauma literature.

Theoretical Orientation Summary
Integrative, but has roots in the Secondary Traumatic Stress literature.

Time Estimate

Administration	Scoring
5–10 minutes self scoring	5–10 minutes

Equipment Needed

Paper & Pencil	Computer	Basic Psychophysiological	Specialized Equipment
X			

Psychometric Maturity

Under Construction	Basic Properties Intact	Mature
X		

Psychometric Properties Summary
The instrument is still being developed. Data from 142 psychotherapy practitioners had alpha reliabilities ranging from .94 to .86. Structural analysis yielded at least one stable factor which is characterized by depressed mood in relationship to work accompanied by feelings of fatigue, disillusionment, and worthlessness. Structural Reliability (stability) of this factor, as indicated by Tucker's Coefficient of Congruence (cc), is .91 (Figley, Stamm, & Bieber, 1995). At this point there is insufficient data to determine the nature of a second structure, although work is continuing on this analysis.

Particular Sensitivity

Age	Change over Time	Culture/ Ethnicity	Gender	Geography/ Climate	Sexual Orientation	Socioeconomic Status	Urban/ Rural
?	X		?		?		

Estimate of Number of In-Process Studies

Numerous

Unpublished References

Published References

Figley, C. R. (Ed.) (1995). *Compassion fatigue: Coping with secondary PTSD among those who treat the traumatized*. New York: Bruner/Mazel.

Figley, C. R. (1995). Compassion fatigue: Toward a new understanding of the costs of caring. In B. H. Stamm (Ed.). *Secondary Traumatic Stress: Self-Care Issues for Clinicians, Researchers, & Educators*. Lutherville, MD: Sidran Press.

Figley, C. R. (1993). Compassion stress and the family therapist. *Family Therapy News* (February), 1–8.

Pines, A. M. (1993). Burnout. In L. Goldberger and S. Breznitz (Eds.). *Handbook of stress: Theoretical and clinical aspects. 2nd ed.*, 386–402. New York: Free Press.

General Comments

This measure is being used in numerous studies across multiple disciplines, including mental health, education, and heath care. An indigenous peoples version is being developed for use in circumpolar regions. At this point in time, the instrument clearly seems capable of describing some level of difficulty to which the worker should attend. It can be used as an indicator of potential problems that should be diagnostically examined rather than as a diagnostic device in and of itself. Because this is a self-test designed as an educational tool and a warning device, it tends to err on the side of over-inclusion, that is, false positive.

Key Words

Population	Stressor	Topic
adults	any secondary traumatic stress care-giving	debriefing ethics measure development research screening self care secondary traumatic stress

Reference Citation for This Review

Figley, C. F., & Stamm, B. H. (1996). Psychometric review of Compassion Fatigue Self Test. In B. H. Stamm (Ed.). *Measurement of stress, trauma, and adaptation*. Lutherville, MD: Sidran Press.

Measure Contact Name

C.R. Figley, Ph.D.

Address:	Psychosocial Stress Research Program
	103 Sandels Hall, R86E
	Florida State University
	Tallahassee, FL 32306 USA
Phone:	904.644.1588
Fax:	904.644.4804
E-mail	CFIGLEY@GARNET.ACNS.FSU.EDU

Compassion Fatigue Self Test for Practitioners

Name _____ Institution _____ Date _____

Please describe yourself: _____ male _____ female; _____ years as practitioner.

Consider each of the following characteristics about you and your *current* situation. Write in the number for the best response. Use one of the following answers.

1=Rarely/Never	2=At Times	3=Not Sure	4=Often	5=Very Often

Answer all items, even if not applicable. Then read the instructions to get your score.

Items about You

1. _____ I force myself to avoid certain thoughts or feelings that remind me of a frightening experience.
2. _____ I find myself avoiding certain activities or situations because they remind me of a frightening experience.
3. _____ I have gaps in my memory about frightening events.
4. _____ I feel estranged from others.
5. _____ I have difficulty falling or staying asleep.
6. _____ I have outburst of anger or irritability with little provocation.
7. _____ I startle easily.
8. _____ While working with a victim I though about violence against the perpetrator.
9. _____ I am a sensitive person.
10. _____ I have had flashbacks connected to my patients and their families.
11. _____ I have had firsthand experience with traumatic events in my adult life.
12. _____ I have had firsthand experience with traumatic events in my childhood.
13. _____ I have thought that I need to "work through" a traumatic experience in my life.
14. _____ I have thought that I need more close friends.
15. _____ I have thought that there is no one to talk with about highly stressful experiences.
16. _____ I have concluded that I work too hard for my own good.

Items about Your Patients and Their Families:

17. _____ I am frightened of things a patient and their family has said or done to me.
18. _____ I experience troubling dreams similar to a patient of mine and their family.
19. _____ I have experienced intrusive thoughts of sessions with especially difficult patients and their families.
20. _____ I have suddenly and involuntarily recalled a frightening experience while working with a patient and their family.
21. _____ I am preoccupied with more than one patient and their family.
22. _____ I am losing sleep over a patient and their family's traumatic experiences.
23. _____ I have thought that I might have been "infected" by the traumatic stress of my patients and their families.
24. _____ I remind myself to be less concerned about the well-being of my patients and their families.
25. _____ I have felt trapped by my work as a practitioner.
26. _____ I have a sense of hopelessness associated with working with patients with certain families.
27. _____ I have felt "on edge" about various things and I attribute this to working with certain patients and their families.
28. _____ I have wished that I could avoid working with some patients and their families.
29. _____ I have been in danger working with some patients and their families.
30. _____ I have felt that some of my patients and their families dislike me personally.

Items about Being a Practitioner and Your Work Environment

31. _____ I have felt weak, tired, run-down as a result of my work as a practitioner.
32. _____ I have felt depressed as a result of my work as a practitioner.

This instrument, by C. R. Figley, may be reproduced without charge and freely distributed, as long as no funds are exchanged.

33. _____ I am unsuccessful at separating work from personal life.

34. _____ I felt little compassion toward most of my coworkers.

35. _____ I feel I am working more for the money than for personal fulfillment.

36. _____ I find it difficult separating my personal life from my work life.

37. _____ I have a sense of worthlessness/disillusionment/resentment associated with my work.

38. _____ I have thoughts that I am a "failure" as a practitioner.

39 _____ I have thoughts that I am not succeeding at achieving my life goals.

40. _____ I have to deal with bureaucratic, unimportant tasks in my work life.

Scoring Instructions: (a) Be certain you respond to all items. (b) Circle the following 23 items: 1–8, 10–13, 17–26, and 29. (c) Add the numbers you wrote next to the item. (d) Note your risks of Compassion Fatigue: 26 or less=Extremely Low Risk; 27–30=Low Risk; 31–35=Moderate Risk; 36–40=High Risk; 41 or more=Extremely High Risk

Then, (e) Add the numbers you write next to the items not circled. (f) Note your risk of burnout: 19 or less=Extremely Low Risk; 20–24=Low Risk; 25–29=Moderate Risk; 30–42=High Risk; 43 or more=Extremely High Risk.

Complex PTSD Interview

Type of Population
Adults

Cost
Free

Copyright

Languages
English

What It Measures
The Complex Posttraumatic Stress Disorder Interview (CPTSD-I) was designed to assess the symptoms of Complex PTSD as defined by Herman (1992), which are described in the *DSM-IV* (1994) as the "Associated Features of PTSD."

Measure Content Survey, Procedure, or Process
The CPTSD-I is a semi-structured interview designed to be administered by a trained clinician. The interview is formatted similarly to the Clinician Administered PTSD Scale (CAPS; Blake et al., 1995) and hence may easily be administered in conjunction with the CAPS. It covers the seven main symptom domains of Complex PTSD as described by van der Kolk et al. (1995) and provides both a continuous score of overall severity and a dichotomous score for the presence or absence of a diagnosis of Complex PTSD.

Theoretical Orientation Summary
Our approach to the interview is atheoretical, in line with *DSM-IV*. Complex PTSD is a descriptive construct thought to account for the characterological consequences of chronic interpersonal violence (Herman, 1992). The relationship between the symptoms of Complex PTSD and chronic childhood trauma has been supported in the *DSM-IV* Field Trial for PTSD (van der Kolk et al., 1995).

Time Estimate

Administration	Scoring
30–90 min	15 minutes

Equipment Needed

Paper & Pencil	Computer	Basic Psychophysiological	Specialized Equipment
X			

Psychometric Maturity

Under Construction	Basic Properties Intact	Mature
X		

Psychometric Properties Summary
The CPTSD-I is currently under study in a sample of adult women with chronic childhood sexual abuse. Reliability (internal consistency, test-retest, inter-rater) and convergent validity of the CPTSD-I with conceptually-related instruments will be examined.

Particular Sensitivity

Age	Change over Time	Culture / Ethnicity	Gender	Geography / Climate	Sexual Orientation	Socioeconomic Status	Urban / Rural
?	?	?	?	?	?	?	?

Estimate of Number of In-Process Studies

Ouimette, P. C., & Saxe, G. Reliability and validity study of the complex PTSD interview.

Unpublished References

van der Kolk, B. A., Roth, S., Pelcovitz, D., Mandel, F. S. (1995). Complex Posttraumatic Stress Disorder: Results from the DSM-IV field trial for PTSD. Unpublished manuscript.

Published References

American Psychiatric Association (1994). *Diagnostic and statistical manual of mental disorders*. 4th ed. Washington, DC: Author.

Blake, D. D., Weathers, F. W., Nagy, L. M., Kaloupek, D. G., Gusman, F. D., Charney, D. S., & Keane, T. M. (1995). The development of a Clinician-Administered PTSD Scale. *Journal of Traumatic Stress, 8*, 75–90.

Herman, J. L. (1992). Complex PTSD: A syndrome in survivors of prolonged and repeated trauma. *Journal of Traumatic Stress, 5*, 377–391.

General Comments

As this instrument is undergoing psychometric study, we ask that those wishing to use the CPTSD-I share their raw data with us to further these efforts. We are very interested in facilitating the use of the CPTSD-I in different populations and will provide copies of the instrument and manual to those who are willing to sign a data sharing agreement. Please contact Paige Ouimette, Ph.D., or Glenn Saxe, M.D., as indicated below. Also, a self-report questionnaire version of the CPTSD-I is in development.

Key Words

Population	Stressor	Topic
adults	sexual assault/abuse chronic interpersonal violence	diagnosis measure development research

Reference Citation for This Review

Ouimette, P. C., Saxe, G., & van der Kolk, B. A. (1996). Psychometric review of The Complex PTSD Interview. In B. H. Stamm (Ed.). *Measurement of stress, trauma, and adaptation*. Lutherville, MD: Sidran Press.

Measure Contact Names

Paige C. Ouimette, Ph.D.
Address: VA Palo Alto Health Care System
            Menlo Park Division (152)
            795 Willow Road
            Menlo Park, CA 94025 USA
Phone: 415.493.5000 x22847
Fax: 415.617.2736
E-mail: Ouimette.Paige_J@Palo-Alto.Va.Gov

The Complex PTSD Interview Sample Items:

I. ALTERATION IN REGULATION OF AFFECT AND IMPULSES

a) Affect Instability
I'm going to ask you about several different feelings that may have caused you difficulty.

1) Do you get too angry? Do you yell? Hit things? Or do you never feel angry at all?
2) Do you get too sad? Do you feel persistently dysphoric, sad? Do you think about suicide?
3) Do you get too anxious (nervous)? Feel very jittery or scared? How do these affect your work and social relationships? What methods do you use to calm down?

Frequency
How often have any of these feelings caused you difficulty in the past year? In the worst month, how often have you felt this way?

0. Never
1. Once or twice
2. Once or twice a week
3. Several times a week
4. Daily or almost every day

Intensity
At their worst how strong were these feelings?

0. No problem with feelings
1. Mild—when my feelings get intense I have little problem calming down/ feeling better.
2. Moderate—when my feelings get intense it is sometimes difficult to calm down/ feel better (takes several hours to self-soothe).
3. Severe—when my feelings get intense I have to put a great deal of effort to calm down/ feel better (several hours to days).
4a. Extreme—when my feelings get intense I cannot control them (unable to self-soothe).
4b. I never have any feelings.

C	L
——	——
F	F
——	——
I	I
——	——
ON SET	ON SET
——	——
OFF SET	OFF SET

b) Impulsivity

Have you ever done things that are harmful?

ai) Have you tried to harm your body (e.g., cutting, burning, suicide attempts)?

aii) Have you ever thought of harming your body?

bi) Have you ever tried to harm others?

bii) Have you ever thought of harming others?

c) Have you exposed yourself to situations that might be dangerous (including impulsive sexual behavior; query about involvement in unsafe sexual practices)?

Frequency

How often have thought of or done anything harmful in the past year? In the worst month, how often have you thought of these things?

0. Never
1. once or twice
2. once or twice a week
3. several times a week
4. daily or almost every day

Intensity

At their worst how strong were these feelings of doing something harmful?

0. No feelings of doing anything harmful.
1. Mild—I only have thoughts of harming myself or someone else.
2. Moderate—I have done something harmful but didn't think that it would really kill me or someone else.
3. Severe—I have done something harmful and thought that it might have killed me or someone else.
4. Extreme—I have tried make myself or someone else die.

C	L
___ F	___ F
___ I	___ I
___ ON SET	___ ON SET
___ OFF SET	___ OFF SET

Computerised 16-Item Visual Analogue Scale of Menstrual Change

Type of Population
Female

Cost
Free

Copyright

Languages
English

What It Measures
The Computerised 16-item Visual Analogue Scale is intended to measure women's mood and somatic changes across the menstrual cycle. The scale can be used as a quick screening instrument (less than 10 minutes), in conjunction with other measures, to aid the diagnosis of Premenstrual Syndrome (PMS) or researches concerning the relationship between cyclical phases and behavioural changes. The scale can also be administered repeatedly to provide information about the mood and somatic fluctuation pattern of a particular individual in relation to the stages of her menstrual cycle.

Measure Content Survey and Procedures
Each item is presented on the computer screen with a 10-cm continuous line which is marked with 0 and 100 at each end. Subjects are asked to point at the appropriate place of the line to represent the degree of that mood or physical state they experience at the moment by a computer mouse as the response device. Scores are calculated automatically, including scores for each individual variable and three Principal-Component factor scores (see below). A practice session prior to the testing phase is included to ensure subjects know how to respond by using the computer mouse.

Theoretical Orientation Summary
These 16 items cover those mood and physical states which are frequently reported to concur with the menstrual cycles. The cyclical pattern in women has often shown to involve a peak of negative mood and uncomfortable physical complaints predominate in the premenstrual or menstrual phase, while the middle of the cycle is most often characterised by positive moods. The common premenstrual changes include depression, irritability, tension, lack of energy, abdominal bloatedness, breast tenderness, headache, urinary frequency, and craving for special foods (Bancroft & Backstrom, 1985).

Time Estimate

Administration	*Scoring*
10–15 minutes	10–15 minutes

Equipment Needed

Paper & Pencil	*Computer*	*Basic Psychophysiological*	*Specialized Equipment*
	An Apple Macintosh computer run with System 6.05 or above and Hyper-Card application (version 2.0 or above) are required.		

Psychometric Maturity

Under Construction	Basic Properties Intact	Mature
	X	

Psychometric Properties Summary

The scale shows high internal-consistent reliability. The scale has also reliably discriminated fluctuation of mood and somatic states among menstrual phases in a normal population of more than 200 women. A Principal-Component Analysis has yielded three factors which have been tentatively labelled as "Negative Mood," "Physical Distress," and "Physical Sensation" (Tseng, et al., 1992). Other studies have found it is sensitive in detecting mood change as a result of a laboratory mood induction procedure (Tseng, et al., submitted for publication). However, subjects who are characterised as suffering from computer anxiety may be biased by the employment of this computerised version. In comparison with the paper-and-pencil version, these subjects report heightened negative mood in the computerised version. Potential users for this programme are cautioned to take the individual characteristics related to Human-Computer Interaction into account.

Particular Sensitivity

Age	Change over Time	Culture / Ethnicity	Gender	Geography / Climate	Sexual Orientation	Socioeconomic Status	Urban / Rural
X	?	?	X	?	?	?	?

Estimate of Number of In-Process Studies

Unknown.

Unpublished References

Tseng, H., Macleod, H. A., & Wright, P. (1995). Computer anxiety and computerised versus paper-and-pencil assessment of induced mood change. Submitted for publication.

Published References

Bancroft, J., & Backstrom, T. (1985). Premenstrual syndrome. *Clinical Endocrinology, 22,* 313–336.

Tseng, H., Wright, P., & Macleod, H. A. (1992). Computerised and conventional mood assessment across the menstrual cycle. In *Abstracts Annual Conference of Society for Reproductive and Infant Psychology.* Strathclyde, Scotland: University of Strathclyde.

General Comments

The Computerised Analogue Scale is especially useful to free psychologists from repetitive work in scoring and administration. However, cautions should be exercised in interpreting scores obtained from subjects who perceive the computer as a stressor (i.e., computer anxiety).

Key Words

Population	Stressor	Topic
adolescent females adult females	menstrual pain menstruation premenstrual tension and distress	diagnosis gynecological medicine premenstrual syndrome research

Reference Citation for This Review

Tseng, Hsu-Min (1996). Psychometric review of Computerised 16-item Visual Analogue Scale of Menstrual Change. In B. H. Stamm (Ed). *Measurement of stress, trauma, and adaptation*. Lutherville, MD: Sidran Press.

Measure Authors

Hsu-Min Tseng, Hamish A. Macleod, Peter Wright

Measure Contact Name

Hsu-Min Tseng, Mr.

Address:	7 George Square
	Department of Psychology
	University of Edinburgh
	Edinburgh EH8 9JZ
	SCOTLAND
Phone:	+44.131.6503454
Fax:	+44.131.6503461
E-mail:	Tsenghm@ed.ac.uk

Concerns and Coping with HIV Scales

Type of Population

Adults anticipating or receiving HIV+ diagnosis

Cost

Free

Copyright

Languages

English, Mexican Spanish

What It Measures

Self-reported major concerns about becoming or being HIV infected, and expected or actual ways of coping, based on the Lazarus and Folkman (1984) theoretical model.

Measure Content Survey, Procedure, or Process

The initial development study gathered data from 278 HIV test clients of the Dallas County Health Department's HIV Clinic who were asked to report their anticipated major concerns and ways of coping if their test should indicate they were HIV infected. Selected items were taken or modified from the Folkman, et al. (1986) Stakes and Ways of Coping Scales; additional items were developed by a focus group of HIV counselors. Principal components factor analysis with oblique rotation was used to derive the scales; maximum likelihood analyses yielded essentially the same measurement models.

The five factor-based scales assessing major concerns (stress appraisals) are Existential Losses, Financial Dependence, Concern for Others, Relationship Losses and Strains, and Loss of Respect. The nine factor-based scales measuring coping dimensions include four familiar coping factors (Social-Emotional Support, Escape Fantasies, Distancing, and Negative Rumination), and five less often seen factors: Optimistic Planning, HIV Community, Self-Isolation, Anger, and Spirituality. Factor structures did not differ between gay/bisexual men, heterosexual women, or heterosexual men.

These findings were cross-validated on a second sample of 227 HIV test clients at the Nelson-Tebedo Community Clinic, Dallas, TX using LISREL confirmatory factor analyses. The Study I factor structures for each scale replicated with no significant or notable factor structure differences found for the sample as a whole or for subgroups defined by gender and sexual preference (men, women, heterosexual women, gay men). Factor loadings, intercorrelations, and errors were again invariant, and most of the subgroup mean differences that appeared were explained by different numbers of HIV+ people known. Psychometric data from these samples enabled detailed item and subscale analyses (Jenkins & Guarnaccia, 1995).

Theoretical Orientation Summary

Based on the Lazarus and Folkman (1984) theoretical model of stress and the coping process, which includes 1) cognitive appraisal of stressors (what is at stake in the stressful encounter) and 2) coping responses. These are seen as process-oriented and stressor-specific, and thus may differ for the same person under different stressors, or with the same stressor at different points in time. Thus, people may cope differently with traumatic stresses associated with disasters as compared to diagnosis of a fatal disease, and also differently with different diseases (e.g., cancer versus HIV, as shown by the validational study) and at different points in the disease course.

Time Estimate

Administration	Scoring
20–45 minutes	15 minutes

Equipment Needed

Paper & Pencil	Computer	Basic Psychophysiological	Specialized Equipment
X			

Psychometric Maturity

Under Construction	Basic Properties Intact	Mature
	X	

Psychometric Properties Summary

Cronbach's alpha reliabilities range from .57 to .82 (Jenkins & Guarnaccia, 1995), and thus are comparable to those reported for the Ways of Coping Scale (Folkman et al., 1986; Reed, Kemeny, Taylor, Wang, & Visscher, 1994).

Particular Sensitivity

Age	Change over Time	Culture / Ethnicity	Gender	Geography / Climate	Sexual Orientation	Socioeconomic Status	Urban / Rural
?	?	X	X	?	X	X	?

Estimate of Number of In-Process Studies

2

Unpublished References

Jenkins, S. R. (1995). Women coping with possible HIV+ diagnosis: Two studies. Presented at the HIV Infection in Women Conference. Washington, DC.

Jenkins, S. R., & Guarnaccia, C. A. (1995). Concerns and coping with HIV: Comparisons across groups. Unpublished manuscript, University of North Texas.

Published References

Jenkins, S. R., & Coons, H. L. (in press). Psychosocial stress and adaptation processes for women coping with HIV/AIDS. In A. O'Leary & L. S. Jemmott (Eds.). *Women and AIDS: Coping and care.* New York: Plenum.

General Comments

Key Words

Population	Stressor	Topic
adults elderly emergency services workers [medical] health care workers men minorities women	AIDS disease HIV physical sexual	appraisal coping measure development psychosocial research social support

Reference Citation for This Review

Jenkins, S. R. (1996). Psychometric review of Concerns and Coping with HIV Scales. In B. H. Stamm (Ed.). *Measurement of Stress, Trauma, and Adaptation.* Lutherville, MD: Sidran Press.

Measure Contact Name

Sharon Rae Jenkins, Ph.D.

Address: Department of Psychology
                P.O. Box 13587
                University of North Texas
                Denton, TX 76203-3587 USA

Phone: 817.565.4107

Fax: 817.565.4682

E-mail: jenkinss@terrill.unt.edu

The Cultural Messages Scale

Type of Population

Women

Cost

There is no cost to using the scale. We would greatly appreciate it if people who choose to use the scale would provide us with either summary data or the raw data that emerge from the use of the scale, as this will facilitate further scale development.

Copyright

Languages

English

What It Measures

The scale assesses familiarity with and endorsement of common cultural constructions (i.e. beliefs, messages, and ideas) about women, heterosexual relations, and sexuality.

Measure Content Survey, Procedure, or Process

The two versions of the scale (created to facilitate pre- and post-testing) assess familiarity with and endorsement of common cultural constructions, (i.e., common beliefs, messages, and ideas) about women, women and men, and sexuality. The scale includes items such as: If you're not a virgin you're a whore; Women exist for men's sexual pleasure; A raped woman is soiled, damaged goods; A woman's attractiveness is her most important trait, etc. The items were empirically derived from varied sources—focus groups of undergraduate students, media productions, transcripts of women who have been raped—and are intended to represent a fairly broad domain of cultural messages about women and sexuality. The scale is organized to evaluate the subjects' degree of *familiarity* with the items as well as their *agreement* with the items on a 5-point interval rating format. Thus, for each item subjects indicate separately the degree to which they are familiar with the item and the degree to which they agree with the item. In addition to the actual scale items, the scale also contains a number of reversed stereotypes and positive statements intended to break response set and provide a way to evaluate the validity of an individual subject's score.

Theoretical Orientation Summary

The scale grew out of an interface between the feminist analysis of social and cultural institutions and our current models of response to trauma (Lebowitz & Roth, 1994). Within the feminist literature, scholars have long argued that our culture is replete with images and messages about women that organize our perceptions and social organizations. Within psychology, trauma's impact on people has frequently been understood in terms of its impact on our organizing schemas. These literatures were used to hypothesize that culturally located schemas about women and sexuality might prove to be an important domain in understanding the impact of sexually traumatic events and the differential effect of various types of treatment interventions.

Time Estimate

Administration	Scoring
15–30 minutes	10–15 minutes

Equipment Needed

Paper & Pencil	Computer	Basic Psychophysiological	Specialized Equipment
X			

Psychometric Maturity

Under Construction	Basic Properties Intact	Mature
	X	

Psychometric Properties Summary

The first version of the scale was given to 417 female undergraduate students. A principal components factor analysis was performed on the 116 items for Familiarity. Both orthogonal and oblique rotations revealed the same factor structure: One main factor of 96 items with factor loadings ranging from .39 to .69 with alpha coefficient of .98. A second factor consisted largely of the items included to break response set. Item-to-total correlations were calculated for Factor 1 and low scoring items were eliminated. The remaining items were then divided into two scales (43 items and 7 reversals/positive items), deemed to be functionally identical. These two new versions of the scale were then administered to 298 undergraduate females. A second factor analysis was performed. For Form 1, alpha coefficients were .97 for Familiarity and .92 for Agreement; for Form 2, alpha coefficents were .97 for Familiarity and .91 for Agreement. The two forms are highly correlated (r=.98, p<.01). The mean inter-item correlation for Form 1 is .45 (minimum correlation is .16, maximum is .69); and for Form 2, the mean inter-item correlation is .44 (minimum correlation is .15, maximum is .70). The overall averages from the second administration (298 undergraduates) are as follows: Familiarity, Form 1=3.48, Form 2=3.46; Agreement, Form 1=1.66, Form 2=1.72. Levels of familiarity and endorsement varied according to victimization history (e.g., sexually traumatized women were more familiar with the scale items than non-traumatized women, and sexually traumatized women were more likely to agree with negative messages) as well as a history of having taken a women's studies course, defining oneself as a feminist, and sexual orientation.

Particular Sensitivity

Age	Change over Time	Culture / Ethnicity	Gender	Geography / Climate	Sexual Orientation	Socioeconomic Status	Urban / Rural
?	X	X	X	?	X	X	?

Estimate of Number of In-Process Studies
Unknown

Unpublished References

Lebowitz, L., & Kieley, M. (October 1993). The Cultural Messages Scale: Assessing cultural constructions of women and sexuality. In L. Lebowitz (Chair). Trauma and Cultural Constructions of Gender: Assessment and Implications. Symposium presented at the International Society for Traumatic Stress Studies. San Antonio, TX.

Published References

Lebowitz, L., & Roth, S. (1994). I felt like a slut: The cultural context and women's response to being raped. *Journal of Traumatic Stress*, 7 (3), 363–390.

General Comments

This scale should prove useful in evaluating differences among traumatized groups, and the effects of different types of treatment interventions. In addition, it should prove a useful tool in teaching about culture and internalized schemas.

Key Words

Population	Stressor	Topic

adolescents
adults
perpetrators
women
	criminal
	   victimization
	domestic violence
	physical
	   abuse/neglect
	sexual assault/abuse
	gender crimes
		internalized social
		   messages
		measure development
		research

Reference Citation for This Review

Lebowitz, L., & Kiely, M. (1996). Psychometric review of The Cultural Messages Scale. In B. H. Stamm (Ed.). *Measurement of stress, trauma, and adaptation*. Lutherville, MD: Sidran Press.

Measure Contact Name

Leslie Lebowitz, Ph.D.

Address: 388 Park Steet
               West Roxbury, MA 02132 USA

Phone: 617.327.1081

Fax: 617.327.1081

E-mail:

Dimensions of Stressful Events (DOSE) Ratings Scale

Type of Population

Children and adolescents (although slight revisions make it useful for adults as well).

Cost

Free.

Copyright

Languages

English

What It Measures

This is essentially a detailed checklist containing 25 items pertaining to particular dimensions of stressful events that the literature suggests are likely to increase the traumatic impact on children. These include items assessing such things as the unexpectedness of the event, who was impacted directly, whether or not anyone the child knows was physically injured or died, who or what the source of the trauma was, etc. twenty-four additional items are included for sexually abused children.

Measure Content Survey, Procedure, or Process

Items are rated by the interviewer in conjunction with feedback from the children and/or parents.

Theoretical Orientation Summary

In order to better assess the equivalence of children's experiences of the same (or different) stressors, it is necessary to measure the DOSE of their exposure to traumatic dimensions of the stressors. That is what this scale is intended to be used for.

Time Estimate

Administration	Scoring
15–30 minutes	5–15 minutes

Equipment Needed

Paper & Pencil	Computer	Basic Psychophysiological	Specialized Equipment
X			

Psychometric Maturity

Under Construction	Basic Properties Intact	Mature
X		

Psychometric Properties Summary

This is not a true scale. It can actually be "scored" in several ways and used in several ways. Scoring suggestions are included.

Particular Sensitivity

Age	Change over Time	Culture/ Ethnicity	Gender	Geography/ Climate	Sexual Orientation	Socioeconomic Status	Urban/ Rural
X	?	?	?	?	?	?	?

Estimate of Number of In-Process Studies

3. One of these is a national effort to gather data for validation for the interview and other related interviews and scales. If you are interested in joining this effort, please contact Ken Fletcher at the address and telephone below.

Unpublished References

Unknown.

Published References

None.

General Comments

In order to better assess the equivalence of children's (or adults') experiences of the same (or different) stressors, it is necessary to measure the DOSE of their exposure to traumatic dimensions of the stressors. That is what this scale is intended to be used for. An IBM-compatible data entry program is available from the author for this scale. The data entry program runs in EPI INFO, a data entry creation program distributed (for free from other users or academic computer departments or for $50 from the Center for Disease Control or the World Health Organization). EPI INFO programs allow data bases to be created which can be analyzed on a basic level within EPI INFO itself and by other statistical programs (such as SPSS, SAS, and Systat) or by databases and spreadsheets that will read dBase file formats.

I feel so strongly that the field needs to take routine measures of the stressful events themselves that I have not copyrighted this scale. Instead, I am placing it in the public domain. You may use it for free, as long as you do not try to sell it, or a computer version, to anyone. I would appreciate hearing about your experiences with it, however, if only to help me revise it and make it a better scale. I would also like to share your raw data with you regarding this scale in order to get some norms. Suggestions for revisions are requested.

Key Words

Population	Stressor	Topic
children	any	assessment measure development research

Reference Citation for This Review

Fletcher, K. E. (1996). Psychometric review of Dimensions of Stressful Events (DOSE) Ratings Scale. In B. H. Stamm (Ed.). *Measurement of stress, trauma, and adaptation*. Lutherville, MD: Sidran Press.

Measure Contact Name

Kenneth E. Fletcher, Ph.D.
Address: University of Massachusetts Medical Center
              Psychiatry Dept.
              55 Lake Avenue North
              Worcester, MA 01655-0001 USA
Phone: 508.856.3329
Fax: 508.856.6426
E-Mail: fletcher@umassmed.ummed.edu

Dimensions of Stressful Events (DOSE) Rating Scale

1. Who were the direct victims of the stressful event(s)? [Check all that apply.]
___ The child   ___ One or both of the child's parents or guardians
___ Siblings   ___ Other adult relatives
___ Other child relatives   ___ Adult mentors (e.g., teacher, minister, coach, etc.)
___ Other children **the child knows well**   ___ Other adults **the child knows well**
       from outside the family   ___ Other adults **the child does not know well**
___ Other children **the child does not know**   ___ A pet of the child or family
       well from outside the family
___ Other (specify): _____

2. How many times was the child exposed to this kind of event?
___ Once ___ More than Once but Has Ceased ___ More than Once and Continues

3a. If a one-time only event, how long did it last? _____

3b. If a more-than-one-time event, how long did the event(s) usually or typically last? _____

3c. If a more-than-one-time event, over what span of time did the events take place from first occurrence to last or latest? _____

4. Was anyone physically injured due to the event(s)? If so, indicate who. [Check all that apply.]
___ No one was physically injured
___ The child   ___ One or both of the child's parents or guardians
___ Siblings   ___ Other adult relatives
___ Other child relatives   ___ Adult mentors (e.g., teacher, minister, coach, etc.)
___ Other children **the child knows well**   ___ Other adults **the child knows well**
       from outside the family   ___ Other adults **the child does not know well**
___ Other children **the child does not know**   ___ A pet of the child or family
       well from outside the family
___ Other (specify): _____

5. Did anyone die as a result of the event(s)?   ___ No   ___ Yes

5a. If so, indicate who. [Check all that apply.]
___ The child   ___ One or both of the child's parents or guardians
___ Siblings   ___ Other adult relatives
___ Other child relatives   ___ Adult mentors (e.g., teacher, minister, coach, etc.)
___ Other children **the child knows well**   ___ Other adults **the child knows well**
       from outside the family   ___ Other adults **the child does not know well**
___ Other children **the child does not know**   ___ A pet of the child or family
       well from outside the family
___ Other (specify): _____

6. Did the child witness violence directed at anyone?   ___ No ___ Yes
7. Did the child witness the physical injury of anyone?   ___ No ___ Yes
8. Did the child witness the death of anyone?   ___ No ___ Yes
9. Did the child witness destruction of property?   ___ No ___ Yes
10. Did the child witness social chaos?   ___ No ___ Yes
11. Did the child view the event(s) as a threat to his or her safety or well-being?   ___ No ___ Yes
12. Did the child view the event(s) as a threat to the safety or well-being of family or friends?   ___ No ___ Yes
13. Who or what was the source of the stressful event(s)? [Check all that apply.]
___ One or both parents   ___ Child relative
___ Other adult relative   ___ Other known child
___ Other known adult   ___ Other unknown child
___ Other unknown adult   ___ Animal(s)

This instrument, by Kenneth E. Fletcher, may be reproduced without charge and freely distributed, as long as no funds are exchanged.

___ Manmade or technological accident or disaster

___ Natural disaster

___ Chronic illness or other physical injury (e.g., burns)

___ Medical interventions (e.g., repeated operations like skin grafts)

___ Other (specify): _____

14. If a one time event, how prepared was the child for the event when it occurred? If an event of more than one occurrence, how well was the child usually prepared for them when the events occurred?

    ___ Not at all   ___ Very Little   ___ Some   ___ Very Much

15. How much control over the course of events did the child feel he or she had?

    ___ None   ___ Very Little   ___ Some   ___ Lots

16. How much control did the child feel his or her parents or other adults in charge at the time had over the course of events?

    ___ None   ___ Very Little   ___ Some   ___ Lots

17. Has the child been exposed to other potentially very stressful events in addition to the event being rated?

    ___ No   ___ Possibly   ___ Yes

    IF SO, WHAT?

    _____

    _____
    _____

18. Was the child separated from the family during or after the stressful event(s)?

    ___ No   ___ Yes, but Is Now Reunited   ___ Yes, and Remains Separated

19. Was the child dislocated from his or her home due to the event(s)?

    ___ No   ___ Yes, but Temporarily   ___ Yes, Permanently

20. Did the child suffer any lasting losses (other than death of friends or relatives) due to the stressful event(s)?

    ___ No

    ___ Yes, but of Minor Importance to the Child

    ___ Yes, and of Major Importance to the Child

21. How long-lasting are the major negative consequences of the stressful event(s) likely to be?

    ___ Less than 6 Months

    ___ 6 Months to a Year

    ___ More than a Year but not into Adulthood

    ___ Into Adulthood and Maybe a Lifetime

22. How specifically does the child define the cause(s) of the stressful event(s)?

    ___ Cause is Seen as Very Specific to the Circumstances (e.g., only the neighbor's German shepherd bites)

    ___ Cause is Seen as Partly Generalized to Some Similar Circumstances (e.g., all German shepherd dogs bite)

    ___ Cause is Seen as Generalized to All People, Places, or Things Like Those Involved (e.g., all dogs bite)

23. Does the child believe the event(s) *will* (rather than *might*) recur?

    ___ No   ___ Yes

24. Did the stressful event(s) lead to moral or religious conflicts for the child?

    ___ No   ___ Yes

25. Did the stressful event(s) lead to stigmatization for the child?

    ___ No, and the Child Has No Such Fear

    ___ No, but It May Happen OR the Child Fears the Possibility

    ___ Yes

Additional DOSE Items For Sexually Abused Children

1. Rate the seriousness of the sexual abuse on the following scale:
   ___ **Least serious**—inappropriate kissing or sexual touching while child was clothed; sexual touching (nongenital) under the clothes or when the child was undressed
   ___ **Serious**—direct genital touching and/or digital penetration of vagina or anus; simulated intercourse
   ___ **Most serious**—cunnilingus, fellatio, anilingus, and/or penile penetration of vagina, anus, or mouth
2. How certain is it that abuse took place?
   ___ Very uncertain; evidence to the contrary
   ___ Somewhat uncertain; questionable evidence
   ___ Somewhat certain; some corroborative evidence
   ___ Very certain; verified
3. How many offenders were involved in the event(s)? _____
4. Approximately how many incidents were there altogether? _____
5. How certain is the evidence for the number of incidents reported in the previous question?
   ___ Very uncertain; evidence to the contrary
   ___ Somewhat uncertain; questionable evidence
   ___ Somewhat certain; some corroborative evidence
   ___ Very certain; verified
6. Did the child ever receive a reward for the event(s)?
   ___ No   ___ Yes
7. Was the child ever physically restrained during the event(s)?
   ___ No   ___ Yes
8. Did the child ever try to avoid, resist, or escape the event(s)?
   ___ No   ___ Yes
9. Was the child ever threatened with harm if abuse was revealed?
   ___ No   ___ Yes
10. Were members of the child's family ever threatened with harm if abuse was revealed?
    ___ No   ___ Yes
11. Does the offender deny event(s) took place?
    ___ No   ___ Yes
12. Was child ever under the influence of alcohol or illicit drugs during the stressful event(s)?
    ___ No   ___ Yes
13. Rate the amount of emotional support provided the child by the mother after the event(s):
    ___ Reactions unknown; not available
    ___ Is committed to the child and provides meaningful support
    ___ Is somewhat committed and supportive
    ___ Vacillates in ability and/or desire to support child
    ___ Unsupportive, yet not hostile or abandoning
    ___ Is threatening or hostile; has abandoned child psychologically or physically or both
14. Rate the amount of emotional support provided the child by the father after the event(s):
    ___ Reactions unknown; not available
    ___ Is committed to the child and provides meaningful support
    ___ Is somewhat committed and supportive
    ___ Vacillates in ability and/or desire to support child
    ___ Unsupportive, yet not hostile or abandoning
    ___ Is threatening or hostile; has abandoned child psychologically or physically or both
15. Rate the extent to which the mother believes the child's version of the event(s):
    ___ Mother's reactions unknown; unavailable
    ___ Makes clear, public statement of belief
    ___ Makes weak statements of belief
    ___ Wavers in belief of child or is undecided
    ___ Makes weak statements of disbelief
    ___ Totally denies event(s) happened as child says it did; denies abuse

16. Rate the extent to which the father believes the child's version of the event(s):
___ Father's reactions unknown; unavailable
___ Makes clear, public statement of belief
___ Makes weak statements of belief
___ Wavers in belief of child or is undecided
___ Makes weak statements of disbelief
___ Totally denies event(s) happened as child says it did; denies abuse

17. Indicate mother's action toward the offender:
___ Not applicable (Mother is offender)
___ No known action taken; unavailable
___ Actively demonstrates disapproval of offender's abusive behavior
___ Remains passive; refuses to take sides
___ Chooses offender over child

18. Indicate father's action toward the offender:
___ Not applicable (Father is offender)
___ No known action taken; unavailable
___ Actively demonstrates disapproval of offender's abusive behavior
___ Remains passive; refuses to take sides
___ Chooses offender over child

Answer the Following Questions if the Child is Living with a Foster, Adoptive, or Step-parent Parent:

19. Rate the amount of emotional support provided the child by the [foster/adoptive/step-] mother after the event(s):
___ Reactions unknown; not available
___ Is committed to the child and provides meaningful support
___ Is somewhat committed and supportive
___ Vacillates in ability and/or desire to support child
___ Unsupportive, yet not hostile or abandoning
___ Is threatening or hostile; has abandoned child psychologically or physically or both

20. Rate the amount of emotional support provided the child by the [foster/adoptive/step-] father after the event(s):
___ Reactions unknown; not available
___ Is committed to the child and provides meaningful support
___ Is somewhat committed and supportive
___ Vacillates in ability and/or desire to support child
___ Unsupportive, yet not hostile or abandoning
___ Is threatening or hostile; has abandoned child psychologically or physically or both

21. Rate the extent to which the [foster/adoptive/step-] mother believes the child's version of the event(s):
___ Reactions unknown; unavailable
___ Makes clear, public statement of belief
___ Makes weak statements of belief
___ Wavers in belief of child or is undecided
___ Makes weak statements of disbelief
___ Totally denies event(s) happened as child says it did; denies abuse

22. Rate the extent to which the [foster/adoptive/step-] father believes the child's version of the event(s):
___ Reactions unknown; unavailable
___ Makes clear, public statement of belief
___ Makes weak statements of belief
___ Wavers in belief of child or is undecided
___ Makes weak statements of disbelief
___ Totally denies event(s) happened as child says it did; denies abuse

23. Indicate [foster/adoptive/step-] mother's action toward the offender:
___ Not applicable (is offender)
___ No known action taken; unavailable
___ Actively demonstrates disapproval of offender's abusive behavior

___ Remains passive; refuses to take sides

___ Chooses offender over child

24. Indicate [foster/adoptive/step-] father's action toward the offender:

___ Not applicable (is offender)

___ No known action taken; unavailable

___ Actively demonstrates disapproval of offender's abusive behavior

___ Remains passive; refuses to take sides

___ Chooses offender over child

Scoring the Dimensions of Stressful Events (DOSE) Rating Scale

The DOSE is actually a multi-purpose rating scale. It is intended to help the clinician, researcher, and child to better delineate the traumatizing dimensions of stressful events. As such it has many different uses.

The DOSE can be used in a qualitative way, allowing different groups of traumatized children to be studied. A researcher might be interested in the differences in children's stress responses depending upon one or more of the dimensions rating by the DOSE. Groups might be formed, for example, of children who had experienced loss or physical injury in a disaster versus children who had experienced neither. Answers to all of the questions should be of interest to therapists. The DOSE is one way of insuring that these questions get considered in the light of each child's own experience.

The DOSE can be used as a scaled instrument as well as a means of categorizing traumatic experiences. One way to do this might be to add together all of those ratings that allow a scaled answer to be derived. Thus, all *yes* answers would be counted as one and *no* answers as zero. Those ratings with answers that range over several answers can generally be scored from some low score (for example, 0 for None or Not at All, 1 for Very Little, 2 for Some, and 3 for Very Much). Most of the first 26 questions lend themselves to such scoring. Only questions 3 and 13 do not. Question 13 could be scaled, however, by scoring A Parent=13, Child or Other adult relative=12, Other known adult=11, Other unknown adult=10, Other known child or Other unknown child=9, etc. But the rating you assigned would have to be subjective in some ways because they would depend upon the type of experiences being rated. Cruder categories might prove more useful, such as Relatives=5, Other adults or Chronic illness/ Medical interventions=4, Other child=3, Disasters=2, Other=depends (you would have to decide this).

Answers to questions 1, 4, and 5 in the first part of the DOSE can also be scored in a manner to that suggested above for question 13. The Child=7, Parents or siblings=6, Other relatives=5, Adult mentors=4, Others child knows well=3, Others child doesn't know well=2, Pet=1, Other=?.

Sexual Abuse Questions

The last 24 questions in the DOSE are to be completed only when sexual abuse is at issue. These questions, too, can be scored in various ways. All *yes* questions could equal 1, for example, and all *no* questions=0. Some methods of scoring the questions might not be obvious. For example, in the first of these questions, Least serious might=1 and Most serious=3. In question 2, Very uncertain might=0 and Very certain might=3. It might make sense to take the scores for question 1 and question 2 and multiply them together. So that if 1 was answered Serious (=2) and 2 was answered Very certain (=3), the score for these two questions would be 2 x 3=6. The answer to question 3 could be added to 1 and 2, or multiplied by them. Or the answers to questions number 3 and 4 could be kept from the total and used separately in statistical analyses of research results.

Questions 13, 14, 19, and 20 in the last half of the DOSE might be scored as –10 for Is Committed to the Child; –5 for Is somewhat committed; 3 for Vacillates; 5 for Unsupportive; and 10 for Is threatening or hostile. Reactions unknown=missing. For questions 15, 16, 21, and 22, Makes clear, public statement=–10; Makes weak statement=–5; Wavers or undecided=3; Weak disbelief=5; and Totally denies abuse=10. Reactions unknown=missing. For questions 17, 18, 23, and 24, Actively demonstrates disapproval of offender=-5; Remains passive=5; Chooses offender over child=10; otherwise=missing.

To score the DOSE when sexual abuse is involved, you can use averages. Divide total scores by the number of questions that did not have missing answers. This provides a rough average level of traumatization score.

Dissociative Experiences Scale (DES)

Type of Population

Adults

Cost

Available as appendix of Carlson & Putnam 1993 (see reference below). Scale manual is also contained in the publication.

Copyright

Journal of Nervous and Mental Disease and Dissociation

What It Measures

Frequency of dissociative experiences in adults

Measure Content Survey, Procedure, or Process

28-item self-report measure of experiences of amnesias, depersonalization, derealization, absorption, and imaginative involvement. Subject is asked to indicate how much of the time each experience happens to them (from 0%=never to 100%=always).

Theoretical Orientation Summary

Scale measures reports of experiences and behaviors and has no theoretical orientation.

Time Estimate

Administration	Scoring
10–20 minutes	5 minutes

Equipment Needed

Paper & Pencil	Computer	Basic Psychophysiological	Specialized Equipment
X			

Psychometric Maturity

Under Construction	Basic Properties Intact	Mature
		X

Psychometric Properties Summary

Scale shows excellent reliability and validity and has been used extensively. Over 120 published studies (to date) report on use of the DES.

Particular Sensitivity

Age	Change over Time	Culture/ Ethnicity	Gender	Geography/ Climate	Sexual Orientation	Socioeconomic Status	Urban/ Rural
?	?	?	?	?	?	?	?

Estimate of Number of In-Process Studies

Unknown

Unpublished References

Unknown.

Published References

Allen, J. G., & Smith, W. H. (1993). Diagnosing dissociative disorders. *Bulletin of the Menninger Clinic, 57,* 328–343.

Anderson, G., Yasenik, L., & Ross, C. A. (1993). Dissociative experiences and disorders among women who identify themselves as sexual abuse survivors. *Child Abuse and Neglect, 17,* 677.

Anderson, G. L. (1992). Dissociation, distress and family function. *Dissociation, 5* (4), 211–215.

Armstrong, J. G., & Loewenstein, R. J. (1990). Characteristics of patients with multiple personality and dissociative disorders on psychological testing. *Journal of Nervous and Mental Disease, 178,* 448–454.

Berger, D., Onon, Y., Nakajima, K., & Suematsu, H. (1994). Dissociative symptoms in Japan. *American Journal of Psychiatry, 151,* 148–149.

Bernstein, E. M., & Putnam, F. W. (1986). Development, reliability, and validity of a dissociation scale. *Journal of Nervous and Mental Disease, 174,* 727–735.

Boon, S., & Draijer, N. (1993). Multiple personality disorder in the Netherlands: A clinical investigation of 71 patients. *American Journal of Psychiatry, 150* (3), 489–494.

Bowman, E. S. (1993). Etiology and clinical course of pseudoseizures: Relationship to trauma, depression, and dissociation. *Psychosomatics, 34* (8), 333–342.

Bowman, E. S., & Coons, P. M. (1992). The use of electroconvulsive therapy in patients with dissociative disorders. *Journal of Nervous and Mental Disease, 180* (8), 524–528.

Branscomb, L. (1991). Dissociation in combat-related post-traumatic stress disorder. *Dissociation, 4* (1), 13–20.

Bremner, J. D., Southwick, S., Brett, E., Fontana, A., Rosenheck, R., & Charney, D.S. (1992). Dissociation and post-traumatic stress disorder in Vietnam combat veterans. *American Journal of Psychiatry, 149,* 328–332.

Briere, J., & Runtz, M. (1993). Childhood sexual abuse: Long-term sequelae and implications for psychological assessment. *Journal of Interpersonal Violence, 8,* 312–330.

Carlson, E. B. (1994). Studying the interaction between physical and psychological states with the Dissociative Experiences Scale. In D. A. Spiegel (Ed.). *Dissociation: Culture, Mind and Body.* Washington, DC: American Psychiatric Press.

Carlson, E. B., & Armstrong, J. (1994). Diagnosis and assessment of dissociative disorders. In S. J. Lynn & J. Rhue (Eds.). *Dissociation: Theoretical, clinical, and research perspectives.* New York: Guilford.

Carlson, E. B., & Putnam, F. W. (1989). Integrating research in dissociation and hypnotic susceptibility. Are there two pathways to hypnotizability? *Dissociation, 2* (1), 32–38.

Carlson, E. B., & Putnam, F. W. (1990). Comment on "A factor analytic study of two scales measuring dissociation" by Fischer and Elinitsky. *American Journal of Clinical Hypnosis, 33,* 133–135.

Carlson, E. B., & Putnam, F. W. (1993). An update on the Dissociative Experiences Scale. *Dissociation, 6,* 16–27.

Carlson, E. B., Putnam, F. W., Ross, C. A., Torem, M., Coons, P., Dill, D. L., Loewenstein, R. J., & Braun, B. G. (1993). Validity of the Dissociative Experiences Scale in screening for multiple personality disorder: A multicenter study. *American Journal of Psychiatry, 150* (7), 1030–1036.

Carlson, E. B., & Rosser-Hogan, R. (1991). Trauma experiences, posttraumatic stress, dissociation, and depression in Cambodian refugees. *American Journal of Psychiatry, 148,* 1548–1551.

Carlson, E. B., & Rosser-Hogan, R. (1993). Mental health status of Cambodian refugees ten years after leaving home. *American Journal of Orthopsychiatry, 63,* 223–231.

Carlson, E.B., & Rosser-Hogan, R. (1994). Cross-cultural response to trauma: A study of traumatic experiences and posttraumatic stress symptoms in Cambodian refugees. *Journal of Traumatic Stress, 7,* 43–58.

Chu, J. A., & Dill, D. L. (1990). Dissociative symptoms in relation to childhood physical and sexual abuse. *American Journal of Psychiatry, 147,* 887–892.

Coons, P., Bowman, E., & Milstein, V. (1988). Multiple personality disorder: A clinical investigation of 50 cases. *Journal of Nervous and Mental Disease, 176,* 519–527.

Coons, P. M. (1992). Dissociative disorder not otherwise specified: A clinical investigation of 50 cases with suggestions for typology and treatment. *Dissociation, 5* (4), 187–195.

Coons, P. M., Bowman, E., Pellow, T. A., & Schneider, P. (1989). Post-traumatic aspects of the treatment of victims of sexual abuse and incest. *Psychiatric Clinics of North America, 12,* 325–335.

Demitrack, M. A., Putnam, F. W., Brewerton, T. D., Brandt, H. A., & Gold, P. W. (1990). Relation of clinical variables to dissociative phenomena in eating disorders. *American Journal of Psychiatry*, *147*, 1184–1188.

Demitrack, M. A., Putnam, F. W., Rubinow, D. R., & Pigott, T. A. (1993). Relation of dissociative phenomena to levels of cerebrospinal fluid monoamine metabolites and beta-endorphin in patients with eating disorders: A pilot study. *Psychiatry Research*, *49* (1), 1–10.

Devinsky, O., Putnam, F. W., Grafman, J., Bromfield, E., & Theodore, W. H. (1989). Dissociative states and epilepsy. *Neurology*, *39*, 835–840.

DiTomasso, M. J., & Routh, D. K. (1993). Recall of abuse in childhood and three measures of dissociation. *Child Abuse and Neglect*, *17*, 477–485.

Draijer, N., & Boon, S. (1993). The validation of the Dissociative Experiences Scale against the criterion of the SCID-D using receiver operating characteristics (ROC) analysis. *Dissociation*, *6*, 28–37.

Dunn, G. E., Paolo, A. M., Ryan, J. J., & Fleet, J. V. (1993). Dissociative symptoms in a substance abuse population. *American Journal of Psychiatry*, *150* (7), 1043–1047.

Ellason, J. W., Ross, C. A., Mayran, L. W., & Sainton, K. (1994). Convergent validity of the new form of the DES. *Dissociation*, *7* (2), 101–104.

Ensink, B. J., & van Otterloo, D. (1989). A validation of the Dissociative Experiences Scale in the Netherlands. *Dissociation*, *2* (4), 221–223.

Fischer, D., & Elnitsky, S. (1990). A factor analytic study of two scales measuring dissociation. *American Journal of Clinical Hypnosis*, *32*, 201–207.

Fischer, D. G. (1990). Reply to Carlson and Putnam letter. *American Journal of Clinical Hypnosis*, *33*, 134–135.

Frischholz, E. J., Braun, B. G., Lewis, J., Schaeffer, D., Sachs, R. G., Schwartz, D. R., Westergaard, C., & Pasquotto, J. (1992). Construct validity of the Dissociative Experiences Scale II: Its relationship to hypnotizability. *American Journal of Clinical Hypnosis*, *35*, 145–152.

Frischholz, E. J., Braun, B. G., Sachs, R. G., Hopkins, L., Shaeffer, D. M., Lewis, J., Leavitt, F., Pasquotto, M. A., & Schwartz, D. R. (1990). The Dissociative Experiences Scale: Further replication and validation. *Dissociation*, *3* (3), 151–153.

Frischholz, E. J., Braun, B. G., Sachs, R. G., Schwartz, D. R., Lewis, J., Shaeffer, D., Westergaard, C., & Pasquotto, J. (1991). Construct validity of the Dissociative Experiences Scale (DES): I. The relation between the DES and other self report measures of dissociation. *Dissociation*, *4* (4), 185–188.

Gilbertson, A., Torem, M., Cohen, R., Newman, I., Radojicic, C., & Patel, S. (1992). Susceptibility of common self-report measures of dissociation to malingering. *Dissociation*, *5*(4), 216–220.

Goff, D. C., Brotman, A. W., Kindlon, D., Waites, M., & Amico, E. (1991). The delusion of possession in chronically psychotic patients. *Journal of Nervous and Mental Disease*, *179* (9), 567–571.

Goff, D. C., Brotman, A. W., Kindlon, D., Waites, M., & Amico, E. (1991). Self-reports of childhood abuse in chronically psychotic patients. *Psychiatry Research*, *37*, 73–80.

Goff, D. C., Olin, J. A., Jenike, M. A., Baer, L., & Buttolph, M. L. (1992). Dissociative symptoms in patients with obsessive-compulsive disorder. *Journal of Nervous and Mental Disease*, *180* (5), 332–337.

Goldner, E. M., Cockhill, L. A., Bakan, R., & Birmingham, C. L. (1991). Dissociation experiences and eating disorders. *American Journal of Psychiatry*, *148*, 1274–1275.

Goodwin, J. M., Cheeves, K., & Connell, V. (1990). Borderline and other severe symptoms in adult survivors of incestuous abuse. *Psychiatric Annals*, *20*, 22–32.

Heber, A. S., Fleisher, W., Ross, C. A., & Stanwick, R. (1989). Dissociation in alternative healers and traditional therapists: A comparative study. *American Journal of Psychotherapy*, *43*, 562–574.

Herman, J. L., Perry, J. C., & van der Kolk, B. A. (1989). Childhood trauma in borderline personality disorder. *American Journal of Psychiatry*, *146*, 490–495.

Herzog, D. B., Staley, J. E., Carmody, S., & Robbins, W. M. (1993). Childhood sexual abuse in anorexia nervosa and bulimia nervosa: A pilot study. *Journal of the American Academy of Child and Adolescent Psychiatry*, *32* (5), 962–966.

Hyer, L. A., Albrecht, J. W., Boudewyns, P. A., Woods, M. G., & Brandsma, J. (1993). Dissociative experiences of Vietnam veterans with chronic posttraumatic stress disorder. *Psychological Reports*, *73*, 519–530.

Kihlstrom, J. F., Glisky, M. L., & Angiulo, M. J. (1994). Dissociative tendencies and dissociative disorders. *Journal of Abnormal Psychology*, *103* (1), 117–124.

Kirby, J. S., Chu, J. A., & Dill, D. L. (1993). Correlates of dissociative symptomatology in patients with physical and sexual abuse histories. *Comprehensive Psychiatry, 34*, 258–263.

Leavitt, F., & Braun, B. (1991). Historical reliability: A key to differentiating populations among patients presenting signs of multiple personality disorder. *Psychological Reports, 69*, 499–510.

Loewenstein, R., & Putnam, F. W. (1990). The clinical phenomenology of males with multiple personality disorder. *Dissociation, 3* (3), 135–143.

Loewenstein, R. J., & Putnam, F. W. (1988). A comparison study of dissociative symptoms in patients with complex partial seizures, multiple personality disorder, and posttraumaticstress disorder. *Dissociation, 1* (4), 17–23.

McCallum, K. E., Lock, J., Kulla, M., Rorty, M., & Wetzel, R. D. (1992). Dissociative symptoms and disorders in patients with eating disorders. *Dissociation, 5* (4), 227–235.

Murphy, P. E. (1994). Dissociative experiences and dissociative disorders in a non–clinical university student group. *Dissociation, 7* (1), 28–34.

Nadon, R., Hoyt, I. P., Register, P. A., & Kihlstrom, J. F. (1991). Absorption and Hypnotizability: Context effects reexamined. *Journal of Personality and Social Psychology, 60*, 144–153.

Norton, G. R., Ross, C. A., & Novotny, M. F. (1990). Factors that predict scores on the Dissociative Experiences Scale. *Journal of Clinical Psychology, 46*, 273–277.

Orr, S. P., Claiborn, J. M., Altmann, B., Forgue, D. F., de Jong, J. B., Pitman, R. K., & Herz, L. R. (1990). Psychometric profile of posttraumatic stress disorder, anxious, and healthy Vietnam veterans: Correlations with psychophysiologic responses. *Journal of Consulting and Clinical Psychology, 58*, 329–335.

Paolo, A. M., Ryan, J. J., Dunn, G. E., & Fleet, J. V. (1993). Reading level of the Dissociative Experiences Scale. *Journal of Clinical Psychology, 49* (2), 209–211.

Pribor, E. F., Yutzy, S. H., Dean, J. T., & Wetzel, R. D. (1993). Briquet's syndrome, dissociation, and abuse. *American Journal of Psychiatry, 150*, 1507–1511.

Putnam, F. W. (1989). *Diagnosis and treatment of multiple personality disorder.* New York: Guilford.

Putnam, F. W. (1991). Recent research on multiple personality disorder. *Psychiatric Clinics of North America, 14*, 489–502.

Quimby, L. C. (1991). Dissociative symptoms and aggression in a state mental hospital. *Dissociation, 4* (1), 21–24.

Ray, W. J., June, K., Turaj, K., & Lundy, R. (1992). Dissociative experiences in a college age population: A factor analytic study of two dissociation scales. *Personality and Individual Differences, 13*, 417–424.

Richards, D. (1991). A study of the correlations between subjective psychic experiences and dissociative experiences. *Dissociation, 4* (1), 83–91.

Ross, C. A. (1991). Epidemiology of multiple personality disorder and dissociation. *Psychiatric Clinics of North America, 14*, 503–517.

Ross, C. A., & Anderson, G. (1988). Phenomenological overlap of multiple personality disorder and obsessive–compulsive disorder. *Journal of Nervous and Mental Disease, 176*, 295–299.

Ross, C. A., Anderson, G., Fleisher, W., & Norton, G. R. (1992). Dissociative experiences among psychiatric inpatients. *General Hospital Psychiatry, 14*, 350–354.

Ross, C. A., Anderson, G., Fleisher, W. P., & Norton, G. R. (1991). The frequency of multiple personality disorder among psychiatric inpatients. *American Journal of Psychiatry, 148*, 1717–1720.

Ross, C. A., Anderson, G., Fraser, G. A., Reagor, P., Bjornson, L., & Miller, S. D. (1992). Differentiating multiple personality disorder and dissociative disorder not otherwise specified. *Dissociation, 5* (4), 87–90.

Ross, C. A., Anderson, G., Heber, S., & Norton, G. R. (1990). Dissociation and abuse in multiple personality patients, prostitutes, and exotic dancers. *Hospital and Community Psychiatry, 41*, 328–330.

Ross, C. A., Anderson, G., Heber, S., Norton, G. R., Anderson, B., del Campo, M., & Pillay, N. (1989). Differentiating multiple personality disorder and complex partial seizures. *General Hospital Psychiatry, 11*, 54–58.

Ross, C. A., Fast, E., Anderson, G., Auty, A., & Todd, J. (1990). Somatic symptoms in multiple sclerosis and MPD. *Dissociation, 3* (2), 102–106.

Ross, C. A., Heber, S., Norton, G. R., Anderson, D., Anderson, G., & Barchet, P. (1989). The Dissociative Disorders Interview Schedule: A structured interview. *Dissociation, 2* (3), 169–189.

Ross, C. A., Heber, S., Norton, G. R., & Anderson, G. (1989). Differences between multiple personality disorder and other diagnostic groups on a structured interview. *Journal of Nervous and Mental Disease, 177*, 487–491.

Ross, C. A., & Joshi, S. (1992). Paranormal experiences in the general population. *Journal of Nervous and Mental Disease, 180*, 357–361.

Ross, C. A., & Joshi, S. (1992). Schneiderian symptoms and childhood trauma in the general population. *Comprehensive Psychiatry, 33,* 269–273.

Ross, C. A., Joshi, S., & Currie, R. (1990). Dissociative experiences in the general population. *American Journal of Psychiatry, 147,* 1547–1552.

Ross, C. A., Joshi, S., & Currie, R. (1991). Dissociative experiences in the general population: Identification of three factors. *Hospital and Community Psychiatry, 42,* 297–301.

Ross, C. A., Kronson, J., Koensgen, S., Barkman, K., Clark, P., & Rockman, G. (1992). Dissociative comorbity in 100 chemically dependent patients. *Hospital and Community Psychiatry, 43,* 840–842.

Ross, C. A., Miller, S. D., Bjornson, L., Reagor, P., Fraser, G., & Anderson, G. (1990). Structured interview data on 102 cases of multiple personality disorder from four centers. *American Journal of Psychiatry, 147,* 596–601.

Ross, C. A., Norton, G. R., & Anderson, G. (1988). The Dissociative Experiences Scale: A replication study. *Dissociation, 1* (3), 21–22.

Ross, C. A., Norton, G. R., & Wozney, K. (1989). Multiple personality disorder: An analysis of 236 cases. *Canadian Journal of Psychiatry, 34,* 413–418.

Ross, C. A., Ryan, L., Anderson, G., Ross, D., & Hardy, L. (1989). Dissociative experiences in adolescents and college students. *Dissociation, 2* (4), 240–242.

Ross, C. A., Ryan, L., Voigt, H., & Eide, L. (1991). High and low dissociators in a college student population. *Dissociation, 4* (3), 147–151.

Russ, M. J., Shearin, E. N., Clarkin, J. F., Harrison, K., & Hull, J. W. (1993). Subtypes of self–injurious patients with borderline personality disorder. *American Journal of Psychiatry, 150* (12), 1869–1871.

Rynearson, E. K., & McCreery, J. M. (1993). Bereavement after homicide: A synergism of trauma and loss. *American Journal of Psychiatry, 150* (2), 258–261.

Sandberg, D. A., & Lynn, S. J. (1992). Dissociative experiences, psychopathology and adjustment, and child and adolescent maltreatment in female college students. *Journal of Abnormal Psychology, 101,* 717–723.

Sanders, B., & Giolas, M. H. (1991). Dissociation and childhood trauma in psychologically disturbed adolescents. *American Journal of Psychiatry, 148,* 50–54.

Sanders, B., & Green, J. A. (1994). The factor structure of the Dissociative Experiences Scale in a non–clinical university student group. *Dissociation, 7* (1), 23–27.

Sanders, B., McRoberts, G., & Tollefson, C. (1989). Childhood stress and dissociation in a college population. *Dissociation, 2* (1), 17–23.

Saxe, G. N., Chinman, G., Berkowitz, R., Hall, K., Lieberg, G., Schwartz, J., & van der Kolk, B. A. (1994). Somatization in patients with dissociative disorders. *American Journal of Psychiatry, 151,* 1329–1334.

Saxe, G. N., van der Kolk, B. A., Berkowitz, R., Chinman, G., Hall, K., Lieberg, G., & Schwartz, J. (1993). Dissociative disorders in psychiatric inpatients. *American Journal of Psychiatry, 150* (7), 1037–1042.

Shearer, S. L. (1994). Dissociative phenomena in women with borderline personality disorder. *American Journal of Psychiatry, 151,* 1324–1328.

Shilony, E., & Grossman, F. K.(1991). Depersonalization as a defense mechanism in survivors of trauma. *Journal of Traumatic Stress, 6,* 119–128.

Silva, C. E., & Kirsch, I. (1992). Interpretive sets, expectancy, fantasy proneness, and dissociation as predictors of hypnotic response. *Journal of Personality and Social Psychology, 63,* 847–856.

Smyser, C. H., & Baron, D. A. (1993). Hypnotizability, absorption, and subscales of the Dissociative Experiences Scale in a nonclinical population. *Dissociation, 6,* 28–37.

Spanos, N. P., Arango, M., & de Groot, H. P. (1993). Context as a moderator in relationships between attribute variables and hypnotizability. *Personality and Social Psychology Bulletin, 19* (1), 71–77.

Spiegel, D., & Cardena, E. (1991). Comments on Hypnotizability and Dissociation. *American Journal of Psychiatry, 148,* 813–814.

Steinberg, M., Rounsaville, B., & Cicchetti, D. (1991). Detection of dissociative disorders in psychiatric patients by a screening instrument and a structured diagnostic interview. *American Journal of Psychiatry, 148,* 1050–1054.

Strick, F. L., & Wilcoxon, S. A. (1991). A comparison of dissociative experiences in adult female outpatients with and without histories of early incestuous abuse. *Dissociation, 4* (4), 193–199.

Swett, C., & Halpert, M. (1993). Reported history of physical and sexual abuse in relation to dissociation and other symptomatology in women psychiatric inpatients. *Journal of Interpersonal Violence, 8,* 545–555.

Tanabe, H., & Ogawa, T. (1992). On the measurement of dissociative experiences: Development of the Dissociative Experiences Scale with a population of Japanese university students. *Tsukuba Psychological Research, 14,* 171–178.

Torem, M. S., Hermanowski, R. W., & Curdue, K. J. (1992). Dissociation phenomena and age. *Stress Medicine, 8,* 23–25.

van der Kolk, B. A., Perry, J. C., & Herman, J. L. (1991). Childhood origins of self–destructive behavior. *American Journal of Psychiatry, 148,* 1665–1671.

Walker, E. A., Katon, W. J., Neraas, K., Jemelka, R. P., & Massoth, D. (1992). Dissociation in women with chronic pelvic pain. *American Journal of Psychiatry, 149,* 534–537.

Warshaw, M. G., Fierman, E., Pratt, L., Hunt, M., Yonkers, K. A., Massion, A. O., & Keller, M. B. (1993). Quality of life and dissociation in anxiety disorder patients with histories of trauma or PTSD. *American Journal of Psychiatry, 150,* 1512–1516.

General Comments

DES can be used to measure frequency of dissociation for clinical or research purposes. When used clinically, it is intended as a screening tool to identify subjects with dissociative disorders. Subjects with PTSD consistently score high on the scale.

Key Words

Population	Stressor	Topic
adult	any	assessment clinical diagnosis dissociation general treatment research

Reference Citation for This Review

Carlson, E. B. (1996). Psychometric review of Dissociative Experiences Scale (DES). In B. H. Stamm (Ed.). *Measurement of stress, trauma, and adaptation.* Lutherville, MD: Sidran Press.

Measure Contact Name

Eve Bernstein Carlson, Ph.D.

Address:	806 Racine Street
	Delavan, WI 53115 USA
Phone:	414.728.5285
Fax:	same (call first)
E-mail:	carlson@wisenet.net

Early Trauma Inventory

Type of Population
Adult Survivors of Childhood Abuse

Cost
Minimal

Copyright

What It Measures
Childhood physical, sexual, and emotional abuse

Measure Content Survey, Procedure, or Process
The Early Trauma Inventory is a systematic assessment of the three domains of abuse. An open-ended introduction is followed by a comprehensive list of abuse experiences grouped by domain, with evaluation of frequency according to three developmental periods, impact immediately, and across the life span on a 7-point dually valenced bipolar rating and perpetrator.

Theoretical Orientation Summary
The Early Trauma Inventory was developed over three years by seven investigators and clinicians at the four sites of the National Center for Post Traumatic Stress Disorder. Preliminary data show that the Early Trauma Inventory, if feasible to administer, accurately identifies individuals with abuse histories, and is not associated with complications of administration. Reliability and validity testing are currently being initiated.

Time Estimate

Administration	Scoring
15–30 minutes	5–15 minutes

Equipment Needed

Paper & Pencil	Computer	Basic Psychophysiological	Specialized Equipment
X			

Psychometric Maturity

Under Construction	Basic Properties Intact	Mature
X		

Particular Sensitivity

Age	Change over Time	Culture / Ethnicity	Gender	Geography / Climate	Sexual Orientation	Socioeconomic Status	Urban / Rural
?	?	?	?	?	?	?	?

Estimate of Number of In-Process Studies
Unknown

Unpublished References

Hiley-Young, B., Blake, D. D., Abueg, F. R., Rozynko, V., & Gusman, F. D. (submitted for publication). Warzone violence in Vietnam: A review and examination of premilitary, military, and postmilitary factors.

Published References

Bremner, J. D., Southwick, S. M., Johnson, D. R., Yehuda, R., & Charney, D. S.(1993). Childhood physical abuse in combat related Post Traumatic Stress Disorder. *American Journal of Psychiatry 150*, 235–239.

Key Words

Population	Stressor	Topic
adults	domestic violence physical abuse sexual assault/abuse	clinical measure development research

Reference Citation for This Review

Bremner, J. D. (1996). Psychometric review of Early Trauma Inventory. In B. H. Stamm (Ed.). *Measurement of stress, trauma, and adaptation.* Lutherville, MD: Sidran Press.

Measure Contact Name

J. Douglas Bremner, M.D.

Address: 116a West Haven VAMC
             950 Campbell Ave.
             West Haven, CT 06516 USA
Phone: 203.932.5711
Fax: 203.937.3886
E-mail:

Evaluation of Lifetime Stressors (ELS) Questionnaire & Interview

Type of Population

Any type of trauma; adults & potentially adolescents

Cost

Free

Copyright

Languages

English

What It Measures

The ELS is a self-report questionnaire and followup semistructured clinical interview package designed to comprehensively assess an individual's lifetime trauma history. The goal is to collect information about all potentially traumatic and traumatic events across the lifespan. *DSM-IV* PTSD Criterion A is utilized as the standard trauma definition, but the ELS is also designed to go beyond *DSM-IV* to collect additional dimensional information about traumatic events, including both objective and subjective dimensions of traumatic experiences. The ELS includes questions about behaviors and events that may serve as "clues" to the existence of childhood trauma, plus a comprehensive section on potentially traumatic events in childhood and adulthood. Specific trauma areas include being confronted with, being threatened with, witnessing, or directly experiencing disasters, illnesses, accidents, street and/or criminal violence, physical assault and abuse, and sexual assault and abuse. The ELS interview (ELS-I) generates a summary list of all traumatic and potentially traumatic events; both objective and subjective dimensions of events are derived, e.g., perpetrator, age, duration, frequency, emotional distress, perceived life threat, presence of a weapon. Additional subjective appraisal information is collected about two (or more) of the worst traumas, including the extent of fear, horror, helplessness, life threat, feelings of responsibility, issues of disclosure, and social support.

Measure Content Survey, Procedure, or Process

The questionnaire (ELS-Q) consists of 56 questions, including an introductory section on clues to childhood trauma, followed by questions that ask about potentially traumatic (criterion A) events more specifically. It takes approximately 15 to 20 minutes to complete. Trauma questions are answered twice, for childhood and adulthood. The ELS-Q is not intended as a stand alone instrument, but rather as a screen for the ELS-I, which follows up on all non-negative answers to the ELS-Q. The process of following up on the questionnaire information allows for a guided exploration of an individual's lifetime trauma history, and also allows for information to be collected in a structured manner. An administration and coding manual is in development.

Theoretical Orientation Summary

The ELS utilizes the *DSM-IV* understanding of traumatic events. The theoretical orientation underlying the development of the ELS combines developmental, cognitive-behavioral, and eclectic perspectives.

Time Estimate

Administration	Scoring
several hours	depends on material gathered

Equipment Needed

Paper & Pencil	Computer	Basic Psychophysiological	Specialized Equipment
X			

Note: ELS Questionnaire and Interview requires experienced clinician

Psychometric Maturity

Under Construction	Basic Properties Intact	Mature
X		

Psychometric Properties Summary

Under construction. Two-year grant received, study of psychometric properties begun 1995. Reliability and validity study being conducted with Vietnam combat and era veterans.

Particular Sensitivity

Age	Change over Time	Culture / Ethnicity	Gender	Geography / Climate	Sexual Orientation	Socioeconomic Status	Urban / Rural
?	?	X	?	?	?	X	?

Estimate of Number of In-Process Studies

The ELS is also about to be used in several studies, most notably with women with sexual abuse histories.

Unpublished References

Krinsley, K. E., Weathers, F. W., Vielhauer, M. J., Newman, E., Walker, E. A., Kaloupek, D. G., Young, L. S., & Kimerling, R. (1994). Evaluation of Lifetime Stressors—Questionnaire and Interview (ELS; ELS-Q, ELS-I). Unpublished manuscript.

As noted, manuals are in development. The ELS has been used in several analyses that were presented at major conferences, but the focus was not on the instrument itself.

Published References

Not currently available. Pilot data being collected.

General Comments

It is important to note that use of the ELS involves a considerable time commitment. The questionnaire is designed to be an independent screening measure, so a face-to-face interview with an experienced clinician is always necessary. That said, the ELS has been tremendously successful at eliciting lengthy trauma histories from men who have never disclosed their stories before. (The ELS has been tested only on male veterans.)

Key Words

Population	Stressor	Topic
some adolescents adults	any	assessment diagnosis measure development

Reference Citation for This Review

Krinsley, K. E. (1996). Psychometric review of The Evaluation of Lifetime Stressors (ELS) Questionnaire & Interview. In B. H. Stamm (Ed.). *Measurement of stress, trauma, and adaptation*. Lutherville, MD: Sidran Press.

Measure Contact Name

Karen E. Krinsley, Ph.D.

Address:	National Center for PTSD (116B-2)
	Boston DVA Medical Center
	150 S. Huntington Ave.
	Boston, MA 02130 USA
Phone:	617.232.9500 x4132 or x4145
Fax:	617.278.4501
E-mail:	KRINSLEY.KAREN@BOSTON.VA.GOV

Family Disruption from Illness Scale

Type of Population
Adults

Cost
Free

Copyright

Languages
English

What It Measures
Degree of difficulty in terms of disruption in daily family routines with symptoms and health problems during the past three months.

Measure Content Survey, Procedure, or Process
Survey.

Time Estimate

Administration	Scoring
10 minutes	10 minutes

Theoretical Orientation Summary
Modified from a Symptom Frequency Scale (which in turn had been modified from the Project Find list of symptoms) developed and used by the author with older adults in community settings. The item list was expanded to be appropriate for all age groups.

Equipment Needed

Paper & Pencil	Computer	Basic Psychophysiological	Specialized Equipment
X			

Psychometric Maturity

Under Construction	Basic Properties Intact	Mature
X		

Psychometric Properties Summary
In process. Being tested with 160 adults in a rural state. Modifications are expected to include both deletion and addition of items.

Particular Sensitivity

Age	Change over Time	Culture/ Ethnicity	Gender	Geography/ Climate	Sexual Orientation	Socioeconomic Status	Urban/ Rural
X	?	?	?	X	?	?	?

Estimate of Number of In-Process Studies

1

Unpublished References

Unknown

Published References

General Comments

Other than the Family Seriousness of Illness Scale (Bigbee, 1988), which is lengthy and includes items of varying degrees of severity, there appears to be nothing available that measures responses to illness at a family level. Contact authors for latest version.

Key Words

Population	Stressor	Topic
adults heads of household	accidents illness	family treatment measure development research

Reference Citation for This Review

Ide, B. A. (1996). Psychometric review of Family Disruption from Illness Scale. In B. H. Stamm (Ed.). *Measurement of stress, trauma, and adaptation*. Lutherville, MD: Sidran Press.

Measure Contact Name

Bette A. Ide, Ph.D., RN

Address:	University of Wyoming School of Nursing
	Laramie, WY 82071 USA
Phone:	307.766.2314
Fax:	307.766.4294
E-mail:	IDE@UWYO.EDU

Family Disruption from Illness Scale
Sample Questions

Below is a list of common symptoms and health problems that can cause difficulties for family members. We'd like to know if any member of your family, including yourself, has had difficulty with any of these symptoms or health problems during the past three (3) months. If there has been difficulty, does it cause a disruption in your family's daily or work routines?

Please circle the appropriate answer(s) for each symptom or health problem listed.

Symptom / Problem	*Difficulty*		*Disruption in Routines*			
1. Poor vision	Yes	No	Major	Minor	Moderate	None
2. Poor hearing	Yes	No	Major	Minor	Moderate	None
3. Anemia	Yes	No	Major	Minor	Moderate	None
4. High blood pressure	Yes	No	Major	Minor	Moderate	None
5. Heart trouble	Yes	No	Major	Minor	Moderate	None
6. Seizures	Yes	No	Major	Minor	Moderate	None
7. Stomach trouble	Yes	No	Major	Minor	Moderate	None
8. Forgetfulness	Yes	No	Major	Minor	Moderate	None
9. Backache	Yes	No	Major	Minor	Moderate	None
10. Sinus trouble	Yes	No	Major	Minor	Moderate	None
11. Speech problems	Yes	No	Major	Minor	Moderate	None
12. Tire too easily	Yes	No	Major	Minor	Moderate	None
13. Injury	Yes	No	Major	Minor	Moderate	None
14. Difficulty walking or climbing stairs	Yes	No	Major	Minor	Moderate	None
15. Feet or legs swelling	Yes	No	Major	Minor	Moderate	None
16. Pain, weakness, or numbness in hand, arm or leg	Yes	No	Major	Minor	Moderate	None
17. Pain in face	Yes	No	Major	Minor	Moderate	None
18. Dizziness	Yes	No	Major	Minor	Moderate	None
19. Noise (in the ear)	Yes	No	Major	Minor	Moderate	None
20. Allergies	Yes	No	Major	Minor	Moderate	None
21. Constipation	Yes	No	Major	Minor	Moderate	None
22. Diarrhea	Yes	No	Major	Minor	Moderate	None
23. Incontinence of stool	Yes	No	Major	Minor	Moderate	None
24. Gas pains	Yes	No	Major	Minor	Moderate	None
25. Shortness of breath	Yes	No	Major	Minor	Moderate	None
26. Skin rash, redness, or itching	Yes	No	Major	Minor	Moderate	None
27. Skin sores or ulcers	Yes	No	Major	Minor	Moderate	None
28. Cough	Yes	No	Major	Minor	Moderate	None
29. Fever	Yes	No	Major	Minor	Moderate	None
30. Cold	Yes	No	Major	Minor	Moderate	None
31. Teeth problems	Yes	No	Major	Minor	Moderate	None
32. Urinary or bladder problems	Yes	No	Major	Minor	Moderate	None
33. Lack of appetite	Yes	No	Major	Minor	Moderate	None
34. Premenstrual tension	Yes	No	Major	Minor	Moderate	None
35. Blackouts	Yes	No	Major	Minor	Moderate	None
36. Memory loss	Yes	No	Major	Minor	Moderate	None

37.	Shakes in the morning	Yes	No	Major	Minor	Moderate	None
38.	Depression	Yes	No	Major	Minor	Moderate	None
39.	Nervousness	Yes	No	Major	Minor	Moderate	None
40.	Anxiety	Yes	No	Major	Minor	Moderate	None
41.	Difficulty sleeping	Yes	No	Major	Minor	Moderate	None
42.	Difficulty communicating or following directions	Yes	No	Major	Minor	Moderate	None
43.	Anti-social behavior	Yes	No	Major	Minor	Moderate	None
44.	Difficulty controlling behavior	Yes	No	Major	Minor	Moderate	None
45.	Suicidal thoughts or actions	Yes	No	Major	Minor	Moderate	None
46.	Thoughts of suspiciousness	Yes	No	Major	Minor	Moderate	None
47.	Mental or emotional illness	Yes	No	Major	Minor	Moderate	None
48.	Prostate problems	Yes	No	Major	Minor	Moderate	None
49.	Difficulty driving or getting around community	Yes	No	Major	Minor	Moderate	None
50.	Uterus or vaginal problems (bleeding, pain, etc.)	Yes	No	Major	Minor	Moderate	None
51.	Menopause problems (hot flashes, sleep disturbances, etc.)	Yes	No	Major	Minor	Moderate	None
52.	Lump or pain in breast	Yes	No	Major	Minor	Moderate	None
53.	Cancer or leukemia	Yes	No	Major	Minor	Moderate	None

Please list any other symptoms or health problems that caused difficulties for a family member during the past three months and rate them as above.

54.	_____	Major	Minor	Moderate	None
55.	_____	Major	Minor	Moderate	None
56.	_____	Major	Minor	Moderate	None

Family Experiences Survey
National Center for PTSD Review

Type of Population

Adults

Cost
Available from author at no charge

Copyright
David Finkelhor, Family Research Laboratory

Languages
English

What It Measures
Assesses retrospectively childhood and adulthood physical and sexual abuse. Scales for Physical Abuse Severity, Sexual Abuse Severity, Witness Violence.

Measure Content Survey, Procedure, or Process
Structured interview, 35 items.

Theoretical Orientation Summary
Empirical approaches to family relations.

Time Estimate

Administration	Scoring
20–30 minutes	5–15 minutes

Equipment Needed

Paper & Pencil	Computer	Basic Psychophysiological	Specialized Equipment
X			

Psychometric Maturity

Under Construction	Basic Properties Intact	Mature
	X	

Psychometric Properties Summary
Internal consistency scores of Item-Total Score r=.54–.93. Concurrent Validity is addressed controlling for the effect of current depression and childhood physical abuse as well as recalled family environment. Sexual abuse severity predicts borderline personality disorder and severity in female psychiatric inpatients. Scoring uses method of Weaver and Clum (1993). Normative data on clinical populations.

Particular Sensitivity

Age	Change over Time	Culture / Ethnicity	Gender	Geography / Climate	Sexual Orientation	Socioeconomic Status	Urban / Rural
?	?	?	X	?	?	?	?

Estimate of Number of In-Process Studies
Unknown

Unpublished References
Unknown

Published References
Finkelhor, D. (1984). *Child sexual abuse*. New York: Free Press.

Finkelhor, D. (1979). *Sexually victimized children*. New York: Free Press.

Weaver, T., & Clum, G. (1993). Early family environments and traumatic experiences associated with borderline personality disorder. *Journal of Consulting and Clinical Psychology, 61*, 1068–1075.

General Comments

Key Words

Population	Stressor	Topic
adults adult psychiatric patients adult sexual abuse survivors	community violence domestic violence physical abuse sexual assault/abuse	research

Reference Citation for This Review
Ford, J. (1996). Psychometric review of Family Experiences Survey. In B. H. Stamm (Ed.). *Measurement of stress, trauma, and adaptation*. Lutherville, MD: Sidran Press.

Reviewer Contact Name
Julian Ford, Ph.D.

Address: National Center for PTSD (116-D)
             VA Medical Center
             White River Junction, VT 05009 USA
Phone: 802.296.5132
Fax: 802.296.5135
E-mail: Julian.Ford@Dartmouth.Edu

Measure Contact Name
David Finkelhor, Ph.D.

Address: Family Research Laboratory
             University of New Hampshire
             Horton Social Science Center
             Durham, NH 03824 USA
Phone:
Fax:
E-mail:

Farm Stressor Inventory

Type of Population
Farm families (particularly oriented toward principal operators of farms)

Cost
Free

Copyright

Languages
English

What It Measures
The Farm Stressor Inventory (FSI) is intended to be an exhaustive inventory of the prevalent and important stressors that farmers experience, including those that are typical of many occupations (such as work overload, role conflict, uncertainty) and those that are more unique to farming (such as seasonal variations in job demands, the relative isolation of farm families, the large financial risk involved in maintaining many farms). The intent of the measure is to assess farmers' exposures (*not* reactions) to psychosocial and physical conditions that are conducive to stress. Major acute stressors, minor acute stressors, and chronic stressors are included.

Measure Content Survey, Procedure, or Process
The FSI is a self-administered questionnaire containing 10 sections and approximately 200 items. Section I asks farmers to report how often major life events and natural disasters (drought, flood, fire) were experienced in the last two years and the severity of the effect of these events on the functioning of the farm. In addition, farmers are asked the number of times that they anticipate certain events to occur in the next two years, and how much of a negative effect these future events are expected to have. This first section could be used as a stand alone measure of major acute stressors. The other sections measure minor and chronic stressors and include the following content: personal finances, workload, equipment, skills and abilities, hazardous tasks and experiences, other job characteristics, geographic isolation, family, and retirement/transfer of farm.

Theoretical Orientation Summary
This instrument stems from the University of Michigan's Institute for Social Research Model of the Stress Process and the model of occupational stress proposed by the National Institute for Occupational Safety and Health. In these models, stressors are rooted in the physical, psychosocial, and organizational structure of the work and non-work environments. Both models emphasize the importance of objective measurement of these environmental stimuli or exposures. Although the FSI is a self-report measure, it attempts to make the measurement of all the stressors as objective and as accurate as possible by asking farmers how often they experience certain things, with no reference to how distressing or bothersome those things were. Clear time frames are provided and recall for minor and chronic stressors is limited to the last month.

Time Estimate

Administration	Scoring
30–45 minutes	15–30 min

Equipment Needed

Paper & Pencil	Computer	Basic Psychophysiological	Specialized Equipment
X			

Psychometric Maturity

Under Construction	Basic Properties Intact	Mature
X		

Psychometric Properties Summary

The FSI is very much a work-in-progress. Psychometric properties for the instrument are not yet established. The process used for developing the FSI included the following steps: review of the literature, review of data gathered through a farmer assistance hotline in Wisconsin, review of data gathered through focus groups of Kentucky farmers, drafting of questionnaire items, review of the drafted items by a focus group of Ohio farmers, revision of the FSI, and review of the revised questionnaire by an expert in questionnaire design. In addition, the revised FSI was calculated to be between a 9th and 10th grade reading level, using the SMOG readability formula. Psychometric testing will aid in paring down the number of items in the instrument.

Particular Sensitivity

Age	Change over Time	Culture / Ethnicity	Gender	Geography / Climate	Sexual Orientation	Socioeconomic Status	Urban / Rural
?	X	?	?	X	?	X	X

Estimate of Number of In-Process Studies

It is likely that the FSI will be administered to large samples of farmers in Ohio and Colorado during 1995–96.

Unpublished References

Heaney, C. A., & Elliott, M. (August, 1994). The development of the Farm Stressor Inventory: Implications for research and preventive intervention. Presented at Agricultural Safety and Health: A National Conference on Detection, Prevention, and Intervention. Columbus, OH.

Heaney, C. A. (September, 1994). Farm Stressor Inventory: Development and early assessment. Final report for the National Institute for Occupational Safety and Health, Division of Biomedical and Behavioral Science, Motivational and Stress Research Section. Cincinnati, OH.

Published References

None.

General Comments

The first three sections of the FSI are provided in this review. The other sections are available from Dr. Heaney at the address listed below. It is desired that those who use the FSI share their results with the author in order to contribute to the assessment of the validity and reliability of the instrument.

Key Words

Population	Stressor	Topic
adults	agriculture economic farming rural	measure development research rural care service delivery

Reference Citation for This Review

Heaney, C. A. (1996). Psychometric review of The Farm Stressor Inventory. In B. H. Stamm (Ed.) *Measurement of stress, trauma, and adaptation*. Lutherville, MD: Sidran Press.

Measure Contact Name

Catherine A. Heaney, Ph.D., MPH

Address: Department of Preventive Medicine

The Ohio State University

320 W. 10th Avenue

Columbus, OH 43210 USA

Phone: 614.293.5837

Fax: 614.293.3937

E-mail: TS4870@OHSTMVSA.ACS.OHIO-STATE.EDU

SECTION I
Weather and Other Factors

Think about **THE PAST 2 YEARS.** For each of the items, enter the number of times you experienced the problem in the past two years in the first column.

For those problems that you experienced at least once, use the scale below to indicate the extent to which each of them <u>negatively affected how you run your farm or how productive your farm is.</u> Enter the appropriate number in the second column.

1	2	3	4	5
Not at All	A Little	A Moderate Amount	Quite A Bit	An Extreme Amount

	Number of Times Experienced in Past 2 Years	Extent To Which Negatively Affected Your Farm
1. drought conditions	_____	_____
2. an early frost	_____	_____
3. a late spring	_____	_____
4. flooding of your fields	_____	_____
5. wind	_____	_____
6. heavy or extended rainfall that held up or interrupted planting or harvesting	_____	_____
7. hail storms	_____	_____
8. disease among your livestock	_____	_____
9. disease among your crops	_____	_____
10. vandalism on your farm	_____	_____
11. fire on your farm	_____	_____
12. loss of hired help at critical times	_____	_____
13. personal injury or illness	_____	_____

Now think about the **FUTURE**. Specifically, think about **THE NEXT 2 YEARS**.

Write in the number of times you expect to experience each of the problems in the next 2 years. Of course, you cannot know for sure. Please provide your best guess.

Then, use the scale below to indicate the extent to which you expect each of them to negatively affect how you run your farm or how productive your farm is. Enter the appropriate number in the second column.

1	2	3	4	5
Not at All	A Little	A Moderate Amount	Quite A Bit	An Extreme Amount

	Number of Times You Expect to Experience	Expected Effect on Your Farm
1. drought conditions	_____	_____
2. an early frost	_____	_____
3. a late spring	_____	_____
4. flooding of your fields	_____	_____
5. wind	_____	_____
6. heavy or extended rainfall that held up or interrupted planting or harvesting	_____	_____
7. hail storms	_____	_____
8. disease among your livestock	_____	_____
9. disease among your crops	_____	_____
10. vandalism on your farm	_____	_____
11. fire on your farm	_____	_____
12. loss of hired help at critical times	_____	_____
13. personal injury or illness	_____	_____

On this page, you will find some more conditions that may or may not have affected your farm over the **PAST 2 YEARS.**

Using the same scale as before, please indicate the extent to which each of the following has negatively affected how you run your farm or how productive your farm is.

1	2	3	4	5
Not at All	A Little	A Moderate Amount	Quite A Bit	An Extreme Amount

Extent to Which Negatively
Affected Your Farm

1. government safety regulations   _____

2. government export policies   _____

3. government farm price supports   _____

4. rapidly changing technology   _____

5. lack of skilled, affordable labor   _____

6. legal liability for your hired help   _____

7. high insurance costs for hired help   _____

8. rapidly changing government policies and regulations   _____

9. fluctuating market prices   _____

10. falling land values   _____

11. regulation of chemical use   _____

12. lack of available farm land   _____

On this page, you will find a list of some major events that may or may not have occurred **DURING THE PAST TWO YEARS.**

Simply circle "YES" or "NO" to indicate whether or not you experienced the event **DURING THE PAST TWO YEARS.**

1. death of a spouse	YES	NO
2. divorce	YES	NO
3. marital separation	YES	NO
4. death of a close family member (other than spouse)	YES	NO
5. getting married	YES	NO
6. marital reconciliation	YES	NO
7. retirement	YES	NO
8. gaining of a new family member	YES	NO
9. death of a close friend	YES	NO
10. foreclosure of a mortgage	YES	NO
11. son or daughter leaving home	YES	NO
12. spouse beginning or stopping off-farm work	YES	NO

SECTION II
Personal Finances

This section asks about your personal finances. Please enter your answer in the blank or circle the appropriate answer.

DURING THE PAST 2 YEARS...

1. How many times have you been behind in repayment of your loans?   ___ times.

2. How many times have you made major purchases
    (e.g., $25,000 or more)?   ___ times.

3. Have you been turned down for a loan for land purchases?

           YES   NO

4. Have you been turned down for an operating loan?

           YES   NO

5. **DURING THE PAST 2 YEARS,** in order to meet your expenses, have you...

    a. Used your savings?   YES   NO

    b. Borrowed money from friends
        or family?   YES   NO

    c. Postponed any major
        farm purchases?   YES   NO

    d. Postponed getting medical care?   YES   NO

    e. Taken on another job off farm   YES   NO

6. Is your debt/asset ratio greater than .40?

           YES   NO   DON'T KNOW

7. Is your current financial situation the same, worse, or better, than it was 5 years ago?

    Much Worse   A Little Worse   About the Same   A Little Better   Much Better

8. How often are you able to purchase the <u>non-essential,</u> <u>non-farm</u> items that you and your family desire?

| Never | A Little of the Time | Sometimes | Most of the Time | Always |

9. To what extent does an <u>irregular cash flow</u> influence your ability to budget effectively?

| Not at All | A Little Bit | A Moderate Amount | Quite a Bit | All the Time |

10. Do you currently work at an off-farm job?

YES   NO
  ↘

    10a. If yes, how many hours per week do you work off the farm? _____ hours

    10b. How long have you worked an off-farm job? _____years _____ months

11. Does your spouse currently work at an off-farm job?

YES   NO   NOT MARRIED
  ↘

    11a. If yes, how many hours per week does your spouse work off the farm?
                                         _____ hours

    11b. How long has your spouse worked an off-farm job? ____years _____ months

SECTION III
Workload

This section asks about how much you work on the farm. Please answer by entering your answer in the blank or by circling the appropriate answer.

DURING THE PAST WEEK...

1. how many days did you work on the farm?   ____ days

2. how many hours did you work each day (on average)?   ____ hours

3. how many days did you have to work extra hard or
    work harder than usual?   ____ days

4. how many days were you not able to complete the tasks you had
    hoped to accomplish that day?   ____ days

5. how many days were you pressured to complete certain tasks
    within a certain time frame?   ____ days

6. how many days did you have to carry over tasks from the previous
    day?   ____ days

7. how many times were you interrupted or forced to leave a task
    before it was completed?   ____ times

8. Describe how your workload this past week compares to a typical week
    for this time of year.   (Circle one)

    Much   Slightly   About the   Slightly   Much
    Lighter   Lighter   Same   Heavier   Heavier

DURING THE PAST TWO YEARS...

9. Did you take a vacation away from the farm?

                    YES   NO

10. If yes, how many days altogether were you away from the farm on vacation?

                    ____ days

Farming/Ranching Stress Scale II

Type of Population
Heads of households of families living on farms and ranches

Cost
Free

Copyright
Mary Araquistain

Languages
English

What It Measures
Severity of stress related to farming and ranching

Measure Content Survey, Procedure, or Process
20-item self-report survey

Theoretical Orientation Summary
Original 13-item Farm/Ranch Stress Scale was developed from the literature on stress related to farming and ranching. The underlying perspective was the widely used ABC-X model of family stress (Hill, 1949), which has been expanded by McCubbin and McCubbin (1989) into the Double ABC and t-Double ABCX models. These models emphasize the cumulative effects of daily life stressors.

Time Estimate

Administration	Scoring
5–10 minutes	5 minutes

Equipment Needed

Paper & Pencil	Computer	Basic Psychophysiological	Specialized Equipment
X			

Psychometric Maturity

Under Construction	Basic Properties Intact	Mature
X		

Psychometric Properties Summary
Needs psychometric evaluation. Developed from validity, reliability, and qualitative analysis of responses of 188 people to original 13-item survey.

Particular Sensitivity

Age	Change over Time	Culture / Ethnicity	Gender	Geography / Climate	Sexual Orientation	Socioeconomic Status	Urban / Rural
?	?	?	?	X	?	X	X

Estimate of Number of In-Process Studies
None at present

Unpublished References
Unknown

Published References

General Comments
Reliability and validity of the original Farm/Ranch Stress Scale were acceptable. The tool was revised based on the qualitative analysis of "other" responses. Contact authors for latest version.

Key Words

Population	Stressor	Topic
adults farmers ranchers	accidents balancing of needs workload variations regulations financial stressors role stress relationship stressors time management stress	measure development research rural care

Reference Citation for This Review
Ide, B. A., & Araquistain, M. (1996). Psychometric review of Farming/Ranching Stress Scale II. In B. H. Stamm (Ed.). *Measurement of stress, trauma, and adaptation.* Lutherville, MD: Sidran Press.

Measure Author Name
Mary Araquistain, MNS, ARNP

Measure Contact Name
Mary Araquistain, MNS, ARNP
Nurse Practitioner
Address: West Coast Community Clinic
               2700 Simpson Avenue
               Aberdeen, WA 98520 USA
Phone: 360.538.1293
Fax:
E-mail: mka@techline.com

Farming/Ranching Stress Scale II

Sample Questions

	Not at all Stressful			Very Stressful
1. Balancing the needs of the farm/ranch with the needs of the family (too much work, putting business before family)	1	2	3	4
2. The weather (water shortage, fog, snow, etc.)	1	2	3	4
3. Governmental policy and/or red tape (loss of water or property rights, environmentalists, etc.)	1	2	3	4
4. Farm/ranch accidents and injuries	1	2	3	4
5. Seasonal variations in workload (planting season, harvest, calving time, marketing time, etc.)	1	2	3	4
6. Not enough money for day to day expenses (purchases, repairs, parts, fence and building maintenance, etc.)	1	2	3	4
7. High debt load	1	2	3	4
8. Working with bankers and loan officers	1	2	3	4
9. Not enough time to spend together as a family in recreation	1	2	3	4
10. Balancing the many roles I perform as a family member and farmer/rancher	1	2	3	4
11. Problems with machinery or livestock (breakdowns, illness, disease, noxious weeds, rodents, etc.)	1	2	3	4
12. Illness at peak times (harvest planting season, etc.)	1	2	3	4
13. Isolation	1	2	3	4
14. Not enough cash/capital for unexpected problems (illnesses, health care, breakdowns, other emergencies)	1	2	3	4
15. Working with extended family members in the farm/ranch operation (parents, in-laws, children, inheritance problems)	1	2	3	4
16. Time management and schedules (deadlines, lack of schedule, not enough time, no free time, sleeping problems, balancing outside work and ranch demands, etc.)	1	2	3	4
17. Agricultural economy (prices, getting and dealing with buyers, lack of stability, future, etc.)	1	2	3	4
18. Taxes (high taxes, figuring taxes, etc.)	1	2	3	4
19. Dealing with non-relative help (incompetent help, finding good help, supervising help)	1	2	3	4
20. Outsiders not understanding nature of farming/ranching	1	2	3	4
21. Please list any other items you find stressful in relation to farming/ranching and rate them.	1	2	3	4

IES Cognitive & Affective Scales

Type of Population

Any and all except children

Cost

Free

Copyright

Languages

English, German

What It Measures

Cognitive and Affective processes in relation to stressful events

Measure Content Survey, Procedure, or Process

These scales were created from existing IES items (scoring is given for old IES and IES—Revised although there has been no data collected on the IES—Revised items). The Cognitive scale reflects the conscious drive to control negative trauma-related experiences. It is conceived as the active intervention on the part of the respondent to consciously control what is happening in his or her world in relation to the trauma, both by acknowledging the problem and by mediating it by the means mentioned in the items. The Affect scale is formed of eight items, four of which are reverse scored. The positive items refer directly to potentially affect-laden experiences like having strong waves of feelings. The negative items can be related to the rising affect in the face of failure to control one's environment (Stamm, 1992; Stamm & Bieber, 1993).

Theoretical Orientation Summary

No particular theoretical underlay, but scale conceptualizations are consistent with Janoff-Bulman's World Assumption Theory. Factorial Invariance (Multigroup & Longitudinal) forms the quantitative theoretical underlay (Bieber, 1986; Bieber & Meredith, 1986).

Time Estimate

Administration	Scoring
5–10 minutes	5 minutes

Equipment Needed

Paper & Pencil	Computer	Basic Psychophysiological	Specialized Equipment
X			

Psychometric Maturity

Under Construction	Basic Properties Intact	Mature
	X	

Psychometric Properties Summary

One study of 1008 cases from a college student population found reliabilities as measured by Tucker's Coefficient of Congruence (cc) of .99 for the Cognitive Scale and .91 for the Affective Scale (Stamm, 1992). In an extension of the first study, a second study in which considered 1081 cases found structural reliability as measured by Tucker's cc to again be cc=.99 for the Cognitive Scale and cc=.91 for the Affective Scale (Stamm & Bieber, 1993). To score the Cognitive Scale sum the items (see table below for item numbers keyed to either the old IES or the IES—Revised). To score the Affective Scale, reverse (1=5, 2=4, 3=3, 0=0) the items indicated by an r in the table below and and add to the sum of the remaining items. Higer scores indicate more difficulty. The samples in these two studies were not independent. Of the 2089 cases considered across the two studies, 746 cases appeared twice, once in each study.

It should be noted that this research was based on a continuous scale of 0 to 5 (e.g. 0, 1, 2, 3, 4, 5) rather than 0, 1, 3, 5 as indicated in the IES and IES—Revised (see IES—R in this volume). While no formal psychometric comparison between the two scorings has been undertaken, the observed means on the Intrusion and Avoidance scales of the IES/IES—R are nearly identical to those reported in the literature. Moreover, a close reading of other papers in the literature indicate that the IES/IES—R have been scored in both manners. Also, subjects were instructed to answer the questions in relation to their *most* stressful event, rather than to a specified event.

Particular Sensitivity

Age	Change over Time	Culture / Ethnicity	Gender	Geography / Climate	Sexual Orientation	Socioeconomic Status	Urban / Rural
?	X	?	?	?	?	?	?

Estimated Number of In-Process Studies
Unknown.

Unpublished References
Stamm, B. H. (1992). Stability and generalizability of the Impact of Events Scale. Presented at the World Conference of the International Society for Traumatic Stress Studies. Amsterdam, The Netherlands.

Stamm, B. H., & Bieber, S. L. (1993). The Impact of Events Scale revisited: Two additional research scales. Presented at the Ninth Annual Meeting of the International Society for Traumatic Stress Studies. San Antonio, TX, USA.

Published References
Bieber, S. L. (1986). A hierarchial approach to multigroup factorial invariance. *Journal of Classification, 3,* 113–134.

Bieber, S. L., & Meredith, W. (1986). Transformation to achieve a longitudinally stationary factor pattern matrix. *Psychometrika, 50* (4), 535–547.

General Comments

Key Words

Population	Stressor	Topic
adult	any	general treatment research structural analysis

Reference Citation for This Review
Stamm, B. H., Bieber, S. L., & Rudolph, J. M. (1996). Psychometric review of IES Cognitive and Affective Scales. In B. H. Stamm (Ed.). *Measurement of stress, trauma, and adaptation.* Lutherville, MD: Sidran Press.

Measure Contact Name
B. Hudnall Stamm, Ph.D.

Address   Traumatic Stress Research Group
PO Box 531
Hanover, NH 03755 USA

Phone/Voice Mail:

Fax:

E-mail: b.hudnall.stamm@dartmouth.edu

Scoring

From Old IES
Cognitive: Sum 1, 3, 4, 5, 7, 9, 10, 11, 12, 13, 14
Affective: Sum 5, 6, 10, 11, 3r, 7r, 9r, 13r
        r=reverse coding, 0=0, 1=5, 2=4, 3=3

From IES-Revised (extrapolated from IES)
Cognitive: Sum 1, 2, 3, 6, 8, 9, 11, 12, 15, 16, 17, 22
Affective: Sum 9, 3, 16, 20, 8r, 11r, 17r, 22r
   r=reverse coding, 0=0 1=5, 2=4, 3=3
Available Norms:
For a definition of the categories, see **Stressful Experiences Content Analysis Coding Scheme** in this volume

Northern Rocky Mountain U.S.A. Sample (n=1081)
Cognitive

	Bad Things		Death		Problems in Living		Sexual Assault	
	X	SD	X	SD	X	SD	X	SD
Males	1.75 n=78	1.59	2.03 n=101	1.46	1.95 n=191	1.52	2.00 n=7	1.34
Females	1.98 n=68	1.40	2.10 n=136	1.41	2.07 n=248	1.53	2.35 n=33	1.75

Affective

	Bad Things		Death		Problems in Living		Sexual Assault	
	X	SD	X	SD	X	SD	X	SD
Males	1.70 n=78	1.33	1.98 n=101	1.28	1.84 n=191	1.31	1.63 n=7	.84
Females	1.94 n=68	1.31	2.11 n=136	1.32	1.89 n=248	1.29	1.76 n=33	1.25

Northeast U.S.A. Sample (n=36)

Cognitive

	Bad Things		Death		Problems in Living		Sexual Assault	
	X	SD	X	SD	X	SD	X	SD
Males	1.91 n=8	1.14	1.05 n=4	1.08	1.79 n=6	1.41		
Females	2.30 n=3	0.34	2.82 n=6	1.41	1.24 n=6	1.13		

Affective

	Bad Things		Death		Problems in Living		Sexual Assault	
	X	SD	X	SD	X	SD	X	SD
Males	1.78 n=8	1.24	1.53 n=4	1.65	2.17 n=6	1.72		
Females	1.75 n=3	0.57	2.69 n=6	0.36	0.85 n=7	0.66		

Impact of Events Scale—Revised

Type of Population

Any and all except children

Cost

Free

Copyright

Languages

English, German

What It Measures

Intrusion, Avoidance, and Hyperarousal. The IES—R is a self-report measure of the three broad domains of response to traumatic stress: intrusive phenomena, avoidant and numbing phenomena, and hyperarousal phenomena. It is targeted to levels of symptoms in the past 7 days. In this way it is linked to provide a subjective companion to the observer-based Stress Response Rating Scale (SRRS). It provides a dimensional method of capturing the severity of symptomatic distress. It is quick and easy and contains the original 15 intrusion and avoidance items, making its use comparable with the IES.

Measure Content Survey, Procedure, or Process

Items tap the standard aspects of both emotional and cognitive experiences of intrusion, avoidance and numbing, and hyperarousal. Items are non-technical and easily understood. Responses are scored on a 4-point Likert response, with anchors ranging from "Not at All" to "Often."

Theoretical Orientation Summary

The IES—R is not derived from a specific narrow theoretical orientation, but rather stems from the large body of observation of stress response syndromes promulgated by Horowitz and further refinement of the diagnostic criteria of PTSD.

Time Estimate

Administration	Scoring
5–10 minutes	5–10 minutes

Equipment Needed

Paper & Pencil	Computer	Basic Psychophysiological	Specialized Equipment
X			

Psychometric Maturity

Under Construction	Basic Properties Intact	Mature
		X

Psychometric Properties Summary

Extensive data from numerous studies exists on the original IES subscales of intrusion and avoidance. Data from a recent study of 439 emergency services workers produced coefficient alpha values of .85 for Intrusion and Avoidance and .77 for Hyperarousal. Test-retest data from a sample of 88 victims of the Northridge earthquake was .47

for Intrusion, .40 for Avoidance, and .51 for Hyperarousal. For 31 emergency services workers these data were .56, .51, and .59 respectively.

Particular Sensitivity

Age	Change over Time	Culture / Ethnicity	Gender	Geography / Climate	Sexual Orientation	Socioeconomic Status	Urban / Rural
?	X	?	?	?	?	?	?

Estimated Number of In-Process Studies
Many

Unpublished References
Weiss, D. S., & Marmar, C. R. (October, 1993). The impact of debriefing on emergency services personnel workers: Effects of site and service. Intentional Society for Traumatic Stress Studies Annual Meeting. San Antonio, TX.

Weiss, D. S. (November, 1994). Peritraumatic experiences across combat and natural disasters. International Society for Traumatic Stress Studies Annual Meeting. Chicago, IL.

Published References (selected)
Marmar, C. R., Weiss, D. S., Metzler, T.J ., Ronfeldt, H. M. , & Foreman, C. (in press). Stress responses of emergency services personnel to the Loma Prieta earthquake Interstate 880 freeway collapse and control traumatic incidents. *Journal of Traumatic Stress*.

Weiss, D. W., Marmar, C. R., Metzler, T. J., & Rondfeldt, H. M. (in press). Predicating symptomatic distress in emergency services personnel. *Journal of Consulting and Clinical Psychology*.

General Comments

Key Words

Population	Stressor	Topic
adult general treatment	any	research

Reference Citation for This Review
Weiss, D. (1996). Psychometric review of the Impact of Events Scale—Revised. In B. H. Stamm (Ed.). *Measurement of stress, trauma, and adaptation*. Lutherville, MD: Sidran Press.

Instrument Contact Name
Daniel S. Weiss, Ph.D

Address: U.C.S.F
             Box 0984
             401 Parnassus Ave.
             San Francisco, CA 94143-0984

Phone: 415.476.7557
Fax: 415.502.7296
E-mail: dweiss@itsa.ucsf.edu

Impact Of Event Scale-Revised

INSTRUCTIONS: Below is a list of comments made by people after stressful life events. Please check each item, indicating how frequently these comments were true for you **DURING THE PAST SEVEN DAYS** with respect to the event. If they did not occur during that time, please mark the "not at all" column.

	Not at all	Rarely	Some-times	Often
1. Any reminder brought back feelings about it.	0	1	3	5
2. I had trouble staying asleep.	0	1	3	5
3. Other things kept making me think about it.	0	1	3	5
4. I felt irritable and angry.	0	1	3	5
5. I avoided letting myself get upset when I thought about it or was reminded of it.	0	1	3	5
6. I thought about it when I didn't mean to.	0	1	3	5
7. I felt as if it hadn't happened or wasn't real.	0	1	3	5
8. I stayed away from reminders about it.	0	1	3	5
9. Pictures about it popped into my mind.	0	1	3	5
10. I was jumpy and easily startled.	0	1	3	5
11. I tried not to think about it.	0	1	3	5
12. I was aware that I still had a lot of feelings about it, but I didn't deal with them.	0	1	3	5
13. My feelings about it were kind of numb.	0	1	3	5
14. I found myself acting or feeling like I was back at that time.	0	1	3	5
15. I had trouble falling asleep.	0	1	3	5
16. I had waves of strong feelings about it.	0	1	3	5
17. I tried to remove it from my memory.	0	1	3	5
18. I had trouble concentrating.	0	1	3	5
19. Reminders of it caused me to have physical reactions such as sweating, trouble breathing, nausea, or a pounding heart.	0	1	3	5
20. I had dreams about it.	0	1	3	5
21. I felt watchful and on-guard.	0	1	3	5
22. I tried not to talk about it.	0	1	3	5

Impact of Event Scale—Revised
Scoring Information

Intrusion Subscale=sum of items 1, 2, 3, 6, 9, 16, 20
Avoidance Subscale=sum of items 5, 7, 8, 11, 12, 13, 17, 22
Hyperarousal Subscale=sum of items 4, 10, 14, 15, 18, 19, 21
Item response levels are:
0=Not at All 1=Rarely 3=Sometimes 5=Often

This instrument, by Daniel S. Weiss, may be reproduced without charge and freely distributed, as long as no funds are exchanged.

Incest History Questionnaire

Type of Population
Adult

Cost
no cost

Copyright
Norton & Co.; 1979, C. A. Courtois

Languages
English

What It Measures
The depth of/and the aftereffects of incest based on survivor's recollections

Measure Content Survey, Procedure, or Process
The 52-item Incest History Questionnaire can be administered as a pencil and paper self-report questionnaire and/or clinical interview. It is divided into five sections that are designed to assist both the incest survivor and the clinician when analyzing the family and its functioning and the incest and its aftermath. This instrument aids in analyzing both direct and and indirect aftereffects. The revised version is designed to assist with information gathering for the therapy process.

Theoretical Orientation Summary
Based upon a review of the available incest clinical literature published pre-1979.

Time Estimate

Administration	Scoring
15–20 minutes	10–15 minutes

Equipment Needed

Paper & Pencil	Computer	Basic Psychophysiological	Specialized Equipment
X			

Psychometric Maturity

Under Construction	Basic Properties Intact	Mature
X		

Psychometric Properties Summary
N/A; content validity based upon a review of pre-1979 incest literature.

Particular Sensitivity

Age	Change over Time	Culture / Ethnicity	Gender	Geography / Climate	Sexual Orientation	Socioeconomic Status	Urban / Rural
?	?	?	X	?	?	?	?

Estimate of Number of In-Process Studies

Unknown

Unpublished References

Unknown

Published References

Courtois, C. A., (1988). *Healing the incest wound: Adult survivors in therapy.* New York: W. W. Norton.

General Comments

This questionnaire was developed for dissertation research with a general adult population who reported a history of incest and who agreed to participate in an in-depth interview about their experience and its aftereffects. In 1988 it was modified somewhat for easier clinical use.

Key Words

Population	Stressor	Topic
adults	sexual abuse	clinical general treatment measure development research

Reference Citation for This Review

Courtois, C. A. (1996). Psychometric review of Incest History Questionnaire. In B. H. Stamm (Ed.). *Measurement of stress, trauma, and adaptation.* Lutherville, MD: Sidran Press.

Measure Contact Name

Christine A. Courtois, Ph.D.

Address:	Washington Circle, Suite 206
	Washington, DC 20037 USA
Phone:	202.955.5652
Fax:	703.847.8708
E-mail:	

Incest History Questionnaire Sample Items

- Describe any family problems, trauma or upheavals you can think of that occurred before, during or after the incest (please note when). (E.g., death in the family, divorce, alcoholism, severe illness or injury, desertion, child running away.)
- Describe the incest situation which you were involved in as a child/adolescent.
- In your opinion, did anyone else besides you and the perpetrator know of the incest without a direct disclose?
- Do you know if you had any observable symptoms that would have cued someone to the incest?
- Describe your current feelings about the perpetrator.
- Describe your current feelings about the incest. How do you understand your incest experience? Does it have any meaning to you?
- Describe your current feelings about yourself.

Life Orientation Inventory (LOI)

Type of Population
Adult

Cost
Minimal

What It Measures
Aspects of spirituality along 4 dimensions.

Measure Content Survey, Procedure, or Process
Revision B consists of 35 items (Likert rating scale). Assesses 4 dimensions of spirituality: belief in and attitude toward the non-material, awareness of and openness to one's experiences, hope and meaning, and a sense of connection with the natural world.

Theoretical Orientation Summary
Constructivist Self-Development Theory

Time Estimate

Administration	Scoring
10–15 minutes	5–15 minutes

Equipment Needed

Paper & Pencil	Computer	Basic Psychophysiological	Specialized Equipment
X			

Psychometric Maturity

Under Construction	Basic Properties Intact	Mature
	X	

Psychometric Properties Summary
Full scale reliability of earlier version=.95 (Cronbach's alpha). Factor analysis yielded the 4 factor solution described above. Further reliability and validity studies ongoing.

Particular Sensitivity

Age	Change over Time	Culture/ Ethnicity	Gender	Geography/ Climate	Sexual Orientation	Socioeconomic Status	Urban/ Rural
?	?	?	?	?	?	?	?

Unpublished References
Unknown

Published References
Unknown

General Comments

Normed on general population. Clinical group norms being established.

Key Words

Population	Stressor	Topic
adult		measure development
		research
		spirituality

Reference Citation for This Review

Neumann, D. A., & Pearlman, L. A. (1996). Psychometric review of Life Orientation Inventory. In B. H. Stamm (Ed.). *Measurement of stress, trauma, and adaptation.* Lutherville, MD: Sidran Press.

Instrument Contact Name

Debra Neumann, Ph.D.

Address: 3939 Cambridge Road, Suite 101
            Cameron Park, CA 95682 USA
Phone: 916.672.2053
Fax:
E-mail:

Life Satisfaction Scale

Type of Population
Adult

Cost
Unknown

Copyright

Languages
Russian, English

What It Measures
Long-term effects of psychosocial stress on the life satisfaction of adults.

Measure Content Survey, Procedure, or Process
35 item self-report measure of psychosocial stressors and their effects on life satisfaction as reported on three sub-scales: Subjective state, Life conditions, and Main needs.

Theoretical Orientation Summary

Time Estimate

Administration	Scoring
5–10 minutes	5–10 minutes

Equipment Needed

Paper & Pencil	Computer	Basic Psychophysiological	Specialized Equipment
X			

Psychometric Maturity

Under Construction	Basic Properties Intact	Mature
X		

Psychometric Properties Summary

Particular Sensitivity

Age	Change over Time	Culture / Ethnicity	Gender	Geography / Climate	Sexual Orientation	Socioeconomic Status	Urban / Rural
?	?	X	?	X	?	X	X

Estimate of Number of In-Process Studies
Unknown

Unpublished References
Unknown

Published References

Kopina, O. S., Souslova, E. A., & Zaikan, E. V. (1995). Method for investigation of life satisfaction and the sources of stress in epidemiological studies. *Voprosy Psychologii, 4.*

General Comments

The Life Satisfaction Scale was originally designed and used as tool to measure the long-term effects of psychosocial stress on the life satisfaction of survivors of the Chernobyl nuclear power plant accident seven years after the catastrophe.

Key Words

Population	Stressor	Topic
adult	any	epidiomology life-satisfaction measure development research

Reference Citation for This Review

Kopina, O. S. (1996). Psychometric review of Life Satisfaction Scale. In B. H. Stamm (Ed.). *Measurement of stress, trauma, and adaptation.* Lutherville, MD: Sidran Press.

Measure Contact Name

O.S. Kopina, Ph.D.

Address: Psychological Laboratory
National Research Center for Preventive Medicine
10, Petroverigsky Lane,
Moscow, 101953, Russia

Phone: 7.095.921.58.43; 7.095.138.42.29

Fax: 7.095.921.44.07; 7.095.928.50.63

E-mail: biostat@micpm.msk.su; eqa@glas.apc.org

Life Satisfaction Scale

Subscale 1. Subjective state

How have you been feeling lately?

	Definitely No	Probably No	Probably Yes	Definitely Yes
1. In general I have been satisfied with my life during the last 12 months	1	2	3	4
2. My psychological well-being is getting worse.	1	2	3	4
3. My life in general is going well.	1	2	3	4
4. My well-being went downhill.	1	2	3	4
5. I feel fairly happy.	1	2	3	4
6. There were changes for the worse in my life.	1	2	3	4
7. I have sources of joy and support in my life.	1	2	3	4
8. I have problems which trouble me.	1	2	3	4
9. My life is turned to the better.	1	2	3	4
10. I fail in doing many things.	1	2	3	4

$S1 = X1 + X3 + X5 + X7 + X9$

$S2 = X2 + X4 + X6 + X8 + X10$

$S = S1 - S2$

Range $-15 < S +15$

Subscale 2. Life conditions

Below is a list of life conditions which can influence your psychological state. Please rate your living conditions using the 5-score scale below:

1=very poor   2=poor   3=satisfactory   4=good   5=very good

LIFE CONDITIONS	SCORES
1. Your apartment/home	_____
2. Daily life activities (shops, services, transportation, etc.)	_____
3. Environmental conditions in your region (air, water, soil, etc.)	_____
4. Your working conditions	_____
5. Your income	_____
6. Availability of goods, possibility of investing money	_____
7. Medical care	_____
8. Access to media (radio, TV, periodicals)	_____
9. Leisure, sports, entertainment	_____
10. Availability of cinema, museums, books, etc.	_____
11. Political situation in your region	_____
12. Your social and personal security (safety in your city)	_____
13. Freedom of religious and political activity	_____

Below is a list of life spheres which can influence your psychological state. Please rate how satisfied you are with these spheres. Use the 5-score scale below:

1=completely satisfied   2=unsatisfied   3=somewhat satisfied   4=mainly satisfied   5=completely satisfied

LIFE SPHERES	**SCORES**
1. Your job (work content, work role, interpersonal relations, possibilities, etc.)	_____
2. Relations in your family	_____
3. Your children: their health and well-being	_____
4. Nutrition	_____
5. Rest and relaxation	_____
6. Your material well-being	_____
7. Communication/interaction with friends	_____
8. Your social status	_____
9. Life prospect, future expectations	_____
10. Intimate relations/ sexual satisfaction	_____
11. Hobbies, creativity, self-expression	_____
12. Your health	_____

Life Stressor Checklist—Revised

Type of Population
Adults

Cost
Free

Copyright
yes

Languages
English

What It Measures
The Life Stressor Checklist—Revised was designed to screen for the occurrence of life events that meet the definition of a trauma according to *DSM-IV*, as well as the presence of other stressful life events that may impact on symptomatology or functioning. The instrument is administered as a self-report inventory, although it may be given in an interview format as well. It yields a dichotomous score for the presence or absence of a range of developmental and adult stressors and traumas and a continuous rating of distress at the time of the event and current impact.

Instrument Content Survey
The LSC—R is composed of 30 "event" items, which are endorsed as having occurred or not occurred. Each event is followed by sub-questions deriving age, duration, beliefs about potential harm or lethality of the event, feelings of fear, hopelessness or horror, general distress at the time of the event, and impact of the event in the past year. However, the questionnaire is designed so that negative endorsements of an event allows the subject to skip sub-questions pertaining to that event. The LSC—R contains questions specific to female gender but can also be used with men. It also includes questions about witnessing traumatic events and the vicarious experience of trauma.

Theoretical Orientation Summary
The LSC—R is an empirically based checklist developed in response to the growing need within the field of trauma for an instrument that identifies potential traumas and/or stressors for diagnostic or research purposes.

Time Estimate

Administration	Scoring
15–30 minutes	15–30 minutes

Equipment Needed

Paper & Pencil	Computer	Basic Psychophysiological	Specialized Equipment
X			

Psychometric Maturity

Under Construction	Basic Properties Intact	Mature
X		

Psychometric Properties Summary

Although the LSC has existed for some time, the revised version is only currently undergoing investigation of its psychometric properties. An earlier version of the LSC—R, which was indexed to *DSM-III-R,* has been used to identify traumatic experiences in female veterans of the Vietnam War and female veterans of Operation Desert Storm. In these studies, endorsement of Criterion A traumatic events (*DSM-III-R*) was highly correlated with PTSD diagnosis.

Particular Sensitivity

Age	Change over Time	Culture / Ethnicity	Gender	Geography / Climate	Sexual Orientation	Socioeconomic Status	Urban / Rural
X	?	?	X	?	?	?	?

Estimate of Number of In-Process Studies

Approximately 14. The LSC is currently administered in the following ongoing research projects in which one of the authors is directly involved:

Ouimette, P. C., & Saxe, G. Reliability and validity study of the Complex PTSD Interview.

Brown, P. J. PTSD and substance abuse relapse.

Kimerling, R., Forehand, R., Armistead, L., Clark, L., Morse, E., & Simon, P. Associations among psychosocial variables and markers of HIV infection in women.

Unpublished References (previous versions only)

Kimerling, R., Wolfe, J., Schnurr, P., Clum G., & Chrestman, K. (November 1994). Differential effects of lifetime stressors and social support on physical health in women. Poster presented at the 28th meeting of the International Society of Traumatic Stress Studies. San Diego, CA.

Wolfe, J. (October 1993). Significance of cognitive changes in PTSD: Implications for survival. In R. Yehuda (Chair). Neuropsychological Changes in PTSD. Symposium conducted at the International Society for Traumatic Stress Studies. San Antonio, TX.

Wolfe, J., & Clum, G. (October 1993). Memory with and without conscious awareness in female trauma survivors: A functional model. In D. Bremner (Chair). Stress and Memory: Part 2. Symposium conducted at the meeting of the International Society for Traumatic Stress Studies. San Antonio, TX.

Wolfe, J., Kimerling, R., & Clum, G. (November 1993). Phenomenology of Post Traumatic Stress Disorder symptoms and self reported health in women. Poster presented at the 27th Annual Meeting of the Association for the Advancement of Behavior Therapy. Atlanta, GA.

Wolfe, J., Proctor, S., Brown, P., Kimerling, R., Duncan, J., Chrestman, K., & White, R. (May 1994). Relationship of physical health and Post-Traumatic Stress Disorder in young adult women. Paper presented at the American Psychological Association's conference on Psychosocial and Behavioral Factors in Women's Health: Creating an Agenda for the 21st Century. Washington, DC.

Published References (current version)

Wolfe, J., & Kimerling, R. (in press). Assessment of PTSD and gender. In J. Wilson & T. M. Keane (Eds.). *Assessing psychological trauma and PTSD: A handbook for practitioners.* New York: Plenum.

General Comments

Because this instrument is designed to elicit material that can be disturbing and disruptive to some individuals, we would caution against using the LSC—R in projects or contexts in which a trained clinician would not be available for debriefing and consultation/referral. As this instrument is undergoing psychometric refinement we ask that those wishing to use the LSCL—R share their raw data with us to further these efforts. We are very interested in facilitating the use of the LSCL in different populations and will provide consultation, normative data, updated copies, and scoring instructions to those who are willing to sign a data sharing agreement. Please contact the office of Jessica Wolfe, Ph.D. as indicated below.

Key Words

Population	Stressor	Topic
adult women	any	assessment measure development research

Reference Citation for This Review

Wolfe, J. W., Kimerling, R., Brown, P. J., Chrestman, K. R., & Levin, K. (1996). Psychometric review of The Life Stressor Checklist-Revised. In B. H. Stamm (Ed.). *Measurement of stress, trauma, and adaptation*. Lutherville, MD: Sidran Press.

Measure Authors

Jessica Wolfe, Rachel Kimerling, Pamela Brown, Kelly Chrestman, and Karen Levin

Measure Contact Name

        Jessica Wolfe, Ph.D. or
        Kelly R. Chrestman, Ph.D.
Address: Women's Health Sciences Division
        National Center for PTSD (116B-3)
        150 S. Huntington Ave.
        Boston MA 02130 USA
Phone: 617.232.9500 x4145
Fax: 617.278.4515
E-mail: wolfe.jessica@boston.va.gov

6. Were you ever put in jail?   **YES**   **NO**

a. How old were you when this first began?_____

b. when it ended?_____

c. At the time of the event did you believe that *you or someone else* could be
  killed or seriously *harmed?*   YES   NO

d. At the time of the event did you experience feelings of *intense helplessness,*
  fear, or horror?   YES   NO

e. How upsetting was the event at the time?   (1)   (2)   (3)   (4)   (5)
                                                  not at all   moderately   extremely

f. How much has it affected your life in the past year? (1)   (2)   (3)   (4)   (5)
                                                  not at all   moderately   extremely

10. Have you ever had a very serious physical or mental illness
(for example, cancer, heart attack, serious operation, felt like
killing yourself, hospitalized because of nerve problems)?   **YES**   **NO**

a. How old were you when this first began?_____

b. when it ended?_____

c. At the time of the event did you believe that *you or someone else* could be
  killed or seriously *harmed?*   YES   NO

d. At the time of the event did you experience feelings of *intense helplessness,*
  fear, or horror?   YES   NO

e. How upsetting was the event at the time?   (1)   (2)   (3)   (4)   (5)
                                                  not at all   moderately   extremely

f. How much has it affected your life in the past year? (1)   (2)   (3)   (4)   (5)
                                                  not at all   moderately   extremely

19. When you were young (before age 16), did you ever see violence
between family members (for example, hitting, kicking,
slapping, punching)?   **YES**   **NO**

a. How old were you when this first began?_____

b. when it ended?_____

c. At the time of the event did you believe that *you or someone else* could be
  killed or seriously *harmed?*   YES   NO

d. At the time of the event did you experience feelings of *intense helplessness,*
  fear, or horror?   YES   NO

e. How upsetting was the event at the time?   (1)   (2)   (3)   (4)   (5)
                                                  not at all   moderately   extremely

f. How much has it affected your life in the past year? (1)   (2)   (3)   (4)   (5)
                                                  not at all   moderately   extremely

26. *After age 16*, were you ever *touched* or made to *touch someone else*
in a *sexual way* because they forced you in some way or threatened
to harm you if you didn't?   **YES**   **NO**

a. How old were you when this first began?_____

b. when it ended?_____

c. At the time of the event did you believe that *you or someone else* could be
  killed or seriously *harmed?*   YES   NO

d. At the time of the event did you experience feelings of *intense helplessness,*
  fear, or horror?   YES   NO

e. How upsetting was the event at the time?   (1)   (2)   (3)   (4)   (5)
                                                  not at all   moderately   extremely

f. How much has it affected your life in the past year? (1)   (2)   (3)   (4)   (5)
                                                  not at all   moderately   extremely

Los Angeles Symptom Checklist (LASC)

Type of Population

Any, Adults, Adolescents

Cost

Free

Copyright

David Foy, Ph.D.

Languages

English

What It Measures

The LASC measures Criteria B, C, and D symptoms of posttraumatic stress disorder (PTSD), plus associated features and complications.

Measure Content Survey, Procedure, or Process

The LASC consists of 43 brief phrases describing symptoms of PTSD or problems associated with it. The respondent is asked to supply a rating for each item, ranging from 0 (no problem) to 4 (extreme problem). There are three ways to score the instrument: (a) a sum of the 17 item ratings that most closely correspond to the diagnostic criteria for PTSD; (b) a trichotomous classification of PTSD positive, partial PTSD, or PTSD negative as a function of the pattern of endorsements of these 17 items; and (c) a sum of all 43 item ratings to obtain a global assessment of psychological distress and adjustment problems that may be a consequence of trauma exposure.

Theoretical Orientation Summary

The items were originally written to mirror the *DSM-III* criteria of reexperiencing, numbing, and other symptom categories, and were coupled with an array of symptoms and problem statements which, in the experience of the original test authors, were frequently seen to occur with a PTSD diagnosis. Subsequent improvements in the definition of PTSD reflected in the *DSM-III-R* and *DSM-IV* criteria of reexperiencing, avoidance and numbing, and hyperarousal are contained in the present LASC item set.

Time Estimate

Administration	Scoring
10–20 minutes	10–15 minutes

Equipment Needed

Paper & Pencil	Computer	Basic Psychophysiological	Specialized Equipment
X			

Psychometric Maturity

Under Construction	Basic Properties Intact	Mature
	X	

Psychometric Properties Summary

High internal consistency reliability has been established: (a) .95 for the full 43-item instrument and .94 for the subset of 17 PTSD items across a large heterogeneous sample (N=874); (b) .94 and .91, respectively, for N=300 Vietnam veterans; (c) .94 and .89, respectively, for a combined all female sample of N=406 battered women, adult survivors of child abuse, maritally stressed women, and psychiatric outpatients; and (d) .94 and .88, respectively, for N=168 high-risk adolescents. For a small group (N=19) of Vietnam veterans, test-retest reliability (2-week interval) was .90 for the 43-item index and .94 for the 17-item PTSD index. Regarding validity, for Vietnam veterans correlations with combat exposure have ranged from .30 to .51. Similar correlations between violence exposure and LASC scores have been found for battered women and high-risk adolescents. Expected relationships with the Impact of Events Scale have been documented and several studies have shown convergence with SCID diagnoses. See the King, King, Leskin, and Foy (1995) reference below.

Particular Sensitivity

Age	Change over Time	Culture / Ethnicity	Gender	Geography / Climate	Sexual Orientation	Socioeconomic Status	Urban / Rural
X	?	?	X	?	?	?	?

Estimate of Number of In-Process Studies

10

Unpublished References

Astin, M. C. (1991). Posttraumatic stress disorder in battered women: Comparisons with maritally distressed controls. Unpublished doctoral dissertation, Fuller Theological Seminary. Pasadena, CA.

Guevara, M. (1991). Exposure to gang violence and the development of PTSD in continuation school youth. Unpublished doctoral dissertation, Fuller Theological Seminary. Pasadena, CA.

Hanley, D. C., Piersma, H. L., King, D. S., Larson, D. B., & Foy, D. W. (October 1992). Women outpatients reporting continuing post-abortion distress: A preliminary inquiry. Paper presented at the meeting of the International Society for Traumatic Stress Studies. Los Angeles, CA.

Ryan, S. (1992). Psychometric analysis of the Sexual Abuse Exposure Questionnaire. Unpublished doctoral dissertation, Fuller Theological Seminary. Pasadena, CA.

Published References

Astin, M. C., Lawrence, K. J., & Foy, D. W. (1993). Posttraumatic stress disorder among battered women: Risk and resiliency factors. *Violence and Victims, 8,* 17–29.

Burton, D., Foy, D.W., Bwanausi, C., Johnson, J., & Moore, L. (1994). The relationship between traumatic exposure, family dysfunction, and posttraumatic stress symptoms in juvenile offenders. *Journal of Traumatic Stress, 7,* 83–93.

Butler, R. W., Foy, D. W., Snodgrass, L., Lea-Hurwicz, M., & Goldfarb, J. (1988). Combat-related posttraumatic stress disorder in a nonpsychiatric population. *Journal of Anxiety Disorders, 2,* 111–120.

Carroll, E. M., Rueger, D. B., Foy, D. W., & Donahoe, C. P. (1985). Vietnam combat veterans with posttraumatic stress disorder: An analysis of marital and cohabiting adjustment. *Journal of Abnormal Psychology, 94,* 329–337.

Foy, D. W., Sipprelle, R. C., Rueger, D. B., & Carroll, E. M. (1984). Etiology of posttraumatic stress disorder in Vietnam veterans: Analysis of premilitary, military, and combat exposure influences. *Journal of Consulting and Clinical Psychology, 52,* 79–87.

Gallers, J., Foy, D. W., Donahoe, C. P., & Goldfarb, J. (1988). Combat-related posttraumatic stress disorder: An empirical investigation of traumatic violence exposure. *Journal of Traumatic Stress, 1,* 181–192.

Houskamp, B. M., & Foy, D. W. (1991). The assessment of posttraumatic stress disorder in battered women. *Journal of Interpersonal Violence, 6,* 368–376.

Lund, M., Foy, D. W., Sipprelle, R. C., & Strachan, A. M. (1984). The Combat Exposure Scale: A systematic assessment of trauma in the Vietnam War. *Journal of Clinical Psychology, 40,* 1323–1328.

King, L. A., King, D. W., Leskin, G., & Foy, D. W. (1995). The Los Angeles Symptom Checklist: A self-report measure of posttraumatic stress disorder. *Assessment*, *2*, 1–17.

Resnick, H. S., Foy, D. W., Donahoe, C. P., & Miller, E. N. (1989). Antisocial behavior and posttraumatic stress disorder in Vietnam veterans. *Journal of Clinical Psychology*, *45*, 860–866.

Rowan, A. B., Foy, D. W., Rodriguez, N., & Ryan, S. (1994). Posttraumatic stress disorder in adults sexually abused as children. *International Journal of Child Abuse and Neglect*, *18*, 51–61.

General Comments

The recent article by King, King, Leskin, and Foy (1995) provides a synopsis of existing psychometric characteristics, normative information, and a summary of prior research in which the LASC has been used.

Key Words

Population	Stressor	Topic
adolescents adults	any	assessment diagnosis general treatment research

Reference Citation for This Review

King, L. A. (1996). Psychometric review of the Los Angeles Symptom Checklist (LASC). In B. H. Stamm (Ed.). *Measurement of stress, trauma, and adaptation*. Lutherville, MD: Sidran Press.

Measure Author

David W. Foy, PhD.

Address: Graduate School of Education and Psychology
             Pepperdine University Plaza
             400 Corporate Pointe
             Culver City, CA 90230 USA
Phone: 310.568.5739.
Fax: 310.568.5755
E-mail: DFOY@PEPPERDINE.EDU.

Measure Contact Name

Lynda A. King, Ph.D.

Address: National Center for PTSD (116B-2)
             Boston DVA Medical Center
             150 S. Huntington Avenue
             Boston, MA 02130 USA
Phone: 617.232.9500, ext. 4938
Fax: 617.248.4515
E-Mail: king.lynda@boston.va.gov

Mississippi Scale For Combat-Related PTSD—Short Form

Type Of Population

War zone veterans seeking treatment for PTSD and related disorders, primarily from traumatic exposure in Vietnam but also in World War II and Korea.

Cost

Free.

Copyright

Languages

English.

What It Measures

This scale is an 11-item version of the 35-item Mississippi Scale for Combat-Related PTSD that was developed originally by Terence Keane and associates (Keane, Caddell, & Taylor, 1988). We developed the short version with two goals in mind. First, we wanted a version of the Mississippi Scale that would be maximally sensitive to changes in the severity of PTSD symptoms. This feature is extremely valuable when conducting studies of treatment outcome. Second, we wanted a version that was more economical to administer than the full scale. Brevity is highly desirable for use in large surveys or in any design where a large number of measures is desired and the time for data collection is limited.

Measure Content Survey, Procedure, or Process

The items were selected from a cross-validation study of 436 war zone veterans who received outpatient treatment from the Department of Veterans Affairs PTSD Clinical Teams program. First, 11 items were identified from a randomly selected subsample of 220 veterans on the basis of showing a significant decrease from the beginning of treatment to 4 months later. Second, another randomly selected subsample of 200 veterans was used to cross-validate the items' ability to identify change and to determine their psychometric adequacy as a scale. Third, the full sample was used to derive a cut-score for the diagnosis of PTSD. Finally, difference scores from intake to 4 and 12 months were compared to clinicians' improvement ratings and the amount of treatment received.

Theoretical Orientation Summary

Eight of the items composing the short scale closely approximate the criterion symptoms for the diagnosis of PTSD as defined by the American Psychiatric Association (1987). There are two items for reexperiencing and intrusion, three items for avoidance and numbing, and three items for hyperarousal. The other three items measure suicidal feelings, substance use, and feeling different from other people.

Time Estimate

Administration	Scoring
5–10 minutes	5 minutes

Equipment Needed

Paper & Pencil	Computer	Basic Psychophysiological	Specialized Equipment
X			

Psychometric Maturity

Under Construction	Basic Properties Intact	Mature
	X	

Psychometric Properties Summary

Construct Validity: The internal consistency (coefficient alpha) of the short form was uniformly high across the year: .83 at intake, .85 at 4 months, and .87 at 12 months. Its correlation with the full Mississippi Scale was also consistently high: .95 at intake and 4 months and .96 at 12 months. Even when overlapping items between the short and full forms were removed from the latter, correlations remained at .90. A cut-score of 107 was used for diagnostic determination of PTSD for the full scale (78% of the sample), since Keane's original study found this to be the value that identified PTSD with maximal precision. A cut-score of 34 for the short form (76% of the sample) produced 93% agreement with the full scale, with a sensitivity of 94% and a specificity of 88%.

Predictive Validity: The short form showed a significant decrease in scores from intake to 4 months ($p < .0001$) and from intake to 12 months ($p < .0001$). This contrasted with results for the full scale that showed a significant decrease from intake to 4 months ($p < .02$) and no significant decrease from intake to 12 months. Comparison of short form change scores with clinicians' improvement ratings revealed a consistently positive relationship over the course of the year, with the improvement ratings at the end of 12 months being related significantly to change scores at that time ($p < .02$). Specifically, 76.6% of those with decreases were rated as improved compared to only 60.5% of those with increases. Further, veterans with decreases received more treatment sessions ($p < .0005$) and were in treatment a greater number of months ($p < .005$) than those with increases.

Particular Sensitivity

Age	Change over Time	Culture / Ethnicity	Gender	Geography / Climate	Sexual Orientation	Socioeconomic Status	Urban / Rural
?	X	?	?	?	?	?	?

Estimate of Number of In-Process Studies

The short form is currently being used in a nationwide monitoring of the Department of Veterans Affairs' specialized inpatient PTSD programs. Experience with the extension of the short form to inpatients will be available when these data are analyzed. We have received several requests for the instrument from VA investigators. We do not know, however, how many have actually proceeded to data collection and are using the short form.

Unpublished References

Published References

American Psychiatric Association (1987). *Diagnostic and statistical manual of mental disorders*, 3rd. ed., rev. Washington, DC: Author.

Fontana, A., & Rosenheck, R. (1994). A short form of the Mississippi Scale for measuring change in combat-related PTSD. *Journal of Traumatic Stress, 7*, 407–414.

Keane, T. M., Caddell, J. M., & Taylor, K. L. (1988). Mississippi Scale for Combat-Related Posttraumatic Stress Disorder: Three studies in reliablity and validity. *Journal of Consulting and Clinical Psychology 56*, 85–90.

General Comments

Interested users can consult the "Design" section of Fontana and Rosenheck (1994) for a general description of the alternatives and the full version of the Mississippi Scale for the specific response alternatives for each individual item.

Key Words

Population	Stressor	Topic
men veterans	combat	assessment diagnosis research

Reference Citation for This Review

Fontana, A. (1996). Psychometric review of Mississippi Scale for Combat-Related PTSD—Short Form. In B. H. Stamm (Ed.). *Measurement of Stress, Trauma, and Adaptation*. Lutherville, MD: Sidran Press.

Measure Contact Name

Alan Fontana, PhD

Address: Northeast Program Evaluation Center (182)
             VA Medical Center
             950 Campbell Avenue
             West Haven, CT 06516 USA
Phone: 203.937.3851 x3708
Fax: 203.937.3433
E-mail:

Mississippi Scale for Combat-Related PTSD-Short Form

	Never, Not at all true, Very unlikely				Always, Very frequently true, Extremely likely
1. I have nightmares of experiences in the military that really happened.	1	2	3	4	5
2. Lately, I have felt like killing myself.	1	2	3	4	5
3. *I fall asleep, stay asleep and awaken only when the alarm goes off.	1	2	3	4	5
4. My dreams at night are so real that I waken in a cold sweat and force myself to stay awake.	1	2	3	4	5
5. I feel like I cannot go on.	1	2	3	4	5
6. I do not laugh or cry at the same things other people do.	1	2	3	4	5
7. *I enjoy the company of others.	1	2	3	4	5
8. Unexpected noises make me jump.	1	2	3	4	5
9. There have been times when I used alcohol (or other drugs) to help me sleep or to make me forget about things that happened while I was in the service.	1	2	3	4	5
10. I lose my cool and explode over minor everyday things.	1	2	3	4	5
11. I have a hard time expressing my feelings, even to the people I care about.	1	2	3	4	5

*Item is reversed in scoring.

Multidimensional Trauma Recovery and Resiliency Measures:
The MTRRI (Interview) and the MTRRQ (Sort)

Type of Population
The MTRRI and the MTRRQ are companion instruments that can be used to assess recovery and resiliency in both clinical and community samples of trauma survivors, including combat vets, accident victims, rape victims, child sexual abuse victims, and other traumatized populations.

Cost
Cost will include postage, handling, and copying fees.

Copyright
Mary Harvey, Ph.D. & Drew Weston, Ph.D.

Languages
English

What It Measures
The MTRR Interview and Q-sort assess recovery and resiliency status of trauma survivors on each of eight domains of functioning (Harvey, 1995).

Measure Content Survey, Procedure, or Process
The MTRRI and MTRRQ are companion instruments. The Q-sort consists of 101 items that provide for the quantitative assessment of psychological recovery and resiliency on targeted domains. The Interview can be reliably Q-sorted by clinical researchers and can be probed for qualitative information about individually variant recovery patterns.

Theoretical Orientation Summary
The Q-sort was developed out of the ecological view of psychological trauma and trauma recovery (Harvey, 1995) and a "stages by dimension" model of treatment (Lebowitz, Harvey, & Herman, 1991). This model states that recovery from trauma occurs over three stages and seven domains (authority over the remembering process, memory linked with affect, affect tolerance, and trauma-related affects, symptom mastery, self esteem and self cohesion, safe attachment, and meaning making).

Time Estimate

Administration	Scoring
30–60 minutes	20-30 minutes

Equipment Needed

Paper & Pencil	Computer	Basic Psychophysiological	Specialized Equipment
X			Sort Cards

Psychometric Maturity

Under Construction	Basic Properties Intact	Mature
X		

Psychometric Properties Summary

Initial reliability and validity studies using the MTRRQ show it to be reliable across raters at a level of .75 or better. In addition, it can distinguish recovered survivors from unrecovered survivors; untraumatized individuals from traumatized individuals, and can detect predicted differences between early recovery trauma groups. For a more complete discription of the psychometrics of the Q-sort, see the paper by Westen, Harvey, Vardi, Harnay, Lebowitz, Aviyonnah, and Saunders. Reliability and validity studies using the MTRRI are currently in process.

Particular Sensitivity

Age	Change over Time	Culture/ Ethnicity	Gender	Geography/ Climate	Sexual Orientation	Socioeconomic Status	Urban/ Rural
X	X	?	X	?	?	?	?

Estimate of Number of In-Process Studies

Unknown

Unpublished References

Westen, D., Harvey, M. R., Vardi, D., Harney, P., Lebowitz, L., Aviyonah, O., & Saunders, E. (1995). Development of a multidimensional observer-rated trauma recovery and resiliency Q-sort: Validity and reliability. Paper submitted for publication.

Published References

Harvey, M. R. (in press). An ecological view of psychological trauma and trauma recovery. *Journal of Traumatic Stress*.

Lebowitz, L., Harvey, M., & Herman, J. (1991). A stage by dimension model of recovery from sexual trauma. *Journal of Interpersonal Violence, 8* (3), 378–391.

General Comments

We would hope that anyone using these instruments would provide us with the data as we are establishing a nationwide normative database.

Key Words

Population	Stressor	Topic
adult	any	assessment diagnosis measure development research general treatment

Reference Citation for This Review

Harvy, M. & Weston, D. (1996). Psychometric review of Multidimensional Trauma Recovery and Resiliency Measures: The MTRRI (interview) and the MTRRQ (sort). In B. H. Stamm (Ed.). *Measurement of stress, trauma, and adaptation*. Lutherville, MD: Sidran Press.

Measure Contact Name

Mary Harvey, Ph. D.

         Director of the Victims of Violence Program

Address: The Cambridge Hospital

         Harvard Medical School

         1493 Cambridge Street

         Cambridge, MA 02139 USA

Phone: 617.492.3539
Fax: 617.491.8151
E-mail:

Measure Contact Name

Drew Westen, Ph.D.
                    Chair, Psychology Training
Address: The Cambridge Hospital
                    Harvard Medical School
                    1493 Cambridge Street
                    Cambridge, MA 02139 USA
Phone: 617.498.1167
Fax:
E-mail:

My Worst Experience and
My Worst School Experience Scale

Type of Population

Children with reading level of 4th grade +

Cost

Free for one copy/$50.00 for manual, scoring key, & 10 copies

Copyright

Irwin A. Hyman and National Center for the Study of Corporal Punishment and Alternatives, Temple University

Languages

English

What It Measures

Post Traumatic Stress Syndrome and stress symptoms.

Measure Content Survey, Procedure, or Process

This instrument has been in development for about 10 years. Factors cover current PTSD categories but several other factors appear. There are over 100 items in the complete clinical list. Factors showed high correlation between duration, frequency and intensity of symptoms. We now use frequency and check off duration as more than one month.

Theoretical Orientation Summary

Developed in the early 1980s while conducting clinical evaluations of children who had experienced corporal punishment (CP). The underlying theme in the development of the scales is that many childhood stressors, such as CP and divorce, are widespread and often intended to be for the good of children, but may result in major traumitization. While the scales include items derived from *DSM-IV,* the majority of items emerged from clinical populations. The factoral structure of the scale includes the major diagnostic indicators for PTSD from *DSM-III-R,* but also has other factors assumed to be specific to the nosology for PTSD in children.

Time Estimate

Administration	Scoring
30-120 minutes	30-45 minutes

Equipment Needed

Paper & Pencil	Computer	Basic Psychophysiological	Specialized Equipment
X			

Psychometric Maturity

Under Construction	Basic Properties Intact	Mature
	X	

Psychometric Properties Summary

Measures of frequency, intensity, and duration of symptoms were found to correlate so highly that only frequency was retained as a Likert item on the final version. Research with the scale has addressed populations abused by educators, victims and survivors of a hurricane, sexual abuse, physical abuse and divorce. Two studies investigated the incidence of co-morbidity of PTSD and Conduct Disorder (CD). The subjects were students who attended special education facilities that service children with social and emotional problems who are sent by the public schools. Subjects were administered the MWES Scale. Comparisons of children diagnosed as CD, a general psychiatric population, and control group indicate a significant difference between groups, with CD having higher mean rates of stress and higher incidence of PTSD than the other groups. In a second study, 400 adolescents were administered the MWES. The worst experiences and symptoms (in terms of frequency, duration, and intensity) of students from families where divorce and separation occurred were compared with those of students who had not experienced divorce or separation. The data indicated that a significant number of the former group indicated that the worst experiences of their lives were related to divorce and many had serious stress syptoms. A third study examined attributional styles of survivors of Hurricane Andrew, 6 months after the disaster, to determine the relation between attributional styles of the children and their responses to MWES. A significant relation was found between pessimistic explanatory style for negative life events and duration of symptoms.

Particular Sensitivity

Age	Change over Time	Culture / Ethnicity	Gender	Geography / Climate	Sexual Orientation	Socioeconomic Status	Urban / Rural
X	X	?	?	X	?	?	?

Estimate of Number of In-Process Studies
5

Unpublished References
Contact author; over 20 available.

Published References
Contact author; 3 available.

General Comments

Key Words

Population	Stressor	Topic
adolescents children students	any emotional abuse school corporal punishment	general treatment forensics measure development research

Reference Citation for This Review
Hyman, I. A. (1996). Psychometric review of My Worst Experience and My Worst School Experience Scale. In B. H. Stamm (Ed.). *Measurement of stress, trauma, and adaptation*. Lutherville, MD: Sidran Press.

Measure Contact Name
Dr. Irwin A. Hyman
Address: 1198 Old Jordan Road
            Holland, PA 18966-2659 USA
Phone: 215.579.4865
Fax   215.579.2428
E-mail

National Women's Study (NWS) Event History—PTSD Module

Type of Population

Adult women

Cost

$10.00 fee for reproduction, mail, provision of relevant literature

Copyright

Kilpatrick, D. G., Resnick, H. S., Saunders, B. E., & Best, C. L., National Crime Victims Research and Treatment Center

Languages

English, Spanish

What It Measures

Lifetime history of *DSM-III-R* and *DSM-IV* relevant PTSD Criterion A events schedule and separate PTSD symptom schedule. The event history and PTSD modules are complementary but may be used separately as well. For example, the event history module may be used with other PTSD diagnostic interviews or any diagnostic measures that may be associated with significant stressor history (e.g. depression, panic disorder, etc.). This instrument description focuses on the event history assessment. The interview was developed for use with adult women. Potentially traumatic events assessed in the event history component of the PTSD module include accidents, natural disasters, witnessing violence, homicide of a loved one, completed rape, completed molestation, attempted rape, aggravated assault with or without a weapon.

The measure allows for assessment of multiple incidents of events and includes followup questions to establish *DSM-IV* characteristics of objective and subjective threat. Specifically, for each event reported respondents are asked whether they feared being killed or seriously injured during the incident(s) and the extent of injury sustained. Age at time of event(s) is also assessed. Additional assault followup questions evaluate relationship to the perpetrator and extent to which assaults were repeated versus acute events. To more comprehensively include other events that may meet new *DSM-IV* Criterion A specifications, questions are asked to determine experience of other events (beyond the defined categories outlined above) that included life threat or experience of injury. Thus, respondent identified events that fit qualitative characteristics in *DSM-IV* may be assessed. All events including sexual and aggravated assault are behaviorally defined using specific questions rather than legal terms that may bias responding. Prefaces for specific traumatic event assessment are included to provide background justification to the respondent for the importance of the assessment questions that follow.

The measure is 11 pages in length, including objective questions and scoring, and can be administered in 15 minutes. The PTSD symptom component of the module is described in detail in Resnick, Kilpatrick, Dansky, Saunders, & Best, 1993. For use with adult women, the instrument is not limited by sexual orientation, cultural or ethnic background, or urban/rural living conditions.

Measure Content Survey, Procedure, or Process

The measure is designed to be used in an interview format. Specific instructions and phrasing of questions and provision of codeable responses are included.

Theoretical Orientation Summary

This interview was developed from earlier instruments constructed by Dr. Kilpatrick to sensitively assess a variety of crime events among women in the community. The NWS module was expanded to include other non-crime Criterion A events such as accidents or disaster to allow for full assessment of *DSM-III-R* and *DSM-IV* stressors associated with PTSD. Based on empirical findings linking particular event histories and event characteristics with increased risk of PTSD, emphasis was placed on inclusion of specific characteristics of fear of being killed or seriously injured during any type of event and extent of injury received during any type of event. This inclusion of both objective and subjective threat characteristics makes this measure consistent with new *DSM-IV* PTSD criteria. Behaviorally specific questions to assess sexual assault were developed to avoid stereotypical biases that might be associated with legal terms, such as rape, that could increase false negative rates. Based on previous findings that individuals may have complex histories of traumatic events, this instrument allows for assessment of multiple types and multiple incidents of events that may constitute a complex developmental history. Finally, based on the high prevalence of crime and other potentially traumatic events, it has been argued that standard screening should be conducted to identify histories of such events in clinical and non-clinical populations. This interview provides structured questions that facilitate the conduct of such screenings by trained nonprofessional interviewers.

Time Estimate

Administration	Scoring
15–30 minutes	5–15 minutes depending on responses

Equipment Needed

Paper & Pencil	Computer	Basic Psychophysiological	Specialized Equipment
X			

Psychometric Maturity

Under Construction	Basic Properties Intact	Mature
	X	

Psychometric Properties Summary

Validity of the instrument in terms of Criterion A event assessment is supported by highly comparable rates for specific event exposure and multiple event exposure obtained using this and other traumatic event assessment instruments across general population studies. Rates of PTSD associated with particular event categories such as sexual assault or aggravated assault and particular event characteristics such as receipt of injury or perception of life threat are consistent with PTSD rates as a function of specific event histories observed across both clinical and non-clinical populations. For review, see Resnick et al., 1993. Evaluation of reliability of reporting of specific event histories at longitudinal assessment periods is in progress.

Particular Sensitivity

Age	Change over Time	Culture / Ethnicity	Gender	Geography / Climate	Sexual Orientation	Socioeconomic Status	Urban / Rural
?	?	X	X	?	X	?	X

Estimate of Number of In-Process Studies

several

Unpublished References

Several; please contact Dr. Kilpatrick for more information.

Published References

Palinkas, L. A., Patterson, J. S., Russell, J., & Downs, M. A. (1993). Community patterns of psychiatric disorders after the Exxon Valdez oil spill. *American Journal of Psychiatry, 150*, 1517–1523.

Resnick, H. S., Falsetti, S. F., Kilpatrick, D. G., & Freedy, J. F. (in press). Assessment of rape and other civilian trauma-related PTSD: Emphasis on assessment of potentially traumatic events. In T. Miller (Ed.), *Theory and assessment of stressful life events*. Madison, CT: International Universities Press, Inc.

Resnick, H. S., Kilpatrick, D. G., Dansky, B. S., Saunders, B. E., & Best, C. L. (1993). Prevalence of civilian trauma and posttraumatic stress disorder in a representative national sample of women. *Journal of Consulting and Clinical Psychology, 61*, 984–99.

General Comments

Key Words

Population	Stressor	Topic
adults women	accidents criminal victimization domestic violence physical abuse sexual assault/abuse other injury other life threat witnessing violence	diagnosis epidemiology forensic measure development research

Reference Citation for This Review

Resnick, H. (1996). Psychometric review of National Women's Study (NWS) Event History—PTSD Module. In B. H. Stamm (Ed.). *Measurement of stress, trauma, and adaptation*. Lutherville, MD: Sidran Press.

Measure Authors

Kilpatrick, D. G., Resnick, H. S., Saunders, B. E., & Best, C. L.

Measure Contact Name

Dean G. Kilpatrick
Address: National Crime Victims Research and Treatment Center
             Department of Psychiatry and Behavioral Sciences
             171 Ashley Avenue
             Charleston, SC 29425-0742 USA
Phone: 803.792.2945
Fax: 803.792.3388
E-mail:

National Women's Study (NWS) Event History-
PTSD Module Sample Items

- Included here are the questions used to identify history of rape:
- Has a man or boy ever made you have sex by using force or threatening to harm you or someone close to you? Just so there is no mistake, by sex we mean putting a penis in your vagina.
- Has anyone ever made you have oral sex by force or threat of harm? Just so there is no mistake, by oral sex we mean that a man or a boy put his penis in your mouth or someone penetrated your vagina or anus with their mouth or tongue?
- Has anyone ever made you have anal sex by force or threat of harm?
- Has anyone ever put fingers or objects in your vagina or anus against your will by using force or threats?
- Incidents are defined as completed rape if they include actual penile, digital, or foreign-object penetration of the victim's vagina, mouth, or anus by the assailant; occur without the victim's consent; and involve the use or threat of force.

NCVC Brief Screening for Assault Questionnaire

Type of Population
Adolescents and adults

Cost
Free

Copyright

Languages
English

What It Measures
The NCVC Brief Screening for Assault Questionnaire is a self-report measure designed to assess history of traumatic events. This measure is primarily designed for retrospective reports of lifetime history of aggravated and other physical assault, completed molestation, and completed rape. Items on the questionnaire are adapted from two sources: a) previous interviews designed by Dean G. Kilpatrick for the assessment of history of traumatic events in adult women; and b) an expanded version of Dr. Kilpatrick's trauma assessment questionnaires designed for use in an ongoing national survey at the NCVC of male and female adolescents funded by Institute of Justice (#93-IJ-CX-0023). The NCVC Brief Screening for Assault Questionnaire provides a quick (15-minute) screening instrument for use in primary care and other clinical settings. The measure may also be used to assess traumatic events over time, with events that occur between administrations being recorded at followup interviews.

Measure Content Survey, Procedure, or Process
The NCVC Brief Screening for Assault Questionnaire assesses occurrence and frequency of assaults, as well as factors associated with trauma as antecedents for PTSD including perceived life threat and injury (including pregnancy). The questionnaire also provides information relationship to the assailant and on use of medical care and reporting of trauma to medical professionals in terms of frequency of these behaviors following the assault(s).

Theoretical Orientation Summary
The NCVC Brief Screening for Assault Questionnaire was created in response for the growing need for a brief, yet comprehensive assessment of traumatic events that pose the greatest risk for Post-traumatic Stress Disorder (PTSD). The theoretical foci of this interview include (1) questions which were sensitive to reports of sexual and physical assault; (2) an assessment of event characteristics which have been empirically linked to PTSD vis-a-vis a conditioning model (i.e. perceived life-threat, injury, and completed rape); (3) an assessment of medical utilization secondary to interpersonal violence; and (4) an assessment of the frequency with which a respondent has communicated with a physician about any category of assault event. The current instrument may be used by male and female adolescents and adults. Use of the instrument is not limited by an individual's sexual orientation, cultural or ethnic background, or urban/rural living conditions. The individual must have a reading level of approximately 8th grade.

Time Estimate

Administration	Scoring
15–20 minutes	10–15 minutes

Equipment Needed

Paper & Pencil	Computer	Basic Psychophysiological	Specialized Equipment
X			

Psychometric Maturity

Under Construction	Basic Properties Intact	Mature
X		

Psychometric Properties Summary

Reliability and validity of the questionnaire have not yet been established. A prospective study of adult female sexual assault victims being conducted currently at the NCVC will assess validity of the scale using interview data on trauma history, objective report of a sexual assault in the past three months and medical data on injuries related to this assault.

Particular Sensitivity

Age	Change over Time	Culture / Ethnicity	Gender	Geography / Climate	Sexual Orientation	Socioeconomic Status	Urban / Rural
X	X	X	X	?	X	?	X

Estimate of Number of In-Process Studies

1

Unpublished References

Kilpatrick, D. G., Saunders, B. E., Resnick, H. S., Hanson, R., Swenson, C. P., & Best, C. L. (1995). National Survey of Adolescents. Interview for "Prevalence and Consequences of Child Victimization: A longitudinal study." NIJ Grant #93-IJ-CX-0023. Authors: Kilpatrick, D. G., Resnick, H. S., Weaver, T. L., Nayak, M. B., Saunders, B. E., & Best, C. L.

Published References

Unknown

General Comments

Key Words

Population	Stressor	Topic
adolescents adults	criminal victimization domestic violence physical abuse sexual assault/abuse terrorism torture	assessment epidemiology forensic general treatment measure development research

Reference Citation

Resnick, H. S. (1996). Psychometric review of the NCVC Brief Screening for Assault Questionnaire. In B. H. Stamm (Ed.). *Measurement of stress, trauma, and adaptation.* Lutherville, MD: Sidran Press.

Measure Author Name

Kilpatrick, D. G.; Resnick, H. S.; Weaver, T. L.; Nayak, M. B.; Saunders, B. E.; & Best, C. L.

Measure Contact Name

Heidi S. Resnick, Ph.D.

Address: National Crime Victims Research and Treatment Center
                  Department of Psychiatry and Behavioral Sciences
                  Medical University of South Carolina
                  171 Ashley Avenue
                  Charleston, SC 29425 USA

Phone: 803.792.2945

Fax: 803.792.3388

E-mail: RESNICKH@MUSC.EDU

NCVC Brief Screening For Assault Questionnaire
Sample Items

Stressful events can have a major impact on people's health. We are interested in learning about stressful events that may have happened to patients at our clinic. This information is important to us because it can help us understand how people deal with stresses in their lives and will help us better meet our patients' needs.

1. Please indicate the number of times the following experiences happened to you with anyone (male or female), whether or not the person was a family member, boyfriend/girlfriend, husband/wife, friend, or stranger? (IF NEVER MARK 0)

NUMBER OF TIMES THIS HAPPENED	0 time	1–3 times	4–10 times	>10 times
How many times has anyone, male or female, hit, strangled, or otherwise physically attacked you so that you suffered some degree of injury, including bruises, cuts, or other marks?				
During how many of these attacks were you afraid that you might be killed or seriously injured?				
How many times have you suffered serious injuries as a result of any of these physical attack(s)?				
FOR WOMEN ONLY: How many times did any of these physical attack(s) happen while you were pregnant?				
How many times did any of these physical attack(s) happen before you were 18 years old?				
After how many of these physical attack(s) did you go to a doctor or to the hospital?				
Of these physical attacks, how many did you tell a doctor/ nurse about?				
Of these physical attacks, how many did you report to police or other authorities?				

If you answered "1 or more times" to any question above, please answer question 1a.

1a. Who physically attacked you (CIRCLE ALL THAT APPLY FOR ANY ATTACKS)

FAMILY MEMBER   BOYFRIEND/GIRLFRIEND   HUSBAND/WIFE

FRIEND   STRANGER   OTHER

Nursing Perception of Distress Instrument

Type of Population
professional nurses

Cost

Copyright

Languages
English

What It Measures
Perception by nurses of distress from abuse in the workplace

Measure Content Survey, Procedure, or Process
self-report survey

Theoretical Orientation Summary
The instrument was developed from the literature on female socialization and nursing identity and image.

Time Estimate

Administration	Scoring
5–15 minutes	5–10 minutes

Equipment Needed

Paper & Pencil	Computer	Basic Psychophysiological	Specialized Equipment
X			

Psychometric Maturity

Under Construction	Basic Properties Intact	Mature
	X	

Psychometric Properties Summary
Initial testing demonstrated content validity, substantial to moderate levels of reliability, and internal model validity.

Expert review was used to establish content validity of the Workplace Abuse Scale, that the items were accurate, appropriate, and representative. The items from this scale included 16 statements that were arranged in a Balanced Incomplete Block Design (BIBD) for analysis. Four blocks were repeated once for testing of reliability. Reliability was good, with the correlation for the least distressing scenarios being 0.973 and that for the most distressing scenarios 0.948. Cohen's Kappa measured the degree of agreement of the nurses' responses to the first set of questions and the nurses' responses to the repeated scenarios. The average Kappa for the most dimension was 0.629 and that for the least distressing dimension 0.527 (p for both <0.000). Internal validity was established using Least/Most Discrete Choice Analysis and McFadden's Rho-square (0.4609); the value fell into the category of reasonable to good. Confidence interval analysis of the resulting coefficients demonstrated eight magnitude groupings, with the most distressful independent categories being "humiliated" and "incompetent." Little or no relationship was found between the Rosenberg Self-Esteem Scale and distress encountered in the workplace. The sum of all frequencies of distress and the sum of all effects on performance for each distress category were correlated at r=0.663 (p<,000).

Particular Sensitivity

Age	Change over Time	Culture / Ethnicity	Gender	Geography / Climate	Sexual Orientation	Socioeconomic Status	Urban / Rural
?	?	?	?	?	?	?	?

Estimate of Number of In-Process Studies

Unpublished References

Montopoli, D.C. (1994). Development of an instrument to measure nursing perception of distress and performance among hospital nurses. Unpublished master's thesis, University of Wyoming. Laramie, WY.

Published References

None

General Comments

The Balanced Incomplete Block Design with the Least-Most Discrete Choice Analysis used for this instrument is new in the literature.

Key Words

Population	Stressor	Topic
adults health care workers nurses	physical abuse/neglect Sexual Assault/abuse Abuse in the workplace	measure development professionals research self care secondary traumatic service delivery stress

Reference Citation for This Review

Montopoli, D. (1996). Psychometric review of Nursing Perception of Distress Instrument. In B. H. Stamm (Ed.). *Measurement of stress, trauma, and adaptation*. Lutherville, MD: Sidran Press.

Measure Contact Name

Delia C. Montopoli, M.S., OB/GYN NP, RNC

Address: 403 Eberhart
              Laramie, WY 82070 USA
Phone: 307.742.2491
Fax: 307.766.4294
E-mail: TETON@UWYO.EDU

Nursing Perception of Distress Instrument

Please think about your current workplace and the environment in which you work. For each of the following, check the ONE alternative that has the most distressing effect on your nursing performance, and the ONE alternative that has the least distressing effect on your nursing performance.

least distressing			most distressing
		being made to feel hopeless or powerless	
		being approached with unwanted sexual comments	
		being unfairly paid	
		being laughed at or belittled	
		being made to feel incompetent	
		experiencing yelling, cursing, swearing, or sarcasm	
		being ignored or having needs negated	
		being unfairly paid	
		being unrecognized for job performance	
		being physically slapped and/or pushed	
		being approached with unwanted sexual comments	
		being undervalued as a person	

Workplace Abuse Scale Items

		not distressing			very distressing
1.	being physically slapped and/or pushed	1	2	3	4
2.	being motivated by fear and intimidation	1	2	3	4
3.	being humiliated in front of a third person	1	2	3	4
4.	being made to feel incompetent	1	2	3	4
5.	experiencing yelling, cursing, swearing, or sarcasm	1	2	3	4
6.	being undervalued as a professional	1	2	3	4
7.	being laughed at or belittled	1	2	3	4
8.	being made to feel hopeless or powerless	1	2	3	4
9.	being undervalued as a person	1	2	3	4
10.	being touched in an uncomfortable or inappropriate way	1	2	3	4
11.	being overloaded, overwhelmed or unsupported	1	2	3	4
12.	being unfairly paid	1	2	3	4
13.	being ignored or having needs negated	1	2	3	4
14.	being unrecognized for job performance	1	2	3	4
15.	being deceived, not told the truth	1	2	3	4
16.	being approached with unwanted sexual comments.	1	2	3	4

This instrument, by Delia C. Montopoli, may be reproduced without charge and freely distributed, as long as no funds are exchanged.

Parent Report of the Child's Reaction to Stress

Type of Population
Parent or guardian paper-and-pencil report regarding stress responses of children and adolescents.

Cost
Free to all of those who agree to share the raw data they collect in order to help establish the scale's psychometric properties.

Copyright
Kenneth E. Fletcher, Ph.D.

Languages
English. A Hebrew version of the first revision of the WBTH scale (which is in its third revision) is available. It has been used to study children's reactions to the Gulf War in Israel.

What It Measures
All *DSM-IV* symptoms of PTSD, additional PTSD symptoms as manifested in children, and associated symptoms (anxiety, sadness, omen formation, survivor guilt, guilt/self-blame, fantasy denial, self-destructive behavior, dissociative responses, antisocial behavior, risk-taking behavior, and changed eating habits). Each symptom is assessed by two or more questions. The report allows diagnoses to be made, and it allows an overall severity score to be computed.

Measure Content Survey, Procedure, or Process
79 questions about the child's symptomatology. Most questions are in Likert form, but some use Yes/No format. Room is provided for explanation of some questions, to allow decisions to be made about answers by the scorer.

Theoretical Orientation Summary

Time Estimate

Administration	Scoring
30–45 minutes	10–20 minutes

Equipment Needed

Paper & Pencil	Computer	Basic Psychophysiological	Specialized Equipment
X			

Psychometric Maturity

Under Construction	Basic Properties Intact	Mature
X		

Psychometric Properties Summary
Yet to be established (but see the review of a related self-report measure, The When Bad Things Happen scale elsewhere in this publication).

Particular Sensitivity

Age	Change over Time	Culture / Ethnicity	Gender	Geography / Climate	Sexual Orientation	Socioeconomic Status	Urban / Rural
X	?	?	?	?	?	?	?

Estimate of Number of In-Process Studies

Four. One of these is a national effort to gather data for validation for the interview and other related interviews and scales. If you are interested in joining this effort, please contact Ken Fletcher at the addresses and telephones below.

Unpublished References

Unknown

Published References

None

General Comments

This scale is intended for both clinical and research use. The intent is to eventually pare down the items during the norming process. The report can be administered to parents or guardians of nontraumatized comparison groups as well, as long as a stressor is provided (either the same stressor as the exposed group or the most stressful event that the nontraumatized child has been exposed to). This scale is one of a set. See also "Childhood PTSD Interview," "Childhood PTSD Interview—Parent Form," and the "The When Bad Things Happen Scale." IBM-compatible data entry programs are available from the author for all of these scales. The data entry programs run in EPI INFO, a data entry creation program distributed (for free from other users or academic computer departments or for $50 from the Center for Disease Control or the World Health Organization). EPI INFO programs allow data bases to be created which can be analyzed on a basic level within EPI INFO itself and by other statistical programs (such as SPSS, SAS, and Systat) or by databases and spreadsheets that will read dBase file formats.

Key Words

Population	Stressor	Topic
adult (parents)	any	assessment diagnosis general treatment measure development research

Reference Citation for This Review

Fletcher, K. E. (1996). Psychometric review of the Parent Report of the Child's Reaction to Stress. In B. H. Stamm (Ed.). *Measurement of stress, trauma, and adaptation.* Lutherville, MD: Sidran Press.

Measure Contact Name

Kenneth E. Fletcher, Ph.D.

Address: University of Massachusetts Medical Center
Psychiatry Dept.
55 Lake Avenue North
Worcester, MA 01655-0001 USA

Phone: 508.856.3329

Fax: 508.856.6426

E-mail: fletcher@umassmed.ummed.edu

Parent Report of the Child's Reaction To Stress Sample Items

- How much did what happened scare your child? (Answered on a 5-point Likert, from "Not at all" to "Completely," or "Don't know.")
- Does your child seem to have a hard time putting the event or events out of his or her mind? (Answered "Yes" or "No" or "Don't know.")
- How often do reminders of the stressful event(s) seem to upset your child? (Answered on a 6-point Likert, from "Never" to "Always," or "Don't know.")
- Does your child seem to have lost interest in activities that he or she used to enjoy before the stressful event(s) occurred? (Answered "No" or "Yes" or "Don't know.")
- Compared to before the stressful event(s), how easy is it for your child to get to sleep at night?
- Compared to before the stressful event(s), how fearful in general does you child seem to feel these days? (Answered on a 5-point Likert, from "Much Less" to "Much More," or "Don't know.")
- Compared to before the stressful event(s), how much does your child eat now? (Answered on a 5-point Likert, from "Much Less" to "Much More," or "Don't know.")

Parent Report of Post-Traumatic Symptoms (PROPS) 1.0

Type of Population
Children, Adolescents

Cost

Copyright
Ricky Greenwald

Languages
English

What It Measures
The Parent Report of Post-Traumatic Symptoms (PROPS) measures a range of children's (to age 14) post-traumatic symptomatology as endorsed by the child's parent. It is more oriented towards responses to Type I (vs. chronic) trauma, and focuses on state rather than trait items. An identified trauma is not required. The PROPS is intended as a screening instrument for possible post-traumatic disturbance, and as a repeated measure to track recovery from post-traumatic reactions.

Measure Content Survey, Procedure, or Process
The PROPS 1.0 is a paper and pencil instrument which consists of 28 items representing post-traumatic symptomatology. The parent marks "0" (not true), "1" (somewhat true), or "2" (very true) to indicate how much each item reflected his/her child's behavior in the past week. A higher level of endorsement indicates greater symptomatology. The TRICQ requires a third-grade reading level (or assistance), and may also be administered orally, in person or by telephone. Administration time: 5 minutes. There is no scoring system yet, and some items may be eliminated or weighted following validation studies.

Theoretical Orientation Summary
The PROPS was formulated using the broad definition of child trauma advocated by Terr (1991), with more attention to clinical impact than to diagnostic boundaries. Some items which reflected DSM criteria for PTSD were taken from the Child Behavior Check List (Achenbach & Edelbrock, 1983), following Wolfe, et al.'s (1989) use of the 20 item PTSD subscale. This was modified and expanded to reflect *DSM-IV* revisions, as well as Fletcher's (1993) meta-analysis of the empirical literature on children's post-traumatic symptoms.

Time Estimate

Administration	Scoring
5 minutes	5 minutes

Equipment Needed

Paper & Pencil	Computer	Basic Psychophysiological	Specialized Equipment
X			

Psychometric Maturity

Under Construction	Basic Properties Intact	Mature
X		

Psychometric Properties Summary

A related measure has been validated for use with sexual abuse victims (Wolfe, et al., 1989).

Particular Sensitivity

Age	Change over Time	Culture / Ethnicity	Gender	Geography / Climate	Sexual Orientation	Socioeconomic Status	Urban / Rural
X	?	?	?	?	?	?	?

Estimate of Number of In-Process Studies

2

Unpublished References

Achenbach, T. M., & Edelbrock, C. S. (1983). Manual for the Child Behavior Checklist and Revised Child Behavior Profile. Unpublished manuscript.

Fletcher, K. E. (October 1993). The spectrum of post-traumatic responses in children. Poster session presented at the meeting of the International Society for Traumatic Stress Studies. San Antonio, TX.

Published References

Terr, L. (1991). Childhood traumas: An outline and overview. *American Journal of Psychiatry, 148,* 10–20.

Wolfe, V., Gentile, C., & Wolfe, D. A. (1989). The impact of sexual abuse on children: A PTSD formulation. *Behavior Therapy, 20,* 215–228.

General Comments

Access to your raw data and research results would be appreciated for use in validation. Intended for use with a companion measure such as the Trauma Reaction Indicators Child Questionnaire (Greenwald, 1995), for a more comprehensive estimate of symptomatology.

Key Words

Population	Stressor	Topic
parents	any	diagnosis individual treatment measure development

Reference Citation for This Review

Greenwald, R. (1996). Psychometric review of Parent Report of Post-Traumatic Symptoms. In B. H. Stamm (Ed.). *Measurement of stress, trauma, and adaptation.* Lutherville, MD: Sidran Press.

Measure Contact Name

Ricky Greenwald, Psy.D.

Address: P.O. Box 575
               Trumansburg, NY 14886 USA

Phone: 607.387.9060

Fax:

E-mail:

Sample of Parent Report of Post-Traumatic Symptoms

Mark how well each item describes your child *in the past week*. Circle *the 2* if the item is *very true* or *often true* of the child. Circle the *1* if the item is *somewhat* or *sometimes true* of the child. If the item is *not true* of the child, circle the *0*. Don't skip any, even if you're not sure.

	not true	somewhat true sometimes true	very true often true
1. Difficulty concentrating	0	1	2
2. Mood swings	0	1	2
3. Thinks of bad memories	0	1	2
4 Spaces out	0	1	2

Penn Inventory for Post Traumatic Stress Disorder

Type of Population
Persons who have been exposed to one or more traumatic stressors.

Cost
$35.00 is requested as a one-time fee for multiple uses.

Copyright

Languages
English

What It Measures
The Penn Inventory is a global measure of the severity of Posttraumatic Stress Disorder based on 26 items related to *DSM-III* criteria. The summary severity score ranges from zero to 78 as an interval measure of intensity or severity of PTSD, given the determination of a traumatic stressor.

Measure Content Survey, Procedure, or Process
The 26 items are sets of sentences scaled from 0 to 3. These sets of sentences range across the symptom clusters that comprise the *DSM-III* symptom criteria, and allow the respondent to refer these sentences to themselves.

Theoretical Orientation Summary
Generally, the instrument reflects a cognitive-behavioral orientation that requires self-assessment of current behavior and current stream of thought and feeling, with reference to the past week.

Time Estimate

Administration	Scoring
5–15 minutes	5–10 minutes

Equipment Needed

Paper & Pencil	Computer	Basic Psychophysiological	Specialized Equipment
X			

Psychometric Maturity

Under Construction	Basic Properties Intact	Mature
	X	

Psychometric Properties Summary
Norms for different groups diagnosed with PTSD were established, with mean scores ranging from 48.8 to 55.2 (SD 7.6 to 12.3). A sample from a general psychiatric (non-psychotic) population had mean scores of 28.2 (SD=14.2), and samples from non-PTSD groups had means in range of 15.3 to 15.5 (SD=8.9). A cut-off score of 35 or above was used for estimates of diagnostic accuracy, with an overall "hit rate" of 93%, based on a prevalence rate of 68% in tested samples.

Particular Sensitivity

Age	Change over Time	Culture / Ethnicity	Gender	Geography / Climate	Sexual Orientation	Socioeconomic Status	Urban / Rural
?	?	?	?	?	?	?	?

Estimate of Number of In-Process Studies

Unknown

Unpublished References

Unknown

Published References

Hammarberg, M. (1992). Penn Inventory for Posttraumatic Stress Disorder: Psychometric properties. *Psychological Assessment: A Journal of Consulting and Clinical Psychology, 4* (1), 67–76.

Hammarberg, M., & Silver, S. (1994). Outcome of treatment for Posttraumatic Stress Disorder in a primary care unit serving Vietnam veterans. *Journal of Traumatic Stress, 7* (2), 1–22.

General Comments

Key Words

Population	Stressor	Topic
adult research	any	diagnosis

Reference Citation for This Review

Hammarberg, M. (1996). Psychometric review of The Penn Inventory for Post Traumatic Stress Disorder. In B. H. Stamm (Ed.). *Measurement of stress, trauma, and adaptation.* Lutherville, MD: Sidran Press.

Measure Contact Name

Dr. Melvyn Hammarberg

Address: Department of Anthropology
             325 Museum
             University of Pennsylvania
             Philadelphia, PA 19104-6398 USA

Phone: 215.898.0981

Fax: 610.896.5646

E-mail: mhammar@ccat.sas.upenn.edu

PENN INVENTORY

Name_____ Date_____

On this questionaire are groups of statements. Please read each group of statements carefully. Then pick out the one statement in each group which best describes the way you have been feeling during the **PAST WEEK, INCLUDING TODAY!** Circle the number beside the statement you picked. *Be sure to read all the statements in each group before making your choice.*

1 0 I don't feel much different than most other people my age.
   1 I feel somewhat different than most other people my age.
   2 I feel so different than most other people my age that I choose pretty carefully who I'll be with and when.
   3 I feel so totally alien to most other people my age that I stay away from all of them at all costs.

2 0 I care as much about the consequences of what I'm doing as most other people.
   1 I care less about the consequences of what I'm doing than most other people.
   2 I care much less about the consequences of what I'm doing than most other people.
   3 Often I think, "Let the consequences be damned!" because I don't care about them at all.

3 0 When I want to do something for enjoyment I can find someone to join me if I want to.
   1 I'm able to do something for enjoyment even when I can't find someone to join me.
   2 I lose interest in doing things for enjoyment when there's no one to join me.
   3 I have no interest in doing anything for enjoyment at all.

4 0 I rarely feel jumpy or uptight.
   1 I sometimes feel jumpy and uptight.
   2 I often feel jumpy or uptight.
   3 I feel jumpy or uptight all the time.

5 0 I know someone nearby who really understands me.
   1 I'm not concerned whether anyone nearby really understands me.
   2 I'm worried because no one nearby really understand me.
   3 I'm very worried because no one nearby understands me at all.

6 0 I'm not afraid to show my anger because it's no worse or better than anyone else's.
   1 I'm sometimes afraid to show my anger because it goes up quicker than other people's.
   2 I'm often afraid to show my anger because it might turn to violence.
   3 I'm so afraid of becoming violent that I never allow myself to show any anger at all.

7 0 I don't have any past traumas to feel overly anxious about.
   1 When something reminds me of my past traumas I feel anxious but can tolerate it.
   2 When something reminds me of my past traumas I feel very anxious and must really make an effort to tolerate it.
   3 When something reminds me of my past traumas I feel so anxious I can hardly stand it and have no ways to tolerate it.

8 0 I have not re-experienced a flashback to a trauma event "as if I were there again."
   1 I have re-experienced a flashback to a trauma event "as if I were there again" for a few minutes or less.
   2 My re-experiencing of a flashback to a trauma event sometimes lasts the better part of an hour.
   3 My re-experiencing of a flashback to a trauma event often lasts for an hour or more.

9 0 I am less easily distracted than ever.
   1 I am as easily distracted as ever.
   2 I am more easily distracted than ever.
   3 I feel distracted all the time.

10 0 My spiritual life provides more meaning than it used to.
   1 My spiritual life provides about as much meaning as it used to.
   2 My spiritual life provides less meaning than it used to.
   3 I don't care about my spiritual life.

11 0   I can concentrate better than ever.

       1   I can concentrate about as well as ever.

       2   I can't concentrate as well as I used to.

       3   I can't concentrate at all.

12 0   I've told a friend or family member about the important parts of my most traumatic experiences.

       1   I've had to be careful in choosing the parts of my traumatic experiences to tell friends or family members.

       2   Some parts of my traumatic experiences are so hard to understand that I've said almost nothing about them to anyone.

       3   No one could possibly understand the traumatic experiences I've had to live with.

13 0   I generally don't have nightmares.

       1   My nightmares are less troubling than they were.

       2   My nightmares are just as troubling as they were.

       3   My nightmares are more troubling than they were.

14 0   I don't feel confused about my life.

       1   I feel less confused about my life than I used to.

       2   I feel just as confused about my life as I used to.

       3   I feel more confused about my life than I used to.

15 0   I know myself better than I used to.

       1   I know myself about as well as I used to.

       2   I don't know myself as well as I used to.

       3   I feel like I don't know who I am at all.

16 0   I know more ways to control or reduce my anger than most people.

       1   I know about as many ways to control or reduce my anger as most people.

       2   I know fewer ways to control or reduce my anger than most people.

       3   I know of no ways to control or reduce my anger.

17 0   I have not experienced a major trauma in my life.

       1   I have experienced one or more traumas of limited intensity.

       2   I have experienced very intense and upsetting traumas.

       3   The traumas I have experienced were so intense that memories of them intrude on my mind without warning.

18 0   I've been able to shape things toward attaining many of my goals.

       1   I've been able to shape things toward attaining some of my goals.

       2   My goals aren't clear.

       3   I don't know how to shape things toward my goals.

19 0   I am able to focus my mind and concentrate on the task at hand regardless of unwanted thoughts.

       1   When unwanted thoughts intrude on my mind I'm able to recognize them briefly and then refocus my mind on the task at hand.

       2   I'm having a hard time coping with unwanted thoughts and don't know how to refocus my mind on the task at hand.

       3   I'll never be able to cope with unwanted thoughts.

20 0   I am achieving most of the things I want.

       1   I am achieving many of the things I want.

       2   I am achieving some of the things I want.

       3   I am achieving few of the things I want.

21 0   I sleep as well as usual.

       1   I don't sleep as well as usual.

       2   I wake up more frequently or earlier than usual and have difficulty getting back to sleep.

       3   I often have nightmares or wake up several hours earlier than usual and cannot get back to sleep.

22 0   I don't have trouble remembering things I should know.

       1   I have less trouble than I used to remembering things I should know.

       2   I have about the same trouble as I used to remembering things I should know.

       3   I have more trouble than I used to remembering things I should know.

23 0 My goals are clearer than they were.
   1 My goals are as clear as they were.
   2 My goals are not as clear as they were.
   3 I don't know what my goals are.
24 0 I'm usually able to let bad memories fade from my mind.
   1 Sometimes a bad memory comes back to me, but I can modify it, replace it, or set it aside.
   2 When bad memories intrude on my mind I can't seem to get them out.
   3 I worry that I'm going crazy because bad memories keep intruding on my mind.
25 0 Usually I feel understood by others.
   1 Sometimes I don't feel understood by others.
   2 Most of the time I don't feel understood by others.
   3 No one understands me at all.
26 0 I have not lost anything or anyone dear to me.
   1 I have grieved for those I've lost and can now go on.
   2 I haven't finished grieving for those I've lost.
   3 The pain of my loss is so great that I can't grieve and don't know how to get started.

Peritraumatic Dissociative Experiences Scale
Self-Report and Rater Versions

Type of Population

All but children

Cost

Free

Copyright

Languages

English

What It Measures

Dissociative experiences at time of trauma

Measure Content Survey, Procedure, or Process

Derealization, depersonalization and other dissociative content.

Theoretical Orientation Summary

None

Time Estimate

Administration	Scoring
5–15 minutes	5–10 minutes

Equipment Needed

Paper & Pencil	Computer	Basic Psychophysiological	Specialized Equipment
X			

Psychometric Maturity

Under Construction	Basic Properties Intact	Mature
	X	

Psychometric Properties Summary

In NVVRS CEC theater veterans coefficient alpha =.80. One factor emerged in factor analysis. Validity data in press.

Particular Sensitivity

Age	Change over Time	Culture / Ethnicity	Gender	Geography / Climate	Sexual Orientation	Socioeconomic Status	Urban / Rural
?	?	?	?	?	?	?	?

Estimate of Number of In-Process Studies
Unknown

Unpublished References
Marmar, C. R., Weiss, D. S., Schlenger, W. E., Fairbank, J. A., Jordan, B. K., Kulka, R. T., & Hough, R. L. (under review). *American Journal of Psychiatry*.

Published References
None

General Comments

Key Words

Population	Stressor	Topic
adults adolescents dissociation research	any	assessment

Reference Citation for This Review
Marmar, C. R., & Weiss, D. S. (1996). Psychometric review of Peritraumatic Dissociative Experience Scale Self-Report and Rater Version. In B. H. Stamm (Ed.). *Measurement of stress, trauma, and adaptation.* Lutherville, MD: Sidran Press.

Measure Contact Name
Charles R. Marmar or Daniel S. Weiss

Address: Box F 0984
               Department of Psychiatry UCSF
               San Francisco, CA 94143-0984 USA
Phone: 415.476.7557
Fax: 415.502.7296
E-mail:

PK Scale of the MMPI and MMPI-2
Embedded and Stand Alone Versions

Type of Population

Primarily combat-related PTSD, possible applications for non-combat PTSD.

Cost

Need to purchase MMPI or MMPI-2.

Copyright

Languages

English

What It Measures

Continuous measure of PTSD symptomatology, with cutoff scores predictive of PTSD diagnosis.

Measure Content Survey, Procedure, or Process

In the MMPI the PK scale consists of 49 items, including 3 duplicate items, that were found to discriminate combat veterans with and without PTSD. In the MMPI-2 the duplicate items were dropped and three items were reworded slightly (most notably the MMPI item "I am a good mixer" was changed in the MMPI-2 to "I am a very sociable person"). Research has been conducted on the PK scale scored either from the MMPI or MMPI-2 (embedded version) or from the items administered as a separate questionnaire (stand alone version).

Theoretical Orientation Summary

Empirical, psychometric approach

Time Estimate

Administration	Scoring
5–15 minutes for stand-alone	5–10 minutes for stand-alone

Equipment Needed

Paper & Pencil	Computer	Basic Psychophysiological	Specialized Equipment
X			

Psychometric Maturity

Under Construction	Basic Properties Intact	Mature
		X

Psychometric Properties Summary

Several studies examining the psychometric properties of the PK scale are listed below. In a recent study (Herman et al., 1993) 60 subjects, on three separate occasions 2 to 3 days apart, completed the full MMPI-2 and twice completed the stand-alone version of the PK scale. Test-retest reliability for the two administrations of the stand-alone version was .94. An additional 63 subjects completed the full MMPI-2 and one stand-alone version of the PK scale. For the total sample of 123 subject the correlation between the PK scale scored from the full MMPI-2 and the stand-alone version was .90. The internal consistency was .95 for the embedded version and .96 for the stand alone version. Both versions were strongly correlated with other measures of PTSD, including the Mississippi Scale, the Impact of Events scale, the PTSD Checklist, and the CAPS. For the prediction of a PTSD diagnosis based on the SCID, the optimal cutoff for the embedded version was 23, yielding a sensitivity of .79, a specificity of .71, an efficiency of .76, and a kappa of .50. The optimal cutoff for the stand-alone version was 24, with a sensitivity of .82, a specificity of .76, an efficiency of .80, and a kappa of .59.

Particular Sensitivity

Age	Change over Time	Culture / Ethnicity	Gender	Geography / Climate	Sexual Orientation	Socioeconomic Status	Urban / Rural
?	?	?	?	?	?	?	?

Estimate of Number of In-Process Studies
Unknown

Unpublished References
Herman, D. S., Weathers, F. W., Litz, B. T., Joaquim, S. G., & Keane, T. M. (1993). The PK scale of the MMPI-2: Reliability and validity of the embedded and stand-alone versions. Paper presented at the Annual meeting of The International Society for Traumatic Stress Studies. San Antonio, TX.

Published References
Unknown

General Comments

Key Words

Population	Stressor	Topic
adult veterans diagnosis general treatment research	any	assessment

Reference Citation for This Review
Weathers, F. W. (1996). Psychometric review of PK Scale of the MMPI and MMPI-2 Embedded and Stand Alone Versions. In B. H. Stamm (Ed.). *Measurement of stress, trauma, and adaptation.* Lutherville, MD: Sidran Press.

Measure Contact Name
Frank W. Weathers, Ph.D.

Address:	National Center for PTSD (116B-2)
	150 S. Huntington Avenue
	Boston, MA 02130 USA
Phone:	617.232.9500 x4130/4136
Fax:	617.278.4501
E-mail:	Weathers.Frank_W@Boston.VA.Gov

Potential Stressful Events Interview (PSEI)

National Center for PTSD Review

Type of Population

Adults

Cost

Copyright

Contact Heidi Resnick, Ph.D. Crime Victims Research and Treatment Center.

Languages

English

What It Measures

Retrospective recall of lifetime trauma exposure, high and low magnitude.

Measure Content Survey, Procedure, or Process

Structured interview which assesses retrospectively recalled low- and high-magnitude stressor occurrence and impact. Scores for Rape, Sexual assault, Physical assault, Homicide of family/close friend, Crime victimization, Non-crime trauma, Nontraumatic stressor, Perceived threat, Actual injury.

Theoretical Orientation Summary

Empirical model of traumatic stress.

Time Estimate

Administration	Scoring
90–120 minutes	15–20 minutes

Equipment Needed

Paper & Pencil	Computer	Basic Psychophysiological	Specialized Equipment
X			

Psychometric Maturity

Under Construction	Basic Properties Intact	Mature
	X	

Psychometric Properties Summary

Reliability Unknown. Validity, Predictive (Sexual, Physical assault, Homicide, or Crime victimization increase risk of PTSD diagnosis 2–3x current and lifetime; Perceived threat and Actual injury predict current and lifetime PTSD diagnosis).

Normative Data. *DSM-IV* field trial of community and psychiatric adult populations.

Particular Sensitivity

Age	Change over Time	Culture/ Ethnicity	Gender	Geography/ Climate	Sexual Orientation	Socioeconomic Status	Urban/ Rural
?	?	?	X	?	?	?	?

Estimate of Number of In-Process Studies

unknown

Unpublished References

unknown

Published References

Falsetti, S., Resnick, H., Kilpatrick, D., & Freedy, J. (1994). A review of the "Potential Stressful Events Interview." *Behavior Therapist, 17* (3), 66–67.

Resnick, H., Kilpatrick, D., Dansky, B., Saunders, B., & Best, C. (1993). Prevalence of civilian trauma and post-traumatic stress disorder in a representative national sample of women. *Journal of Consulting and Clinical Psychology, 61*, 984–991.

Resnick, H., Falsetti, S., Kilpatrick, D., & Freedy, J. (in press). Assessment of rape and other civilian trauma-related Post-Traumatic Stress Disorder. In T. W. Miller (Ed.). *Stressful life events.* New York: International Universities Press.

General Comments

The PSEI was used to assess traumatic stress in the *DSM-IV* Field Trial. A Trauma Assessment for Adults (TAA) has been developed as a briefer (20–30 minutes) structured interview to assess lifetime trauma (high magnitude stressor) exposure and resultant fear of death or severe injury and actual occurrence of physical injury.

Key Words

Population	Stressor	Topic
adults women	domestic violence physical abuse sexual assault/abuse	assessment diagnosis research

Reference Citation for This Review

Ford, J. (1996). Psychometric review of Potential Stressful Events Interview (PSEI). In B. H. Stamm (Ed). *Measurement of stress, trauma, and adaptation.* Lutherville, MD: Sidran Press.

Reviewer Contact Name

Julian Ford, Ph.D.

National Center for PTSD (116-D)
VA Medical Center
White River Junction, VT 05009 USA

Phone: 802.296.5132
Fax: 802.296.5135
E-mail: Julian.Ford@Dartmouth.Edu

Measure Contact Name

Heidi Resnick, Ph.D.

Address: Medical University of South Carolina
Crime Victims Research and Treatment Center
171 Ashley Ave
Charleston, SC 29425-0742 USA

Phone: 803.792.2945
Fax: 803.792.3388
E-mail:

Problem Rating Scale (PRS)

Type of Population

Children, Adolescents, Adults

Cost

Copyright

Ricky Greenwald

Languages

English

What It Measures

The Problem Rating Scale (PRS) quantifies the subject's (or parent's) assessment of the magnitude of the primary presenting complaints. Used as a repeated measure, it can be a simple and meaningful way of tracking emotional or behavioral disturbances in trauma victims over time.

Measure Content Survey, Procedure, or Process

The subject (or parent) is asked to describe the presenting complaints in some detail, as might be done in the context of a therapy intake interview. The complaints are then organized and labeled by the interviewer (e.g., nightmares, fears, short temper), and the subject (or parent) is asked to rate the magnitude of the three primary complaints in the past week. A 0 to 10 scale is used, with 0 representing none of the problem, to 10 representing the maximum possible. When a traumatic memory has been identified as the source of the problems, the PRS can be used on a recall basis (for the pre-trauma week) for an estimate of baseline or prior functioning. Can be done in person or by telephone.

Theoretical Orientation Summary

The PRS was developed according to the following premises: (1) people experience a variety of post-traumatic reactions which may or may not meet *DSM* criteria, despite the distress value of the symptoms; (2) the self-rated magnitude of presenting complaints represents part of the process by which people choose to access treatment; and (3) in many research contexts, it is advantageous to use simple, quick measures with face validity that can be easily integrated with the clinical interview.

Time Estimate

Administration	Scoring
5–10 minutes	5 minutes

Equipment Needed

Paper & Pencil	Computer	Basic Psychophysiological	Specialized Equipment
X			

Psychometric Maturity

Under Construction	Basic Properties Intact	Mature
X		

Psychometric Properties Summary

Greenwald (1994) found that the PRS scores were closely correlated with children's Subjective Units of Disturbance Scale (SUDS) ratings of their memories of a traumatic event; when the high SUDS scores were eliminated following treatment, the PRS scores also fell precipitously, to premorbid levels. Formal validation has not yet been completed. However, the PRS is fairly similar to the widely used SUDS (Wolpe, 1982) and to the Goal Attainment Scale (Kirusek & Sherman, 1968; reviewed by Emmerson & Neely, 1988), both of which have documented reliability and validity.

Particular Sensitivity

Age	Change over Time	Culture / Ethnicity	Gender	Geography / Climate	Sexual Orientation	Socioeconomic Status	Urban / Rural
X	X	?	?	?	?	?	?

Estimate of Number of In-Process Studies

2

Unpublished References

Unknown

Published References

Emmerson, G. J., & Neely, M. A. (1988). Two adaptable, valid, and reliable data-collection measures: Goal attainment scaling and the semantic differential. *Counseling Psychologist, 16,* 261–271.

Greenwald, R. (1994). Applying eye movement desensitization and reprocessing (EMDR) to the treatment of traumatized children: Five case studies. *Anxiety Disorders Practice Journal, 1,* 83–97.

Kiresuk, T. J., & Sherman, R. E. (1968). Goal attainment scaling: A general method for evaluating comprehensive community mental health programs. *Community Mental Health Journal, 4,* 443–453.

Wolpe, J. (1982). *The practice of behavior therapy.* New York: Pergamon.

General Comments

If more information is desired, detailed instructions are available from the author. Access to your raw data and research results would be appreciated for use in validation. It is my hope that the PRS may help to bridge the clinician-researcher gap: it can be useful in communicating the relevance of research results and it is conducive to use by clinicians.

Key Words

Population	Stressor	Topic
adolescents children parents	any	diagnosis individual treatment measure development

Reference Citation for This Review

Greenwald, R. (1996). Psychometric review of Problem Rating Scale. In B. H. Stamm (Ed.). *Measurement of stress, trauma, and adaptation.* Lutherville, MD: Sidran Press.

Measure Contact Name

Ricky Greenwald, Psy.D.
Address: P.O. Box 575
             Trumansburg, NY 14886 USA
Phone: 607.387.9060
Fax:
E-mail:

Psychobiological Assessment of PTSD

Type of Population

To date primarily male veterans. Promising results exist for female sexual assault survivors, sexually/physically abused children and vehicle accident survivors.

Cost

Variable, depending on routine capacity of the hospital's clinical laboratory.

Copyright

Languages

English

What It Measures

See tables

Measure Content Survey, Procedure, or Process

Psychological Reactivity, Dexamethasome Suppression Test (DST), Startle Response, Urinary Neurohormone Profiles, Thyroid Function Tests, Stress-induced Analgesia.

Theoretical Orientation Summary

Each test is based on a laboratory abnormality found in PTSD patients. The theoretical basis for each test (a) support stimulus-response conditioning models of PTSD and (b) suggest that basic neurobiological systems activated during traumatic exposure function abnormally in PTSD patients.

Time Estimate

Administration	Scoring
varies	varies

Equipment Needed

Paper & Pencil	Computer	Basic Psychophysiological	Specialized Equipment
		X	X

Psychometric Maturity

Under Construction	Basic Properties Intact	Mature
	varies	

Psychometric Properties Summary

1. Psychophysiological reactivity: specify 61–88%, sensitivity 100%.
2. DST supersuppression: preliminary results suggest that this may have excellent specificity and sensitivity.

Particular Sensitivity

Age	Change over Time	Culture/ Ethnicity	Gender	Geography/ Climate	Sexual Orientation	Socioeconomic Status	Urban/ Rural
?	X	X	X	X	X	X	X

Estimate of Number of In-Process Studies

Several

Unpublished References

Unknown

Published References

Bremner, J. D., et. al. (1993). Neurobiology of Posttraumatic Stress Disorder. In J. M. Oldham, M. B. Riba, & A. Tagman (Eds.). *Review of psychiatry*, vol. 12. Washington, D.C.: American Psychiatric Press, Inc.

Friedman, M. J., & Yehuda, R. (1995). PTSD and comorbidity: Psychobiological approaches to differential diagnosis. In M. J. Friedman, D. S. Charney, & A. Y. Deutch (Eds.). *Neurobiological and clinical consequences to stress: From normal adaptation to PTSD* (pp. 429–44). Philadelphia: Lippincott-Raven.

Pitman R. K., et al. (1987). Psychophysiologic assessment of posttraumatic stress disorder imagery in Vietnam combat veterans. *Archives of General Psychiatry*, *44*, 970–975.

Yehuda, R. et al. (1993). Enhanced suppression of cortisol following a low dose of dexamethasome in combat veterans with posttraumatic stress disorder. *American Journal of Psychiatry*, *150*, 83–96.

General Comments

This is an emerging field. Stay tuned.

Key Words

Population	Stressor	Topic
adults veterans men women	any	assessment neurobiology diagnosis psychophysiological research

Reference Citation for This Review

Friedman, M. J. (1996). Psychometric review of Psychbiological Assessment of PTSD. In B. H. Stamm (Ed.). *Measurement of stress, trauma, and adaptation*. Lutherville, MD: Sidran Press.

Measure Contact Name

Matthew J. Friedman M.D., Ph.D.

Address:	National Center for PTSD (116-D)
	VA Medical Center
	White River Junction, VT 05009 USA
Phone:	802.296.5132
Fax:	802.296.5135
E-mail:	Matthew.Friedman@Dartmouth.Edu

Figure 1

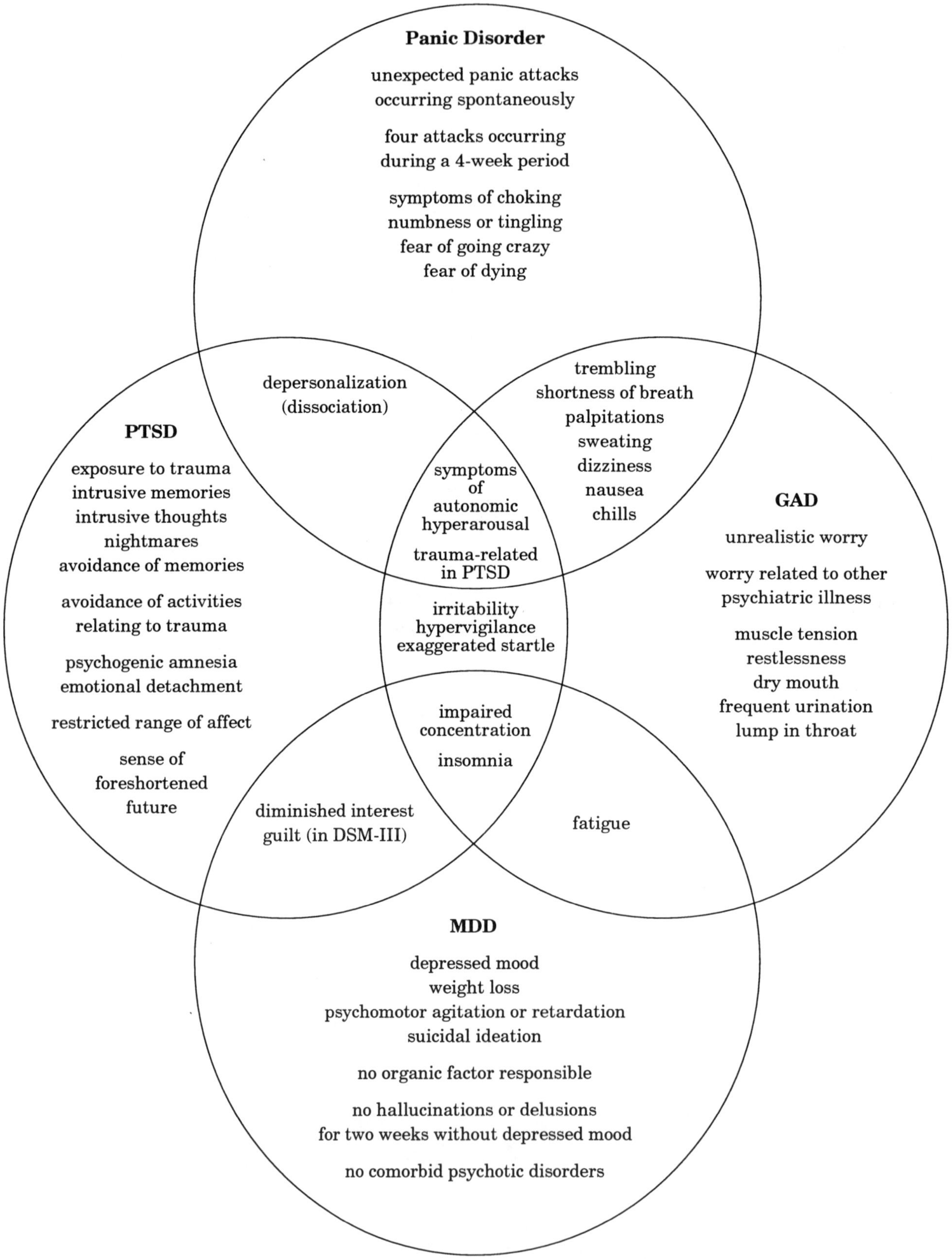

Panic Disorder

unexpected panic attacks
occurring spontaneously

four attacks occurring
during a 4-week period

symptoms of choking
numbness or tingling
fear of going crazy
fear of dying

depersonalization
(dissociation)

trembling
shortness of breath
palpitations
sweating
dizziness
nausea
chills

PTSD

exposure to trauma
intrusive memories
intrusive thoughts
nightmares
avoidance of memories

avoidance of activities
relating to trauma

psychogenic amnesia
emotional detachment

restricted range of affect

sense of
foreshortened
future

symptoms
of
autonomic
hyperarousal

trauma-related
in PTSD

irritability
hypervigilance
exaggerated startle

impaired
concentration

insomnia

GAD

unrealistic worry

worry related to other
psychiatric illness

muscle tension
restlessness
dry mouth
frequent urination
lump in throat

diminished interest
guilt (in DSM-III)

fatigue

MDD

depressed mood
weight loss
psychomotor agitation or retardation
suicidal ideation

no organic factor responsible

no hallucinations or delusions
for two weeks without depressed mood

no comorbid psychotic disorders

Table 1 *Criteria for Clinical Usefulness of a Psychobiological Assessment Procedure*

1. The biological finding obtained through the testing procedure should be highly replicable within and across different laboratories. Furthermore, to have true clinical utility, the testing paradigm should be relatively easy to set up and the information obtained be subject to a relatively unambiguous interpretation by a trained professional.
2. The biological alteration should be reliably present in individuals with PTSD regardless of the type of trauma that has been sustained, and should be differentiable from normals.
3. The biological alteration should not be present in individuals who do not meet criteria for PTSD even though they may have been exposed to trauma.
4. The biological abnormality should be relatively specific to PTSD and as such, afford the opportunity of distinguishing PTSD from other diagnostic possibilities.
5. The biological finding, ideally, should be present in individuals with PTSD even if they meet the comorbid criteria for other psychiatric disorders.

Table 2 *Laboratory Abnormalities in PTSD*

Physiological assessment techniques:
    Psychophysiological Reactivity
    Startle Response
    EEG/Sleep Physiology
    Event-Related Brain Potentials
    Odor-induced EEG
Baseline Neurohormone levels:
    catecholamines
    cortisol
    testosterone
    thyroid
    ACTH
    endorphins
    urinary neurohormone profile

Baseline receptor levels:
    lymphocyte glucocorticoid
    Platelet alpha-2 adrenergic
    Lymphocyte beta adrenergic
*Challenge Tests:
    DST
    yohimbine
    stress-induced analgesia (with/without naloxone)
    clonidine (growth hormone)
    L-dopa (growth hormone)
    CRF (ACTH)
    TRH (TSH)
*Most physiological assessment approaches are also challenge tests.

Table 3 *Feasible Psychobiological Approaches to Differential Diagnosis*

Test	Feasibility Criteria				
	1	2	3	4	5
Psychophysiological Reactivity	X	X	X	?3	X
DST	X	?1,2	X	?3	X
Startle	X	X	U	?1,3	?4
Thyroid Function Tests	X	U	U	No	U
Yohimbine	X	?1,2	U	?1,2,3	X
Urinary Neurohormone Profile	X	?1,2	U	X	U

X Definitely meets criterion.
? Probably meets criteria but hasn't been adequately tested.
    ?1: only tested in one laboratory.
    ?2: only tested on Vietnam veterans.
    ?3: not adequately tested in other anxiety disorders.
    ?4: not adequately tested in PTSD patients with comorbid diagnosis.
U Unknown.
NoDoes not meet criterion.

Psychological (PSY) and Physical (PHY) Maltreatment Scales
National Center for PTSD Review

Type of Population

Adults

Cost

Available from author at no charge

Copyright

John Briere, M.D.

Languages

English

What It Measures

Assesses retrospectively perceived maltreatment by mother and father.

Measure Content Survey, Procedure, or Process

Questionnaire; 24 seven-point frequency of occurrence items which include physical maltreatment by mother, physical maltreatment by father, psychological maltreatment by mother, and psychological maltreatment by father. Sum items designated for each scale.

Theoretical Orientation Summary

Empirical approaches to family relations.

Time Estimate

Administration	Scoring
5–10 minutes	5–10 minutes

Equipment Needed

Paper & Pencil	Computer	Basic Psychophysiological	Specialized Equipment
X			

Psychometric Maturity

Under Construction	Basic Properties Intact	Mature
	X	

Psychometric Properties Summary

Reliability Internal Consistency: Cronbach's Alpha=.75–.87.

Validity Concurrent: PSYf predicts HSCL anxiety, depression, interpersonal sensitivity; and dissociation; PHYm predicts HSCL interpersonal sensitivity; dissociation; suicide attempts, in a sample of 252 female college students.

Normative Data: College students.

Particular Sensitivity

Age	Change over Time	Culture / Ethnicity	Gender	Geography / Climate	Sexual Orientation	Socioeconomic Status	Urban / Rural
?	?	?	?	?	?	?	?

Estimate of Number of In-Process Studies

unknown

Unpublished References

unknown

Published References

Briere, J., & Runtz, M. (1990). Differential adult symptomatology associated with three types of child abuse histories. *Child Abuse & Neglect, 14*, 357–364.

Briere, J., & Runtz, M. (1988). Multivariate correlates of childhood psychological and physical maltreatment among university women. *Child Abuse & Neglect, 12*, 333–341.

General Comments

Key Words

Population	Stressor	Topic
adult	childhood emotional abuse physical abuse	research

Reference Citation for This Review

Ford, J. (1996). Psychometric review of Psychological (PSY) and Physical (PHY) Maltreatment Scales. In B. H. Stamm (Ed). Measurement of stress, trauma and adaptation. Lutherville, MD: Sidran Press.

Reviewer Contact Name

Julian Ford, Ph.D.

National Center for PTSD (116-D)
VA Medical Center
White River Junction, VT 05009 USA

Phone: 802-296-5132
Fax: 802-296-5135
E-mail: Julian.Ford@Dartmouth.Edu

Measure Contact Name

John Briere, M.D.

Address: Dept. of Psychiatry
USC School of Medicine
1934 Hospital Place
Los Angeles, CA 90033 USA

Phone: 213.226.5697
Fax: 213.226.5550
E-mail: jbriere@hsc.usc.edu

PTSD Checklist (PCL-C, PCL-S, PCL-M, PCL-PR)

Type of Population

Veterans (PCL-M); Adult civilians (PCL-S, PCL-C); Parent Report on Child (PCL-PR)

Cost

Available from Author at no charge

Copyright

Languages

What It Measures

Post traumatic stress disorder symptomatology severity. PCL-S, PCL-C, and PCL-PR are keyed to any stressful life experience and the PCL-M is keyed to stressful military experiences.

Measure Content Survey, Procedure, or Process

17 items directly adapted from the *DSM-IV* PTSD Criteria B–D. Respondent is asked to rate on a 5-point scale (with anchors ranging from 1=Not at All to 5= Extremely) how much "you have been bothered by that problem IN THE PAST MONTH." All versions are identical except for: (a) target population specified (PCL-M="veterans"; PCL-C and PCL-S="people"; PCL-PR="children"), (b) type of stressor (PCL-M="stressful military experiences"; PCL-S=a specified "stressful life experience"; PCL-C and PCL-PR=any (unspecified) "stressful life experiences"). Separate scores for Criteria B, C, and D and Total PTSD severity.

Time Estimate

Administration	Scoring
5-7 minutes	5 minutes

Equipment Needed

Paper & Pencil	Computer	Basic Psychophysiological	Specialized Equipment
X			

Psychometric Maturity

Under Construction	Basic Properties Intact	Mature
All Versions for *DSM-IV*	PCL-M for *DSM-III-R*	

Psychometric Properties Summary

Reliability

The *DSM-III-R* PCL-M (with samples of Vietnam veterans and Persian Gulf veterans) showed Coefficient alpha .90–.93 for Criterion B symptoms, .89–.92 for Criterion C symptoms, .91–.92 for Criterion D symptoms, and .96–.97 for a total score. Item-Total Score correlations ranged from .52 to .80 for Persian Gulf veterans and .62 to .87 for Vietnam veterans). Test-retest reliability over a 2–3 day period was r=.96.

Data from a sample of child psychiatry outpatients on the *DSM-IV* PCL-PR showed Coefficient alpha .88 for Criterion B symptoms, .82 for Criterion C symptoms, .91 for Criterion D symptoms, and .88 for a total score. Item-Total Score correlations ranged from .47 to .79.

Convergent / Discriminant Validity

The *DSM-III-R* PCL-M with a sample of Vietnam veterans showed correlations of r=.93 with the Mississippi Scale, r=.90 with the Impact of Events Scale, and r=.77 with the MMPI PK scale. A lower but significant correlation (r=.46) with the Combat Exposure Scale suggested the PCL is related to combat exposure but less strongly (discriminant validity) than with direct measures of PTSD severity. For Persian Gulf veterans, a correlation of r=.85 with the Mississippi Scale (ODS Version) was observed. There is preliminary testing underway with the *DSM-IV* PCL-C, PCL-S, and PCL-M with veteran and civilian samples. There is also preliminary testing using the CBCL, RCMAS, and the CAPS-C underway on the *DSM-IV* PCL-PR.

Diagnostic Utility

The *DSM-III-R* PCL-M showed the following results: For Vietnam veterans, SCID PTSD diagnoses were predicted with optimal efficiency with a cutoff score of 50 (sensitivity of .82; specificity of .84; Kappa=.64). Mean PCL-M total scores were 63.6 (SD=14.1) for PTSD participants, 34.3 (SD=14.1) for participants not diagnosed with PTSD.

Preliminary testing is underway with the *DSM-IV* PCL-C, PCL-S, and PCL-M with the CAPS-L as criterion, while the *DSM-IV* PCL-PR is being tested with the CAPS-C.

Particular Sensitivity

Age	Change over Time	Culture / Ethnicity	Gender	Geography / Climate	Sexual Orientation	Socioeconomic Status	Urban / Rural
X	?	?	?	?	?	?	?

Estimated Number of In-Process Studies

Unpublished References

Weathers, F., Litz, B., Herman, D., Huska, J., & Keane, T. (October 1993). The PTSD Checklist (PCL): Reliability, Validity, and Diagnostic Utility. Paper presented at the Annual Convention of the International Society for Traumatic Stress Studies, San Antonio. (*DSM-III-R* PCL-M)

Published References

General Comments

Key Words

Population	Stressor	Topic
adults parents (PCL-PR)	any (PCL-S, PCL-PR) military (PCL-M)	diagnosis research

Reference Citation for This Review

Weathers, F., & Ford, J. (1996). Psychometric review of PTSD Checklist (PCL-C, PCL-S, PCL-M, PCL-PR). In B. H. Stamm (Ed.). *Measurement of stress, trauma, and adaptation*. Lutherville, MD: Sidran Press.

Measure Contact Names

PCL-M, PCL-C, PCL-S
Frank Weathers, Ph.D.
Address: National Center for PTSD, VAMC 116B-2
          150 South Huntington Ave
          Boston, MA 02130
Phone/Voice Mail: 617-232-4130
Fax: 616-278-4501
Email: Frank.Weathers@Boston.va.gov

PCL-PR

Julian Ford, Ph.D.

Address: National Center for PTSD, VAMC 116D
              White River Junction, VT 05009
Phone/Voice Mail: 802-296-5132
Fax: 802-296-5135
Email: Julian.Ford@Dartmouth.edu

PTSD Inventory

Type of Population
Adolescent, Adults, Elderly.

Cost
Free

Copyright
Zahava Solomon, Ph.D.

Languages
English, Hebrew

What It Measures
The PTSD Inventory aims to diagnose PTSD, based on the *DSM* criteria. In addition, it assesses both the intensity and the differential symptom profile of the syndrome.

Measure Content Survey, Procedure, or Process
The self-report scale consists of 17 statements corresponding to the 17 PTSD symptoms listed in the *DSM-IV*. Subjects are asked to indicate for each statement whether or not they suffered the symptom during the last month. In accordance with *DSM-IV*, the subject is diagnosed as having PTSD if he/she experienced a traumatic event, suffers from a significant distress or impairment in functioning, and if he/she endorsed 1 or more intrusive symptoms, 3 or more avoidance symptoms, and 2 or more arousal symptoms.

Theoretical Orientation Summary

Time Estimate

Administration	Scoring
5–10 minutes	5–10 minutes

Equipment Needed

Paper & Pencil	Computer	Basic Psychophysiological	Specialized Equipment
X			

Psychometric Maturity

Under Construction	Basic Properties Intact	Mature
	X	

Psychometric Properties Summary
The psychometric merits of the version based on the *DSM-III-R* have been well-proven. Internal consistency among the 17 items is high (Cronbach alpha=.86) and the scale as found to have high convergent validity when compared with diagnoses based on the Structured Clinical Interview for *DSM-III-R* (SCID).

Particular Sensitivity

Age	Change over Time	Culture/ Ethnicity	Gender	Geography/ Climate	Sexual Orientation	Socioeconomic Status	Urban/ Rural
X	?	X	?	?	?	?	?

Estimate of Number of In-Process Studies

Unknown

Unpublished References

Unknown

Published References

Schwarzwald, J., Weisenberg, M., Solomon, Z., & Waysman, M. (1994). Stress reactions of school-age children to the bombardment by Scud missiles: A 1-year follow-up. *Journal of Traumatic Stress, 7,* 657–667.

Solomon, Z., Benbenishty, R., Neria, Y., Abramowitz, M., Ginzburg, K., & Ohry, A. (1993). Assessment of PTSD: Validation of the Revised PTSD Inventory. *Israel Journal of Psychiatry and Related Sciences, 30,* 110–115.

Solomon, Z., Laor, N., Weiler, D., Muller, U. F., Hadar, O., Waysman, M., Koslosky, M., Ben Yaker, M., & Bleich, A. (1993). The psychological impact of the Gulf War: A study of acute stress in Israeli evacuees. *Archives of General Psychiatry, 50,* 320–321.

Solomon, Z., Neria, Y., Ohry, A., Waysman, M., & Ginzburg, K. (1994). PTSD among Israeli former prisoners of war and soldiers with combat stress reactions: A longitudinal study. *American Journal of Psychiatry, 151,* 554–559.

General Comments

Key Words

Population	Stressor	Topic
adolescents adults elderly	any	assessment diagnosis research

Reference Citation for This Review

Solomon, Z. (1996). Psychometric review of PTSD Inventory. In B. H. Stamm (Ed.). *Measurement of stress, trauma, and adaptation.* Lutherville, MD: Sidran Press.

Measure Contact Names

Zahava Solomon, Ph.D.

Address: Bob Shapell School of Social Work
             Tel Aviv University
             Ramat Aviv, Tel Aviv, 699 78 Israel
Phone: 972.9.506.906
Fax: 972.9.503.318
E-mail:

Purdue PTSD Scale

Type of Population

Survivors of a potentially traumatic incident, disaster, etc.

Cost

Free

Copyright

Don M. Hartsough, Ph.D.

Languages

English

What It Measures

The degree of endorsement (1–5 scale) of diagnostic criteria for PTSD on *DSM-III-R* and two general questions.

Measure Content Survey, Procedure, or Process

There are 15 items on the scale, 13 reflecting specific symptoms of PTSD as described in the criteria and 2 questions about levels of general distress. The respondent is asked about symptoms in the last seven days, including today.

Theoretical Orientation Summary

The scale reflects the same theoretical orientation as the list of criteria in *DSM-III-R*. Both describe PTSD in terms of the physiological, emotional, and cognitive reactions experienced following a stressor that would be considered potentially traumatic for most people. In a validation study of rescue workers, the average PTSD Scale score was 29.08. The Scale correlated .89 with judges ratings of post-traumatic stress based on interviews. Test-retest reliability has been demonstrated in several studies.

Time Estimate

Administration	Scoring
5–10 minutes	5–10 minutes

Equipment Needed

Paper & Pencil	Computer	Basic Psychophysiological	Specialized Equipment
X			

Psychometric Maturity

Under Construction	Basic Properties Intact	Mature
X		

Psychometric Properties Summary

(See above.) There are currently no norms for the Purdue PTSD Scale. The Scale has a consistent high correlation (high .70s to middle .80s) with the Brief Symptom Inventory and less high correlation with the Impact of Events Scale.

Particular Sensitivity

Age	Change over Time	Culture / Ethnicity	Gender	Geography / Climate	Sexual Orientation	Socioeconomic Status	Urban / Rural
?	?	?	?	?	?	?	?

Estimate of Number of In-Process Studies
Unknown

Unpublished References
Unknown

Published References
Unknown

General Comments
The Scale is easily biased, if the respondent so wishes. It is easily understood and read.

Key Words

Population	Stressor	Topic
adult	any	measure development research

Reference Citation for This Review
Hartsough, D. M. (1996). Psychometric review of Purdue PTSD Scale. In B. H. Stamm (Ed.). *Measurement of Stress, trauma, and adaptation*. Lutherville, MD: Sidran Press.

Measure Contact Name
Don M. Hartsough, Ph.D.

Address: White River Psychology, Inc.
             303 North Alabama Street, Suite 390
             Indianapolis, IN 46204 USA
Phone:.   317.684.7171
Fax:.   317.684.7172
E-mail:

Quality of Life Barometer

Type of Population
Combat Veterans

Cost
Minimal

Copyright

Languages
English

What It Measures
Eudaemonia (Aristotle)—A good life for a human being.

Measure Content Survey, Procedure, or Process
The scale consists of mostly subjective items about the experienced quality of life. Responses are clearly affected by mood. There are opportunities for limited open ended responses as well as the opportunity to dispute validity of items that make no sense to the subject. This instrument was developed in PTSD med-group.

Theoretical Orientation Summary
Survivors of severe trauma may achieve very satisfying, valuable, and meaningful lives while still being highly symptomatic and disabled from normal social and occupational lives. This instrument attempts to address the features associated with a satisfying and meaningful life even in the presence of trauma symptomatology.

Time Estimate

Administration	Scoring
45–60 minutes	varies

Equipment Needed

Paper & Pencil	Computer	Basic Psychophysiological	Specialized Equipment
X			

Psychometric Maturity

Under Construction	Basic Properties Intact	Mature
X		

Psychometric Properties Summary
Piloting was done only for quality of instructions and items. At this time there are no psychometric data available.

Particular Sensitivity

Age	Change over Time	Culture / Ethnicity	Gender	Geography / Climate	Sexual Orientation	Socioeconomic Status	Urban / Rural
?	?	?	?	?	?	?	?

Estimate of Number of In-Process Studies
Unknown

Unpublished References
Unknown.

Published References
No references for this instrument are available at this time and no cognate literature has been identified.

General Comments

Key Words

Population	Stressor	Topic
combat veterans research measure development	combat	general treatment

Reference Citation for This Review
Shay, J. (1996). Psychometric review of Quality of Life Barometer. In B. H. Stamm (Ed.). *Measurement of stress, trauma, and adaptation*. Lutherville, MD: Sidran Press.

Measure Contact Name
Jonathan Shay, M.D., Ph. D.

Address:	Boston VA OPC
	251 Causeway St.
	Boston, Ma. 2114 USA
Phone:	617.248.1076
Fax:	
Email:	Shay.Jonathan@Boston.VA.Gov

Quality of Life Barometer
Recording How Often Things Were Good and What Was Good

A good life for a combat Veteran is not simply the absence of suffering. To give you the best possible advice on medications, we need to know where you started and what has changed for you each month in the things that make life worth living. Some people have both great suffering and great satisfaction in the same period of their lives. We believe it is important to ask separately about both symptoms of injury (in the Combat Stress Barometer) and positive indicators of life quality (in this Quality of Life Barometer).

Just as there were items in the Combat Stress Barometer that were never a problem for you, there will be items in the Quality of Life Barometer that simply aren't part of your picture of what is good in life, or that you reject as something that you would even want for yourself.

There is no universally accepted picture of the good life for a human being. We are trying to find out how your life has been in the last month in terms that *make sense to you*.

Many items will be activities or experiences that you yourself feel make up a good life, if you have them. Please mark each item for how often you experienced this in the last month. If the item is something you think is good for your life, but you never had it in the last month, mark "N" for never.

Some items will be things you reject as part of your picture of a good life for a human being. Cross out each item that you reject. Do not reject an item that you think is good for your life, simply because you have not experienced it.

We are bound to have missed items that are really important to your picture of the good life. There are blank items on every page and at the end for you to fill in the important things we have missed. These items may be pleasures that you currently have that we have not mentioned, or they may be things that you see as part of a good life that you want to have but have not experienced in the last month. Don't write in anything that you don't actually want for yourself, just because you think you <u>should</u> want it.

A filled in example is on the next page.

		Never	1–2 Per Month	Weekly	1–2 Per Week	Daily or Almost Daily
	Example: Twice a week as a volunteer you help your wife with her job, which is at a day care center in the project. You really like being around your wife when she is with small children, because of what it brings out of her. When your own kids were this small you were too wired to enjoy it, working seven days three jobs, both to give them a good home and to keep so busy you didn't think about the 'Nam. You also like the big yell you get from the older kids in the day care when you come, and they race over and climb on you. Some of the single mothers who use the center have gone out of their way to tell you how important they think you are to their children.					
A.	Felt pleasure *when you saw that someone enjoyed your company*				X	
B.	Had pleasure from the *respect of others*				X	
D.	*Enjoyed someone's company*			X		
C.	Felt you were a *good adult figure to a child* in your life, whether the child is your own or not	X				
..	(Other items . . .)					

Be sure to put your name and the date at the top of each page.
Complete your Barometer for this month on the pages that follow

	name: date:	Never	1–2 Per Month	Weekly	1–2 Per Week	Daily or Almost Daily
1.	Felt pleasure *when you saw that someone enjoyed your company*					
2.	Respected your own *sense of justice*					
3.	Had balance, moderation, and good judgment in a relationship *with a close friend*					
4.	Respected the *value and truth in your own life story*					
5.	Felt *in control of your own mental functions*, such as attention, memory, thought					
6.	Met someone new *who really excited you*					
7.	Felt that a particular moment of time was *abundant enough* for you to live it well					
8.	Had balance, moderation and good judgment in a relationship *with a family member*					
9.	Felt *safe about making commitments* to other people					
10.	Enjoyed *something beautiful* and wanted to remember that moment					
11.	Allowed other people to *matter to you*, and allowed yourself to *matter to them*					
12.	Was able to take in and understand what another person said was *his or her way of seeing reality*, when it was different from your way					
13.	Had balance, moderation, and good judgment *in a love relationship*					
14.	Had a really *great time with friends*					
15.	Had confidence in your ability to *see and understand reality*					
16.	Felt *good in your body*					
17.	Felt like you really *belong at your job*, that this was your place among your people, and it felt right					

This instrument, by Jonathan Shay, may be reproduced without charge and freely distributed, as long as no funds are exchanged.

18.	Felt a sense of your *own value and dignity*					
19.	Felt *alive*					
20.	Experienced *peacefulness*, tranquility					
21.	Felt sufficiently strong and knowledgeable about the real dangers in the world to feel you *got around safely and with confidence*					
22.	Respected your *own fortitude and endurance of hardship*					
23.	Accurately judged the *real safety or danger* of the situations you encountered					
24.	Felt satisfaction in the something *you did, accomplished, or created*					
25.	*Freed yourself* from an idea, activity, or relationship that imprisoned or enslaved you					
26.	Felt like you really *belong in your religious community*, that this was your place among your people, and it felt right					
27.	*Found pleasure and enjoyment* without harming yourself or others					
28.	Felt *released from suffering*					
29.	Were able to *remember things* you wanted to recall, **and** could *put memories away* when you chose to					
30.	Enjoyed *giving someone a real good laugh*					
31.	Had balance, moderation and good judgment in a relationship *with a neighbor*					
32.	Gave **and** got *sexual pleasure*, if that was right in the relationship at the moment					
33.	*Enjoyed someone's company*					
34.	Felt that the *movements of your mind and body* were strong, supple, and good to watch					
35.	Had pleasure from the *respect of others*					
36.	Had balance, moderation and good judgment in a relationship *with a fellow worker*					

No.						
37.	Comfortably, with good humor, *refrained from sex*, if it was not right in the relationship					
38.	Your sense of rightness in the way you inhabited your body was *not threatened by minor health problems*					
39.	Felt *OK about the effects of age* on your body					
40.	*Embraced your fate as your own*					
41.	Enjoyed *something you read*					
42.	Had balance, moderation and good judgment in a relationship *with a stranger*					
43.	Felt you were carrying out *God's purpose for you* in the world					
44.	Felt *free to decide* how you were going to act to get closer to what you value **and** *free to choose not to destroy* what you value					
45.	Felt like you really *belong in your family*, that this was your place among your people, and it felt right					
46.	Experienced *ecstasy*					
47.	Used your personal resources effectively to *protect yourself from real dangers*					
48.	Fulfilled one of *your ideals for yourself*					
49.	Felt supported and loved by *your religious community*					
50.	Had the personal strength to *live a moment well*					
51.	Had balance, moderation, and good judgment in a relationship *with a fellow Veteran*					
52.	*Did not waste* personal resources protecting yourself from dangers that did not exist or going after things that gave no pleasure or satisfaction					
53.	Felt satisfaction *helping someone else*					
54.	Felt secure that you *have a safety net of self-respect* that even someone you respect and trust cannot destroy					
55.	Felt a wonderful *sense of power* running through you					

56.	Did not allow anyone to force *total responsibility* for his or her existence on you					
57.	Felt satisfaction at *help you were able to offer another person*, despite having no godlike power to do more					
58.	Felt *master of yourself*, of your passions and desires					
59.	Enjoyed something *you saw in a theater or on TV*					
60.	Felt like something that you did or made *really mattered and had meaning*					
61.	Had balance, moderation and good judgment in a relationship with a *family member*					
62.	Felt pleasure *in the enjoyment of others*					
63.	Felt *God's love*					
64.	Felt like you really belong *in your neighborhood*, that this was your place among your people, and it felt right					
65.	Respected the *dignity of your own suffering*					
66.	Earned a *really good living* for yourself and your family					
67.	Were aware of *what you want* for yourself and for people who matter to you					
68.	Felt satisfaction *in the accomplishments of others*					
69.	Made progress toward important life goals					
70.	Felt there was someone whom you really trusted and could rely on in your life					
71.	Felt *connected to other people*					
72.	Improved your standing compared to other people					
73.	Used *your personal resources effectively*, without waste, to bring you pleasure and enjoyment					
74.	Felt you were a really *good adult figure to a child* in your life, whether the child is your own or not					
75.	Enjoyed a *good laugh*					
76.	*Felt secure* that your value and dignity could not be touched by someone you didn't respect and trust					

77.	Respected your own efforts to see things *justly* done, even if you did not succeed in making it happen					
78.	Enjoyed your own mental activities, such as problem solving, imagining things, strategy in a game, planning a piece of work					

Retrospective Assessment of Traumatic Experiences (RATE)
National Center for PTSD Review

Type of Population

Adult psychiatric patients

Cost

Available from author at no charge

Copyright

Stephen W. Hurt, Ph.D.

Languages

English

What It Measures

Retrospectively recalled severity of childhood trauma

Measure Content Survey, Procedure, or Process

Structured interview to assess retrospectively recalled severity of childhood trauma. Scales for Loss, Physical abuse, Verbal abuse, and Sexual abuse with a 0–1 rating for occurrence, 0–4 rating for severity of trauma.

Theoretical Orientation Summary

Emprical model based on association of childhood trauma with personality disorders.

Time Estimate

Administration	Scoring
45-70 minutes	varies

Equipment Needed

Paper & Pencil	Computer	Basic Psychophysiological	Specialized Equipment
X			

Psychometric Maturity

Under Construction	Basic Properties Intact	Mature
	X	

Psychometric Properties Summary

Reliability Interrater (2 clinicians conducting interview) K=.84+ for occurrence of trauma, Intraclass r=.94+ for severity.

Normative Data available on 22 female psychiatric patients.

Particular Sensitivity

Age	Change over Time	Culture / Ethnicity	Gender	Geography / Climate	Sexual Orientation	Socioeconomic Status	Urban / Rural
?	?	?	X	?	?	?	?

Estimate of Number of In-Process Studies
Unknown

Unpublished References
Unknown

Published References
Gallagher, R., Flye, B., Hurt, S., Stone, M., & Hull, J. (1989). Retrospective assessment of traumatic experiences. *Journal of Personality Disorders, 6,* 99–108.

General Comments

Key Words

Population	Stressor	Topic
adult psychiatric patients	loss physical abuse sexual abuse verbal abuse	research

Reference Citation for This Review
Ford, J. (1996). Psychometric review of Retrospective Assessment of Traumatic Experiences (RATE). In B. H. Stamm (Ed.). *Measurement of stress, trauma, and adaptation.* Lutherville, MD: Sidran Press.

Reviewer Contact Name
Julian Ford, Ph.D.
Address: National Center for PTSD (116-D)
               VA Medical Center
               White River Junction, VT 05009 USA
Phone: 802.296.5132
Fax: 802.296.5135
E-mail: Julian.Ford@Dartmouth.Edu

Measure Contact Name
Stephen W. Hurt, Ph.D.
Address: New York Hospital/Cornell Medical Center, Westchester Division
               21 Bloomingdale Rd.
               White Plains, NY 10605 USA
Phone:
Fax:
E-mail:

Schillace Loss Scale (SLS)

Type of Population

Adults; older adolescents (14–19)

Cost

Free

Copyright

Ralph Schillace, Ph.D.

Languages

English

What It Measures

The impact of an event perceived by the respondent as a loss: a choiceless change removes something positive.

Measure Content Survey, Procedure, or Process

Thirty declarative statements answered true or false at the time of taking the test. The higher the score, the greater the impact of an event perceived as a loss. A typical item is, "I have a sense that something or someone is missing and that I am searching for it."

Theoretical Orientation Summary

Primarily psychodynamic, but sequelae of loss are also thought to be cognitive and behavioral. Instrument is based on clinical reactions of grief-stricken individuals and attempts to measure intensity of responses by surveying a broad sample of reactions.

Time Estimate

Administration	Scoring
5–10 minutes	5–10 minutes

Equipment Needed

Paper & Pencil	Computer	Basic Psychophysiological	Specialized Equipment
X			

Psychometric Maturity

Under Construction	Basic Properties Intact	Mature
	X	

Psychometric Properties Summary

41 items reduced to 30 by item analysis. All 30 correlate with total score. With 80 adult volunteers, some reporting loss, some not, a Cronbach alpha=.88 was obtained for reliability. Test-retest over 12 weeks for 51 undergraduates in a course on loss and trauma yielded a reliability r=.90. Significant relationships were found between the SLS and the Saunder Grief Inventory (N=21 undergraduates), especially with r=.77. The Schillace Loss Scale was correlated with the Schillace Trauma and Schillace Vulnerability Scales, r=.80 and r=.70 respectively.

Particular Sensitivity

Age	Change over Time	Culture / Ethnicity	Gender	Geography / Climate	Sexual Orientation	Socioeconomic Status	Urban / Rural
X	?	?	?	?	?	?	?

Estimate of Number of In-Process Studies

Unknown

Unpublished References

Papers and poster sessions presented upon request.

Published References

General Comments

Key Words

Population	Stressor	Topic
adults older adolescents	grief loss	research

Reference Citation for This Review

Schillace, R. (1996). Psychometric review of Schillace Loss Scale (SLS). In B. H. Stamm (Ed.). *Measurement of stress, trauma, and adaptation.* Lutherville, MD: Sidran Press

Measure Contact Name

Ralph Schillace, Ph.D.

Address: Psychology Department-Pryale Hall
            Oakland University
            Rochester, MI 48309-4401 USA
Phone: 810.652.6285
Fax: 810.370.4612
E-mail: Schillac@oakland.edu

L-Scale Sample Items

Please indicate if you believe the statements below are either True or False as they apply to you.

I am not especially irritable these days.

I have frequent periods of weeping.

I have felt a profound lack of preparation for certain important and recent events in my life.

I used to feel life made sense and was understandable; now it seems confusing and meaningless.

Schillace Post-Traumatic Vulnerability Scale

Type of Population

Adults; Older adolescents (16–19)

Cost

Free

Copyright

Ralph Schillace, Ph.D.

Languages

English

What It Measures

A perceived sense of defenselessness; a sense of insecurity and expectation that danger exists and harm will occur; overvigilance and caution to protect self and loved ones.

Measure Content Survey, Procedure, or Process

Twenty-four declarative statements answered (t-f) at time of taking test; prototypical item, "Sometimes I feel 'exposed' and unprotected and that I could easily be hurt (either physically or emotionally)." Statements are typical of post-trauma victims report as they struggle to reestablish their sense of safety.

Theoretical Orientation Summary

Based on psychodynamic clinical observations of trauma victims and adjustment/adaption reactions. Vulnerability is a gauge of the state of the personality as it changes to accommodate a (traumatic) event. Reestablished invulnerability or reduced vulnerability is considered a sign of recovery (adaptation).

Time Estimate

Administration	Scoring
10–15 minutes	5–10 minutes

Equipment Needed

Paper & Pencil	Computer	Basic Psychophysiological	Specialized Equipment
X			

Psychometric Maturity

Under Construction	Basic Properties Intact	Mature
	X	

Psychometric Properties Summary

Item analysis reduced items from 32 to present 24. All statistically significantly correlated with the total score (point biserial r analysis, N=457). Cronbach's alpha=.79 for 24 item instrument, split-half reliability (N=80). Test-retest reliability r=.85 (N=51, 12-week time period). Significant correlations with Keane's Trauma Scale (MMPI), BDI, State-Trait Anxiety Scales and IES Scales (N=57). Significant findings using instrument: (a) sense of vulnerability changes over life span (N=500); (b) females reliably report greater sense of vulnerability than males; (c) sense of vulnerability significantly related to specific incidents of both loss and trauma.

Particular Sensitivity

Age	Change over Time	Culture / Ethnicity	Gender	Geography / Climate	Sexual Orientation	Socioeconomic Status	Urban / Rural
X	X	?	X	?	?	?	?

Estimate of Number of In-Process Studies

Unpublished References
Hallmark paper on concept of sense of vulnerability and trauma.
Schillace, R. Presentation papers available upon request.

Published References
Perloff, L.(1983) Perceptions of vulnerability to vicitimization. *Journal of Social Issues, 39,* 41–46.

General Comments
Helpful gauge for recovery from trauma; insightful theoretically for understanding of intrapsychic adaptation.

Key Words

Population	Stressor	Topic
adults older adolescents	loss sense of vulnerability	research

Reference Citation for This Review
Schillace, R. (1996). Psychometric review of Schillace Post-Traumatic Vulnerability Scale. In B. H. Stamm (Ed.). *Measurement of stress, trauma, and adaptation.* Lutherville, MD: Sidran Press.

Measure Contact Name
Ralph Schillace, Ph.D.
Address: Psychology Department-Pryale Hall
            Oakland University
            Rochester, MI 48309-4401 USA
Phone: 810.652.6285
Fax: 810.470.4612
E-mail: Schillac@oakland.edu

V-Scale Sample Items

Please indicate if you believe the statements below are either true or false as they apply to you.

I have had many narrow escapes in life and feel as though my "nine lives" are almost used up.

Regarding disappointment and tragedy, I am no longer sure that it will happen to the other guy/gal, not me.

I am confident I will be spared terrible misfortunes.

I control my well-being.

I welcome challenges.

Schillace Trauma Scale (STS)

Type of Population

Adults; Older Adolescents (16–19)

Cost

Free

Copyright

Ralph Schillace, Ph.D.

Languages

English

What It Measures

The emotional, behavioral, and cognitive impact of a traumatic event. The higher the score, the greater the impact of the trauma

Measure Content Survey, Procedure, or Process

Thirty-seven declarative statements answered true or false for the time of the test and indicating the degree of disruption and adaption in an individual's life. Example item: "I feel overwhelmed with fear when I talk about certain events."

Theoretical Orientation Summary

A traumatic event is conceptualized as a physical or psychological injury which produces emotion (fear) and behavioral (avoidance responses) and cognitive (intrusive thoughts, e.g. flashbacks) sequelae. The items on the STS inventory are a sampling of these responses. The more items endorsed as reflecting a trauma, the higher the traumatic impact of the event.

Time Estimate

Administration	Scoring
10–15 minutes	5–10 minutes

Equipment Needed

Paper & Pencil	Computer	Basic Psychophysiological	Specialized Equipment
X			

Psychometric Maturity

Under Construction	Basic Properties Intact	Mature
	X	

Psychometric Properties Summary

45 items from clinical practice reduced to 37 by item analysis. All 37 items correlate with total score. Preliminary item analysis, excluding low correlation items, resulted in a Cronbach's alpha =.87 for the 37 item scale. Test-retest reliability over a 12 week span resulted in r=.89. Correlate with Keane Trauma Scale, r=.51 (Keane, Malloy, & Fairbank, 1984).

Particular Sensitivity

Age	Change over Time	Culture/ Ethnicity	Gender	Geography/ Climate	Sexual Orientation	Socioeconomic Status	Urban/ Rural
X	?	?	?	?	?	?	?

Estimate of Number of In-Process Studies

Unpublished References

Copies of papers/poster presentations available on request.

Published References

Keane, T. M., Malloy, P. F., & Fairbank, J. A. (1984). Empirical development of an MMPI subscale for the assessment of combat-related post-traumatic stress disorder. *Journal of Consulting and Clinical Psychology, 52,* 888–891.

General Comments

The STS seems to be a global estimate of impact of negative events and is correlated with measures of vulnerability, loss, and depression.

Key Words

Population	Stressor	Topic
adult older adolescents	any	research

Reference Citation for This Review

Schillace, R. (1996). Psychometric review of Schillace Trauma Scale. In B. H. Stamm (Ed.). *Measurement of stress, trauma, and adaptation.* Lutherville, MD: Sidran Press.

Measure Contact Name

Ralph Schillace, Ph.D.
Address: Psychology Department-Pryale Hall
                Oakland University
                Rochester, MI 48309-4401 USA
Phone: 810.652.6285
Fax: 810.370.4612
E-mail: Schillac@oakland.edu

T-Scale—Sample Items

Please indicate if you believe the statements below are either True or False as they apply to you.

I feel very hurt (emotionally) by recent events in my life.

I believe that I am safe even if the world is dangerous.

I used to feel that the world was fair and just—now it seems unfair.

I just don't understand it.

I have a kind of nervous energy these days which keeps me from resting.

Secondary Traumatic Stress Disorder Scale

Type of Population
Adult. Human service field, family members, and others exposed to a traumatized person for which they feel responsible in some way to relieve their suffering.

Cost
Free

Copyright
Charles R. Figley, Ph.D.

Languages
English

What It Measures
Secondary traumatic stress disorder and its separate symptoms and the sources of stress connected with them. The measure replicates the items in the symptom criteria for Posttraumatic Stress Disorder in the American Psychiatric Association's *Diagnostic and Statistical Manual of Mental Disorders* (4th ed.) by orienting the Criterion A wording to fit exposure to a traumatized person or persons, rather than being traumatized by an event or events.

Measure Content Survey, Procedure, or Process
Instrument is under development. Face validity was established through a panel of 23 specialists. A study to establish the instrument's psychometric properties is currently underway.

Theoretical Orientation Summary
Figley's empathic response theory that links the empathic ability, sense of competence, and differentiation ability of the helper and the helper's secondary traumatic stress. The helper's unresolved traumatic conflicts also play a role, as does the fatigue, in the emergence of PTSD.

Time Estimate

Administration	Scoring
10–15 minutes	5–10 minutes

Equipment Needed

Paper & Pencil	Computer	Basic Psychophysiological	Specialized Equipment
X			

Psychometric Maturity

Under Construction	Basic Properties Intact	Mature
X		

Psychometric Properties Summary
Data are being collected and analyzed.

Particular Sensitivity

Age	Change over Time	Culture / Ethnicity	Gender	Geography / Climate	Sexual Orientation	Socioeconomic Status	Urban / Rural
?	?	?	?	?	?	?	?

Estimate of Number of In-Process Studies
Several

Unpublished References

Published References

General Comments
The measure is designed to document the cost of caring for those suffering from PTSD and other traumatic symptoms. Results of current research are expected to reveal a high correlation with measures of PTSD and be able to differentiate those helpers who are coping well with exposure to traumatized persons and those who are absorbing and retaining the suffering of traumatized persons.

Key Words

Population	Stressor	Topic
adult caregivers	caregiving secondary trauma exposure	measure development research secondary traumatic stress

Reference Citation for This Review
Figley, C. R. (1996). Psychometric review of Secondary Trauamtic Stress Disorder Scale. In B. H. Stamm (Ed.). *Measurement of stress, trauma, and adaptation*. Lutherville, MD: Sidran Press.

Measure Contact Name
Charles R. Figley, Ph.D.

Address: Psychosocial Stress Research Program
Florida State University
103 Sandels Building
Tallahassee, FL 32306-4097 USA

Phone: 904.644.1588
Fax: 904.644.4804
E-Mail: CFIGLEY@GARNET.ACNS.FSU.EDU

Sexual Abuse Exposure Questionnaire (SAEQ)
National Center for PTSD Review

Type of Population
Preadolescents, adolescents

Cost
Available from author at no charge.

Copyright
Ned Rodriguez & David Foy, Ph.D.

Languages
English

What It Measures
Assesses retrospectively recalled sexual abuse.

Measure Content Survey, Procedure, or Process
Assesses retrospectively recalled sexual abuse with scores for Exposure, Perpetrator, Duration, Age of Onset/Termination, Frequency, Betrayal of Trust, Special Favors, Threats to Others/Self, Force, Injury, Life Threat, Amnesia, Disclosure During/After, and Response to Disclosure

Theoretical Orientation Summary
Foy's trauma exposure model.

Time Estimate

Administration	Scoring
30-60 minutes	varies

Equipment Needed

Paper & Pencil	Computer	Basic Psychophysiological	Specialized Equipment
X			

Psychometric Maturity

Under Construction	Basic Properties Intact	Mature
	X	

Psychometric Properties Summary
Reliability Retest (2 weeks, 117 survivors): r=.52-.99; K=.60-1.0 for all items. Internal Consistency (Split Half) r=.73 for Exposure Type.

Validity Predictive (Lifetime PTSD SCID diagnosis predicted by Exposure, Perpetrator, Duration, Age, Frequency, Betrayal of Trust, Special Favors, Threats to Self, Force, Injury, Injury, Life Threat, Amnesia).

Normative data from recruited childhood sexual abuse survivors in treatment, primarily white females.

Particular Sensitivity

Age	Change over Time	Culture / Ethnicity	Gender	Geography / Climate	Sexual Orientation	Socioeconomic Status	Urban / Rural
X	?	X	X	?	?	X	?

Estimate of Number of In-Process Studies

5+

Unpublished References

Ryan, S., Rodriguez, N., Rowan, A., & Foy, D. (1992). Psychometric analysis of the Sexual Abuse Exposure Questionnaire (SAEQ). Paper presented at the annual convention of the American Psychological Association. Washington, DC.

Published References

General Comments

Key Words

Population	Stressor	Topic
adolescents preadolescents	sexual abuse	diagnosis research

Reference Citation for This Review

Ford, J. (1995). Psychometric review of the Sexual Abuse Exposure Questionnaire (SAEQ). In B. H. Stamm (Ed.). *Measurement of stress, trauma, and adaptation*. Lutherville, MD: Sidran Press.

Reviewer Contact Name

Julian Ford, Ph.D.
Address: National Center for PTSD (116-D)
             VA Medical Center
             White River Junction, VT 05009 USA
Phone: 802.296.5132
Fax: 802.296.5135
E-mail   Julian.Ford@Dartmouth.Edu

Measure Contact Name

Ned Rodriguez   David Foy, Ph.D.
Address: Box 1238   Graduate School of Education and Psychology
             Graduate School of Psychology   Pepperdine Univ.
             Fuller Theological Seminary   400 Corporate Pointe
             Pasadena, CA 91182   4th Floor GSEP
             USA   Culver City, CA
                                             90230-7627 USA
Phone: 310.568.5739
Phone: 310.568.5755
E-mail: DFOY@PEPPERDINE.EDU

Somatic Inkblot Series Test

Type of Population
Clinical psychiatric cases, post traumatic stress victims, adults, adolescents, and children over 6 years of age.

Cost
1. SIS-II Booklet form $60 (Sets of 20 with manual)
2. SIS-II Video $99 (Set with manual)
3. SIS-I Card Set $60 (Manual & set of 20 cards)

Copyright
Wilfred A. Cassell

Languages
English. Some items available in Italian, German, and Hindi. Spanish available soon.

What It Measures
Personality, diagnosis, therapeutic intervention, prognosis.

SIS is a structured projective diagnostic instrument and an adjunct to psychotherapy. It helps in hearing the inner cry of suffering individuals and brings out unprocessed unconscious material that needs processing. It has been able to assess the personality and is used as a diagnostic instrument. It is a self-administered test and the first inkblot test in video setting. Because of its unique characteristic of individualized self administration, it penetrates into the deeper inner self and brings out the buried material through projection. It has also been used as a screening test during selection interviews in India. People with traumatic experiences go back in time and start revealing the painful materials that need verbalization and catharsis.

Measure Content Survey, Procedure, or Process
1. SIS-I 20 card set—used like the Rorschach Test. About 30 minutes for administration.
2. SIS-II Booklet form has 62 images. Self-administered test. About 45 minutes for administration.
3. SIS-II Video form is the video of 62 images. Self administered. 45 minutes for administration.

All three sets of SIS are scored for indices such as number of responses (R), human (H), animal (A), anatomical (At), Sex (S), movement (M), most-typical (MT), typical (T), atypical (At), and four pathological categories—Hostility Association Scale (HAS), Pathological Anatomy Scale (PAS), Depression (D), and Paranoia (P). Quantitative analysis may help in diagnosis and comparison with other groups, whereas content analysis helps in understanding the psychopathology of the case and hearing the inner cry of the suffering individual.

Theoretical Orientation Summary
SIS is backed by theory of somatic imagery, theory of body symbolism and theory of inner cry (Cassell, Dubey, & Pershad, 1995). Theories explain how SIS helps in understanding somatic imagery and body symbolism as the responses to SIS images are language of the unconscious.

Time Estimate

Administration	Scoring
30–45 minutes	10–30+ minutes

Equipment Needed

Paper & Pencil	Computer	Basic Psychophysiological	Specialized Equipment
Patient needs nothing except for SIS-II booklet			VCR and TV for SIS-II Video set.

Psychometric Maturity

Under Construction	Basic Properties Intact	Mature
	X	X

Psychometric Properties Summary

The retest reliability, split-half reliability and parallel form reliability of SIS-II and SIS-II Video was found ranging from .51 to .71. (Pershad & Dubey, 1994). The test has high construct validity. The SIS series is able to discriminate normal subjects from clinical groups (anxiety, depressive disorder, schizophrenic disorders). Adult subjects responded differently than adolescents (Dwivedi, Mishra, & Cassell, 1994). The test is able to take the subject back in time and bring out unconscious material that needs processing. This is proved by various cases studied and presented through video tapes. No consistent sex differences have been found in studies to date. Work with the SIS series is being conducted by researchers in different countries. Kendall's coefficient of concordance between the nine scoring indices of SIS-II and research proved that both the tests are similar in their construct and measurement. However, because of its emphasis on content analysis, SIS is beyond the Rorschach test.

Particular Sensitivity

Age	Change over Time	Culture/ Ethnicity	Gender	Geography/ Climate	Sexual Orientation	Socioeconomic Status	Urban/ Rural
X	?	X	X	?	?	?	?

Estimate of Number of In-Process Studies

many

Unpublished References

Cassell, W. A. (1987). The SIS Video Version. Paper presented at the annual meeting of the Society for Personality Assessment. San Francisco, CA.

Cassell, W. A. (1988). Validity study of the SIS-II Booklet in pregnant and nonpregnant women. Paper presented at the meeting of the International Congress of Psychology. Sydney, Australia.

Cassell, W. A. (1989). Therapeutic application of the SIS. Paper presented at the meeting of the Society for Personality Assessment. New York, NY.

Cassell, W. A. & Dubey, B. L. (1995). The Use of the Rorschach and SIS in Relieving Somatized Grief. SIS Center, 504 Sector 15A, Chandigarh - 160015 (India).

Dubey, B. L., Dwivedi, P., Cassell, W. A., & Mishra, M. (August 1993). Inner cry through Somatic Inkblot Series. Proceedings of 51st International Council of Psychologists. Montreal, Canada.

Dubey, B. L., Pershad, D., & Cassell, W. A. (July 1992a). Clinical utility of Somatic Inkblot Series Video. Proceedings of 50th International Council of Psychologists. Amsterdam, The Netherlands.

Dubey, B. L., Pershad, D., & Cassell, W. A. (July 1992b). Diagnostic utility of Somatic Inkblot Series Video. Proceedings of 25th International Congress of Psychology, Brussels, Belgium.

Dwivedi, P., Dubey, B. L., Cassell, W. A., & Pershad, D. (July 1992). Somatic Inkblot Series video in adolescents. Proceedings of 25th International Congress of Psychology. Brussels, Belgium.

Goel, D. S., Rathee, S. P., Sardhana, M., & Dubey, B. L. (April 1990). SIS-I in coronary heart disease. Proceedings of First National Workshop on SIS and Rorschach. Chandigarh, India, April.

Mishra, M. (1995). Compatibility of SIS-II and the Rorschach Indices in normal, neurotics and schizophrenics. Ph.D. thesis, Benarus Hindu University. Varanasi, India (in progress for submission).

Published References

Cassell, W. A. (1965a). Body Perception and Symptom Localization. *Psychosomatic Medicine*, *27*, 171–176.

Cassell, W. A. (1965b). Responses to inkblot configurations resembling the heart. *Journal of Projective Techniques and Personality Assessment*, *3*, 123–126.

Cassell, W. A. (1971). Body consciousness in exhibitionism. *British Journal of Projective Techniques, 16,* 21–23.

Cassell, W. A. (1972). Individual differences in somatic perception. *Advances in Psychosomatic Medicine, 8,* 86–104.

Cassell, W. A. (1977a). Aggressive imagery and clinical symptoms in schizophrenia. *British Journal of Projective Techniques, 16,* 21–31.

Cassell, W. A. (1977b). Desensitization therapy for body image anxiety. *Canadian Psychiatric Association Journal, 22,* 239–242.

Cassell, W. A. (1979). Anatomical Rorschach Responses and Death Symbolism. *British Journal of Projective Technique and Personality Study, 24,* 7–16.

Cassell, W. A. (1980a). Body awareness and somatic delusions involving sexual organs. *American Journal of Psychoanalysis, 40,* 125–135.

Cassell, W. A. (1980b). *Body symbolism and the Somatic Inkblot Series.* Anchorage, Alaska: Aurora Publishing.

Cassell, W. A. (1980c). Computerized projective testing as an aid in medical diagnosis. *Alaska Medicine, 26,* 1–9.

Cassell, W. A. (1994). The Somatic Inkblot Series: Continuing Rorschach's Conceptualization. *SIS J. Proj. Psy. & Mental Health, 1,* 3–14.

Cassell, W. A. (1984). *Somatic Inkblot Series Video.* Anchorage, Alaska: SIS Center.

Cassell, W. A. (1990). *Somatic Inkblot Series Manual.* Anchorage, Alaska: SIS Center.

Dharamvir, R., Pershad, D., Dubey, B. L., & Mann, S. B. S. (1994). Body imagery in vertigo patients. *SIS J. Proj. Psy., & Mental Health, 1,* 65–72.

Dubey, B. L., Dwivedi, P., Cassell, W. A., & Sahay, M. (1993). Projective value of Somatic Inkblot Series II in a case of stammering. *Journal of Personality and Clinical Studies, 8,* 173–176.

Dubey, B. L., & Cassell, W. A. (1993). Some experiences with Somatic Inkblot Series II. *British Journal of Projective Psychology, 38* (1), 19–41.

Dubey, B. L., & Pershad, D. (1994). Reliability and Validity of Somatic Inkblot Series in India. *SIS J. Proj. Psy. & Mental Health, 1,* 33–38.

Dubey, B. L., Cassell, W. A., Pershad, D., & Dwivedi, P. (1995). Diagnostic Utility of Somatic Inkblot Series. *SIS J. Proj. Psy. & Mental Health, 2,* 77–84.

Dwivedi, P., Mishra, M. & Cassell, W. A. (1994). Somatic Inkblot Series-Video in Adolescents. *SIS J. Proj. Psy. & Mental Health, 1,* 27–32.

Ramachandra, S., & Chaturvedi, S. K. (1995). Body Imagery in SIS Test. *SIS J. Proj. Psy. & Mental Health, 2,* 53–60.

Rathee, S. P., Goel, D. S., Chawla, M. L., & Saldanha, D. (1994). A Study of Somatic Inkblot Series-I in Coronary Cases. *SIS J. Proj. Psy. & Mental Health, 1,* 51–64.

Rathee, S. P., Pandey, V., & Singh, A. (1995). Diagnostic efficacy of Somatic Inkblot Series-II amongst psychiatric patents of armed forces. A preliminary study. *SIS J. Proj. Psy. & Mental Health, 2,* 61–66.

Sahay, M., & Srivastava, P. K. (1994). Somatic Inkblot Series-II in male transsexuals. *SIS J. Proj. Psy. & Mental Health, 1,* 73–78.

Saldanha, D., & Dubey, B. L. (1995). Effect of sodium pentothal on SIS-Video-A Inkblot images. *SIS J. Proj. Psy. & Mental Health, 2,* 19–28.

Savage, George (1995). Bereavement and hypnosis: A case study. *SIS J. Proj. Psy. & Mental Health, 2,* 29–40.

Verma, S. K. (1995). Reliability and validity of Somatic Inkblot Series Test. *SIS J. Proj. Psy. & Mental Health, 2,* 67–71.

Verma, S. K., Pershad, D., & Nehra, R. (1994). Cross-validation of SIS-II Psychiatric Population. *SIS J. Proj. Psy. & Mental Health, 1,* 15–18.

Key Words

Population	Stressor	Topic
children	accident	diagnosis
adolescents	combat	general treatment
adults	domestic violence	stimulate of
veterans	physical abuse	therapeutic dreams
police	sexual abuse	substance abuse
	traumatic grief	

Reference Citation for This Review

Cassell, W. A. (1996). Psychometric review of Somatic Inkblot Series Test. In B. H. Stamm (Ed.). *Measurement of stress, trauma, and adaptation.* Lutherville, MD: Sidran Press.

Measure Contact Name

Dr. Wilfred A. Cassell

Address:	4450 Cordova Street, Suite 100
	Anchorage, Alaska 99503 USA
Phone:	907.563.4325
Fax:	907.563.3746
E-mail:	sis@owt.con

Research Contact Name

Dr. B. L. Dubey, Ph.D.

Address:	504 Sector-15A
	Chandigarh-160015
	India
Phone:	91.172.701800
E-mail:	

Spiritual Assessment Structured Interview

Type of Population

Adult hospice patients; may be adapted for family members of patient.

Cost

Free.

Copyright

Languages

English.

What It Measures

The purpose of this assessment is to determine whether an individual has a spiritual support system in place or whether (s)he is seeking a spiritual understanding of her/his circumstance.

Measure Content Survey, Procedure, or Process

The interview consists of 25 questions which identify existing spiritual support systems, self-examination of existing beliefs, need to talk to hospice personnel regarding spiritual concerns, satisfaction and dissatisfaction with life, and information about future thinking.

Theoretical Orientation Summary

Structured interview.

Time Estimate

Administration	Scoring
10–30 minutes	NA

Equipment Needed

Paper & Pencil	Computer	Basic Psychophysiological	Specialized Equipment
X			

Psychometric Maturity

Under Construction	Basic Properties Intact	Mature
X		

Psychometric Properties Summary

None established.

Particular Sensitivity

Age	Change over Time	Culture / Ethnicity	Gender	Geography / Climate	Sexual Orientation	Socioeconomic Status	Urban / Rural
?	?	X	?	?	?	?	?

Estimate of Number of In-Process Studies

Unknown

Unpublished References

Unknown

Published References

None

General Comments

This information may be helpful in identifying appropriate care assignments of volunteers, chaplains, or nurses within the hospice setting. It is important to note that no assumption is made that each individual must have or should need a spiritual support system. The assessment does, however, give opportunity to address such issues.

Key Words

Population	Stressor	Topic

adults
terminal patients and
  their families
	death
	life-threatening illness
	terminal illness
	traumatic grief
		secondary traumatic
		  stress service delivery

Reference Citation for This Review

McNeill, F. (1996). Psychometric review of Spiritual Assessment Structured Interview. In B. H. Stamm(Ed.). *Measurement of stress, trauma, and adaptation*. Lutherville, MD: Sidran Press.

Measure Contact Name

Fran McNeill

Address:	12021 Portage Dr
	Anchorage, AK 99515
E-Mail:	asfrm@uaa.alaska.edu

Sometimes when people are facing serious illness, they think about their beliefs a lot. When they think about their beliefs, they are often comforted, reassured, concerned, bothered, worried, anxious, or just confused. They often feel scared, angry, sad, hurt, lonely, or resentful.

1.   How do you feel?
2.   Has your illness made you think a lot about your beliefs?
3.   Do you have spiritual beliefs?
4.   Do they help you?
5.   Is it important to you to talk about your beliefs?
6.   Do you want to talk to someone about your beliefs?
7.   Do you want to talk to someone about your feelings?
8.   Are you a member of a spiritual community?
9.   What do you call that community?
10. Does your spiritual community have a leader?
11. What do you call your spiritual community leader?

(For future questions the interviewer should use name of the spiritual leader identified in question 11--for example, pastor, minister, priest, rabbi, shaman, teacher, healer, medicine person)

12. Does your _____ know about your illness? (for example, fill in the blank with *rabbi, priest, pastor, etc.*)
13. Is your _____ someone you are comfortable talking to?
14. Would you want us to call your _____ in case of an emergency?
     a. If so, who is your _____?
     b. If not, who should we contact? ("No one" is an appropriate response.)
15. Is your spiritual community and your _____ providing the kind of support you want and need at this time?
16. Do you feel that your _____ and others who support you understand what you are going through?
17. Do you wish to talk with someone on our staff about your feelings?
18. What are your worries for now?
19. What are your worries for the future?
20. How do you feel about what you have done with your life up to now?
21. Do you have regrets about your life?
22. Are there things you feel guilty about?
23. What are you proud of in your life?
24. How do you feel about the future at this time?
25. What do you want to do with your life in the future?

Standards of Practice & Ethical Issues Questionnaire

Type of Population
Professionals

Cost
Free

Copyright

Languages
English

What It Measures
This questionnaire addresses attitudes, values, beliefs, practices, and concerns in the area of ethical provision of treatment, research, training, and education. The instrument is also being used as tool for assessing what needs to be included in an ethical code for working with trauma survivors.

Measure Content Survey, Procedure, or Process
The questionnaire is self-administered, utilizing both Likert scale (0–5, never to always, with don't know option) and open-ended questions. At this time, scoring is for the entire scale using a summative scoring technique with a higher score representing higher ethical standards.

Theoretical Orientation Summary
Bias of instrument is at the intersection of ethics and trauma.

Time Estimate

Administration	Scoring
45 minutes	varies

Equipment Needed

Paper & Pencil	Computer	Basic Psychophysiological	Specialized Equipment
X			

Psychometric Maturity

Under Construction	Basic Properties Intact	Mature
X		

Psychometric Properties Summary
The instrument has undergone peer review by trauma experts and ethicists. At this time, no psychometric data is available. Data have been collected and are being analyzed.

Particular Sensitivity

Age	Change over Time	Culture/ Ethnicity	Gender	Geography/ Climate	Sexual Orientation	Socioeconomic Status	Urban/ Rural
?	?	?	?	?	?	?	?

Estimate of Number of In-Process Studies

1

Unpublished References

Williams, M. B., & Sommer, J. F. (1990). Ethics and Trauma. Presented in The Research and Methodology Interest Group Pre-Meeting Institute of Sixth Annual Meeting of The International Society for Traumatic Stress Studies. Washington, DC.

Williams, M. B., Sommer, J. F., & Stamm, B.H. (1991). Developing ethical priniciples for the ISTSS: Developing comprehensive guidelines. Symposium presented at the Seventh Annual Meeting of The International Society for Traumatic Stress Studies. Washington, DC.

Williams, M. B., Sommer, J. F., & Stamm, B. H. (1992). Establishment of a code of ethics for the International Society for Traumatic Stress Studies. Symposium presented at the First World Conference of The International Society for Traumatic Stress Studies. Amsterdam, The Netherlands.

Williams, M. B., Sommer, J. F., & Stamm, B. H. (1993). Developing ethical principles for trauma research, education and treatment. Presented at the Ninth Annual Meeting of The International Society for Traumatic Stress Studies. Los Angeles, CA.

Williams, M. B., Sommer, J. F., Stamm, B. H., Harris, C.J., & Hammarberg, M. (1992). Developing ethical priniciples for the ISTSS-II: Developing comprehensive guidelines. Symposium presented at the Eighth Annual Meeting of The International Society for Traumatic Stress Studies. Los Angeles, CA.

Published References

Sommer, J. F., Williams, M. B., Harris, C. J., & Stamm, B. H. (1994). The development of ethical principles for post traumatic research, practice, training and publication. In M. B. Williams & J. F. Sommer, (Eds.). *Handbook of Post Traumatic Therapy*. Westport, CT: Greenwood Press.

Key Words

Population	Stressor	Topic
adult professional		ethics research

General Comments

It should be noted that there is a potential for a faking good response set. Faking good is hopefully detectable via the open-ended questions.

Reference Citation for This Review

Williams, M. B., & Sommer, J. F. (1996). Psychometric review of Standards of Practice and Ethical Issues Questionnaire. In B. H. Stamm (Ed.). *Measurement of stress, trauma, and adaptation*. Lutherville, MD: Sidran Press.

Measure Contact Name

Mary Beth Williams, Ph.D.

Address:	Trauma Recovery Education and Counseling Center
	9 N. 3rd St.
	Suite 100 #14
	Warrenton, VA 22186 USA
Phone:	703.341.7339
Fax:	703.341.7339
E-mail:	mbethwms@internext.com

Standards of Practice and Ethical Issues Questionnaire

Rate each item using the following scale

Never	Seldom		Sometimes		Always
0	1	2	3	4	5

____ 1. People who work with traumatized individuals, as therapists, should keep an emotionally neutral stance.

____ 2. Conferring a diagnosis is a moral act.

____ 3. Diagnosis defines client needs and treatment methods.

____ 4. The use of the PTSD diagnosis helps predict the course and outcome of the disorder.

____ 5. Insurance constraints impact the choice of diagnosis.

____ 6. Therapists should share the process of making a diagnosis with their clients.

____ 7. The therapeutic relationship provides a framework for making ethical decisions.

____ 8. Therapy is a reciprocal relationship.

____ 9. It is acceptable for therapists to disclose personal information.
     If so, when and under what conditions?_____

____ 10. It is acceptable for therapists to use clients' works of art (poetry, paintings, essays) in presentations.
     If so, when? With or without permission?_____

____ 11. Relating one's story in research study can be retraumatizing.
     If so, when?_____

____ 12. The choice of a research instrument impacts results.

____ 13. The choice of a statistical test impacts results.

____ 14. Clients need to give input into research projects.

____ 15. Therapists are responsible for establishing safe boundaries in the therapeutic relationship.

____ 16. Sexual involvement with a client is unethical.

____ 17. Maintaining social contact with clients outside therapy is unethical.
     When is it not?_____

____ 18. Clients interests are primary in therapy.

____ 19. Therapy is a partnership.

____ 20. Therapists working with traumatized persons should make them aware of their rights at the outset of the beginning of therapy.

____ 21. Therapists need to be self-aware, continuously reexamining the impact of personal life experiences on the work of therapy.

____ 22 Therapists need to understand differences between clients and self when clients are of other genders, races, ages, social classes or sexual orientations.

____ 23. Therapists have an ethical obligation to recognize the type(s) of clients and cases he/she is unable to treat effectively and seek referrals for them elsewhere.

____ 24. The therapist who works with trauma survivors clarifies personal values and is aware how those values enter into therapeutic practice.

____ 25. The PTSD diagnosis creates a theoretical framework for therapy.

____ 26. The PTSD diagnosis offers a specialized model for helping.

____ 27. Use of the PTSD diagnosis helps determine what techniques, procedures or methods are used in therapy as well as when and why they are used.

____ 28. The initial focus of post-traumatic therapy is working through the traumas which have occurred.

____ 29. It is not necessary to structure the process of therapy.

____ 30. The physical setting and arrangement of an office has an impact upon therapy.

____ 31. Maintenance of detailed records is essential.

____ 32. Sharing records with insurance companies is acceptable.

____ 33. Asking clients to tell their stories outside the therapy setting/session is ethical.
     If so, when? _____

____ 34. Therapists should expect trauma survivors to trust them within a relatively few number of sessions (e.g. 6–8).

This instrument, by Mary Beth Williams, may be reproduced without charge and freely distributed, as long as no funds are exchanged.

_____ 35. Maintaining emotional distance with traumatized clients is important to avoid client dependency.
_____ 36. The therapist needs to set limits for clients.
　　　　If so, when and in what areas?

_____

_____ 37. The locus of responsibility for effective treatment lies with the therapist.
_____ 38. Abreactive work (working through traumatic memories) should occur only after a safety context (i.e., establishing boundaries, creating a safe setting, developing a therapeutic alliance) has been developed.
_____ 39. Therapists may assume the role of abuser in the eyes or mind of the client.
_____ 40. Therapists are susceptible to secondary post-traumatic stress reactions.
_____ 41. Therapists may _take on_ the memories of clients.
_____ 42. Therapists are responsible for their own self care (networking, training, continuing education).
　　　　If so, what activities are most helpful to you?

_____

_____ 43. Working with PTSD leads to vicarious traumatization of therapists.
_____ 44. It is ethical to work in solo private practice.
_____ 45. Paradoxical techniques can be used successfully with victims of trauma.
_____ 46. The goals of therapy for trauma survivors are set by client and therapist working together.
_____ 47. Therapists who work with trauma survivors should be professionally licensed.
_____ 48. Ethical guidelines for supervision of persons working with trauma at all levels of practice are necessary.
　　　　By whom and under what conditions should supervision occur?

_____

_____ 49a. It is important to demonstrate continuing competency in clinical work with trauma victims and survivors.
　　　　It is important to demonstrate continuing competency in research with trauma victims and survivors.
_____ 49b. If so, how?

_____

　　　　What requirements and standards should there be?

_____

_____ 50. Non-degreed persons/counselors can deliver effective therapeutic services to trauma victims.
　　　　If so, when?

_____

　　　　How should they be credentialed, if at all?

_____

_____ 51. Non-degreed individuals can be effective in critical incident stress debriefings.
　　　　If so, how and when?

_____

_____ 52. It is ethical to begin research projects with survivors of a traumatic event immediately after that event has occurred.
_____ 53. Debriefings should occur as soon after an event as is possible.
_____ 54. Debriefings should be led by a certified mental health professional.
_____ 55. Persons knowledgeable about trauma have a responsibility to train paraprofessionals through workshops, consulting, courses, or continuing education programs.
_____ 56. Paraprofessionals need appropriate training to work in the trauma field.
_____ 57. Training for any trauma therapist should include a supervised field experience.
_____ 58. Persons working with trauma should be willing to share their knowledge and skills with others.
_____ 59. Training is an ongoing need in the trauma field.
_____ 60. Credentialing of persons working with trauma survivors is necessary.
_____ 61. Credentialing should be based on experience not on education.
_____ 62. The field of traumatology should allow for varying levels of professional education, training, and competence.
　　　　If so, what levels?

_____

_____ 63. Persons who work with traumatized individuals need to be culturally sensitive.

_____ 64. It is unethical to work for a government or organization that treats employees or citizens inhumanely.

_____ 65. It is necessary to provide equal access to treatment, regardless of an individual's ability to pay for services. If so, how?

_____

_____ 66. Retelling one's story in therapy can be retraumatizing. If so, when?

_____

_____ 67. Traumatology is a profession.

_____ 68. A code of ethics for persons who work with trauma should be educational in nature.

_____ 69. A code of ethics for persons who work with trauma needs to be regulatory, containing prescriptions and rules as well as providing for sanctions.

_____ 70. Therapy is a moral enterprise.

_____ 71. Power in a therapeutic relationship needs to be shared.

_____ 72. All clients should have access to therapy.

_____ 73. Fidelity (keeping promises) should be a value held by persons working with trauma survivors.

_____ 74. Beneficence (helping others) should be a value held by persons working with trauma survivors.

_____ 75. Values are the foundations of an ethical code.

_____ 76. Dual relationships are not always harmful in therapy. If they are not, then when?

_____

_____ 77. Therapists have the responsibility to provide safety for traumatized clients. If so, how is this done?

_____

_____ 78. If a therapist is presented with a symptom picture that might indicate abuse, it is ethical and permissible to suggest to the client that abuse occurred.

_____ 79. Therapists should believe everything clients tell them about their past experiences.

_____ 80. A trauma is in the _eye of the beholder:_ traumatic events are traumatic due to the perceptions of those involved.

_____ 81. Traumatic events are traumatic in and of themselves.

82. I believe the mission of a traumatologist (a person who works with trauma victims and survivors) is:

_____

_____

83. I believe that the functions of an ethical code for persons working in the trauma field are:

_____

_____

84. The basic principles that guide my professional efforts are:

_____

_____

85. To me, professional competence means:

_____

_____

86. To me, the major values that guide my professional efforts are:

_____

_____

87. What I would want to add about my practice in the trauma field is:

_____

_____

88. What specifically would you like to see in a code of ethics for the trauma field?

_____

_____

If you are a helping professional please complete this information:

Name (optional)

Age _____ Gender _____ Nationality/Ethnicity _____

Professional Background _____

Educational Background _____

Experience/training in the trauma field _____

Education/training needs _____

Total Years in Practice _____

Present Setting and Length of Time _____

Previous Settings and Length of Time _____

What I have found to be _most_ helpful therapeutically in treating survivors of trauma is _____

_____

What I have found to be _least_ helpful therapeutically in treating survivors of trauma is _____

_____

If you are a client/patient please complete this information:

Age _____ Gender _____ Nationality/Ethnicity _____ Highest Educational Level _____

Trauma(s) Experienced _____

Years in Therapy _____ Years in Trauma-related Therapy _____

What have you found (techniques, types of treatment, medications, etc.) most helpful in your therapy? _____

_____

What have you found least helpful? _____

_____

What therapist characteristics are most conducive to personal healing? _____

_____

What characteristics are least conducive? _____

_____

Please add any other information, ethical concerns, case examples, dilemmas, in this space or on the back. _____

_____

Stanford Acute Stress Reaction Questionnaire (SASRQ)

Type of Population
Adults

Cost
Free. Available from the authors.

Copyright

Languages
English, Spanish

What It Measures
The current version of the SASRQ evaluates the presence of Acute Stress Disorder (ASD) diagnosis and symptoms. ASD is a new diagnosis in the *DSM-IV* for posttraumatic pathology shortly after a traumatic event. The SASRQ is a self-administered, short (10 minutes) scale and to our knowledge it is currently the only measure that assesses all diagnostic criteria for Acute Stress Disorder.

Measure Content Survey, Procedure, or Process
The SASRQ evaluates the following criteria: a) presence of a traumatic event and psychological impact on the individual, b) dissociative symptomatology (numbing/detachment, reduction in awareness, derealization, depersonalization and dissociative amnesia), c) reexperiencing of the traumatic event, d) avoidance, e) hyperarousal. The scale consists of a free-form description of the most traumatic event, a rating on how disturbing that event was for the individual, 30 items on a 6-point Likert-type scale, and a question on the number of days that the individual experienced the worst symptoms. The scale can be scored for all of the items, or for subscales that assess each of the diagnostic criteria. This scale was developed from a previous and longer version. Items with high reliability and consistent with the ASD criteria were maintained, and a few questions were added to address all diagnostic criteria.

Theoretical Orientation Summary
There is consistent evidence, from research on different types of trauma and with different populations, that dissociative symptomatology (i.e., alterations of consciousness characterized by a detachment from the self and/or the environment) is typically present during or shortly after a traumatic event (e.g., Cardeña & Spiegel, 1993; Cardeña et al, 1996; Spiegel & Cardeña, 1991). It is also now known from retrospective (Marmar et al., 1994; Bremner et al., 1992) and prospective studies (Classen, Koopman, Hales, & Spiegel, submitted; Koopman, Classen, & Spiegel, 1994; Shalev et al., 1996) that dissociative symptomatology is one of the best predictors, if not the best, of long-term posttraumatic symptomatology.

Time Estimate

Administration	Scoring
5–10 minutes	5–10 minutes

Equipment Needed

Paper & Pencil	Computer	Basic Psychophysiological	Specialized Equipment
X			

Psychometric Maturity

Under Construction	Basic Properties Intact	Mature
	X	

Psychometric Properties Summary

We are currently conducting an extensive analysis of the psychometric properties of the measure. Previous analyses have showed very high measure reliability (Cronbach's alpha=.92) and good 3-week test-retest correlation when no trauma intervened (r=.78). The measure has obvious face validity with the ASD criteria, and its longer version showed significant convergent validity with the IES (Impact of Events Scale). Furthermore, the SASRQ has significantly predicted the incidence of long-term PTSD, as the theory predicts. The measure has been or is being currently used in a number of studies, including those with sexual abuse survivors (Koopman, Gore-Felton, & Spiegel, submitted) Gulf War PTSD veterans (Cardeña, in preparation), witnesses to a random shooting (Classen, Koopman, & Spiegel, 1995; Koopman et al., in preparation), rescue workers of a plane crash (Grieger et al., in preparation), witnesses to mass shootings (Classen, Koopman, Hales, & Spiegel, submitted), and Mexican nationals reacting to a political assassination (Maldonado et al., in preparation).

Particular Sensitivity

Age	Change over Time	Culture / Ethnicity	Gender	Geography / Climate	Sexual Orientation	Socioeconomic Status	Urban / Rural
?	X	X	?	?	?	?	?

Estimated Number of In-Process Studies

Unpublished References

Cardeña, E. (in preparation). Dissociativity among Gulf War veterans.

Classen, C., Koopman, C., Hales, R., & Spiegel, D. (submitted). Acute stress disorder predicts posttraumatic stress disorder.

Grieger, T., et al. (in preparation). Acute stress disorder among rescue helpers in the Pittsburgh plane crash.

Koopman, C., Gore-Felton, C., & Spiegel, D. (submitted). Acute stress disorder symptoms among sexual abuse survivors seeking treatment.

Maldonado, J., Page, K., Koopman, C., Stein, H., & Spiegel D. (in preparation). Acute stress reactions to the assassination of a Mexican presidential candidate.

Spiegel, D., Koopman, C., Classen, C., & Cardeña, E. The development of a state measure of dissociative reactions to trauma. (Final report to the NIMH.) Manuscript. Stanford University.

Published References

Bremner, J. D., Southwick, S., Brett, E., Fontana, A., Rosenheck, R., & Charney, D. S. (1992). Dissociations and posttraumatic stress disorder in Vietnam combat veterans. *American Journal of Psychiatry, 149,* 328–332.

Cardeña, E., Lewis-Fernandez, R., Beahr, D., Pakianathan, I., & Spiegel, D. (1996). Dissociative disorders. In Sourcebook for the *DSM-IV,* Vol. II (pp. 973–1005). Washington, DC: American Psychiatric Press.

Cardeña, E., & Spiegel D. (1993) Dissociative reactions to the Bay Area Earthquake. *American Journal of Psychiatry, 150,* 474–478.

Koopman, C., Classen, C., & Spiegel, D. (1994). Predictors of posttraumatic stress symptoms among survivors of the Oakland/Berkeley, Calif. firestorm. *American Journal of Psychiatry, 151,* 888–894.

Marmar, C. R., Weiss, D. S., Schlenger, W. E., Fairbank, J. A., Jordan, B. K., Kulka, R. A., & Hough, R. L. (1994). Peritraumatic dissociation and post-traumatic stress in male Vietnam theater veterans. *American Journal of Psychiatry, 151,* 902–907.

Shalev, A. Y., Peri, T., Canetti, L., & Schreiber, S. (1996). Predictors of PTSD in injured trauma survivors: A prospective study. *American Journal of Psychiatry, 153,* 219–225.

Spiegel, D., & Cardeña, E. (1991). Disintegrated experience: The dissociative disorders revisited. *Journal of Abnormal Psychology, 100,* 366–378.

General Comments

Scoring keys, subscale information, and preliminary norms are available upon request. We ask that all who use the instrument agree to share their raw data with us to further our validation efforts. If applicable, any modification to the scale will be communicated to authors sharing the data with us.

Key Words

Population	Stressor	Topic
adults minorities (Spanish speaking)	any	acute stress disorder assessment diagnosis epidemiology research

Reference Citation for This Review

Cardeña, E. (1996). Psychometric review of the Stanford Acute Stress Reacion Questionnaire (SASRQ). In B. H. Stamm (Ed.). *Measurement of stress, trauma, and adaptation*. Lutherville, MD: Sidran Press.

Measure Contact Name

Etzel Cardeña, Ph.D.
Address: Department of Psychiatry
                        USUHS
                        4301 Jones Bridge Rd.
                        Bethesda, MD 20814
Phone/Voice Mail: 202-782-5098
Fax: 202-782-7003
Email: Cardena@usuhsb.usuhs.mil

David Spiegel, M.D.
Address: Department of Psychiatry & Behavioral Sciences
                        Stanford University School of Medicine
                        Stanford, CA 94305
Phone/Voice Mail: (415) 723-6421
Fax: 415.725.3762
Email: dspiegel@leland.stanford.edu

SASRQ

DIRECTIONS:
Recall the stressful events that occurred during _____ .

Briefly describe the one event that was the most disturbing on the lines below:

_____

_____

_____

How disturbing was this event to you? (Please mark one):
____ Not at all disturbing   ____ Somewhat disturbing   ____ Moderately disturbing
____ Very disturbing   ____ Extremely disturbing

DIRECTIONS: Below is a list of experiences people sometimes have during and after a stressful event. Please read each item carefully and decide how well it describes your experience during the month after the event described above. Refer to this event in answering the items that mention "the stressful event." Use the 0–5 point scale shown below and circle the number that best describes your experience.

0	1	2	3	4	5
not experienced	very rarely experienced	rarely experienced	sometimes experienced	often experienced	very often experienced

____ 1. I had difficulty falling or staying asleep.
____ 2. I felt restless.
____ 3. I felt a sense of timelessness.
____ 4. I was slow to respond.
____ 5. I tried to avoid feelings about the event.
____ 6. I had repeated distressing dreams of the stressful event.
____ 7. I felt extremely upset if exposed to events that reminded me of an aspect of the stressful event.
____ 8. I would jump in surprise at the least thing.
____ 9. The stressful event made it difficult for me to perform work or other things I needed to do.
____ 10. I did not have the usual sense of who I am.
____ 11. I tried to avoid activities that reminded me of the stressful event.
____ 12. I felt hypervigilant or "on edge."
____ 13. I experienced myself as though I were a stranger.
____ 14. I tried to avoid conversations about the event.
____ 15. I had a bodily reaction when exposed to reminders of the stressful event.
____ 16. I had problems remembering important details about the stressful event.
____ 17. I tried to avoid thoughts about the stressful event.
____ 18. Things I saw looked different to me from how I know they really looked.
____ 19. I had repeated and unwanted memories of the event.
____ 20. I felt distant from my own emotions.
____ 21. I felt irritable or had outbursts of anger.
____ 22. I avoided contact with people who reminded me of the stressful event.
____ 23. I would suddenly act or feel as if the stressful event was happening again.
____ 24. My mind went blank.
____ 25. I had amnesia for large periods of the event.
____ 26. The stressful event caused problems in my relationships with other people.
____ 27. I had difficulty concentrating.
____ 28. I felt estranged or detached from other people.
____ 29. I had a vivid sense that the event was happening all over again.
____ 30. I tried to stay away from places that reminded me of the event.

How many days did you experience the worst symptoms of distress? (Please mark one):
   none   one   two   three   four   five or more

Scoring of the Stanford Acute Stress Reaction Questionnaire

The questionnaire can be scored as the total sum of raw scores for the scale and/or subscales, or for "caseness." For the latter purpose, we score a symptom as present if the respondent marks it as occurring at least "sometimes," which includes a response of 3 or higher. The definition of acute stress disorder requires the presence of trauma (criterion A), at least 3 dissociative symptoms, and one symptom each of: 1) reexperiencing trauma, 2) avoidance, and 3) marked anxiety or arousal.

A. Traumatic Event
The initial sentence in the "Directions" can be tailored to a specific time span (e.g., the past week, the past month). The initial narrative helps to establish whether the person has experienced, witnessed, or confronted an event involving actual of threatened death or serious injury, or threat to the physical integrity of oneself or others. The rating scale from "not at all disturbing" to "extremely disturbing" assesses the intensity of the person's response.

B. Dissociative symptoms
    1) Subjective sense of numbing, detachment, or absence of emotional responsiveness
        items 20, 28
    2) A reduction in awareness of one's surroundings
        items 4, 24
    3) Derealization
        items 3, 18
    4) Depersonalization
        items 10, 13
    5) Dissociative amnesia, i.e., inability to recall an important aspect of trauma
        items 16, 25
C. The traumatic event is persistently reexperienced
        items 6, 7, 15, 19, 23, 29
D. Marked avoidance of stimuli that arouse recollections of the trauma
        items 5, 11, 14, 17, 22, 30
E. Marked symptoms of anxiety or increased arousal
        items 1, 2, 8, 12, 21, 27
F. Impairment in functioning
        items 9, 26

Stanford Loss of Personal Autonomy Scale

National Center for PTSD Review

Type of Population
    Adults

Cost
    Available from author at no charge.

Copyright
    Contact Cheryl Koopman, Ph.D.

Languages
    English

What It Measures
    Assesses retrospectively recalled loss of personal autonomy in stressful event(s).

Measure Content Survey, Procedure, or Process
    Questionnaire. 11-item 6-point ratings to assess retrospectively-recalled loss of personal autonomy in stressful event(s). Scores for Loss of Personal Autonomy.

Theoretical Orientation Summary
    D. Spiegel's trauma and dissociation model.

Time Estimate

Administration	Scoring
5–10 minutes	5–10 minutes

Equipment Needed

Paper & Pencil	Computer	Basic Psychophysiological	Specialized Equipment
X			

Psychometric Maturity

Under Construction	Basic Properties Intact	Mature
	X	

Psychometric Properties Summary
    Reliability Internal Consistency (Cronbach's Alpha=.63).
    Validity, Predictive (r=.35–.46 with Mississippi PTSD Scale and IES Scale).
    Normative data on 154 adult survivors of Oakland/Berkeley firestorm.

Particular Sensitivity

Age	Change over Time	Culture / Ethnicity	Gender	Geography / Climate	Sexual Orientation	Socioeconomic Status	Urban / Rural
?	?	?	?	?	?	?	?

Estimate of Number of In-Process Studies

2+

Unpublished References

Unknown

Published References

Koopman, C., Classen, C., & Spiegel, D. (1994). Predictors of posttraumatic stress symptoms among survivors of the Oakland/Berkeley, Calif., firestorm. *American Journal of Psychiatry, 151*, 888–894.

General Comments

Key Words

Population	Stressor	Topic
adult emergency service workers	any fire	research

Reference Citation for This Review

Ford, J. (1996). Psychometric review of Stanford Loss of Personal Autonomy Scale. In B. H. Stamm (Ed.). *Measurement of stress, trauma, and adaptation*. Lutherville, MD: Sidran Press.

Reviewer Contact Name

Julian Ford, Ph.D.

Address: National Center for PTSD (116-D)
             VA Medical Center
             White River Junction, VT 05009 USA
Phone: 802.296.5132
Fax: 802.296.5135
E-mail: Julian.Ford@Dartmouth.Edu

Measure Contact Name

Cheryl Koopman, Ph.D.

Address: Department of Psychiatry
             Stanford University Medical Center
             Stanford, CA 94305 USA
Phone: 415.723.9081
Fax:
E-mail:

Stressful Events Content Analysis Coding Scheme (SECACS)

Type of Population

    any

Cost

Copyright

    B. Hudnall Stamm, Ph.D. Traumatic Stress Research Group

Languages

    English; can be applied to any language if the coders are bilingual or if there is a team for translation of either the content coding scheme or the event text. The original measure to be coded can be in any language.

What It Measures

    This is a data coding scheme designed to facilitate the compilation of qualitative data and for the creation of categorical (classification) variables used to classify data for statistical tests such as ANOVA and Discriminant Analysis. There are three distinct levels of specificity referring to the *event* (a) *meta*, (b) *general*, (c) and *specific*. Two other classes apply to the *person-in-event:* (a) *to whom* did the event happen and (b) *by whom* was the action taken.

    This classification system was created to preserve as much of the qualitative aspect of the information as possible. The coder creates an outline of each individual story. These outlines can be considered individually or it is possible to look at the impact of a specific *event* or *person-in-event* across an entire sample.

    The SECACS methodology was constructed over several years for use with the Structural Assessment of Stressful Experiences (SASE) (Stamm, 1993) and has subsequently been used successfully in other studies (Malnekoff, 1995; Rudolph, 1994).

Measure Content Survey, Procedure, or Process

    Depending on the originating measure, each scenario is rated in an *event* progression through *meta, general, specific* as well as for *person-in-event, to whom* and *by whom.* Data can generate from checklists, written essays, clinical interviews, etc. The only necessary information is a basic description of the event to be coded.

Coding Guidelines

Event Related Classifications

    The event related levels, *meta* (4 classes), *general* (up to 10 classes) and *specific* (up to 99 classes), provide progressively detailed levels of information about an *event*. Events (with a few exceptions) are coded without regard to *person-in-event*. To differentiate between victim, perpetrator, and secondary *person-in-event* participation, one need only examine the *to whom / by whom* information (see description below).

Meta Level Classes

    At the *meta* level the four classes denote stressor categories of (1) bad things, (2) death, (3) problems-in-living, and (4) sexual assault. The *death* class is the easiest to define: death precedes all categories in the *meta* level; any occurrence of death is classified in this group. The sexual assault class is also fairly easy to code. Any life experience that describes a sexual assault, regardless of age of perpetrator or victim is coded here. Problems in living is used to code those things that we think of as daily hassles or as V codes in the *DSM* system. Bad Things is a catch all class of those things that are not death nor sexual assault nor a problem-in living. This class refers to accidents, disasters, and combat and those things that a person might describe as a "bad thing that happened."

General Level Classes

    The *general* level further delineates the event into seven types of events. These classes group events that share many qualities. Again, in trying to maximize both similarity and dissimilarity, the groups were created keeping events which are the most similar with each other while keeping in mind the dissimilarity to other groups. The seven classes are (1) war/combat, (2) violence, (3) problems in living, (4) duty related, (5) accident/disaster, (6) sexual assault, and (7) health related, with (9) as a code for unspecified.

Specific Level Classes

The *specific* categories were designed to make fine distinctions between events, such as child sexual abuse and rape. With extremely large data sets these numbers can be meaningfully analyzed. However, with smaller data sets it is more difficult. This is illustrated by the normative data sets in this review. The *specific* level information is also particularly helpful when interpreting single cases or for clinical applications.

Person-in-Event Related Classifications

The *to whom* and *by whom* classifications help identify people's perceived roles in the events. This allows further clarification of the event. The coding scheme was designed specifically to help clarify the confusion between primary and secondary victims of events. Take, for example, a combat scenario. A subject may report killing an enemy (primary, perpetrator), being shot by an enemy (primary, victim), watching a fellow soldier kill an enemy (secondary, perpetrator), watching a friend be killed or wounded by an enemy (primary as bereaved *and* secondary as witness), or be a therapist hearing about the battle (secondary, victim). This aspect of the analysis can also be useful in identifying relationships that may have a significant traumatic impact, such as the death of a child.

The classes used for coding *to whom* and *by whom* are the same. The difference is only in their level; either *to whom* or *by whom*. Coding is always done from the perspective of the *person of interest* in the scenario. For example, if a child reported being sexually assaulted by a neighbor, the coding would be *to whom: self* and *by whom: neighbor*. If the mother reported this event, the coder would ask if the data were being collected in respect to the mother. If yes, (*to whom: child, by whom: neighbor*) clearly recognizes the mother's role as the Secondary victim. If the mother reported this event FOR the child, and the child were the subject of interest, then it would be coded from the child's perspective (*to whom: self, by whom: neighbor*). A case note could indicate that the mother provided the information on behalf of the child. This would clarify the child as the primary event target. It is even possible to have a self-inflicted event, such as an attempted suicide. In this case the event would have been *to whom: self* and *by whom: self*.

Identifying Secondary Traumatic Stress, Victims, and Perpetrators

To identify Secondary Traumatic Stress, sort the *to whom / by whom* classifications to separate those events without self in either class. Those scenarios that do not have self listed as either the victim nor the perpetrator will be secondary events. To identify Perpetrators, sort *by whom* for self. Those with "self" as the *by whom* will consider themselves to be the perpetrator of the event. Care should be taken in interpreting this information as the literature has shown that victims may blame themselves inappropriately for events. To identify the direct or primary victims, sort *to whom* for self.

Theoretical Orientation Summary

This content analysis coding scheme was designed using the concepts of similarity and dissimilarity. The logic used was taken from the several multivariate analyses, including cluster analysis, multidimensional scaling and factor analysis. Whenever possible, groupings were made with attention to both similarity and dissimilarity. However, in practice, classes were organized with more attention to either dissimilarity or to similarity. This was necessary because the more attention paid to similarity, the larger the number of classes required to organize the data meaningfully.

Thus, when attention to the similarity of experience of a single class is the key organizing heuristic, many classes were required. For example, all physical attacks could be grouped together, but the literature has suggested that a mugging is not completely similar to an interpersonal, intrafamilar attack such as spousal abuse. Thus, these two attacks, while similar, have an element of dissimilarity that suggests that the two should not be grouped together. The advantage of grouping with similarity as the key heuristic with dissimilarity as the secondary heuristic is that there is better preservation of the original quality of the information. The disadvantage is that it creates so many categories that some quantitative analyses are not possible.

For this reason, two classes were created that had fewer sub-categories. In these broader classes, dissimilarity is the main organizing heuristic with similarity as the second heuristic. In these cases, assignment to a particular class is determined more by dissimilarity to other classes than it is to similarity within that class. For example, while child sexual abuse and rape are not necessarily similar events, they are qualitatively equally dissimilar to experiencing an industrial accident or moving. While it is clear that a great deal of information is lost by using such forced categorization, as suggested above, it is sometimes necessary to create these more global classes, such as when large data sets must be grouped logically into 5 or fewer groups for use in an ANOVA.

Time Estimate

Administration	Scoring
Depends on instrument being coded	trained coders can rate scenario in 1–3 minutes depending on length of description of event

Equipment Needed

Paper & Pencil	Computer	Basic Psychophysiological	Specialized Equipment
X			

Psychometric Maturity

Under Construction	Basic Properties Intact	Mature
	X	

Psychometric Properties Summary

Use with the SASE indicates adequate to excellent congruence between trained raters. Congruence of as high 100% has been observed at the *meta* and *general* levels. Other inter-rater reliability studies, including the *specific* level, are in progress as the data pool increases in size.

Particular Sensitivity

Age	Change over Time	Culture / Ethnicity	Gender	Geography / Climate	Sexual Orientation	Socioeconomic Status	Urban / Rural
X	X	X	X	X	X	X	X

Estimate of Number of In-Process Studies
4

Unpublished References

Malnekoff, D. (1995). Secondary traumatic stress in the family members of soldiers of the Gulf Wars. unpublished dissertation, Pacific Graduate School of Psychology. Palo Alto, CA.

Rudolph, J. M. (1994). Perceptions of resource need in disaster situations. Unpublished manuscript, University of Alaska Anchorage, Anchorage, AK.

Stamm, B. H., & Bieber, S. L. (1992). A metatheoretical instrument: The Structural Assessment of Traumatic Stress. Presented at the Eighth Annual Meeting of The International Society for Traumatic Stress Studies. Los Angeles, CA.

Stamm, B. H., & Bieber, S. L. (1994). Perceptions of stressful life experiences: Comparisons across sex and stressor classes. Manuscript under review.

Stamm, B. H., & Bieber, S. L. (1995). Conceptualizing stressful life experiences: A metatheoretical structural approximation. Manuscript under review.

Stamm, B. H., Green, B. L., Figley, C. R., Lebowitz, L., Keily, M. C., Friedman, M., Pearlman, L. A., Weiss, D., Hammarberg, M., Weathers, F. W., Plecovitz, D., & Hartsough, D. (1993). *Instrumentation in the field of traumatic stress.* Ninth Annual conference of the International Society for Traumatic Stress Studies. San Antonio, TX.

Stamm, B. H., Varra, E. M., & Sandberg, C. T. (1993). *When it happens to another: Direct and indirect trauma.* Ninth Annual conference of the International Society for Traumatic Stress Studies. San Antonio, TX.

Published References

Stamm, B. H. (1995). Contextualizing death and trauma: A preliminary attempt. In C. F. Figley (Ed.), *Death and trauma.* New York: Bruner/Mazel.

General Comments

There is a computer program written in SPSS that is available upon request. The best method for obtaining this program is via e-mail.

Key Words

Population	Stressor	Topic
adolescents adults children elderly minority	any	content analysis qualitative analysis research

Reference Citation for This Review

Stamm, B. H., Varra, E. M., & Rudolph, J. M. (1996). Psychometric review of Stressful Events Content Analysis Coding Scheme (SECACS). In B. H. Stamm (Ed.). *Measurement of stress, trauma, and adaptation.* Lutherville, MD: Sidran Press.

Measure Contact Name

B. Hudnall Stamm, Ph.D.

Address   Traumatic Stress Research Group
PO Box 531
Hanover, NH 03755 USA

Phone/Voice Mail:
Fax:
E-mail: b.hudnall.stamm@dartmouth.edu

Coding Scheme and Normative Data
across Four "Stressful Life Experiences"

The normative data below were collected from two different college student populations in the US—Northern Rocky Mountain (n=1081) and Northeastern (n=36). Because of a peculiarity in the Northern Rocky Mountain data collection, 95 cases were not coded for the meta levels listed but do but appear later in the general and specific levels.

The tables outline the frequency each class was coded and the percentage of that frequency to the total subject population. All information recorded in the tables was coded from the stressful life experiences essays collected with the SASE (see Stamm, in this volume). The categories of most stressful, second, third and fourth most stressful are based on subjects' stress ranking of their life experiences.

Frequencies Rocky Mountain US Sample (N=1081)

Meta Category	Most Stressful		Second Most Stressful		Third Most Stressful		Fourth Most Stressful	
	N	%	N	%	N	%	N	%
Bad Things Code=1	154	14.2%	64	5.9%	32	3%	6	.006%
Death Code=2	249	23%	130	12%	43	4%	5	.005%
Problems in Living (Code=3)	471	43.6%	328	30.3%	154	14.2%	19	.018%
Sexual Assault Code=4)	44	4.1%	20	1.9%	13	1.2%	2	.002%

Frequencies Northeastern US Sample (n=36)

Meta Category	Most Stressful		Second Most Stressful		Third Most Stressful		Fourth Most Stressful	
Bad Things Code=1	11	30.6%	5	13.9%	4	11.1%	1	2.8%
Death Code=2	10	27.8%	4	11.1%	5	13.9%	-	-
Problems in Living (Code=3)	13	36.1%	11	30.6%	7	19.4%	6	16.7%
Sexual Assault Code =4)	-	-	2	0.06%	-	-	-	-

Frequencies Rocky Mountain US Sample (n=1081)

General	Most Stressful		Second Most Stressful		Third Most Stressful		Fourth Most Stressful	
war/combat (code=1)	20	1.9%	7	.006%	9	.008		
violence (code=2)	73	6.8%	43	3.97%	16	1.4%	2	.002
problem in living (code=3)	364	33.7%	254	23.5%	118	10.9%	14	1.3%
duty related (code=4)	8	.007%	5	.005%	2	.002%		
accident/disaster (code=5)	127	11.7%	54	5.00%	25	2.3%	7	.006%
sexual assault (code=6)	37	3.4%	20	1.85%	13	1.2%	2	.002%
health related (code=7)	117	10.8%	72	6.66%	36	3.3%	5	.005%
unspecified (code=9)	312	28.9%	97	8.97%	31	2.9%	3	.003%

This instrument, by B. Hudnall Stamm, may be reproduced without charge and freely distributed, as long as no funds are exchanged.

Frequencies Northeastern US Sample (n=36)

General	Most Stressful		Second Most Stressful		Third Most Stressful		Fourth Most Stressful	
war/combat (code=1)	1	2.8%						
violence (code=2)	5	13.9%	5	13.9%	2	5.6%	2	5.6%
problem in living (code=3)	13	36.1%	11	30.6%	6	16.7	14	38.9%
duty related (code=4)								
accident/disaster (code=5)	5	13.9%			2	5.6%	7	19.4%
sexual assault (code=6)					1	2.8%	2	5.6%
health related (code=7)	6	16.7%	4	11.1%	3	8.3%	5	13.9%
unspecified (code=9)							3	8.3%

Specific

The following is the full event list. There are spaces to allow for additions or alterations based upon the *specific* project and types of traumatic events. The tables list the most frequently designated events and percentages based upon the total population (n=1081). Information on *specific* events was not reported for the Northeastern US sample due to the limited size.

1 terrorism
2. pow
3. holocaust
4. refugee
5. combat
6. torture
7.
8.
9.
10. caused death
11. witness death
12. homicide
13. suicide
14. fight
15. mugging
16. theft/rob
17. physical abuse
18. harassment/ threats
19. sex harassment
20. rape
21. incest
22. dysfunction
23. extrafamilial sexual abuse
24. intrafamilial sexual abuse

25. kidnap
26.
27.
28.
29.
30. waiting/ ambiguity
31. moving
32. wedding/ marriage
33. divorce
34. grief
35. punishment
36. breakup
37. poor relationship
38. abortion
39. pregnancy
40. unwanted pregnancy
41. basic training
42. school
43. career change
44. fired
45. graduation/ vocation
46. grades/flunk
47. job overload
48. unemployment
49. living adjustment
50. money

51. legal
52. competition
53.
54.
55. therapist
56. crisis worker
57. EMS
58. police
59. firefighter
60. human disaster, other
61. plane crash
62. train wreck
63. shipwreck
64. car wreck
65. toxic disaster
66. industrial accident
67. riot
68. natural disaster, other
69. earthquake
70. fire
71. flood
72. tornado
73. tsunami
74. winter storm
75. volcano
76.

77.
78.
79.
80. surgery
81. accident injury
82. HIV/AIDS
83. cancer
84. dismemberment
85. chronic physical illness
86. chronic mental illness
87. terminal illness
88. alcoholism/
89. substance abuse
90. illness
91. heart attack/ stroke
92. mortality
93.
94.
95.
96.
97.
98.
99. unspecified

Frequencies for Northern Rocky Mountain US Sample (N=1081) *Specific*

Specific

(all over 2%)	Most Stressful	
	N	%
Divorce	64	5.9%
Car Wreck	64	5.9%
Poor Relation	40	3.7%
Living Adjustment	37	3.4%
Surgery	34	3.1%
Suicide	29	2.7%
Accident-Injury	28	2.6%
Abuse	27	2.5%
Breakup	23	2.1%
Legal	23	2.1%
Chronic Illness	23	2.1%

Specific

(all over 1%)	2nd Stressful	
	N	%
Divorce	47	4.3%
Poor Relation	36	3.3%
Living Adjustment	25	2.3%
Car Wreck	23	2.1%
Abuse	22	2.0%
Moving	19	1.8%
Suicide	18	1.7%
Breakup	15	1.4%
Cancer & Illness	14	1.3%
Surgery	12	1.1%
Alcoholism/Sub Abuse	12	1.1%

Specific

(over 1%)	3rd Stressful	
	N	%
Car Wreck	15	1.4%
Divorce	13	1.2%
Living Adjust	13	1.2%
Moving	11	1.0%

Specific

(top 2)	4th Stressful	
	N	%
Car Wreck	4	.37%
Divorce	3	.28%

To Whom/By Whom

100. self
101. husband
102. wife
103. baby own
104. child own
105. 1st degree relative
106. mother
107. father
108. parent unspec
109. stepparent unspec
110. stepmother
111. stepfather
112. multiple birth sib
113. older sib unspec
114. older brother
115. older sister
116. younger sib unspec
117. younger brother
118. younger sister
119. sib unspecified
120.
121.
122.
123.
124.

125.
126.
127.
128. 2nd degree relative
129. grandmother
130. grandfather
131. aunt
132. uncle
133. cousin
134. foster parent unspec
135. foster mother
136. foster father
137. shelter worker
138. nanny
139. babysitter
140.
141.
142.
143.
144.
145.
146.
147.
148. friend
149. good friend

150. significant other
151. ex-significant other
152. acquaintance
153. date
154. baby not own
155. child not own
156. roommate
157. workmate
158. schoolmate
159. enemy
160.
161.
162.
163.
164.
165. shop keep
166. military officer
167. judge
168. police
169. physician/ primary care provider
170. therapist
171. live-in help
172. counselor
173. minister

174. teacher
175. boss
176. employee
177. criminal
178. bystander
179. stranger
180.
181.
182. pet, own
183. pet, not own
184. domestic animal
185. wild animal
186.
187. property
188. environment
189.
190. corporation
191. government
192. invaders
193. own military
194.
195. illness
196.
197.
198. unspecified

Stress Response Rating Scale

Type of Population

Any and all except children

Cost

Minimal

Copyright

Languages

English

What It Measures

Intrusion, Avoidance, and General Arousal

The SRRS is a clinician-report measure of the three broad domains of response to traumatic stress: intrusive phenomena, avoidant and numbing phenomena, and hyperarousal phenomena. It is targeted to levels of symptoms in the past 7 days. In this way it is linked to provide an objective observer-based companion to the Impact of Event Scale—Revised. It provides a dimensional method of capturing the severity of symptomatic distress.

Measure Content Survey, Procedure, or Process

Forty items tap the standard aspects of both emotional and cognitive experiences of intrusion, avoidance and numbing, and hyperarousal. Stem definitions further refine the exact psychological construct of each item. Responses are scored on a 4-point Likert response with anchors ranging from "Not present" to "Major."

Theoretical Orientation Summary

The SRRS is not derived from a specific narrow theoretical orientation, but rather stems from the large body of observation of stress response syndromes promulgated by Horowitz and further refinement of the diagnostic criteria of PTSD.

Time Estimate

Administration	Scoring
10–20 minutes	10–15 minutes

Equipment Needed

Paper & Pencil	Computer	Basic Psychophysiological	Specialized Equipment
X			

Psychometric Maturity

Under Construction	Basic Properties Intact	Mature
		X

Psychometric Properties Summary

Coefficient alpha of .84–.86 for sample of 439 respondents rated by expert clinicians in the National Vietnam Veterans Readjustment Study Clinical Examination Component subsample. In previous research, interrater reliability using intraclass correlations for the pooled rating of two judges was .87 for Intrusion, .60 for Avoidance, and .78 for General Arousal.

Particular Sensitivity

Age	Change over Time	Culture / Ethnicity	Gender	Geography / Climate	Sexual Orientation	Socioeconomic Status	Urban / Rural
	X						

Estimate of Number of In-Process Studies

many

Unpublished References

unknown

Published References (Selected)

Horowitz, M. J., Marmar, C. R., Weiss D. S., DeWitt, K. N., & Rosenbaum, R. (1984). Brief psychotherapy of bereavement reactions: The relationship of process to outcome. *Archives of General Psychiatry, 41,* 438–448.

Jordan, B. K., Marmar, C. R., Fairbank, J. A., Schlenger, W. E., Kulka, R. A., Hough, R. L., & Weiss, D. S. (1992). Problems in families of male Vietnam veterans with posttraumatic stress disorder. *Journal of Consulting and Clinical Psychology, 60,* 916–926.

Kulka, R. T., Schlenger, W. E., Fairbank, J. A., Hough, R. L., Jordan, B. K., Mannar, C. R., & Weiss, D. S. (1990). *Trauma and the Vietnam War generation: Report of findings from the national Vietnam veterans readjustment study.* New York: Brunner/Mazel.

Mariner, C. M., Horowitz, M. J., Weiss, D. S., Wilner, N. R., & Kaltreider, N. B. (1988). A controlled trial of brief psychotherapy and mutual-help group treatment of conjugal bereavement. *American Journal of Psychiatry, 145,* 203–209.

Marmar, C. R., & Weiss, D. S. (1992). The prevalence of post-traumatic stress disorder in the Vietnam generation: A multimethod, multisource assessment of psychiatric disorder. *Journal of Traumatic Stress, 5,* 333–363.

Marmar, C. R., Weiss, D. S., Schlenger, W. E., Fairbank, J. A., Jordan, B. K., Kulka, R. A., & Hough, R. L. (1994). Peritraumatic dissociation and posttraumatic stress in male Vietnam theater veterans. *American Journal of Psychiatry, 151,* 902–907.

Weiss, D. S. (1993). Structured clinical interview techniques. In J. P. Wilson & B. Raphael (Ed.)., *International Handbook of Traumatic Stress Syndromes.* New York: Plenum Press.

Weiss, D. S., DeWitt, K. N., Kaltreider, N. B., & Horowitz, M. J. (1985). A proposed method for measuring change beyond symptoms. *Archives of General Psychiatry, 42,* 703–708.

Weiss, D. S., Horowitz, M .J., & Wilner, N. R. (1984). The Stress Response Rating Scale: A clinician's measure for rating the response to serious life events. *British Journal of Clinical Psychology, 23,* 202–215.

Weiss, D. S., Marmar, C. R., Schlenger, W. E., Fairbank, J. A., Jordan, B. K., Hough, R. L., & Kulka, R. A. (1992). The prevalence of lifetime and partial post-traumatic stress disorder in Vietnam theater veterans. *Journal of Traumatic Stress, 5,* 365–376.

General Comments

Key Words

Population	Stressor	Topic
adolescents adults any elderly	any	assessment general treatment

Reference Citation for This Review

Weiss, D.S. (1996). Psychometric review of Stress Response Rating Scale. In B. H. Stamm (Ed.). *Measurement of stress, trauma, and adaptation.* Lutherville, MD: Sidran Press.

Measure Contact Name

Daniel S. Weiss, Ph.D.

Address: UCSF Box 0984

Department of Psychiatry

San Francisco, CA 94143-0984 USA

Phone: 415.476.7557

Fax: 415.502.7296

E-mail: dweiss@itsa.ucsf.edu

STRESS RESPONSE RATING SCALE

Directions: Please judge the degree to which the following forty (40) signs and symptoms describe the subject **IN THE PAST (7) SEVEN DAYS.** Base your judgements on either the history as reported to you or your own observations during the interview. Circle the appropriate response for each item.

1. **HYPERVIGILANCE** - Excessively alert, overly scanning the surrounding environment, overly aroused in perceptual searching, tensely expectant:

0	1	3	5
NOT PRESENT	MINOR	MODERATE	MAJOR

2. **STARTLE REACTIONS** - Flinching after noises, unusual orienting reactions, blanching or otherwise reacting to stimuli that usually do not warrant such responses:

0	1	3	5
NOT PRESENT	MINOR	MODERATE	MAJOR

3. **ILLUSIONS OR MISPERCEPTIONS** - A misappraisal of a person, object, or scene as something or someone else (e.g., a bush is seen for a moment as a person; a person is misrecognized as someone else):

0	1	3	5
NOT PRESENT	MINOR	MODERATE	MAJOR

4. **INTRUSIVE THOUGHTS OR IMAGES WHEN TRYING TO SLEEP** - Unwelcome and unbidden mental contents that may be difficult to dispel; include trains of thought that begin volitionally but develop an out-of-control quality:

0	1	3	5
NOT PRESENT	MINOR	MODERATE	MAJOR

5. **BAD DREAMS** - Any dreams experienced as unpleasant, not just the classical nightmare with anxious awakenings:

0	1	3	5
NOT PRESENT	MINOR	MODERATE	MAJOR

6. **HALLUCINATIONS, PSEUDOHALLUCINATIONS** - An emotional reaction to imagined stimuli, experienced as if it were real, regardless of the person's belief in its reality. "Felt presences" of others as well as sensations of smell, taste, touch, movement, sound, and vision are included along with out-of-body experiences:

0	1	3	5
NOT PRESENT	MINOR	MODERATE	MAJOR

7.   **INTRUSIVE IMAGES WHILE AWAKE** - Unbidden sensations which occurs in a nonvolitional manner either in visual or other sensory systems. Awareness of these images is unwanted and occurs suddenly:

0	1	3	5
NOT PRESENT	MINOR	MODERATE	MAJOR

8.   **INTRUSIVE THOUGHTS OR FEELINGS WHILE AWAKE** - Unwilled entries of simple ideas or trains of thought and feeling taking unwilled directions:

0	1	3	5
NOT PRESENT	MINOR	MODERATE	MAJOR

9.   **RE-ENACTMENTS** - Any behavior that repeats any aspects of the serious life event, from minor tic-like movements and gestures to acting out in major movements and sequences, including retelling the event. Repeated enactments of personal responses to the life event, whether or not they actually occurred at the time of the event:

0	1	3	5
NOT PRESENT	MINOR	MODERATE	MAJOR

10.   **RUMINATION OR PREOCCUPATION** - Continuous conscious awareness about the event and associations to the event that go beyond ordinary thinking through. The key characteristic is a sense of uncontrolled repetition:

0	1	3	5
NOT PRESENT	MINOR	MODERATE	MAJOR

11.   **DIFFICULTY IN DISPELLING THOUGHTS AND FEELINGS** - Once a thought or feeling has come to mind, even if it was deliberate, awareness of it cannot be stopped:

0	1	3	5
NOT PRESENT	MINOR	MODERATE	MAJOR

12.   **PANGS OF EMOTION** - A wave of feeling that increases and then decreases rather than remaining constant:

0	1	3	5
NOT PRESENT	MINOR	MODERATE	MAJOR

13.   **FEARS OR SENSATIONS OF LOSING BODILY CONTROL** - Sensations of urinating, vomiting, or defecating without will, fear of suffocating, fear of being unable to control voluntary behavior as well as somatic responses such as sweating, diarrhea, tachycardia:

0	1	3	5
NOT PRESENT	MINOR	MODERATE	MAJOR

14. **INATTENTION, DAZE** - Staring off into space, failure to determine the significance of stimuli, flatness of response to stimuli:

0	1	3	5
NOT PRESENT	MINOR	MODERATE	MAJOR

15. **MEMORY FAILURE** - Inability to recall expectable details, sequences of events, or specific events:

0	1	3	5
NOT PRESENT	MINOR	MODERATE	MAJOR

16. **LOSS OF TRAIN OF THOUGHT** - Temporary or micro-momentary lapses in continuation of a communication, or a report of inability to concentrate on a train of thought:

0	1	3	5
NOT PRESENT	MINOR	MODERATE	MAJOR

17. **NUMBNESS** - Sense of not having feelings, or being "benumbed." (<u>Note</u>: Either patient report or your inference is acceptable here.)

0	1	3	5
NOT PRESENT	MINOR	MODERATE	MAJOR

18. **SENSE OF UNREALITY** - Experiences of depersonalization, derealization, or altered sense of time and place:

0	1	3	5
NOT PRESENT	MINOR	MODERATE	MAJOR

19. **WITHDRAWAL** - Feeling or actions indication social isolation or experiences of being isolated and detached:

0	1	3	5
NOT PRESENT	MINOR	MODERATE	MAJOR

20. **MISDIRECTION OF FEELINGS** - Displacement of positive or negative feelings:

0	1	3	5
NOT PRESENT	MINOR	MODERATE	MAJOR

21. **EXCESSIVE USE OF ALCOHOL OR DRUGS** - Avoidance of implications of event by increased usage. Alcohol: excessive usage. Drugs: abuse of prescription agents, as well as abuse of other drugs, legal and illegal:

0	1	3	5
NOT PRESENT	MINOR	MODERATE	MAJOR

22. **INHIBITION OF THINKING** - Attempts to block thinking about the event. Success or awareness of the attempt is not a consideration:

0	1	3	5
NOT PRESENT	MINOR	MODERATE	MAJOR

23. **UNREALISTIC DISTORTION OF MEANINGS** - Effects of the event on day-to-day living are inaccurately appraised:

0	1	3	5
NOT PRESENT	MINOR	MODERATE	MAJOR

24. **EXCESSIVE SLEEPING** - Avoidance of implications of the event by increased sleeping as well as by simply staying in bed:

0	1	3	5
NOT PRESENT	MINOR	MODERATE	MAJOR

25. **AVOIDANCE OF REMINDERS** - Staying away from certain places, foods, activities; avoiding photographs or other mementos:

0	1	3	5
NOT PRESENT	MINOR	MODERATE	MAJOR

26. **SEEKING OF DISTRACTING STIMULATION OR ACTIVITY** - Avoidance of the implications of the event by seeking excessive exposure to external stimuli or activities such as television, loud must, fast driving, sexual activity, voracious reading, or other diversions:

0	1	3	5
NOT PRESENT	MINOR	MODERATE	MAJOR

27. **HYPERACTIVITY** - Fidgeting, markedly increased pace of activity, inability to slow down or stop sequences of actions; periods of frenzied activity:

0	1	3	5
NOT PRESENT	MINOR	MODERATE	MAJOR

28. **RETARDED PACE OF ACTIONS** - Psychomotor retardation; clear slowing, either continuous or episodic, of thought or behavior:

0	1	3	5
NOT PRESENT	MINOR	MODERATE	MAJOR

TREMORS OR TICS - Tremors or tics, including tics about the eyes or mouth. (Note: Basis of tremor or tic as neurological or characterological is irrelevant.)

0	1	3	5
NOT PRESENT	MINOR	MODERATE	MAJOR

30. **CLUMSINESS OR CARELESSNESS** - Dropping objects, bumping into furniture, actions that are more than awkward:

0	1	3	5
NOT PRESENT	MINOR	MODERATE	MAJOR

31. **AUTONOMIC HYPERAROUSAL** - Sweating, palpitations, frequent urination, altered skin color, altered pupil size, or other autonomic signs:

0	1	3	5
NOT PRESENT	MINOR	MODERATE	MAJOR

32. **TROUBLED SLEEP** - An inability to fall and stay asleep; bad feeling about or during sleep:

0	1	3	5
NOT PRESENT	MINOR	MODERATE	MAJOR

33. **RESTLESSNESS OR AGITATION** - Report of inner sensations of agitation or action and behavior which is restless or agitated:

0	1	3	5
NOT PRESENT	MINOR	MODERATE	MAJOR

34. **EXCITED STATES** - Thought and action is dominated by excessively high rate of arousal, information processing, and expression. May include excessively high levels of sexuality, creativity, productivity, exercise:

0	1	3	5
NOT PRESENT	MINOR	MODERATE	MAJOR

35. **SELF-HATRED** - Uncontrollable suicidal preoccupation or gestures, self-loathing, or hostility towards a part of the body:

0	1	3	5
NOT PRESENT	MINOR	MODERATE	MAJOR

36. **RAGE AT OTHERS** - Uncontrollable hostility and anger, even if the target is unclear:

0	1	3	5
NOT PRESENT	MINOR	MODERATE	MAJOR

37. **PANIC OR DISINTEGRATION** - Periods of high pressure, confusion, chaos, anxiety, and purposelessness:

0	1	3	5
NOT PRESENT	MINOR	MODERATE	MAJOR

38. **SADNESS** - Uncontrollable sadness or grief; floods of despair, longing, pining, or hopelessness:

0	1	3	5
NOT PRESENT	MINOR	MODERATE	MAJOR

39. **GUILT OR SHAME** - Out-of-control experience of remorse, sense of wrongdoing, or exposure of personal evil or defectiveness:

0	1	3	5
NOT PRESENT	MINOR	MODERATE	MAJOR

40. **IRRITABILITY OR TOUCHINESS** - Relations with peers, children, or strangers that are either inwardly irritating or outwardly abrupt, hostile, and bristling:

0	1	3	5
NOT PRESENT	MINOR	MODERATE	MAJOR

Stress Response Rating Scale
Scoring Information

Intrusion Scale=sum of items 1, 2, 3, 4, 5, 6, 7, 8, 9, 10, 11, 12, 14
Denial/avoidance Scale=sum of items 14, 15, 16, 17, 18, 19, 20, 21, 22, 23, 24, 25, 26
General Arousal Scale=sum of items 27, 28, 29, 30, 31, 32, 33, 34, 35, 36, 37, 38, 39, 40

Item response levels are:

0=Not present
1=Minor
3=Moderate
5=Major

Stressful Life Experiences Screening
Short and Long Forms (SLES-S, SLES-L)

Type of Population

Adult

Cost

Copyright

B. Hudnall Stamm, Ph.D., Traumatic Stress Research Group

Languages

English

What It Measures

Screens for major life events that could be stressful or important in a person's life. Depending on how it is used, it can provide a simple list of experiences or a scale score of experiences with or without the person's perception of the event's stressfulness.

Measure Content Survey, Procedure, or Process

This is a very fast (20-item) screening to use for things such as intake assessment in clinical settings or to identify potential traumatic stressors as possible confounds in research situations. Two forms are available with multiple scoring options. The short form provides a list of events that can be scored in a dichotomous or continuous fashion. The long form asks the person how stressful the event was for them at the time of the event and how stressful they find it now.

Theoretical Orientation

The screening draws from the extant literature and the *DSM* although it is not intended to be used for diagnosis of PTSD. The underlying theory of the screening is Structural Conceptualization of Stressful Experiences (SCSE, Stamm, 1995; Stamm, in press; also see SECACS and SASE in this volume); a contextual model which incorporates, but is not limited to, the *DSM* PTSD diagnosis. SCSE makes the assumption that stressful life experiences are an integral part of being human. Stressful events can motivate growth in positive or negative ways depending on the person-event interaction, mediated by the distance from the event (time post-event, psychological and/or physical). From SCSE, the stronger the event-induced demand for psychological reorganization and/or the fewer the psychological resources available to accomplish the reorganization, the greater the risk for negative stress of the experience.

Time Estimate

Administration	Scoring
1–5 min short form 5–10 min long form	1–5 minutes

Equipment Needed

Paper & Pencil	Computer	Basic Psychophysiological	Specialized Equipment
X			

Psychometric Maturity

Under Construction	Basic Properties Intact	Mature
X		

Psychometric Properties Summary

The instrument was developed based on extant instruments and research of the Traumatic Stress Research Group. Data were collected on a beta version from military physical health care workers (n=15). Following this, the instrument was reworked to reduce inter-item correlation and increase overall scale stability. Data were gathered from mental health care workers (n=30) and university students (n=30). Data from the university students on the "experienced this" scale (n=30) showed an alpha reliabilities for internal consistency at .7. Item-to-scale correlations generally ranged from .0 to .3 with a few as high as .5. The low item-to-scale correlations, coupled with nearly nonexistent changes in overall alpha reliabilty of the scale, suggest that the instrument is addressing a single overall concept. But most of the questions were unique and separate from other items of the test. Additional data are in the process of being collected for structural and test-retest analyses.

Particular Sensitivity

Age	Change over Time	Culture / Ethnicity	Gender	Geography / Climate	Sexual Orientation	Socioeconomic Status	Urban / Rural
	X (long form)						

Estimated Number of In-Process Studies

three

Unpublished References

Published References

Stamm, B. H. (1996). Contextualizing death and trauma: A preliminary attempt. In C. F. Figley (Ed.). Death and trauma. New York: Brunner/Mazel.

Stamm, B. H. (Ed.) (1995). Secondary traumatic stress: Self-care issues for clinicians, researchers and educators. Lutherville, MD: Sidran Press.

General Comments

Data can be obtained in two forms, discrete or continuous. If categories of present/not present are desired, scores can be summed as 0 (did not happen) or 1 (did happen, any response 1 to 10). If continuous data are desired, the entire scale, 0 to 10, can be used. If there is a need for the person's report of the stressfulness of the event is needed, the long form yields stress levels from 0 (not at all stressful) to 10 (extremely stressful). This can also be asked as a "then" (at the time of the event) and/or "now" question.

Key Words

Population	Stressor	Topic
Adults	Any	Clinical Screening/Intake Research

Reference Citation for This Review

Stamm, B. H., Rudolph, J. M., Dewane, S., Gaines, N., Gorton, K., Paul, G., McNeil, F., Bowen, G., & Ercolano, M. (1996). Psychometric review of Stressful Life Experiences Screening. In B. H. Stamm (Ed.). *Measurement of stress, trauma, and adaptation*. Lutherville, MD: Sidran Press.

Measure Contact Name

B. Hudnall Stamm, Ph.D.

Address   Traumatic Stress Research Group
               PO Box 531
               Hanover, NH 03755 USA

Phone/Voice Mail:

Fax:

E-mail: b.hudnall.stamm@dartmouth.edu

Stressful Life Experiences Screening—Short Form

We are interested in learning about your experiences. Below is a list of experiences that some people have found stressful. Please fill in the number that best represents how much the following statements describe your experiences. If you are not sure of your answer, just give us your best guess.

Describes your Experience (use in Describes Experiences Column)

0	1	2	3	4	5	6	7	8	9	10

I did not experience | a little like like my experiences | | | | somewhat like my experiences | | | | | exactly like my experiences

Describes Experience	Life Experience
	I have witnessed or experienced a natural disaster; like a hurricane or earthquake.
	I have witnessed or experienced a human made disaster like a plane crash or industrial disaster.
	I have witnessed or experienced a serious accident or injury.
	I have witnessed or experienced chemical or radiation exposure happening to me, a close friend or a family member.
	I have witnessed or experienced a life threatening illness happening to me, a close friend or a family member.
	I have witnessed or experienced the death of my spouse or child.
	I have witnessed or experienced the death of a close friend or family member (other than my spouse or child).
	I or a close friend or family member has been kidnapped or taken hostage.
	I or a close friend or family member has been the victim of a terrorist attack or torture.
	I have been involved in combat or a war or lived in a war affected area.
	I have seen or handled dead bodies other than at a funeral.
	I have felt responsible for the serious injury or death of another person.
	I have witnessed or been attacked with a weapon other than in combat or family setting.
	As a child/teen I was hit, spanked, choked or pushed hard enough to cause injury.
	As an adult, I was hit, choked or pushed hard enough to cause injury.
	As an adult or child, I have witnessed someone else being choked, hit, spanked, or pushed hard enough to cause injury.
	As a child/teen I was forced to have unwanted sexual contact.
	As an adult I was forced to have unwanted sexual contact.
	As a child or adult I have witnessed someone else being forced to have unwanted sexual contact.
	I have witnessed or experienced an extremely stressful event not already mentioned. Please Explain:

Stressful Life Experiences Screening—Long Form

We are interested in learning about your experiences. Below is a list of experiences that some people have found stress-ful. Please fill in the number that best represents how much the following statements describe your experiences. You will need to use two scales, one for how well the statement describes your experiences and one for how stressful you found this experience. If you are not sure of your answer, just give us your best guess.

Describes your Experience (use in Describes Experiences Column)

0	1	2	3	4	5	6	7	8	9	10

I did not experi-ence   a little like like my experiences   somewhat like my experiences   exactly like my experiences

Stressfulness of Experience (Use in Stressfulness Then and Stressfulness Now Column)

0	1	2	3	4	5	6	7	8	9	10

Not at all stress-ful   not very stressful   somewhat stressful   extremely stressful

Describes Experience	Life Experience	Stressfulness Then	Stressfulness Now
	I have witnessed or experienced a natural disaster like a hurricane or earthquake.		
	I have witnessed or experienced a human made disaster like a plane crash or industrial disaster.		
	I have witnessed or experienced a serious accident or injury.		
	I have witnessed or experienced chemical or radiation exposure happening to me, a close friend or a family member.		
	I have witnessed or experienced a life threatening illness happening to me, a close friend or a family member.		
	I have witnessed or experienced the death of my spouse or child.		
	I have witnessed or experienced the death of a close friend or family member (other than my spouse or child).		
	I or a close friend or family member has been kidnapped or taken hostage.		
	I or a close friend or family member has been the victim of a terrorist attack or torture.		
	I have been involved in combat or a war or lived in a war affected area.		
	I have seen or handled dead bodies other than at a funeral.		

I have felt responsible for the serious injury or death of another person.		
I have witnessed or been attacked with a weapon other than in combat or family setting.		
As a child/teen I was hit, spanked, choked or pushed hard enough to cause injury.		
As an adult, I was hit, choked or pushed hard enough to cause injury.		
As an adult or child, I have witnessed someone else being choked, hit, spanked, or pushed hard enough to cause injury.		
As a child/teen I was forced to have unwanted sexual contact.		
As an adult I was forced to have unwanted sexual contact.		
As a child or adult I have witnessed someone else being forced to have unwanted sexual contact.		
I have witnessed or experienced an extremely stressful event not already mentioned. Please Explain:		

Scoring for SLES

For Dichotomous (Categorical) Data
<u>Experience Subscale</u>
if score =0, category=0 (did not experience)
if score >0, category=1 (did experience at some level stressful)
<u>Stress Then or Stress Now Subscale</u>
if score =0, category=0 (did not experience)
if score >0, category=1 (did experience at some level stressful)

For Continuous Data
<u>Experience Subscale</u>
sum all items for total exposure score
<u>Stress Then or Stress Now Subscale</u>
sum all items for total perceived stress score

NOTE: Contact the authors for preliminary norms.

Structural Assessment of Telemedical Systems (SATS)

Type of Population

    Any

Cost

    Depends on application. Basic tables are included here to be used free of charge.

Copyright

    B. Hudnall Stamm and Mark E. N. Agnew

Languages

    Depends on application. Currently being used in English and several arctic languages.

What It Measures

    At the most fundamental level, the SATS is designed to measures (a) cost, (b) acceptance, and (c) satisfaction with telemedicine by both patients and providers. It addresses both technology and medical/social concerns. The SATS can be adapted to assess health care outcomes in clinical trials.

Measure Content Survey, Procedure, or Process

    The SATS begins with an overview of the entire health care system in the telemedical environment. From that overview, based on the sites and the needs of the sites, an assessment program can be designed to answer specific questions drawing from the range of potential tools.

Theoretical Orientation Summary

    The SATS is based on Longitudinal Multigroup Factorial Invariance (Bieber, 1986; Bieber & Meredith, 1986; Stamm, 1992). This methodology assumes that across any system there are sets of variables common to everything in that system. Beyond those universal sets, there are subsets that are unique to only parts of the system. Because of the complex nature of the interaction between technology and medical/social content areas in telemedicine, LMFI was deemed to be particularly appropriate. In addition, Primary and Secondary Traumatic Stress are included as fundamental parts of the medical/social content area.

Time Estimate

Administration	Scoring
depends on measure	depends on measure

Equipment Needed

Paper & Pencil	Computer	Basic Psychophysiological	Specialized Equipment
X	X	X	X

Psychometric Maturity

Under Construction	Basic Properties Intact	Mature
X (method)	X (uses tools and methodologies that have been previously validated)	

Psychometric Properties Summary

SATS employs methodologies and tools that have been previously validated. The structural assessment process has been previously used (for example, see Compassion Fatigue Self Test, Impact of Events Scale Research Scales: Cognitive and Affective, TSI Autonomy and Connection Scales, TSI Belief Scales, Structural Assessment of Traumatic Stress, all in this volume). The actual instruments with which to collect data can be selected depending on sites and questions of interest.

Particular Sensitivity

Age	Change over Time	Culture / Ethnicity	Gender	Geography / Climate	Sexual Orientation	Socioeconomic Status	Urban / Rural
?	X (long form)	X	?	X	?	X	X

Estimate of Number of In-Process Studies

Unpublished References

Pearce, F. W., Stamm, B. H., Agnew, M., Rieder, R. M., Boucha, K., & Eussen, L. (1995). Alaska telemedicine: The trail ahead. Alaska Telemedicine Conference, Anchorage, Alaska.

Stamm, B. H. (1992). Stability and generalizability of the Impact of Events Scale. Presented at the World Conference of the International Society for Traumatic Stress Studies. Amsterdam, The Netherlands.

Stamm, B. H., & Bieber, S. L. (1993). The Impact of Events Scale revisited: Two additional research scales. Presented at the Ninth Annual Meeting of the International Society for Traumatic Stress Studies. San Antonio, Texas, USA.

Stamm, B. H., & Rudolph, J. M. (1994). Rural communities and the information superhighway. Alaska Psychological Association Convention. Anchorage, Alaska.

Published References

Bieber, S. L. (1986). A hierarchical approach to multigroup factorial invariance. *Journal of Classification, 3,* 113–134.

Bieber, S. L., & Meredith, W. (1986). Transformation to achieve a longitudinally stationary factor pattern matrix. *Psychometrika, 50* (4), 535–547.

Bills, L. J. (1995). Trauma based psychiatry for primary care. in B. H. Stamm, B. H. (Ed.). *Secondary traumatic stress: Self-care issues for clinicians, researchers and educators.* Lutherville, MD: Sidran Press.

Stamm, B. H., & Pearce, F. W. (1995). Creating virtual community: Telemedicine and self care. in B. H. Stamm (Ed.). *Secondary traumatic stress: Self-care issues for clinicians, researchers, and educators.* Lutherville, MD: Sidran Press.

Terry, M. J. (1995). Kelengakutelleghpat: an Arctic Community-based approach to trauma. in B. H. Stamm (Ed.). *Secondary traumatic stress: Self-care issues for clinicians, researchers, and educators.* Lutherville, MD: Sidran Press.

General Comments

The authors wish to thank the members of the Alaska Telemedicine Project for feedback on drafts of this measurement template, including Dr. Frederick W. Pearce of the University of Alaska Anchorage Journalism and Public Communications Department and Kathe Boucha-Roberts of Providence Alaska Medical Center. We also wish to thank the U.S. Airforce 3rd Medical Group, in particular Col. Emma Forkner and Capt. Greg Carson for their contributions. Finally, we wish to thank Mike Terry of the Norton Sound Health Corporation; Douglas Perednia of the Telemedicine Information Exchange at the University of Oregon Health Sciences program, and Dr. Rhett Drugie of the Internet Dermatology Society for their reviews of drafts of the project.

Key Words

Population	Stressor	Topic

adolescents
adults
children
computers
elderly
providers
telecommunications
   equipment
telecommunications
   networks
	accidents
	air evacuations
	caregiving
	combat
	extreme climate/
	   geography
	health care
	   transportation
	isolation
	lack of access to
	   supervision
	limited resources
	remote locations
		assessment
		ethics
		research
		rural care
		secondary traumatic
		   stress
		service delivery
		telemedicine

Reference Citation for This Review

Stamm, B. H., Agnew, M. E. N., & Rudolph, J. M. (1996). Psychometric review of Structural Assessment of Telemedical Systems. in Stamm (Ed.). *Measurement of stress, trauma, and adaptation.* Lutherville, MD: Sidran Press.

Measure Authors

B. Hudnall Stamm, Ph.D. & Mark E. N. Agnew, M.A., M.B., M.R.C.G.P.

Measure Contact Name

B. Hudnall Stamm, Ph.D.

Address	Traumatic Stress Research Group PO Box 531 Hanover, NH 03755 USA

Phone/Voice Mail:
Fax:
E-mail: b.hudnall.stamm@dartmouth.edu

Measure Contact Name

Mark E. N. Agnew, M.A., M.B., M.R.C.G.P.

Address:	Director of Medical Staff Education Providence Alaska Medical Center 3200 Providence Drive Anchorage, AK 99508 USA

Phone: 907.261.3011
Fax: 907.261.4911
E-mail: magnew0434@aol.com

Overview of Technology and Human Content

Structural Assessment of Telemedical Systems

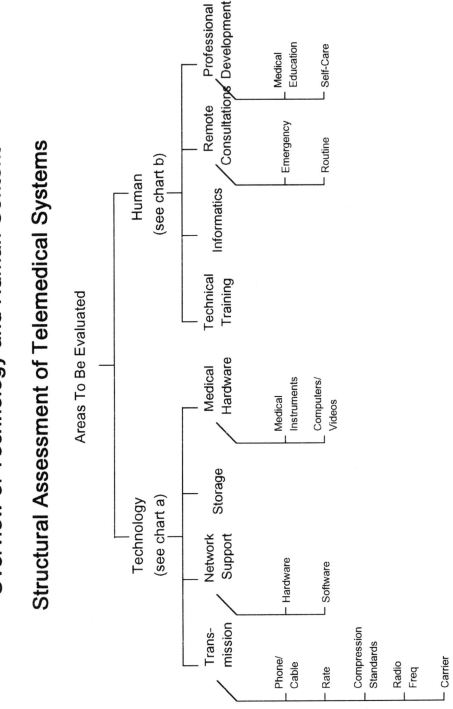

Copyright, B.H. Stamm & M.E.N. Agnew, 1995

This instrument, by B. Hudnall Stamm and Mark E. N. Agnew, may be reproduced without charge and freely distributed, as long as no funds are exchanged.

Overview of Technology Content
Structural Assessment of Telemedical Systems
(chart a)

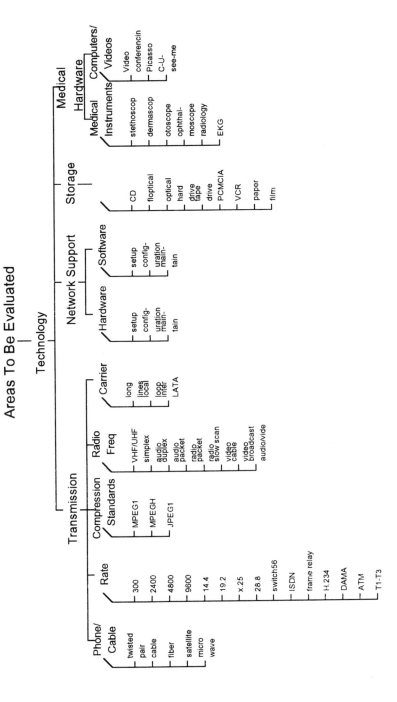

Overview of Human Content

Structural Assessment of Telemedical Systems
(chart b)

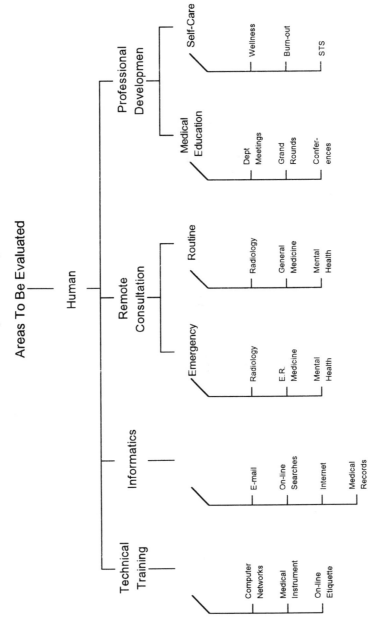

Areas To Be Evaluated

Human

Technical Training
- Computer Networks
- Medical Instrument
- On-line Etiquette

Informatics
- E-mail
- On-line Searches
- Internet
- Medical Records

Remote Consultation

Emergency
- Radiology
- E.R. Medicine
- Mental Health

Routine
- Radiology
- General Medicine
- Mental Health

Professional Developmen

Medical Education
- Dept Meetings
- Grand Rounds
- Confer-ences

Self-Care
- Wellness
- Burn-out
- STS

Copyright. B.H. Stamm & M.E.N. Agnew, 1995

Expanded Chart a
Structural Assessment of telemedical Systems: Technology Content
Assessment (Baseline, Interim, Outcome)

| Location | Need | Project | Transmission | | | | | Network Support | | Storage | Medical Hardware | Expected Outcomes | |
			Phone Cable	Rate	Compress Standards	RF	Carrier	Hardware	Software			Financial	Medical/ Social

Expanded Chart b
Structural Assessment of Telemedical Systems: Human Content

Location	Need	Project	Technical Training	Informatics	Assessment (Baseline, Interim, Outcome)					Expected Outcomes	
					Remote Consultation		Professional Development				
					Emergency	Routine	Medical Education	Self-Care		Financial	Medical/ Social

©B. H. Stamm & M.E.N. Agnew, 1995, 1996

Technology Content
Structural Assessment of Telemedical Systems Tracking Sheet

LOCATION:
PROJECT:
Need 1:
Need 2:
Need 3:

Evaluation Elements	Transmission					Network Support		Storage	Medical Hardware	
	Phone/ Cable	Rate	Compressio Standards	RF	Carrier	Hardware	Software		Medical Instruments	Computers/ Video-conference
Measure What										
Measure How										
Planned Data Analysis										
Identify Outcome										

©B. H. Stamm & M.E.N. Agnew, 1995, 1996

Human Content
Structural Assessment of Telemedical Systems Tracking Sheet

LOCATION:
PROJECT:
Need 1:
Need 2:
Need 3:

Evaluation Elements	Technical Training	Informatics	Consultations		Professional Development	
			Emergency	Routine	Medical Education	Self-Care
Measure What						
Measure How						
Planned Data Analysis						
Identify Outcome						

©B. H. Stamm & M.E.N. Agnew, 1995, 1996

Structural Assessment of Stressful Experiences (SASE)

Type of Population
Adult; any.

Cost

Copyright
B. H. Stamm, Traumatic Stress Research Group

What It Measures
Perceptions and reactions, both positive and negative, across a range of stressful life experiences from little or no stress to extreme stress. Issues which could be described as transpersonal relating to spirituality and meaning form an integral part of the scales.

Measure Content Survey, Procedure, or Process
The instrument is composed of three parts, each of which contains several subscales. There are approximately 200 items plus a written trauma history. The instrument takes about 45 minutes to complete. An overview of the scales is below.

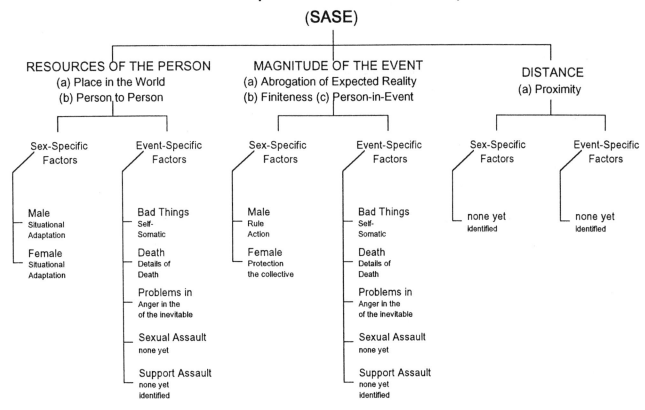

© B. Hudnall Stamm, 1992, 1993, 1996

Part I. Resources of the Person Scales
Universal Scales (apply to males and females, all types of events)
    1. Place in the World
    2. Person to Person
Sex-Specific Scales (apply to all types of events)
    1. Masculine Situational Adaptation (specific to males)
    2. Feminine Situational Adaptation (specific to females)
Trauma-Specific Scales (apply to males and females)
    1. Survivor Maturity (Specific to Accidents/Disasters)
    2. Public Coping/Private Pain (Specific to Death)
    3. Overload (Specific to Problems in Living)
    4. Disempowered Self (Sexual Assault)
5. Vacant Self in Harsh World (Specific to Vicarious)

Part II. Magnitude of the Event Scales
Universal Scales (apply to males and females, all types of events)
    1. Abrogation of Expected Reality
    2. Finiteness
    3. Person in Event
Sex-Specific Scales (apply to all types of events)
    1. Rule Confusion/Action Paradox (male)
    2. Protection within the Collective (female)
Trauma-Specific Scales (apply to males and females)
    1. Self-Focused Somatic Arousal (Specific to Accidents/Disasters)
    2. Details of Death (Specific to Death)
    3. Anger in the Face of the Inevitable (Specific to Problems in Living)

Part III. Distance Scales
Universal Scales (apply to males and females, all types of events)
    1. Proximity—measured in terms of physical and psychological distance

Theoretical Orientation Summary

The instrument is based in the Structural Conceptualization of Stressful Experiences (SCSE). SCSE is a quantitatively derived, metatheoretical structural orientation to stress and traumatic stress (Stamm & Bieber, 1993).

Time Estimate

Administration	Scoring
20–45 minutes	10–20 minutes

Equipment Needed

Paper & Pencil	Computer	Basic Psychophysiological	Specialized Equipment
X			

Psychometric Maturity

Under Construction	Basic Properties Intact	Mature
	X	

Psychometric Properties Summary

Extensive psychometric work has been done using the structural technique of Factorial Invariance, in both longitudinal and multigroup (sex and classes of stressful experiences) form. Structural Reliability (stability) on the Universal scales as measured by Tucker's Coefficient of Congruence (cc) ranges from .82 to .96. Test-retest values ranged between cc=.72 and cc=.82. The specific scales were more varied. Measures for the sex-related scales ranged between cc=.60 and cc=.68. Measures for the trauma-specific subscales generally ranged between cc=.58 and cc=.88, with the exception of the Sexual Assault and the Vicarious groups, which had very modest ccs of .33. This lack of stability in these two groups may be an artifact of small sample size for these two cells. More specific information is available upon request. Norms from college students are available across five broad classes of stressors: accidents/disasters, death, problems in living, sexual assault, and a vicarious trauma/helper group.

Particular Sensitivity

Age	Change over Time	Culture / Ethnicity	Gender	Geography / Climate	Sexual Orientation	Socioeconomic Status	Urban / Rural
?	X	?	X	?	?	?	?

Unpublished References

Malnekoff, D. (1995). Secondary traumatic stress in the family members of soldiers of the Gulf Wars. Unpublished dissertation, Pacific Graduate School of Psychology, Palo Alto, CA.

Stamm, B. H., & Bieber, S. L. (1995). Conceptualizing stressful life experiences: A metatheoretical structural approximation. Manuscript under review.

Stamm, B. H., & Bieber, S. L. (1992). *A metatheoretical instrument: The Structural Assessment of Traumatic Stress.* Presented at the Eighth Annual Meeting of The International Society for Traumatic Stress Studies. Los Angeles, CA

Stamm, B. H., & Bieber, S. L. (1994). Perceptions of stressful life experiences: Comparisons across sex and stressor classes. Manuscript under review.

Stamm, B. H., Green, B. L., Figley, C. R., Lebowitz, L., Keily, M. C., Friedman, M., Pearlman, L. A., Weiss, D., Hammarberg, M., Weathers, F.W., Plecovitz, D., & Hartsough, D. (1993). *Instrumentation in the field of traumatic stress.* Ninth Annual Conference of the International Society for Traumatic Stress Studies. San Antonio, TX.

Stamm, B. H. , Varra, E. M., & Sandberg, C. T. (1993). *When it happens to another: Direct and indirect trauma.* Ninth Annual conference of the International Society for Traumatic Stress Studies. San Antonio, TX.

Published References

Stamm, B. H. (1995). Contextualizing death and trauma: A preliminary attempt. In C. F. Figley (Ed.), *Death and trauma.* New York: Brunner/Mazel.

Key Words

Population	Stressor	Topic
adult	any	assessment measure development spirituality secondary traumatic stress research

Reference Citation for This Review

Stamm, B. H., & Bieber, S. L. (1996). Psychometric review of Structural Assessment of Stressful Experiences (SASE). In B. H. Stamm (Ed.). *Measurement of stress, trauma, and adaptation.* Lutherville, MD: Sidran Press.

Measure Contact Name

B. Hudnall Stamm, Ph.D.

Address   Traumatic Stress Research Group
PO Box 531
Hanover, NH 03755 USA

Phone/Voice Mail:

Fax:

E-mail: b.hudnall.stamm@dartmouth.edu

Resources of the Person

Place in the World Scale

	Males			Females		
	X	SD	n	X	SD	n
Bad Things	7.2	1.2	78	7.3	.95	73
Death	7.4	1.0	108	7.4	.91	138
Living	7.4	1.0	209	7.4	1.0	260
Sexual Assault	7.5	1.0	7	7.4	1.2	37
Support Assault Victim	7.6	1.0	26	7.7	1.1	7

Person to Person Interactions

	Males			Females		
	X	SD	n	X	SD	n
Bad Things	5.37	1.4	79	5.7	1.1	72
Death	5.2	1.3	109	5.8	1.3	133
Living	5.1	1.3	203	5.6	4.4	251
Sexual Assault	5.0	1.0	6	5.7	1.0	35
Support Assault Victim	5.5	1.6	25	5.6	1.5	66

Masculine Situational Adaptation

	Males			Females		
	X	SD	n	X	SD	n
Bad Things	6.3	.8	78			
Death	6.5	.8	108			
Living	6.5	.8	209			
Sexual Assault	6.6	.7	7			
Support Assault Victim	6.6	.7	26			

Feminine Situational Adaptation

	Males			Females		
	X	SD	n	X	SD	n
Bad Things				6.8	.7	73
Death				6.8	.8	138
Living				6.8	.9	260
Sexual Assault				6.7	.8	37
Support Assault Victim				7.0	.9	67

Survivor Maturity

	Males			Females		
	X	SD	n	X	SD	n
Bad Things	6.59	.9	78	6.8	.7	73
Death						
Living						
Sexual Assault						
Support Assault Victim						

Public-Coping/Private-Pain

	Males			Females		
	X	SD	n	X	SD	n
Bad Things						
Death	6.3	.7	108	6.2	.6	138
Living						
Sexual Assault						
Support Assault Victim						

Overload

	Males			Females		
	X	SD	n	X	SD	n
Bad Things						
Death						
Living	6.4	.7	209	6.4	.8	260
Sexual Assault						
Support Assault Victim						

Disempowered Self

	Males			Females		
	X	SD	n	X	SD	n
Bad Things						
Death						
Living						
Sexual Assault	6.8	.9	7	6.7	.8	37
Support Assault Victim						

Vacant-Self-in-a-Harsh-World

	Males			Females		
	X	SD	n	X	SD	n
Bad Things						
Death						
Living						
Sexual Assault						
Support Assault Victim	6.1	.6	26	6.1	.7	67

Magnitude of the Event

Abrogation of Expected Reality

	Males			Females		
	X	SD	n	X	SD	n
Bad Things	7.8	2.0	78	8.4	1.7	68
Death	7.9	1.8	100	8.7	1.8	131
Living	7.1	1.9	191	7.6	1.8	246
Sexual Assault	8.8	1.0	6	9.0	1.7	32
Support Assault Victim	7.4	2.1	23	7.9	2.0	59

Finiteness

	Males			Females		
	X	SD	n	X	SD	n
Bad Things	1.7	1.4	78	1.8	.9	70
Death	2.0	1.3	103	1.6	.9	131
Living	1.3	1.0	196	1.4	.9	247
Sexual Assault	1.5	.6	7	1.6	.9	35
Support Assault Victim	1.7	1.3	24	1.8	1.2	59

Person-in-Event

	Males			Females		
	X	SD	n	X	SD	n
Bad Things	3.8	1.8	78	4.5	1.5	68
Death	4.7	1.4	106	4.9	1.4	133
Living	3.9	1.7	187	4.1	1.7	241
Sexual Assault	4.0	1.0	6	3.5	1.5	31
Support Assault Victim	4.3	1.8	24	4.6	1.7	58

Rule-Confusion/Action-Paradox

	Males			Females		
	X	SD	n	X	SD	n
Bad Things	4.1	1.9	78			
Death	4.4	1.9	102			
Living	3.9	1.9	196			
Sexual Assault	5.4	1.4	7			
Support Assault Victim	3.7	1.7	25			

Protection-Within-the-Collective

	Males			Females		
	X	SD	n	X	SD	n
Bad Things				3.4	1.6	70
Death				3.8	1.3	136
Living				2.8	1.6	244
Sexual Assault				2.6	1.1	33
Support Assault Victim				3.5	1.9	56

Reactive-Self-Focused-Somatic-Arousal

	Males			Females		
	X	SD	n	X	SD	n
Bad Things	3.1	1.7	78	3.2	1.3	70
Death						
Living						
Sexual Assault						
Support Assault Victim						

Details of Death

	Males			Females		
	X	SD	n	X	SD	n
Bad Things						
Death	2.3	1.6	105	2.2	1.5	134
Living						
Sexual Assault						
Support Assault Victim						

Anger-in-the-Face-of-the-Inevitable

	Males			Females		
	X	SD	n	X	SD	n
Bad Things						
Death						
Living	3.7	2.1	198	3.8	1.9	244
Sexual Assault						
Support Assault Victim						

Scoring of the SASE

Pattern for reverse items—marked with an r
0=0 1=10 2=9 3=8 4=7 5=6 6=5 7=4 8=3 9=2 10=1

Place in the World
5,6,7,8,10,15,19,25,26,27,28,29,31r,35r,37r

Person to Person
2r,9r,11r,12r,14r,16r,18r,20r,21r,22r,30r,36r,37r,38r

Masculine Situational Adaptation
1,2,11,12,14,15r,30,34,38r

Feminine Situational Adaptation
3,4,8,16,18r,21r,26,38

Survivor Maturity
1r,3,17,18r,19,26,30r,32r,36,38

Private-Coping/Public-Pain
3,4,10,11r,12r,13,14r,15,28r,29r,36

Overload
3r,4r,5,13r,20,23r,24,26r,36r,38r

Disempowered-Self
1,4,12r,13r,14r,18r,20r,32r,36,38

Vacant Self in a Harsh World
1r,6r,13,17,27r,32r,36,38

Abrogation of Reality
46,47,49,50,51,54,55,56,57,58,59,60,61,62,63,67,80,84,85,86,87,88,89,
104,105,106,107,108,109,110,111,112,113,117,118,121,122,123,124,125,126

Finiteness
54r,55r,56r,62,63,64,65,68,69,70,71,72,73,74,75,76,77,78,79,82,86r,87r, 88r,89r,90r,116r,117r

Person in Event
49r,51r,59r,67r,90r,94,95,96,97r,98,99,100r,101r,115,116r,117,120,122,123,124,125,126

Rule-Confusion/Action-Paradox
47,48,49,50,51,53,90,91,92,93,95,96

Protection-within-the-Collective
88,89,92,93,98,99,101r,102r,110r,111r

Reactive-Self-Focused-Somatic-Arousal
61r,62r,66,76r,87r,88r,89r,91r,92r,93r,100,101,102,108,109,110,111

Details of Death
66r,68r,72,74,75,81,85,86r,87r,88r,89r,103,112

Anger-in-the-Face-of-the-Inevitable
54r,55r,56r,57r,86,87,88,89,90,91,92,93,106

Structural Assessment of Stressful Experiences (SASE)

This is a questionnaire about stressful life experiences. We are interested in anything you have to tell us. In this first section, we want to get to know a bit about you and your life in general. Throughout the questionnaire we ask that you respond as honestly as you can.

Birth date: _____ Month _____ Day _____ Year

Race/Ethnic Group: _____

Sex: _____ Male _____ Female

Marital Status:
_____ Single _____ Married _____ Divorced _____ Living with someone _____ Widowed

Number of Children living with you _____
_____ under 3 years _____ 3–5 years old
_____ 6–11 years old _____ 12–15 years old
_____ 16–18 years old _____ over 18 years old

Number of Children not living with you

Work (check all that apply):
_____ unemployed _____ work more than one job
_____ full time, year round _____ full-time, seasonal
_____ part-time, seasonal _____ part-time seasonal
_____ student, full time _____ student, part-time

Highest Grade Level (in years) _____
Highest Degree /Technical Certification Earned:

Occupation (check all that apply):
_____ Professional/Technical
_____ Manager/Proprietor
_____ Service worker _____ Laborer
_____ Factory line worker
_____ Farmer or fisheries

Total Annual Household Income:
_____ less than $5000 _____ $35,001–$40,000
_____ $5000–$10,000 _____ $40,001–$45,000
_____ $10,001–$15,000 _____ $45,001–$50,000
_____ $15,001–$20,000 _____ $50,001–$60,000
_____ $20,001–$25,000 _____ $60,001–$75,000
_____ $25,001–$30,000 _____ $75,001–$100,000
_____ $30,001–$35,000 _____ over $100,000

If you work, what kind of job do you have?_____

Is this the field in which you were trained? _____ yes _____ no

If no, what type work were you trained to do? _____

If you are working outside of the field in which you were trained, is this by choice? _____ yes _____ no

What kind of work would you like to do? _____

Religious Affiliation (be as specific as possible, e.g. Southern Baptist, LDS, Muslim, Native American, atheist, etc.)

Using the scale below, how important are your religious beliefs to you?

0	1	2	3	4	5	6	7	8	9	10
Not at all important		Somewhat important							Extremely important	

SECTION I

In this section you will be asked to respond to a number of questions about how you view the world. You should rate each statement with the number from the scale below which best represents your thoughts or feelings about the statement. Since each person is unique, there are no right or wrong answers.

0	1	2	3	4	5	6	7	8	9	10
Not true at all	strongly disagree, I rarely feel/think this							strongly agree, I often feel/think this		

____ 1. I try to avoid thoughts about my death.
____ 2. I do not like to be around sick people.
____ 3. There are some things that I do not have the physical ability to do.
____ 4. At times I wish I had a different body.
____ 5. I feel like I have a place in this world.
____ 6. I feel like I can make a positive contribution to the world.
____ 7. I make decisions to pursue my goals.
____ 8. When things are different than I expect, I can adapt.
____ 9. When I have to make changes I feel like I am losing part of myself.
____ 10. I can use what is in my environment to solve problems.
____ 11. I avoid getting into situations where I have to adapt.
____ 12. I am more comfortable when my friends are just like me.
____ 13. I enjoy being around people who are different from myself.
____ 14. If people were more alike there would be fewer problems in the world.
____ 15. I enjoy people who take a new approach to old problems.
____ 16. Sometimes people act in ways that are just unnatural.
____ 17. People learn best when they discover something for themselves.
____ 18. By the time a person is grown, they know what they need to know to get along in the world.
____ 19. I do things because I believe in them, not just for money.
____ 20. I like my work because it makes me feel powerful.
____ 21. In order to get what you need, you have to take it.
____ 22. If you do not watch out, people will take things from you.
____ 23. At times you have to do what is right regardless of the cost.
____ 24. When I see someone in pain I want to help.
____ 25. When things are difficult, I can find comfort in my beliefs.
____ 26. Sometimes I have to just take time out for me.
____ 27. I care about me.
____ 28. Even when I feel alone, I realize that I am not truly alone.
____ 29. My faith supports me.
____ 30. When I am feeling low, I can only find comfort from other people.
____ 31. Sometimes when I think about myself there is not anything to think about.
____ 32. The strong people have the right to command the weaker people.
____ 33. I have an obligation to preserve resources for future generations.
____ 34. I have a community on whom I can count.
____ 35. There is no one I can turn to.
____ 36. Bad things happen to me.

_____ 37. I never get a break.

_____ 38. I have been a victim before.

The following statements describe how children are sometimes treated by their parent(s) [parental figures or primary caretaker(s)] as well as others in their life. Please read each paragraph and then decide how well the information in the paragraph describes how you were treated by your parent(s) or parental figures or others in your life. Use the following rating scale.

0	1	2	3	4	5	6	7	8	9	10
Not true at all	**a little bit/ I think this is true**								**a great deal I am sure this is true**	

Sometimes birth parents or parental figures belittle their children's accomplishments, feelings, or physical appearance. They may make the child feel stupid for making mistakes, unloved unless they do what the parents wants, or unappreciated no matter what they do. They may make the child feel that he or she is inadequate and not really lovable.

_____ How much does this paragraph describe the way *your parent(s) or parent figure(s)* treated you?

Who was this person(s)? Check all that apply.

_____ birth parents   _____ parental figures   _____ both birth parents and other parental figures

Sometimes it is not a parent or parental figure but an outsider, friend, sibling, or other relative who belittles a child's accomplishments, feelings, or physical appearance. They may make the child feel stupid for making mistakes, unloved unless they do what the person wants, or unappreciated no matter what they do. They may make the child feel that he or she is inadequate and not really lovable. How much does this paragraph describe the way someone *other* than your parent(s) or parental figure(s) treated you?

Where did this happen? _____

What was this person's relationship to you? _____

Sometimes birth parents or parental figures get very angry and spank a child too hard. They may do a variety of things like beat the child, hit the child with objects, choke the child, or shove the child around. How much does this paragraph describe the way your *parent(s) or parental figure(s)* treated you? Check all that apply.

_____ How much does this paragraph describe the way *your parent(s) or parent figure(s)* treated you?

Who was this person(s)? Check all that apply.

_____ birth parents   _____ parental figures   _____ both birth parents and other parental figures

Sometimes it is not a birth parent or parental figure but an outsider, friend, sibling, or other relative who gets very angry and spanks a child too hard. They may do a variety of things like beat the child, hit the child with objects, choke the child, or shove the child around.

_____ How much does this paragraph describe the way someone *other* than your birth parent(s) or parental figure(s) treated you?

Where did this happen? _____

What was this person's relationship to you? _____

Sometimes birth parents or parental figures use the child to satisfy their own sexual needs. They may fondle the child or have the child fondle him or her. They may engage in oral sex or have intercourse with the child. How much does the above paragraph describe the way *your birth parent(s) or parental figure(s)* treated you? Check all that apply.

_____ How much does this paragraph describe the way *your parent(s) or parent figure(s)* treated you?

Who was this person(s)? Check all that apply.

_____ birth parents   _____ parental figures   _____ both birth parents and other parental figures

Sometimes it is not a birth parent or parental figure but an outsider, friend, sibling, or other relative who uses the child to satisfy their own sexual needs. They may fondle the child or have the child fondle him or her. They may engage in oral sex or have intercourse with the child. How much does this paragraph describe the way someone *other* than your birth parent(s) or parental figure(s) treated you?

Where did this happen? _____

What was this person's relationship to you? _____

SECTION II

Most people experience events they find stressful. These questions ask about your stressful experiences. These experiences could be your own or those of somebody you know. Stressful experiences could include but are not limited to things that threaten your life or health or cause severe physical harm or injury. It could be exposure to other persons who have been severely injured or are dead, the violent or sudden loss of a loved one, learning of exposure to a noxious agent, or causing death or severe harm to another.

Examples of the types of experiences which most people find stressful are natural disasters like earthquakes and tornadoes or human made disasters such as toxic waste spills. Transportation accidents such as car or plane crashes or serious medical problems such as accidents, terminal diseases, or chronic life threatening conditions can be stressful. Other stressful events could be assaults and crimes such as mugging, berating, battering, rape, incest, kidnapping, or murder. The loss of a loved one such as the death of a parent or friend or even the loss of a special pet could be stressful. Life events such as divorce, moving, moving away from home, test anxiety, the loss of a job, or chronic unemployment are stressful for some. Many family experiences include negative emotional, physical, or sexual interactions which can be stressful. These interactions can be between parents or parental figures, between siblings, or between parents and children.

Please think of your stressful life experiences, regardless of whether it occurred when you were an adult or a child, and record the approximate date or time period and the event below.

A. On _____ (or from about _____ to
         date   *beginning date*

about _____) you experienced _____
      ending date   *life event*

_____ .

Many people have experienced multiple stressful life events. If you have experienced more than one stressful life event, please list the other event(s) which you consider stressful below.

B. On _____ (or from about _____ to
         date   *beginning date*

about _____) you experienced _____
      ending date   *life event*

_____ .

C. On _____ (or from about _____ to
         date   *beginning date*

about _____) you experienced _____
      ending date   *life event*

_____ .

D. On _____ (or from about _____ to
　　　　　date　　　　　　　　　　　　*beginning date*

about _____) you experienced _____
　　　ending date　　　　　　　　　　　　　　　　*life event*

_____ .

(If you need more room, please use the back of this sheet.)

Consider the list of events above. Please rank them in the order you consider their stressfulness with 1 being the most stressful.

RANK

Experience A _____　　　　　Experience C _____

Experience B _____　　　　　Experience D _____

Below are some statements about stressful life events. Please respond with a rating of how well each of the statements describes your *most* stressful life experience.

0	1	2	3	4	5	6	7	8	9	10

Not true　**strongly disagree, I**　　　　　　　　　　　　　　　　**strongly agree, I**
at all　　**rarely feel/think this**　　　　　　　　　　　　　　　　**often feel/think this**

_____ 46. It all seemed too horrible to believe.
_____ 47. Time seemed to stand still.
_____ 48. It seemed to go on forever.
_____ 49. I could not trust what I thought was true.
_____ 50. It was like someone changed the rules.
_____ 51. I did not know what rules to believe.
_____ 52. What I learned growing up just was not true.
_____ 53. I do not know when it started.
_____ 54. It seemed like a dream.
_____ 55. It seemed unreal.
_____ 56. It was like watching a movie.
_____ 57. It seemed like it all happened to someone else, not me.
_____ 58. I could not believe it was happening.
_____ 59. I just wanted to get away.
_____ 60. I thought I would die.
_____ 61. I thought my family would die.
_____ 62. I thought my friends would die.
_____ 63. I thought people I did not know would die.
_____ 64. I died.
_____ 65. I had a life-after-death experience.
_____ 66. I thought I had died.
_____ 67. I wanted to die.
_____ 68. My family member died.
_____ 69. My family member had a life-after-death experience.
_____ 70. I thought my family member had died.
_____ 71. My family member wanted to die.
_____ 72. My friend died.
_____ 73. My friend had a life-after-death experience.
_____ 74. I thought my friend had died.
_____ 75. My friend wanted to die.
_____ 76. People I did not know died.

_____ 77. People I did not know had a life-after-death experience.

_____ 78. I thought people I did not know had died.

_____ 79. People I did not know wanted to die.

_____ 80. I realized life is not forever.

_____ 81. There was so much blood.

_____ 82. Parts of bodies seemed to be everywhere.

_____ 83. I never thought I would see people look like that.

_____ 84. I never thought things like that would really happen.

_____ 85. It all seemed so violent.

_____ 86. There was nothing I could do.

_____ 87. There was nothing my family member(s) could do.

_____ 88. There was nothing my friend(s) could do.

_____ 89. There was nothing others around me could do.

_____ 90. There was nothing I could do to help myself.

_____ 91. There was nothing I could do to help my family member(s).

_____ 92. There was nothing I could do to help my friend(s).

_____ 93. There was nothing I could do to help others around me I did not know.

_____ 94. I am proud of what I could do to help.

_____ 95. I did not know I could do so much to help.

_____ 96. I was able to do things that I did not know I could do.

_____ 97. I felt totally and absolutely alone.

_____ 98. I felt close to the others.

_____ 99. I felt as if I were really part of the group.

_____ 100. I caused it.

_____ 101. It was directed at me.

_____ 102. I was (one of) the victim(s).

_____ 103. I could not go home after it happened.

_____ 104. I felt invaded.

_____ 105. I was afraid.

_____ 106. I was very angry.

_____ 107. I felt like throwing up.

_____ 108. I felt like I could not breathe.

_____ 109. My heart was pounding.

_____ 110. My body felt limp.

_____ 111. My head was throbbing.

_____ 112. A person the age I was should not have to experience that.

_____ 113. It made me grow up before I should have.

_____ 114. I had to act like an adult.

_____ 115. I was more willing to understand others.

_____ 116. I learned new things.

_____ 117. I realized what was really important.

_____ 118. It seemed like the end of the world was coming.

_____ 119. I felt more in touch with my environment.

_____ 120. I found my faith strengthened.

_____ 121. I knew if I survived this, I could survive anything.

_____ 122. I appreciated being alive more.

_____ 123. I felt numb.

_____ 124. I appreciate people more now.

_____ 125. I appreciate things more now.

_____ 126. I remember the good times.

_____ 127. I feel more for other people now.

_____ 128. I am more understanding of others problems now.

_____ 129. I understand others more.

_____ 130. Talking about this to other people would be wrong.
_____ 131. If people know about this they would think less of me.
_____ 132. I should not be made to pay.
_____ 133. Somebody should be made to pay.
_____ 134. Because I survived this I'll be more prepared in the future.

SECTION III

In the following questions, you will be asked to estimate a number of things about your relationships to people, time, and distance in the event. If you cannot remember exactly, estimate to the best of your ability as you remember the event now. It is very important that you try to answer all of the questions, even if you have to guess. So that you will be able to understand how to use the scale, there is an example below.

EXAMPLE

Make a slash on the line so that it corresponds to your answer. For instance, if the questions is "I LIKE ORANGES," and you hate oranges with a passion, make a slash through the 0. If you love them with a passion, you might slash through 100. If you fall somewhere in between, just mark the line so that you feel it best represents your feelings.

0	/	50	100
not true			absolutely true

On the scale below, rate your actual physical closeness to the experience with 0 being no contact at all and 100 being in direct contact with yourself.

0	50	100
no contact at all		direct contact with your person

135. If you were a witness, rate your degree of emotional closeness to the direct victim on a scale of 0 to 100 with 0 being strangers and 100 being very emotionally close such as a twin, parent/child, or spouse/mate relationship.
    I was not a witness

0	50	100
victim was a a stranger		victim was very close; a twin, parent/child or spouse/mate

136. Who was this person? Be as specific as possible, for example, was this person a stranger, a school mate, a spouse, etc.

_____

137. If you were the/one of the causes of the experience, rate your degree of emotional closeness to the direct victim on a scale of 0 to 100 with 0 being strangers and 100 being very emotionally close such as a twin, parent/child, or spouse/mate relationship.
    _____ I was not a cause

0	50	100
victim was a a stranger		victim was very close; a twin, parent/child or spouse/mate

138. Who was this person? Be as specific as possible, for example, was this person a stranger, a school mate, a spouse, etc.

_____

139. Please estimate your physical distance from when the experience took place. Make sure to indicate the unit of measure you use. For example, use feet, miles, meters, kilometers, etc.

_____distance _____unit of measure

For instance, if you were 100 feet from the site, write 100 for distance and feet for unit of measure.

140. How long did it last? You may use minutes, hours, days, months, or years, etc.

_____time _____unit of measure

For instance, if it was 5 hours, write 5 for time and hours for unit of measure.

141. In some cases, experiences are sudden and unexpected, in other cases, people have some warning. How much time did you have to prepare? You may use seconds, minutes, hours, days, months, or years. If the event was totally unexpected, write 0 in the space for time.

_____time _____unit of measure

For instance, if it was 5 hours, write 5 for time and hours for unit of measure.

142. Although some people may feel like the experience has never "ended," how long has it been since it ended? You may use minutes, hours, days, months, or years.

_____time _____unit of measure

For instance, if it was 5 years since it ended, write 5 for time and years for unit of measure.

143. If it feels like it never ended, how close does it feel now?

0	50	100
not close at all/		very close
like it happened		like it is
a million years ago		still going on

144. At times, the event happens and a person finds out later. If you were not aware of the event at the time it happened, how much later was it that you heard the news? You may use minutes, hours, days, months, or years. The event might have been directed at you such as in a toxic waste spill; or not such as in the loss of a loved one.

_____ I found out at the time it happened

_____time _____unit of measure

For instance, if you found out 5 hours after the event happened, write 5 for time and hours for unit of measure.

145. If you found out after the event, how long has it been since you found out? You may use minutes, hours, days, months, or years.

_____ I found out at the time it happened.

_____time _____unit of measure

For instance, if it has been 5 weeks since you first found out about the event, write 5 for time and weeks for unit of measure.

146. Regardless of when you first became aware of the event, how long has it been since the actual time of the event? You may use minutes, hours, days, months, or years.

_____time _____unit of measure

For instance, if it has been 5 years since the event actually happened, write 5 for time and years for unit of measure.

Structured Clinical Interview for *DSM-IV* Dissociative Disorders—Revised (SCID-D-R)

Type of Population

Adults, Adolescents

Cost

The SCID-D and *Interviewer's Guide to the SCID-D* are published by the American Psychiatric Press in Washington, DC (telephone 1-800-368-5777). The SCID-D is available in packets of 5 interviews for $21.95; *Interviewer's Guide,* $43.95.

Copyright

American Psychiatric Press

Languages

English, Spanish, Dutch, Norwegian, & Portuguese

What It Measures

Presence and severity of five core dissociative symptoms (amnesia, depersonalization, derealization, identity confusion, identity alteration). It diagnoses the five dissociative disorders and Acute Stress Disorder based on *DSM-IV* criteria.

Measure Content Survey, Procedure, or Process

The SCID-D is a semi-structured interview consisting of 277 items, in which *DSM-IV* criteria are embedded. It can be used to diagnose the 5 *DSM-IV* dissociative disorders (dissociative amnesia, dissociative fugue, depersonalization disorder, DID, and DDNOS) and Acute Stress Disorder.

Theoretical Orientation Summary

Embeds *DSM-IV* criteria; can be used by clinicians from any theoretical background or training.

Time Estimate

Administration	Scoring
30–90 minutes	10–30 minutes

Equipment Needed

Paper & Pencil	Computer	Basic Psychophysiological	Specialized Equipment
X			

Psychometric Maturity

Under Construction	Basic Properties Intact	Mature
		X

Psychometric Properties Summary

Good-to-excellent reliability and discriminant validity were reported for the SCID-D with respect to the five dissociative symptoms and the dissociative disorders, on the basis of over 500 administrations of the instrument (Steinberg, Rounsaville, & Cicchetti, 1990; Steinberg, Cicchetti, Buchanan, Hall, & Rounsaville, 1989–1992). These results were replicated by researchers at Harvard (Goff, Olin, Jenike, Baer, & Buttolph, 1992) and in the Netherlands (Boon & Draijer, 1991). Preliminary results regarding SCID-D psychometrics led to the award of an NIMH grant to field test the instrument (Steinberg, et al., 1990). The SCID-D was field tested on 140 patients with a variety of psychiatric disorders, including the affective, psychotic, anxiety, substance abuse, and personality disorders. SCID-D interviews were rated by 2 of 5 interviewers blind to the referring clinician's diagnosis. Each subject was given two interviews with 1-week interval, and 50 were given a third interview at 6-month followup. Analysis of the results of this field testing has indicated good-to-excellent reliability and validity for dissociative symptoms and disorders (Steinberg, et al., 1989–1992). In addition, multicenter field trials of the SCID-D have been completed with expert researchers at four sites: in Philadelphia (Drs. Kluft, Fine, and Fink), Indianapolis (Drs. Coons and Bowman), Summit, New Jersey (Dr. Pamela Hall), and New Haven (Drs. Steinberg, Rounsaville, and Cicchetti) (Steinberg, Kluft, Coons, Bowman, Buchanan, Fine, et al., 1989–1993). SCID-D interviews were performed at each of the four sites and then co-rated by experts at the other sites. Analysis (based on results from three of the four sites) continues to indicate good-to-excellent inter-rater reliability for each of the five dissociative symptoms as well as the diagnosis of the dissociative disorders.

Particular Sensitivity

Age	Change over Time	Culture / Ethnicity	Gender	Geography / Climate	Sexual Orientation	Socioeconomic Status	Urban / Rural
X	X	X	X	?	?	X	X

Estimate of Number of In-Process Studies
Many other investigations using the SCID-D, including cross-cultural studies, are being conducted by researchers internationally.

Unpublished References
Unknown

Published References
Boon, S., & Draijer, N. (1991). Diagnosing dissociative disorders in the Netherlands: A pilot study with the Structured Clinical Interview for *DSM-III-R* Dissociative Disorders. *American Journal of Psychiatry, 148,* (4) 458–462.

Boon, S., & Draijer, N. (1993). Multiple personality disorder in the Netherlands: A clinical investigation of 71 patients. *American Journal of Psychiatry, 150* (3), 489–494, 1993.

Coons, P. M., & Bowman, E. S. (1993). Dissociation and eating (letter). *American Journal of Psychiatry, 150,* 171–172.

Goff, D. C., Botman, A. W., Kindlon, D., Waites, M., & Amico, E. (1991). The delusion of possession in chronically psychotic patients. *Journal of Nervous and Mental Disease, 179* (9), 567–571.

Goff, D. C., Olin, J. A., Jenike, M. A., Baer, L., & Buttolph, M. L. (1992). Dissociative symptoms in patients with obsessive-compulsive disorder. *Journal of Nervous and Mental Disease, 180* (5), 332–337.

Hall, P., & Steinberg, M. (1994). Systematic assessment of dissociative symptoms and disorders in a clinical outpatient setting. *Dissociation, 7* (2), 112–116.

Kluft, R. P., Steinberg, M., & Spitzer, R. L. (1987). *DSM-III-R* revisions in the dissociative disorders: An explanation of their derivation and rationale. *Dissociation, 1* (1), 39–46.

Kolodner, G., & Frances, R. (1993). Recognizing dissociative disorders in patients with chemical dependency. *Hospital and Community Psychiatry, 44* (2), 1041–1043.

Steinberg, M. (1985). *Structured Clinical Interview for DSM-III-R Dissociative Disorders (SCID-D).* New Haven: Yale University School of Medicine.

Steinberg, M. (1990). Transcultural issues in psychiatry: The Ataque and multiple personality. *Dissociation, 3* (1), 31–33.

Steinberg, M. (1991a). Commentary on Toth and Baggaley. *Psychiatry, 54,* 184–186.

Steinberg, M. (1991b). The spectrum of depersonalization: Assessment and treatment. In A. Tasman and S. M. Goldfinger (Eds.). *Psychiatric update,* vol. 10. Washington, DC: American Psychiatric Press, pp. 223–247.

Steinberg, M. (1993, 1994a). *The interviewers' guide to the Structured Clinical Interview for DSM-IV Dissociative Disorders—Revised.* Washington, DC: American Psychiatric Press.

Steinberg, M. (1993, 1994b). *The Structured Clinical Interview for DSM-IV Dissociative Disorders—Revised (SCID-D-R).* Washington, DC: American Psychiatric Press.

Steinberg, M. (1994). Systematizing dissociation: Symptomatology and diagnostic assessment. In D. Spiegel (Ed.). *Dissociation: Culture, mind, and body.* Washington, DC: American Psychiatric Press.

Steinberg, M. (1995). *Handbook for the assessment of dissociation: A clinical guide.* Washington, DC: American Psychiatric Press.

Steinberg, M. (1996). Assessment of dissociation in trauma survivors and PTSD. In J. Wilson and T. Keane (Eds.). *Assessing psychological trauma and PTSD: A handbook for practitioners.* New York: Guilford Press.

Steinberg, M. (in press, a). Psychological assessment of dissociative disorders. In L. K. Michelson and W. J. Ray (Eds.). *Handbook of dissociation: Theroretical, empirical, and research perspectives.* New York: Plenum Press.

Steinberg, M. (in press, b). Psychological assessment of dissociative disorders in children and adolescents. In F. Putnam and D. Lewis (Eds.). *Psychiatric Clinics of North America.*

Steinberg, M. (in press, c). Treatment of depersonalization. In G. Gabbard (Ed.). *Treatment of psychiatric disorders: The DSM-IV edition.* Washington, DC: American Psychiatric Press,.

Steinberg, M., & Bancroft, J. (1993). Multiple personality disorder and crimnal law. *Bulletin of the American Academy of Psychiatry and the Law, 21* (3), 345–356.

Steinberg, M., Buchanan, J., Cicchetti, D. V., Hall, P. E., & Rounsaville, B. J. (1989–1992). *NIMH field trials of the Structured Clinical Interview for DSM-III-R Dissociative Disorders (SCID-D).* New Haven, CT: Yale University School of Medicine.

Steinberg, M., Cicchetti, D., Buchanan, J., Hall, P. E., & Rounsaville, B. J. (1993). Clinical assessment of dissociative symptoms and disorders: The Structured Clinical Interview for DSM-IV Dissociative Disorders (SCID-D). *Dissociation, 6* (1), 3–15.

Steinberg, M., Cicchetti, D., Buchanan, J., Raakfeldt, J., & Ronsaville, B. (1994). Distinguishing between multiple persoanlity disorder and schizophrenia using the Sturctured Clinical Interview for DSM-IV Dissociative Disorder (SCID-D). *Journal of Nervous and Mental Disease* 182 (Sept), 495–502.

Steinberg, M., Howland, F., & Cicchetti, D. V. (1986). The Structured Clinical Interview for DSM-III-R Dissociative Disorders: A preliminary report. In B. Braun (Ed.). *Dissociative disorders.* Proceedings of the International Conference on Multiple Personality and Dissociative States. Rush Presbyterian Hospital, Chicago, IL.

Steinberg, M., Kluft, R. P., Coons, P. M., Bowman, E. S., Buchanan, J., Fine, C. G., Fink, D. L., Hall, P. E., Rounsaville, B. J., & Cicchetti, D. V. (1989–1993). A multi-center study of the Structured Clinical Interview for DSM-IV Dissociative Disorders (SCID-D).

Steinberg, M., Rounsaville, B. J., & Cicchetti, D. V. (1990b). Dr. Steinberg and associates reply (letter). *American Journal of Psychiatry, 147* (12), 1699.

Steinberg, M., Rounsaville, B. J., & Cicchetti, D. V. (1990a). The Structured Clinical Interview for *DSM-III-R* Dissociative Disorders: Preliminary report on a new diagnositic instrument. *American Journal of Psychiatry, 147* (1), 76–82.

Steinberg, M., Rounsaville, B. J., & Cicchetti, D. V. (1991). Detection of dissociative disorders in psychiatric patients by a screening instrument and a structured diagnostic interview. *American Journal of Psychiatry, 148* (8), 1050–1054.

Steinberg, M., & Steinberg, A. (1995).Using the SCID-D to assess Dissociative Identity Disorder in adolescents: Three case studies. *Bulletin of the Menninger Clinic,* 59, 222–231.

General Comments

The American Psychiatric Press publishes the *Stuctured Clinical Interview for DSM-IV Dissociative Disorders (SCID-D)* as well as the *Interviewer's Guide to the SCID-D.* The Interviewer's Guide is intended to provide clinicians with a theoretical and practical introduction to the dissociative symptoms and disorders, together with information about the administration and interpretation of the SCID-D. Clinicians wishing to use the SCID-D should familiarize themselves with the SCID-D and the Interviewer's Guide. In addition, they should attend workshops for additional training. For further information about SCID-D workshops call/fax 203.776.7733.

Key Words

Population	Stressor	Topic
adults adolescents	any	assessment clinical trials diagnosis treatment

Reference Citation for This Review

Steinberg, Marlene, (1996). Psychometric review of Structured Clinical Interview for DSM-IV Dissociative Disorders—Revised (SCID-D-R). In B. H. Stamm (Ed.). *Measurement in Stress, Trauma, and Adaptation.* Lutherville, MD: Sidran Press.

Measure Contact Name

Marlene Steinberg, M. D.
Address: Yale University School of Medicine
                    Department of Psychiatry
                    New Haven, CT 06508 USA
Phone: 203.776.7733, 203.777.7575
Fax: 203.776.7733
E-mail:

Structured Interview for Measurement of Disorders of Extreme Stress

Type of Population
Victims of interpersonal trauma, illness, disaster, and combat.

Cost
Free

Copyright
Contact David Pelcovitz and Bessel A. van der Kolk for information.

Languages
English

What It Measures
Alterations in regulation of affect, attention or consciousness, self-perception, relations with others, somatization, systems of meaning.

Measure Content Survey, Procedure, or Process
Using structured interview format, this measure evaluates 27 criteria often seen in response to extremely traumatic events. The instrument is designed to be used only in conjunction with a structured measure assessing the presence of PTSD.

Theoretical Orientation Summary
The 27 criteria were generated based on a systematic review of the literature on the emotional and behavioral sequelae of extreme stress and a survey of 50 experts.

Time Estimate

Administration	Scoring
5-20 minutes	5–10 minutes

Equipment Needed

Paper & Pencil	Computer	Basic Psychophysiological	Specialized Equipment
X			

Psychometric Maturity

Under Construction	Basic Properties Intact	Mature
	X	

Psychometric Properties Summary
Inter-rater reliability as measured by Kappa coefficients for lifetime and current Disorders of Extreme Stress were 0.81 and 0.67 respectively. Internal consistency using coefficient alpha ranged from 0.53 to 0.96. In the *DSM-IV* PTSD Field Trials, (N=520) construct validity was supported by the finding that 33 out of 34 comparisons showed a

significant difference in the percentage of interpersonal abuse subjects who endorsed SIDES items when compared to those who experienced disaster.

Particular Sensitivity

Age	Change over Time	Culture / Ethnicity	Gender	Geography / Climate	Sexual Orientation	Socioeconomic Status	Urban / Rural
?	?	?	?	?	?	?	?

Estimate of Number of In-Process Studies

Unknown

Unpublished References

Pelcovitz, van der Kolk, Roth, et al. A structured interview for measurement of disorders of extreme stress (manuscript submitted for review).

Published References

Unknown

Key Words

Population	Stressor	Topic
adults	any	assessment diagnosis research

Reference Citation for This Review

Pelcovitz, D., & van der Kolk, B. A. (1996). Psychometric review of Structured Interview for Measurement of Disorders of Extreme Stress. In B. H. Stamm (Ed.). *Measurement of stress, trauma, and adaptation*. Lutherville, MD: Sidran Press.

Measure Contact Name

David Pelcovitz, Ph.D.

Address: Trauma Clinic
             North Shore Hospital
             300 Community Drive
             Manhassett, NY 11030 USA
Phone: 516.562.3005
Fax: 516.562.3997
E-mail

Measure Contact Name

Bessel A. van der Kolk, M.D.

Address   Mass. General Hospital
             Department of Psychiatry
             Harvard Medical School
             25 Staniford Street
             Boston, MA 02114 USA
Phone: 617.727.5500 x949
Fax: 617.248.0630
E-mail:

Structured Interview(s) of Post-Disaster Adjustment

Type of Population
Adults and adolescents

Cost
Free

Copyright
Contact John R. Freedy, Ph.D., National Crime Victims Research & Treatment Center.

Languages
English

What It Measures
Several alternate interview forms were developed by our research team in the course of conducting studies concerning adult and adolescent adjustment following major natural disasters. To date, these interviews have been used in general population surveys following these disasters: Hurricane Hugo (September 1989); the Loma Prieta earthquake (October 1989); the Sierra Madre earthquake (June 1991); the Oakland Hills fire (October 1991); and Hurricane Andrew (August 1992). Depending on the particular disaster studied, adult or adolescent interviews are available. These measures assess a range of individual and environmental predictors of post-disaster adjustment, in addition to post-disaster mental health. Specific constructs assessed are provided in the instrument content summary.

Measure Content Survey, Procedure, or Process
Available interviews assess a range of variables from three time periods: pre-disaster, within-disaster (i.e., at the time of the disaster), and post-disaster. Owing to the difficulties in conducting prospective studies, these instruments rely on retrospective reports. These pre-disaster factors are assessed: demographics, mental health history (depression, anxiety, and substance abuse), prior exposure to traumatic events (e.g., violent crime, combat, other disasters), and past-year exposure to non-traumatic life events (e.g., work problems, marital problems). The within-disaster variables assessed include a number of questions concerning objective (e.g., serious injury, deaths, property damage) and subjective (e.g., perception of life threat, fear for family members) indicators of disaster exposure. The post-disaster variables measured include disruption of basic goods and services, measures of the intensity of initial psychological distress, traumatic and non-traumatic life events, personal and social resource loss, social support, and coping behavior. Mental health measures include the assessment of Major Depressive Episodes, PTSD, and Alcohol Abuse. All of the above content areas are assessed for adult respondents. Adolescent interviews delete some sensitive content areas (e.g., alcohol abuse, sexual abuse).

Theoretical Orientation Summary
These interviews were formatted as telephone interviews and used to gather information regarding short-term (less than one year) and long-term (up to three years) adjustment following natural disaster exposure. Thus, the research team considers these instruments to be empirical tools. The content of the questionnaires reflect a conceptualization of post-disaster adjustment as determined by a combination of pre-, within-, and post-disaster variables. A particular strength of this approach lies in the emphasis on a range of variables in addition to disaster exposure (e.g., prior trauma history, post-disaster resource loss) as potential determinants of post-disaster adjustment. Empirical findings have confirmed the importance of prior trauma history and resource loss as important determinants of adjustment, among other variables (Freedy, et al., 1994; Freedy, et al., 1995).

Time Estimate

Administration	Scoring
20–60 minutes	5–30 minutes

Equipment Needed

Paper & Pencil	Computer	Basic Psychophysiological	Specialized Equipment
X			telephone

Psychometric Maturity

Under Construction	Basic Properties Intact	Mature
	X	

Psychometric Properties Summary

When possible, questions to assess the various constructs were derived from published, standardized instruments. In other cases, an appropriate measure was not available and so the research team developed items to assess the construct of interest (Freedy, Kilpatrick, & Resnick, 1993). Prior to utilization, these instruments were pilot-tested in both in-person and telephone interview formats. Based upon interviewer feedback, items were revised for the sake of clarity and comprehension. To date, the various constructs assessed by available interviews have behaved consistently across samples and disasters (e.g., similar lifetime trauma rates, similar lifetime prevalence rates for mental health disorders). This has involved interviewing thousands of adults and adolescents. This consistency lends support to the utility of these interviews. The research team can be contacted regarding specific interview properties.

Particular Sensitivity

Age	Change over Time	Culture/ Ethnicity	Gender	Geography/ Climate	Sexual Orientation	Socioeconomic Status	Urban/ Rural
X	X	X	?	X	?	X	X

Estimate of Number of In-Process Studies

Unknown

Unpublished References

Freedy, J. R., Addy, C. L., Kilpatrick, D. G., Resnick, H. S., Garrison, C. Z., & Spurrier, P. G. (1995). Disasters impact upon adults and adolescents. Final report for NIMH Grant #R01-MH47507. Violence and Traumatic Stress Research Branch, NIMH.

Freedy, J. R., Kilpatrick, D. G., & Resnick, H. S. (1993). The psychological impact of the Oakland Hills fire. Final report for supplement for NIMH Grant #R01-MH47508-01A1. Violence and Traumatic Stress Research Branch, NIMH.

Freedy, J. R., Kilpatrick, D. G., & Saunders, B. E. (1993). Adult psychological functioning after earthquakes. Final report for NIMH Grant #R03-MH49485. Violence and Traumatic Stress Research Branch, NIMH.

Published References

Freedy, J. R., & Kilpatrick, D. G. (1994). Everything you wanted to know about natural disasters and mental health (well almost!). *National Center for Post-traumatic Stress Disorder Clinical Quarterly, 4* (Spring, 2), 6–8.

Freedy, J. R., Kilpatrick, D. G., & Resnick, H. S. (1993). Natural disasters and mental health: Theory, assessment, and intervention. *Journal of Social Behavior and Personality, 8* (5), 49–103.

Freedy, J. R., Saladin, M., Kilpatrick, D. G., Resnick, H. S., & Saunders, B. E. (1994). Understanding acute psychological distress following natural disaster. *Journal of Traumatic Stress, 7* (2), 257–273.

General Comments

The available interviews provide good starting points for researchers interested in assessing adult or adolescent adjustment following major natural disasters or other community-based traumatic events. We ask that those who use all or part of any interview appropriately reference the interview to the research team. Appropriate references for specific purposes are available from the research team. We also ask that researchers send copies of any presentations or publications to the research team, to assist us in developing a broad information pool based on these instruments.

Key Words

Population	Stressor	Topic
adolescents adults	natural disasters	assessment intervention research

Reference Citation for This Review

Freedy, J. R., Kilpatrick, D. G., & Resnick, H. S. (1996). Review of Structured Interview(s) of Post-Disaster Adjustment. In B. H. Stamm (Ed.). *Measurement of stress, trauma, and adaptation.* Lutherville, MD: Sidran Press.

Measure Contact Name

John R. Freedy, Ph.D.

Address: National Crime Victims Research & Treatment Center
Department of Psychiatry & Behavioral Sciences
Medical University of South Carolina
171 Ashley Ave.
Charleston, SC 29425 USA

Phone: 803.792.2945
Fax: 803.792.3388
E-mail:

Tough Times Checklist
Teen Tough Times Checklist
Child's Upsetting Times Checklist
Young Adult's Upsetting Times Checklist

Type of Population

The Tough Times Checklist is for children aged 8 to 12. The Teen Tough Times Checklist is for adolescents 12 or older. The Child's Upsetting Times Checklist is for adults to complete concerning their children and/or adolescents. The Young Adult's Upsetting Times Checklist is for adults 19 and older.

Cost

Free to all of those who agree to share the raw data they collect in order to help establish the scale's psychometric properties.

Copyright

Kenneth E. Fletcher, Ph.D.

Languages

English

What It Measures

These scales are designed to assess stressful life events to which children and young adults have been exposed.

Instrument Content Survey

Sixty-eight stressful life events are listed, ranging from moving to a new home, getting into trouble in school, exposure to violence in the community, violence against the self and/or the family, deaths of friends and/or family, natural disasters, and, in The Young Adult's Checklist, physical and/or sexual abuse. The Tough Times Checklist is for younger children and is simply a list of events that the child checks off if he or she has ever experienced it. All other versions ask the respondent to indicate how upsetting the worst experience of each checked stressor was for the respondent. For the Teen Tough Times Checklist and the Child's Upsetting Times Checklist responses are either "Not at all," "A little," or "Very much." On the Young Adult's Upsetting Times Checklist responses are either "Not at all," "Some," "Lots," or "Very much." Respondents are asked to describe the worst (or scariest) thing that ever happened to them, and they are asked to describe the worst (or scariest) thing that happened to them in the past two years.

Theoretical Orientation Summary

There is a vast literature on the impact of past stressful experience and current stress. These scales were designed to help assess life stress.

Time Estimate

Administration	Scoring
20–30 minutes	10–20 minutes

Equipment Needed

Paper & Pencil	Computer	Basic Psychophysiological	Specialized Equipment
X			

Psychometric Maturity

Under Construction	Basic Properties Intact	Mature
X		

Psychometric Properties Summary

None so far

Particular Sensitivity

Age	Change over Time	Culture / Ethnicity	Gender	Geography / Climate	Sexual Orientation	Socioeconomic Status	Urban / Rural
X	?	?	?	?	?	?	?

Estimate of Number of In-Process Studies

2

Unpublished References

Published References

General Comments

I created these scales for two reasons. First, none of the life events scales that I could find assess some of the more horrendous violent experiences children are often exposed to these days, such as shootings, robberies, etc. Second, when I tried to assess stressful life events with more detailed scales that included references to physical and sexual abuse, I was told that parents and clinicians would not like them (and I could not get them approved by IRBs). Therefore, I reduced the number of items, made sure they were on a continuum from mild to severe, and did not directly mention physical or sexual abuse in any of the scales but the Young Adult's Upsetting Events Checklist (which is very specific about these types of events; see examples below). The closest the scales for children or teens gets to abuse issues is to ask if other children or adults (in family or out) have ever made the child do something horrible (see examples below). It is expected that that something more specific can be elicited through followup interviews.

These scales are not restricted to use with trauma populations. An IBM-compatible data entry program is available from the author for these scales. The data entry program runs in EPI INFO, a data entry creation program distributed (for free from other users or academic computer departments or for $50 from the Center for Disease Control or the World Health Organization). EPI INFO programs allow data bases to be created which can be analyzed on a basic level within EPI INFO itself and by other statistical programs (such as SPSS, SAS, and Systat) or by databases and spreadsheets that will read dBase file formats.

Key Words

Population	Stressor	Topic
adolescents young adults children	any	assessment research

Reference Citation for This Review

Fletcher, K. E. (1996). Psychometric review of Tough Times Checklist, Teen Tough Times Checklist, Child's Upsetting Times Checklist, and Young Adult's Upsetting Times Checklist. In B. H. Stamm (Ed.). *Measurement of stress, trauma, and adaptation.* Lutherville, MD: Sidran Press.

Measure Contact Name

Kenneth E. Fletcher, Ph.D.

Address: University of Massachusetts Medical Center
Psychiatry Dept.
55 Lake Avenue North
Worcester, MA 01655-0001 USA

Phone: 508.856.3329

Fax: 508.856.6426

E-Mail: Fletcher@umassmed.ummed.edu

Tough Times/Upsetting Times Checklist Sample Items

Have the following ever happened to you?

Moved to a new home.

A teacher embarrassed you.

Did not get invited to a party that your other friends went to.

Had to go live with relatives.

A parent put you down or yelled at you.

Did something bad you knew you should not do.

Shot at.

A grown up stranger made you do something horrible.

A pet died.

From the Young Adult's Upsetting Times Checklist:

One parent beat you up or hurt you physically in some way.

Before you were 18, someone at least 5 years older than you masturbated in front of you.

After you were 18, someone tried to rape you.

Trauma Assessment for Adults (TAA)

Type of Population
Adult men and women

Cost
free

Copyright
Contact Resnick, H. S., Best, C. L., Kilpatrick, D. G., Freedy, J. R., & Falsetti, S. A., National Crime Victims Research and Treatment Center.

Languages
English

What It Measures
A brief interview to assess lifetime history of multiple Criterion A PTSD events, modified from the NWS Event History and PTSD Module and the Potential Stressful Events Interview (PSEI) described elsewhere in this book. The TAA is two pages in length and contains 13 specific event questions. A series of four simple followup questions assess number of times each type of event has occurred, age at first and most recent incident, and respondent's report of fear of death or injury during any experiences of a given type of event. Event types assessed include military/combat, accident, disaster, completed molestation, completed rape, aggravated assault, witnessing violence, other situations that include injury, other situations that include fear of being killed or seriously injured.

Measure Content Survey, Procedure, or Process
The TAA is administered as an interview that includes structured questions and response options; it takes approximately 10 minutes and can be given in clinical or nonclinical settings. The instrument is not restricted based on sexual orientation, gender, culture/ethnicity, or rural/urban background. A self-report version has been developed but has not yet been evaluated.

Theoretical Orientation Summary
Designed as a brief clinically useful instrument to screen for history of Criterion A PTSD events. To maintain brevity and simplicity minimal followup questions to assess qualitative characteristics were restricted to focus on the element of subjective threat in relation to specific events, a factor that leads to increased risk of PTSD; incidence of multiple events that put individuals at increased risk of negative mental health outcomes, and age (to allow for developmental/chronological factors).

Time Estimate

Administration	Scoring
10–15 minutes	5–10 minutes

Equipment Needed

Paper & Pencil	Computer	Basic Psychophysiological	Specialized Equipment
X			

Psychometric Maturity

Under Construction	Basic Properties Intact	Mature
X		

Psychometric Properties Summary

One study has been conducted using the TAA with a sample of 23 adults within a local mental health center population. The first author of this paper, Robert Mirabella, conducted this project on internship at the National Crime Victims Research and Treatment Center. Although the sample was small, the study revealed that the measure was practical for use in this population and questions were understood by clients and the brevity of the interview was an advantage in that it could be added to standard intake assessments. Thus, clinical utility was supported. Validity of the measure was supported by findings of rates of general trauma and crime exposure that were highly consistent with those previously observed in this population using a different structured assessment measure of traumatic events (Saunders, Kilpatrick, Resnick, & Tidwell, 1989). In addition, archival data from mental health center records were compared with TAA interview data for a subset of 15 cases with both sources of data. For these 15 cases, rates of identified stressor events noted in archival records were in every case identified positively using the TAA. In addition, the TAA also identified additional assault incidents not noted in the archival records as would be expected with the introduction of consistent use of a structured assessment measure.

Particular Sensitivity

Age	Change over Time	Culture/ Ethnicity	Gender	Geography/ Climate	Sexual Orientation	Socioeconomic Status	Urban/ Rural
?	X	X	X	?	?	X	X

Estimate of Number of In-Process Studies

Several, including our clinic.

Unpublished References

Mirabella, R. (unpublished manuscript). The identification of traumatic event history and trauma related symptoms among a mental health center population.

Published References

(Brief description of measure only)

Resnick, H. S., Falsetti, S. A., Kilpatrick, D. G., & Freedy, J. R. (in press). Assessment of rape and other civilian trauma-related PTSD: Emphasis on assessment of potentially traumatic events. In T. Miller (Ed.). *Theory and assessment of stressful life events*. Madison, CT: International Universities Press, Inc.

Saunders, B. E., Kilpatrick, D. G., Resnick, H. S., & Tidwell, R. P. (1989). Brief screening for lifetime history of criminal victimization at mental health intake: A preliminary study. *Journal of Interpersonal Violence, 4*, 267–277.

General Comments

Key Words

Population	Stressor	Topic
adults women	accidents criminal victimization domestic violence other injuries or life-threats physical abuse sexual assault/abuse witnessing violence	diagnosis epidemiology measure development

Reference Citation for This Review

Resnick, H. S. (1996). Psychometric review of Trauma Assessment for Adults (TAA). In B. H. Stamm (Ed.). *Measurement of stress, trauma, and adaptation.* Lutherville, MD: Sidran Press.

Measure Authors

Resnick, H. S., Best, C. L., Kilpatrick, D. G., Freedy, J. R., & Falsetti, S. A.

Measure Contact Name

Heidi Resnick, Ph.D.

Address:	National Crime Victims Research and
	Treatment Center
	Department of Psychiatry and Behavioral Sciences
	171 Ashley Avenue
	Charleston, SC 29425-0742
Phone:	803.792.2945
Fax:	803.7923388
E-mail:	RESNICKH@MUSC.EDU

Trauma Assessment for Adults (TAA) Sample Items

16a. Now I'd like to talk about events that may be extraordinarily stressful or disturbing—things that may not happen often, but when they do, they can be frightening, upsetting, or distressful to almost everyone. During your life, have any of the following types of things happened to you?

16b. *(For each "YES" recorded in Q.16a, ask:)* How old were you when this happened (the first time)? *(Record below)*

16c. *(For each "YES" recorded in Q.16a, ask:)* How old were you when this happened most recently? *(Record below)*

16d. *(For each "YES" recorded in Q.16a, ask:)* Did you ever think you might be killed or seriously injured during this/these events? *(Record below)*

| | 16a | | 16b | 16c | 16d |
	No Yes	Age at	Age at	No	Yes
a. Military combat experience, or military service in a war zone?	0 1	_____	_____	0	1
b. A serious accident at work, in a car, or somewhere else?	0 1	_____	_____	0	1
c. A natural disaster such as a tornado, hurricane, flood, major earthquake, or similar natural disaster, counting Hurricane Hugo?	0 1	_____	_____	0	1

Sometimes people have experienced other incidents in their lives that include unwanted sexual advances. People do not always report such experiences to the police or discuss them with family or friends. The person making the advances isn't always a stranger but can be a friend, date, or even a family member. Such experiences can occur anytime in a person's life—even as a child. Regardless of how long ago it happened or who made the advances.... Other than any events that you have already told us about....

| | 16a | | 16b | 16c | 16d |
	No Yes	Age at	Age at	No	Yes
d1. Did you ever have sexual contact with anyone who was five years or more older than you before you reached the age of thirteen? When we say sexual contact, we mean any sexual contact between someone else and your sexual organs (genitals for males, genitals and breasts for females) or between you and someone else's sexual organs.	0 1	_____	_____	0	1
d2. Before you were age eighteen, has anyone ever used pressure, coercion, or nonphysical threats to have sexual contact with you? Again, by sexual contact, we mean any sexual contact between someone else and your sexual organs (genitals for males, genitals and breasts for females) or between you and someone else's sexual organs.	0 1	_____	_____	0	1
d3. At any other time in your life, have you experienced a situation in which someone used physical force or threat of force to make you have some type of unwanted sexual contact? By sexual contact, we mean any sexual contact between someone else and your sexual organs or between you and someone else's sexual organs.	0 1	_____	_____	0	1

If YES in d1, d2, or d3, ask e.

| | 16a | | 16b | 16c | 16d |
	No Yes	Age at	Age at	No	Yes
e. Did this incident (any of these incidents) include forced unwanted vaginal, oral, or anal penetration either by an assailant's penis or the use of fingers, tongue, or some other object?	0 1	_____	_____	0	1
f. Has anyone—including family members or friends—ever attacked you with a gun, knife, or some other weapon, regardless of when it happened or whether you reported it or not?	0 1	_____	_____	0	1
g. Has anyone—including family members or friends—ever attacked you without a weapon but with the intent to kill or seriously injure you?	0 1	_____	_____	0	1

Trauma History Questionnaire (Self-Report)

Type of Population

General or clinical

Cost

Free

Copyright

Contact Bonnie L. Green, Ph.D.

Languages

English

What It Measures

History of exposure to potentially traumatic events that may meet the "A" (stressor) criterion for *DSM* post-traumatic stress disorder.

Measure Content Survey, Procedure, or Process

The instrument has 24 items addressing the lifetime occurrence of a variety of traumatic events in three categories: crime, general disaster/trauma, and sexual and physical assault experiences. The subject indicates, for the first two sets of items, whether or not they have ever had the experience (yes/no), and if yes, the number of times and the age of occurrence. For the latter set of items, the subject indicates whether they have had the experience (yes/no), whether it was repeated, and, if yes, how often and at what age(s). A final item, *"Have you experienced any other extraordinarily stressful situation or event that is not covered above? If yes, please specify,"* is included to allow subjects to report experiences that they considered extremely stressful, regardless of whether these events would be considered traumatic by the investigators. This item also may identify traumatic experiences that are more appropriately recorded elsewhere. In this latter case, the item is rescored in the appropriate category. Otherwise, the item is not scored.

Theoretical Orientation Summary

No specific orientation. The goal was to cover a broad range of events that could objectively be considered potentially traumatic, and that would therefore potentially meet the Criterion A (1) (stressor) criterion for *DSM-III-R* and *DSM-IV* PTSD.

Thus, items focus primarily on situations involving life threat, assaults to physical integrity, tragic/accidental loss of loved ones, and witnessing death or violence. No assessment of the person's response, i.e. Criterion A (2), is included. Questions and coverage are based on the high magnitude stressor events interview, designed by Kilpatrick and Resnick for the *DSM-IV* field trials for PTSD.

Time Estimate

Administration	Scoring
10–15 minutes	5–15 minutes depending on information sought

Equipment Needed

Paper & Pencil	Computer	Basic Psychophysiological	Specialized Equipment
X			

Psychometric Maturity

Under Construction	Basic Properties Intact	Mature
X		

Psychometric Properties Summary

No final scoring system has been devised at this point. We are presently exploring the relationships of the individual items with outcome. A total score can also be calculated (without Item 24), but given the possibility of false positives on some items (see below) we would recommend screening of responses first.

We generally use this instrument in conjunction with an interview to clarify the specific nature of the person's trauma experience, preparatory to a diagnostic interview for PTSD. With few exceptions, the items theoretically would meet the A (1) criterion for PTSD. However, some items routinely result in false positives, e.g., Item 16: *"Have you ever received news of a serious injury, life-threatening illness or unexpected death of someone close to you?"*

Data have been collected on 423 college students and 186 psychiatric outpatients, and THQ information from these two groups, by gender, are available. A test-retest study of 25 college women showed fairly good stability over a 2–3 month period for reporting of most events.

Particular Sensitivity

Age	Change over Time	Culture / Ethnicity	Gender	Geography / Climate	Sexual Orientation	Socioeconomic Status	Urban / Rural
?	?	?	X	?	?	?	?

Estimate of Number of In-Process Studies

Unknown

Unpublished References

Unknown

Published References

None

General Comments

We are also using this instrument in a study of women with breast cancer, in conjunction with an interview. Users of the instrument are asked to give us feedback concerning its use.

Key Words

Population	Stressor	Topic
adult	any	assessment general treatment measure development research

Reference Citation for This Review

Green, B. L. (1996). Psychometric review of Trauma History Questionnaire (Self-Report). In B. H. Stamm (Ed.). *Measurement of stress, trauma, and adaptation*. Lutherville, MD: Sidran Press.

Measure Contact Name

Bonnie L. Green, Ph.D.

Address: Department of Psychiatry

Georgetown University

611 Kober Cogan Hall

Washington, DC 20007 USA

Phone: 202.687.4812

Fax: 202.687-6658

E-mail:

Trauma History Questionnaire (Self Report) Sample Items

Crime-related events:

1. "Has anyone ever tried to take something from you by using force or the threat of force, such as a stick-up or mugging?"

General Disaster and Trauma

6. "Have you ever experienced a natural disaster such as a tornado, hurricane, flood, major earthquake, etc., [where you felt you or your loved ones were in danger of death or injury*]? If yes, please specify."

[*bracketed portion added more recently]

Physical and Sexual Experiences

18. "Has anyone ever made you have intercourse, oral or anal sex against your will? If yes, please indicate nature of relationship with person (e.g., stranger, friend, relative, parent, sibling)."

Trauma Reaction Indicators Child Questionnaire (TRICQ) 1.1

Type of Population
children

Cost
Free

Copyright
Ricky Greenwald

Languages
English

What It Measures
The Trauma Reaction Indicators Child Questionnaire (TRICQ) measures a range of children's post-traumatic symptomatology as endorsed by the child (to age 14). It is more oriented towards responses to Type I (vs. chronic) trauma, and focuses on state rather than trait items. An identified trauma is not required. The TRICQ is intended as a screening instrument for possible post-traumatic disturbance, and as a repeated measure to track recovery from post-traumatic reactions.

Measure Content Survey, Procedure, or Process
The TRICQ 1.1 is a paper and pencil instrument which consists of 26 statements representing post-traumatic symptomatology. The subject marks "0" (none), "1" (some), or "2" (lots) to indicate how much each statement represented his/her experience in the past week. A higher level of endorsement indicates greater symptomatology, except for the last two items, in which the reverse is true. The TRICQ requires a third-grade reading level (or assistance) and may also be administered orally, in person or by telephone. Administration time: 5–10 minutes. There is no scoring system yet, and some items may be eliminated or weighted following validation studies.

Theoretical Orientation Summary
The TRICQ was formulated using the broad definition of child trauma advocated by Terr (1991), with more attention to clinical impact than to diagnostic boundaries. Items were selected on the basis of the *DSM-IV* criteria for PTSD, and on Fletcher's (1993) meta-analysis of the empirical literature on children's post-traumatic symptoms.

Time Estimate

Administration	Scoring
5–15 minutes	5 minutes

Equipment Needed

Paper & Pencil	Computer	Basic Psychophysiological	Specialized Equipment
X			

Psychometric Maturity

Under Construction	Basic Properties Intact	Mature
X		

Psychometric Properties Summary

Validated for content and clarity by a team of child trauma experts, and piloted on child trauma victims, who endorse fewer items following treatment.

Particular Sensitivity

Age	Change over Time	Culture / Ethnicity	Gender	Geography / Climate	Sexual Orientation	Socioeconomic Status	Urban / Rural
X	X	?	?	?	?	?	?

Estimate of Number of In-Process Studies

2

Unpublished References

Unknown

Published References

Unknown

General Comments

Access to your raw data and research results would be appreciated for use in validation. Intended for use with a companion measure such as the Parent Report of Post-traumatic Symptoms (Greenwald, 1995), for a more comprehensive estimate of symptomatology.

Key Words

Population	Stressor	Topic
adolescents children	any	assessment individual treatment measure development

Reference Citation for This Review

Greenwald, R. (1996). Psychometric review of Trauma Reaction Indicators Child Questionnaire. In B. H. Stamm (Ed.). *Measurement of stress, trauma, and adaptation*. Lutherville, MD: Sidran Press.

Measure Contact Name

Ricky Greenwald, Psy.D.
Address: P.O. Box 575
               Trumansburg, NY 14886
Phone: (607)387-9060
Fax:
E-mail:

Trauma Reaction Indicators Child Questionnaire Sample Items

Mark how true each statement feels for you **in the past week**. Don't skip any, even if you're not sure. There is no right or wrong answer. Answer by circling **0 for none, 1 for some**, and **2 for lots**.

None	Some	Lots	
0	1	2	I "space out" when people are talking to me.
0	1	2	I do special things to make sure nothing bad happens.
0	1	2	I get headaches or stomach aches.
0	1	2	I think I will get married and have a family someday.

Trauma Symptom Checklist 33 and 40 (TSC 33 and 40)

Type of Population
Adults

Cost
Free

Copyright
John Briere, Ph.D.

Languages
English

What It Measures
The TSC-40 is a research measure that evaluates symptomatology in adults arising from childhood or adult traumatic experiences. It measures not only posttraumatic stress, but also other symptom clusters found in some traumatized individuals. The TSC-40 is a revision of the earlier TSC-33 (Briere & Runtz, 1989).

Measure Content Survey, Procedure, or Process
The TSC-40 is a 40-item self report instrument consisting of six subscales: *Anxiety, Depression, Dissociation, Sexual Abuse Trauma Index (SATI), Sexual Problems,* and *Sleep Disturbance,* as well as a total score. Each symptom item is rated according to its frequency of occurrence over the prior two months, using a 4-point scale ranging from 0 ("never") to 3 ("often").

Theoretical Orientation Summary
This measure is essentially atheoretical, focusing on the phenomenology of posttraumatic difficulties.

Time Estimate

Administration	Scoring
10–15 minutes	5–10 minutes

Equipment Needed

Paper & Pencil	Computer	Basic Psychophysiological	Specialized Equipment
X			

Psychometric Maturity

Under Construction	Basic Properties Intact	Mature
		X

Psychometric Properties Summary
Studies using the TSC-40 indicate that it is a relatively reliable measure (subscale alphas typically range from .66 to .77, with alphas for the full scale averaging between .89 and .91). The TSC-40 and its predecessor, the TSC-33, have predictive validity with reference to a wide variety of traumatic experiences (e.g., Bagley, 1991; Briere, Evans, Runtz, & Wall, 1988; Demare & Briere, 1995; Elliott & Briere, 1992; Gold, Milan, Mayall, & Johnson, 1994; Magana, 1990; Russ, Shearin, Clarkin, Harrison, & Hull, 1993; Wind & Silvern, 1992). The TSC-40 also appears to predict perpetrators of intimate violence (Dutton, 1995).

Particular Sensitivity

Age	Change over Time	Culture / Ethnicity	Gender	Geography / Climate	Sexual Orientation	Socioeconomic Status	Urban / Rural
?	?	?	?	?	?	?	?

Estimate of Number of In-Process Studies

10+, including doctoral dissertations.

Unpublished References

Alter-Reid, K. (1989). The long-term impact of incest: An investigation of traumagenic factors and effects in four types of childhood abuse. Unpublished manuscript.

Cole, C. B. (May 1986). Differential long-term effects of child sexual and physical abuse. Paper presented at the National Conference on Sexual Victimization of Children. New Orleans, LA.

Demare, D., & Briere, J. (1995). Trauma Symptom Checklist-40: Validation with sexually abused and nonabused university students. Paper presented at the annual meeting of the American Psychological Association. New York, NY.

Garabedian, M. I. (1993). Relationship of child sexual, physical, and psychological abuse to eating disorders and post-traumatic stress disorder in adult women. Unpublished doctoral dissertation. University of Southern California.

Lipinski, B. J. (1992). Psychological correlates of childhood sexual abuse and adult criminal victimization in women's experiences. Unpublished doctoral dissertation. University of Southern California.

Magana, D. (1990). The impacts of client-therapist sexual intimacy and child sexual abuse on psychosexual and psychological functioning. Unpublished doctoral dissertation. University of California at Los Angeles.

Schlaff, K. L. (1992). An investigation of the relationship between chronic pelvic pain in adult women and child sexual abuse utilizing the Trauma Symptom Checklist-40. Unpublished doctoral dissertation. University of Southern California.

Williams, M. B. (1990). Child sexual abuse and posttraumatic stress disorder: The enduring effect. Unpublished doctoral dissertation. Fielding Institute. Santa Barbara, CA.

Published References

Bagley, C. (1991). The prevalence and mental health sequels of child sexual abuse in a community sample of women aged 18 to 27. *Canadian Journal of Community Mental Health, 10*, 103–116.

Briere, J. (1989). *Therapy for adults molested as children: Beyond survival*. New York: Springer.

Briere, J., Evans, D., Runtz, M., & Wall, T. (1988). Symptomatology in men who were molested as children: A comparison study. *American Journal of Orthopsychiatry, 58*, 457–461.

Briere, J., & Runtz, M. (1989). The Trauma Symptom Checklist (TSC-33): Early data on a new scale. *Journal of Interpersonal Violence, 4*.

Dutton, D. G. (1995). Trauma symptoms and PTSD-like profiles in perpetrators of intimate violence. *Journal of Traumatic Stress, 8*, 299–316.

Elklit, A. (1990). Maling af belastninger efter voldeligt overfald med TSC-33 (traume symptom checklist). [Measurement of stress after a violent attack using the TSC-33 (Trauma Symptom Checklist)]. *Nordisk Psukologi, 42*, 281–289.

Elliott, D. M., & Briere, J. (1991). Studying the long-term effects of sexual abuse: The Trauma Symptom Checklist (TSC) scales. In A.W. Burgess (Ed.). *Rape and sexual assault III*. New York: Garland.

Elliott, D. M., & Briere, J. (1992). Sexual abuse trauma among professional women: Validating the Trauma Symptom Checklist-40 (TSC-40). *Child Abuse and Neglect, 16*, 391–398.

Gold, S. R., Milan, L. D., Mayall, A., & Johnson, A.E. (1994). A cross-validation study of the Trauma Symptom Checklist: The role of mediating variables. *Journal of interpersonal Violence, 9*, 12–26.

Russ, M. J., Shearin, E. N., Clarkin, J. F., Harrison, K., & Hull, J. W. (1993). Subtypes of self-injurious patients with borderline personality disorder. *American Journal of Psychiatry, 150*, 1869–1871.

Wind, T. W., & Silvern, L. E. (1992). Type and extent of child abuse as predictors of adult functioning. *Journal of Family Violence, 7*, 261–281.

General Comments

The TSC-40 is a research instrument only. Those requiring a validated psychological test of posttraumatic response, using a similar format, should consider the Trauma Symptom Inventory (TSI) (Briere, 1995). The TSC-40 is freely available to researchers.

No additional permission is required for use or reproduction of this measure, although the author should be cited.

Key Words

Population	Stressor	Topic
adults	any	assessment
		research

Reference Citation for This Review

Briere, J. (1996). Psychometric review of Trauma Symptom Checklist 33 & 40. In B. H. Stamm (Ed.). *Measurement of stress, trauma, and adaptation*. Lutherville, MD: Sidran Press.

Measure Contact Name

John Briere, Ph.D.
USC School of Medicine
1934 Hospital Place
Los Angeles, CA 90033
Phone:
Fax:
E-mail: jbriere@hsc.usc.edu

Trauma Symptom Checklist-40 (TSC-40)

How often have you experienced each of the following in *the last two months*?

	Never			Often
1. Headaches	0.	1.	2.	3.
2. Insomnia (trouble getting to sleep)	0.	1.	2.	3.
3. Weight loss (without dieting)	0.	1.	2.	3.
4. Stomach problems	0.	1.	2.	3.
5. Sexual problems	0.	1.	2.	3.
6. Feeling isolated from others	0.	1.	2.	3.
7. "Flashbacks" (sudden, vivid, distracting memories)	0.	1.	2.	3.
8. Restless sleep	0.	1.	2.	3.
9. Low sex drive	0.	1.	2.	3.
10. Anxiety attacks	0.	1.	2.	3.
11. Sexual overactivity	0.	1.	2.	3.
12. Loneliness	0.	1.	2.	3.
13. Nightmares	0.	1.	2.	3.
14. "Spacing out" (going away in your mind)	0.	1.	2.	3.
15. Sadness	0.	1.	2.	3.
16. Dizziness	0.	1.	2.	3.
17. Not feeling satisfied with your sex life	0.	1.	2.	3.
18. Trouble controlling your temper	0.	1.	2.	3.
19. Waking up early in the morning and can't get back to sleep	0.	1.	2.	3.
20. Uncontrollable crying	0.	1.	2.	3.
21. Fear of men	0.	1.	2.	3.
22. Not feeling rested in the morning	0.	1.	2.	3.
23. Having sex that you didn't enjoy	0.	1.	2.	3.
24. Trouble getting along with others	0.	1.	2.	3.
25. Memory problems	0.	1.	2.	3.
26. Desire to physically hurt yourself	0.	1.	2.	3.
27. Fear of women	0.	1.	2.	3.
28. Waking up in the middle of the night	0.	1.	2.	3.
29. Bad thoughts or feelings during sex	0.	1.	2.	3.
30. Passing out	0.	1.	2.	3.
31. Feeling that things are "unreal"	0.	1.	2.	3.
32. Unnecessary or over-frequent washing	0.	1.	2.	3.
33. Feelings of inferiority	0.	1.	2.	3.
34. Feeling tense all the time	0.	1.	2.	3.
35. Being confused about your sexual sexual feelings	0.	1.	2.	3.
36. Desire to physically hurt others	0.	1.	2.	3.
37. Feelings of guilt	0.	1.	2.	3.
38. Feelings that you are not always in your body	0.	1.	2.	3.
39. Having trouble breathing	0.	1.	2.	3.
40. Sexual feelings when shouldn't have them	0.	1.	2.	3.

Subscale Composition and Scoring for the TSC-40:
Items (add together for subscale score)

Dissociation	7,14,16,25,31,38
Anxiety	1,4,10,16,21,27,32,39
Depression	2,3,9,15,19,20,26,33,37
SATI*	5,7,13,21,25,29,31
Sleep Disturbance	2,8,13,19,22,28
Sexual Problems	5,9,11,17,23,29,35,40
TSC-40 total score	1–40

*Sexual Abuse Trauma Index: Expansion and replacement of the PSAT-H, based on Elliott & Briere (1992).

Taken from: Briere, J., & Runtz, M. (1989). The Trauma Symptom Checklist (TSC-33). Early data on a new scale. *Journal of Interpersonal Violence*, *4*, 151–163, using the additional (formerly "experimental") items to form a 40-item scale.

See also: Elliott, D., & Briere, J. (1992). Sexual abuse trauma among professional women: Validating the Trauma Symptom Checklist-40 (TSC-40). *Child Abuse and Neglect*, *16*, 391–398.

Trauma Symptom Checklist for Children (TSCC)

Type of Population

Children and adolescents (8–16)

Cost

To be determined

Copyright

Psychological Assessment Resources (PAR)

Languages

English

What It Measures

The TSCC evaluates traumatic symptomatology in children, including the effects of child abuse (sexual, physical, and psychological) and neglect, other interpersonal violence, witnessing trauma to others, major accidents, and disasters. The scale measures not only posttraumatic stress, but also other symptom clusters found in some traumatized children.

Measure Content Survey, Procedure, or Process

The TSCC is a 54-item self-report instrument consisting of six subscales: *Anxiety*, *Depression*, *Posttraumatic Stress*, *Sexual Concerns*, *Dissociation*, and *Anger*. The items of the TSCC are explicitly written at a level thought to be understood by children eight years of age or older. The items of the TSCC are contained in a test booklet. Respondents complete a separate answer sheet that facilitates rapid scoring. Each symptom item is rated according to "how often it happens to you," using a 4-point scale ranging from 0 ("never") to 3 ("almost all of the time").

Theoretical Orientation Summary

This measure is essentially atheoretical, focusing on the phenomenology of posttraumatic difficulties.

Time Estimate

Administration	Scoring
10–20 minutes	10 minutes

Equipment Needed

Paper & Pencil	Computer	Basic Psychophysiological	Specialized Equipment
X Item booklet, answer sheets, profile forms, and the professional manual.			

Psychometric Maturity

Under Construction	Basic Properties Intact	Mature
		X

Psychometric Properties Summary

Various studies using the TSCC indicate that it is (a) reliable (alphas in the mid to high 80s for all scales but Sexual Concerns, which tends to be in the high 60s and low 70s) and (b) has convergent and predictive validity in samples of traumatized and nontraumatized children, including those who have experienced sexual abuse (Elliott & Briere, 1994; Elliott & McNeil, 1995; Evans, Briere, Boggiano & Barrett, 1994; Friedrich, 1991; Lanktree & Briere, in press; Singer, Anglin & Lunghofer, 1995; Smith, Swenson, Hanson & Saunders, 1994). In addition to tapping posttraumatic difficulties, the TSCC appears to be sensitive to the effects of therapy for abused children (Cohen & Mannarino, 1992; Lanktree & Briere, in press). Normative data on the TSCC was derived from large samples of nonclinical children across the United States (Evans, et al., 1994; Friedrich, 1995; Singer, et al., 1995), the results of which are currently being analyzed. Preliminary results suggest that separate norms and T scores will be necessary according to sex and several levels of age.

Particular Sensitivity

Age	Change over Time	Culture / Ethnicity	Gender	Geography / Climate	Sexual Orientation	Socioeconomic Status	Urban / Rural
X	?	?	?	?	?	?	?

Estimate of Number of In-Process Studies

10+, including doctoral dissertations.

Unpublished References

Cohen, J. A., & Mannarino, A. P. (November 1992). The effectiveness of short-term group psychotherapy for sexually abused girls: A pilot study. University of Pittsburgh School of Medicine. Pittsburgh, PA.

Elliott, D. M., & McNeil, D. B. (April 1995). Multivariate impacts of sexual molestation, physical abuse, and neglect in older children. Paper presented at the annual meeting of the Western Psychological Association. San Francisco, CA.

Evans, J. J., Briere, J., Boggiano, A. K., & Barrett, M. (January 1994). Reliability and validity of the Trauma Symptom Checklist for Children in a normal sample. San Diego Conference on Responding to Child Maltreatment. San Diego, CA.

Friedrich, W. N. (August 1991). Assessing sexual behavior in sexually abused children: Parents and self-report. Paper presented at the annual meeting of the International Academy of Sex Research. Barrie, Ontario, Canada.

Friedrich, W. N. (1995). Normative data on the TSCC. Unpublished dataset. Mayo Clinic. Rochester, MN.

Lanktree, C. B., Briere, J., & Hernandez, P. (August 1991). Further data on the Trauma Symptom Checklist for Children (TSC-C): Reliability, validity, and sensitivity treatment. American Psychological Association. San Francisco, CA.

Smith, D. W., Swenson, C. C., Hanson, R. F., & Saunders, B. E. (May 1994). The relationship of abuse and disclosure characteristics to Trauma Symptom Checklist for Children scores. Poster presented at the American Professional Society on the Abuse of Children Second Annual Colloquium. Boston, MA.

Published References

Briere, J. (in progress). *Trauma Symptom Checklist for Children (TSCC) professional manual.* Odessa, FL: Psychological Assessment Resources.

Elliott, D. M., & Briere, J. (1994). Forensic sexual abuse evaluations of older children: Disclosures and symptomatology. *Behavioral Sciences and the Law, 12,* 261–277.

Friedrich, W. N. (1994). Assessing children for the effects of sexual victimization. In J. Briere (Ed.), *Assessing and treating victims of violence.* New Directions for Mental Health Services series (MHS #64). San Francisco: Jossey-Bass.

Lanktree, C. B., & Briere, J. (in press). Outcome of therapy for sexually abused children: A repeated measures study. *Child Abuse & Neglect: The International Journal.*

Schmidt-Hirsch, S. E. (1993). A validation study of the Trauma Symptom Checklist for Children. *Dissertation Abstracts International, 54* (1-B), 544.

Singer, M. I., Anglin, T. M., Song, L. Y., & Lunghofer, L. (1995). Adolescents' exposure to violence and associated symptoms of psychological trauma. *Journal of the American Medical Association, 273*, 477–482.

General Comments

In development and testing since 1989, the TSCC is due to be published by PAR in late 1995. Because of concerns by some that asking sexual questions of children (albeit relatively mild ones) may be problematic, the TSCC will appear in two forms: one with all subscales, including Sexual Concerns, and one with all scales except Sexual Concerns. The clinician is advised to use the Sexual Concerns scale, however, in cases where sexual trauma has occurred or is suspected.

Key Words

Population	*Stressor*	*Topic*
adolescents children	any	assessment research

Reference Citation for This Review

Briere, J. (1996). Psychometric review of Trauma Symptom Checklist for Children (TSCC). In B. H. Stamm (Ed.). *Measurement of stress, trauma, and adaptation.* Lutherville, MD: Sidran Press.

Measure Author Name

John Briere, Ph.D.,

Address:	USC School of Medicine
	1934 Hospital Place
	Los Angeles, CA 90033 USA
Phone:	
Fax:	
E-mail:	jbriere@hsc.usc.edu

Measure Contact Name

Psychological Assessment Resources, Inc.

Address:	P.O. Box 998
	Odessa, FL, 33556 USA
Phone:	1.800.331.TEST
Fax:	
E-mail:	

Trauma Symptom Inventory (TSI)

Type of Population
Adults

Cost
Varies according to test component or package

Copyright
Psychological Assessment Resources (PAR)

Languages
English

What It Measures
The TSI evaluates acute and chronic posttraumatic symptomatology, including the effects of rape, spouse abuse, physical assault, combat experiences, and natural disasters, as well as the lasting sequelae of childhood abuse and other early traumatic events. The various scales of the TSI assess a wide range of psychological impacts. These include not only symptoms typically associated with posttraumatic stress disorder or acute stress disorder but also those intra- and interpersonal difficulties often associated with more chronic psychological trauma.

Measure Content Survey, Procedure, or Process
The 100 items of the TSI are contained in a reusable test booklet. Respondents complete a separate answer sheet that facilitates rapid scoring. Each symptom item is rated according to its frequency of occurrence over the prior six months, using a four point scale ranging from 0 ("never") to 3 ("often"). The TSI does not generate *DSM-IV* diagnoses; instead, it is intended to evaluates the relative level of various forms of posttraumatic distress and dysfunction. The TSI requires approximately 20 minutes to complete for all but the most traumatized or clinically impaired individuals and can be scored and profiled in approximately 10 minutes. This measure has 3 validity scales and 10 clinical scales, all of which yield sex- and age-normed T scores. There are 12 critical items.

The validity scales of the TSI are: Response Level (RL) (measuring a tendency toward defensiveness, a general under-endorsement response set, or a need to appear unusually symptom-free); Atypical Response (ATR) (measuring psychosis or extreme distress, a general over-endorsement response set, or an attempt to appear especially disturbed or dysfunctional); and Inconsistent Response (INC) (measuring inconsistent responses to TSI items, potentially due to random item endorsement, attention or concentration problems, or reading/language difficulties).

The clinical scales are: Anxious Arousal (AA) (symptoms of anxiety, including those associated with posttraumatic hyperarousal); Depression (D) (depressive symptomatology, both in terms of mood state and depressive cognitive distortions); Anger/Irritability (AI) (angry or irritable affect, as well as associated angry cognitions and behavior); Intrusive Experiences (IE) (intrusive symptoms associated with posttraumatic stress, such as flashbacks, nightmares, and intrusive thoughts); Defensive Avoidance (DA) (posttraumatic avoidance, both cognitive and behavioral); Dissociation (DIS) (dissociative symptomatology, such as depersonalization, out-of-body experiences, and psychic numbing); Sexual Concerns (SC) (sexual distress, such as sexual dissatisfaction, sexual dysfunction, and unwanted sexual thoughts or feelings); Dysfunctional Sexual Behavior (DSB) (sexual behavior that is in some way dysfunctional, because of either its indiscriminate quality, its potential for self-harm, or its inappropriate use to accomplish nonsexual goals); Impaired Self-Reference (ISR) (problems in the "self" domain, such as identity confusion, self-other disturbance, and a relative lack of self-support); and Tension Reduction Behavior (TRB) (the tendency to turn to external methods of reducing internal tension or distress, such as self-mutilation, angry outbursts, and suicide threats).

Theoretical Orientation Summary
This measure is essentially atheoretical, focusing on the phenomenology of posttraumatic difficulties.

Time Estimate

Administration	Scoring
20 minutes	depends on method, 5–10 minutes

Equipment Needed

Paper & Pencil	Computer	Basic Psychophysiological	Specialized Equipment
Test manual, item booklet, answer sheet, profile/scoring sheet.	Computer program (optional)		

Psychometric Maturity

Under Construction	Basic Properties Intact	Mature
		X

Psychometric Properties Summary

The TSI has been standardized on a random sample of men and women from the general population (N=828), age 18 or older, and includes separate norms for male and female Navy recruits (N=3,659). Because separate norms are available for different combinations of sex and age (18–54; 55 or older), the TSI is appropriate for all adult sex and age combinations. TSI scores vary slightly as a function of race (accounting for 2–3% of the variance in most scales), and slight adjustments for validity scale cutoffs are suggested for certain racial groups. Results of readability analyses indicate that a 5th to 7th grade reading ability is required to complete the TSI. The 10 clinical scales of the TSI are internally consistent (mean alphas of .86, .87, .84, and .84 in standardization, clinical, university, and military samples, respectively) and exhibit reasonable convergent, predictive, and incremental validity. Validity scales covary as expected with similar scales from other measures. In a standardization subsample (n=449), TSI scales predicted independently-assessed PTSD status in over 90% of cases. Similarly, in a psychiatric inpatient sample, TSI scales identified 89% of those independently diagnosed with borderline personality disorder. Studies indicate that specific TSI scale elevations are associated with a wide variety of traumatic experiences in both childhood and adulthood, including various types of interpersonal violence, natural disasters, and witnessing violence to others (Briere & Elliott, in press; Briere, Elliott, Harris, & Cotman, 1995; Elliott & Briere, 1995; Elliott & Mok, 1995).

Particular Sensitivity

Age	Change over Time	Culture / Ethnicity	Gender	Geography / Climate	Sexual Orientation	Socioeconomic Status	Urban / Rural
X	?	X	X	?	?	?	?

Estimated Number of In-Process Studies

10+, including doctoral dissertations.

Unpublished References

Elliott, D. M., & Mok, D. (1995, April). Adult sexual assault: Prevalence, symptomatology, and sex differences. Paper presented at the annual meeting of the Western Psychological Association, San Francisco, CA.

Shapiro, B. L., & Schwarz, J. C. (1995, August). Date rape: Its relationship to trauma symptoms and sexual self-esteem. Paper presented at the annual meeting of the American Psychological Association, New York, NY.

Smiljanich, K., & Briere, J. (1993, August). Sexual abuse history and trauma symptoms in a university sample. Paper presented at the annual meeting of the American Psychological Association, Toronto, Canada.

Published References

Briere, J. (1995). Trauma Symptom Inventory professional manual. Odessa, FL: Psychological Assessment Resources.

Briere, J. (in press). Psychological assessment of posttraumatic states in adults. Washington, DC: American Psychological Association.

Briere, J., & Elliott, D. M. (in press). Appendix I: Trauma Symptom Inventory scores as a function of sexual abuse status in male and female psychiatric inpatients and outpatients. In J. Briere, *Therapy for adults molested as children: Beyond survival,* 2nd ed. New York: Springer.

Briere, J., Elliott, D. M., Harris, K., & Cotman, A. (1995). Trauma Symptom Inventory: Psychometrics and association with childhood and adult trauma in clinical samples. *Journal of Interpersonal Violence, 10,* 387–401.

Briere, J., & PAR staff (1995). Computer scoring system for the Trauma Symptom Inventory (TSI). Computer program. Odessa, FL: Psychological Assessment Resources.

Elliott, D. M., & Briere, J. (1995). Posttraumatic stress associated with delayed recall of sexual abuse: A general population study. *Journal of Traumatic Stress, 8,* 629–647.

General Comments

Common TSI scale profiles/configurations are presented in the professional manual, with brief interpretive suggestions based on clinical experience, normative information, and the results of scale-level factor analyses (exploratory and confirmatory). There is also a scoring program available for the TSI (Briere & PAR staff) which scores and profiles TSI validity and clinical scales, controls for race on validity scales (if requested), and yields three factorial summary scores: Trauma, Self, and Dysphoria.

Key Words

Population	Stressor	Topic
Adult	Any	Assessment Research

Reference Citation for This Review

Briere, J. (1996). Psychometric review of Trauma Symptom Inventory (TSI). In B. H. Stamm (Ed.). *Measurement of stress, trauma, and adaptation.* Lutherville, MD: Sidran Press.

Measure Author

John Briere, Ph.D.

Address: Associate Professor of Psychiatry and Psychology
USC School of Medicine, Graduate Hall
1937 Hospital Place
Los Angeles, CA 90033, U.S.A.

Email: jbriere@hsc.usc.edu

Measure Contact Name

Psychological Assessment Resources, Inc.

Address: P.O. Box 998
Odessa, FL 33556 U.S.A.

Phone/Voice Mail: 1-800-331-TEST

Fax:

Email:

Traumagram Questionnaire

Type of Population

Adult. Those exposed to one or more traumatic events.

Cost

Free

Copyright

Jossey-Bass

Languages

English

What It Measures

The stressfulness of all highly stressful events in a person's life, how long and when it was stressful (including delayed periods and periods of remission), a list of the names of at least one person who also experienced this stressor, and the methods by which the person coped with these stressors. Similar to a genogram, the above data can be represented in a chart that identifies by letter each stressor and when it was stressful during the person's life.

Measure Content Survey, Procedure, or Process

Theoretical Orientation Summary

Figley's theory of traumatic induction and reduction suggests that cognitive review of traumatic experiences lead to successful coping. Those suffering from various trauma-induced emotional problems are employing poor memory management. The Traumagram enables clients to recall more if not all of their traumatic experiences, how the stress decreased over time, and whether this decrease was due to their ability to develop effective methods of coping that could be applied to their challenges with more recent traumatic events.

Time Estimate

Administration	Scoring
5–15 minute	5–10 minutes

Equipment Needed

Paper & Pencil	Computer	Basic Psychophysiological	Specialized Equipment
X			

Psychometric Maturity

Under Construction	Basic Properties Intact	Mature
	X qualitative	

Psychometric Properties Summary

The instrument has at least face validity, based on a review by a panel of clinicians. Used with several dozen clients by over a dozen clinicians and found to be a useful way to gather information about clients' traumatic experiences and how they were able to develop methods for reducing or eliminating the traumatic stress they experienced.

Particular Sensitivity

Age	Change over Time	Culture / Ethnicity	Gender	Geography / Climate	Sexual Orientation	Socioeconomic Status	Urban / Rural
?	?	?	?	?	?	?	?

Estimate of Number of In-Process Studies

Unknown

Unpublished References

Unknown

Published References

Figley, C. R. (1989). *Helping traumatized families*. San Francisco: Jossey-Bass.

Figley, C. R. (1988). Toward a field of traumatic stress studies. *Journal of Traumatic Stress, 1* (1), 3–11.

General Comments

The measure is designed to help the client realize that her or his life has included other experiences with traumatic events; that these events and the way they dealt with them hold the key to their empowerment; that they can build upon past successes in overcoming the unwanted consequences of highly stressful events to overcome their current difficulties with traumatic events.

Key Words

Population	Stressor	Topic
adults	any	assessment

Reference Citation for This Review

Figley, C. F. (1996). Psychometric review of Traumagram Questionnnaire. In B. H. Stamm (Ed.). *Measurement of stress, trauma, and adaptation*. Lutherville, MD: Sidran Press.

Measure Contact Name

Charles R. Figley, Ph.D.

Address:	Psychosocial Stress Research Program
	Florida State University
	103 Sandels Building
	Tallahassee, FL 32306-4097 USA
Phone:	904.644.1588
Fax:	904.644.4804
E-mail:	CFIGLEY@GARNET.ACNS.FSU.EDU

Traumatic Event Screening Instrument for Children (TESI-C)

Type of Population
Children and adolescents (especially those at risk for PTSD), ages 7 to 18. See also TESI-P for completion by parents of children and adolescents at risk for PTSD.

Cost
Free (may be put up for ftp access; call the contact person for details).

Copyright

Languages
English

What It Measures
The TESI-C is a 18-item semi-structured clinical interview for use as a lifetime screening for exposure to several domains of potentially traumatic experiences ranging from accidents, abuse and domestic violence, natural disaster, to separation from primary caregiver. Responses are coded "Yes," "No," "Unsure," "Refuse," and "Questionable Validity." For positive or unsure responses, open-ended questions regarding "What happened?" age of onset, age of offset, frequency, relationship of others involved, consequences, etc. are included. Also available in a checklist format (TESI-Ccl). A computerized data entry program is available for this instrument (using FileMaker Pro™ for the Macintosh).

Measure Content Survey, Procedure, or Process
The TESI-C can be administered as a clinical interview or as a checklist administered by a clinician or completed by an adolescent (TESI-Ccl). Usually administered in conjunction with the parent form (TESI-P or TESI-Pcl).

Theoretical Orientation Summary
No particular theory; based in historical exposure only. Derived in part from J. A. Lipovsky's and R. Hanson's Brief Assessment of Traumatic Event (BATE) interview, as well as from overlapping typologies in the child trauma literature of traumas relatively commonly experienced by treatment-seeking children and adolescents. Items are behaviorally anchored.

Time Estimate

Administration	Scoring
10-30 minutes	5–15 minutes

Equipment Needed

Paper & Pencil	Computer	Basic Psychophysiological	Specialized Equipment
X	Can be used interactively on a Macintosh computer with FileMaker Pro™ software. A FileMaker Pro™ data entry program is available.		

Psychometric Maturity

Under Construction	Basic Properties Intact	Mature
X		

Psychometric Properties Summary

To date, no psychometric properties have been examined.

Particular Sensitivity

Age	Change over Time	Culture / Ethnicity	Gender	Geography / Climate	Sexual Orientation	Socioeconomic Status	Urban / Rural
X	?	?	?	?	?	?	?

Estimate of Number of In-Process Studies

One

Unpublished References

Published References

General Comments

The child version includes clinician action checklist if reporting of possible sexual or physical abuse is indicated. Of particular interest are parent-child comparisons on TESI-C and TESI-P forms. Available for clinical or research use, but clinical use will be difficult before norms are developed. We ask that users provide us with feedback about the clinical and research utility of this instrument.

Key Words

Population	Stressor	Topic
adolescents children	any	measure development research

Reference Citation for This Review

Ribbe, D. (1996). Psychometric review of Traumatic Event Screening Instrument For Children (TESI-C). In B. H. Stamm (Ed.). *Measurement of stress, trauma, and adaptation*. Lutherville, MD: Sidran Press.

Measure Author Names

David Ribbe, Patricia Cone, Margaret Lukovits, Robert Racusin, Karen Rogers, Jason Edwards [National Center for PTSD & Dartmouth Child Trauma Research Group, see address below]

Measure Contact Name

Julian Ford, Ph.D.
Address: The National Center for PTSD (116-D)
             VA Medical & Regional Office Center
             White River Junction, VT 05009 USA
Phone: 802.296.5132
Fax: 802.296.5135
E-mail: Julian.Ford@dartmouth.edu

Traumatic Event Screening Instrument For Parents (TESI-P)

Type of Population

For completion by parent(s) of children and adolescents (especially those at risk for PTSD), ages 7 to 18. See also TESI-C for completion by children and adolescents at risk for PTSD.

Cost

Free (may be put up for ftp access; call the contact person for details).

Copyright

Languages

English

What It Measures

The TESI-P is a 17-item semi-structured clinical interview for use as a lifetime screening for exposure to several domains of potentially traumatic experiences ranging from accidents, abuse and domestic violence, natural disaster, to separation from primary caregiver. Responses are coded "Yes," "No," or "Unsure." For positive or unsure responses, open-ended questions regarding "What happened?" age of onset, age of offset, frequency, relationship of others involved, consequences, etc. are included. Also available in a checklist format (TESI-Pcl). A computerized data entry program is available for this instrument (using FileMaker Pro™ for the Macintosh).

Measure Content Survey, Procedure, or Process

The TESI-P can be administered as a clinical interview or as a checklist administered by a clinician or completed by a parent or parents (TESI-Pcl). Usually administered in conjunction with the child/adolescent form (TESI-C or TESI-Ccl).

Theoretical Orientation Summary

None in particular; uses historical exposure only. Derived in part from J. A. Lipovsky's and R. Hanson's Brief Assessment of Traumatic Event (BATE) interview, as well as from overlapping typologies in the child trauma literature of traumas relatively commonly experienced by treatment-seeking children and adolescents. Items are behaviorally anchored.

Time Estimate

Administration	Scoring
5–10 minutes	5–10 minutes

Equipment Needed

Paper & Pencil	Computer	Basic Psychophysiological	Specialized Equipment
X	Can be used interactively on a Macintosh computer with FileMaker Pro™ software. A FileMaker Pro™ data entry program is available.		

Psychometric Maturity

Under Construction	Basic Properties Intact	Mature
X		

Psychometric Properties Summary

To date, no psychometric properties have been examined.

Particular Sensitivity

Age	Change over Time	Culture / Ethnicity	Gender	Geography / Climate	Sexual Orientation	Socioeconomic Status	Urban / Rural
X	?	?	?	?	?	?	?

Estimate of Number of In-Process Studies

one

Unpublished References

Unknown

Published References

Unknown

General Comments

Child version includes clinician action checklist if reporting of possible sexual or physical abuse is indicated. Of particular interest are parent-child comparisons on TESI-C and TESI-P forms. Available for clinical or research use, but clinical use will be difficult before norms are developed. We ask that users provide us with feedback about the clinical and research utility of this instrument.

Key Words

Population	Stressor	Topic
parents	any	measure development research

Reference Citation for This Review

Ribbe, D. (1996). Psychometric review of Traumatic Event Screening Instrument For Parents (TESI-P). In B. H. Stamm (Ed.). *Measurement of stress, trauma, and adaptation.* Lutherville, MD: Sidran Press.

Measure Author Names

David Ribbe, Margaret Lukovits, Patricia Cone, Robert Racusin, Karen Rogers, Jason Edwards [National Center for PTSD & Dartmouth Child Trauma Research Group, see address below]

Measure Contact Name

Julian Ford, Ph.D.
Address: The National Center for PTSD (116-D)
                VA Medical & Regional Office Center
                White River Junction, VT 05009 USA
Phone: 802.296.5132
Fax: 802.296.5135
E-mail: Julian.Ford@Dartmouth.edu

Traumatic Memory Inventory (TMI)

Type of Population

Adults with trauma histories.

Cost

$10.00 if sent for. Free if copied.

Copyright

Contact Bessel A. van der Kolk, M.D.

Languages

English

What It Measures

1) nature of recall of traumatic memories
2) (sensory, affective & semantic) modalities in which memories are experienced
3) precipitants of intrusive memories
4) nature of flashbacks
5) nature of nightmares
6) ways of controlling flashbacks and nightmares
7) changes in memory recall and content over time
8) comparisons with non-traumatic memories

Measure Content Survey, Procedure, or Process

Structured interview

Theoretical Orientation Summary

None.

Time Estimate

Administration	Scoring
120 minutes	varies

Equipment Needed

Paper & Pencil	Computer	Basic Psychophysiological	Specialized Equipment
X			

Psychometric Maturity

Under Construction	Basic Properties Intact	Mature
	X	

Psychometric Properties Summary

Particular Sensitivity

Age	Change over Time	Culture / Ethnicity	Gender	Geography / Climate	Sexual Orientation	Socioeconomic Status	Urban / Rural
?	?	?	?	?	?	?	?

Estimate of Number of In-Process Studies

2

Unpublished References

Unknown

Published References

van der Kolk, B. A., & Fisler, R. (199). Dissociation and the fragmentary nature of traumatic memories. *Journal of Traumatic Stress, 8,* 505–526.

General Comments

This interview takes about two hours and takes a detailed history of the content, recall, and precipitants of traumatic memories, comparing them with the same in a non-traumatic memory.

Key Words

Population	Stressor	Topic
adults	accidents civil unrest combat criminal victimization domestic violence holocaust, genocide industrial disaster natural disaster physical abuse/neglect political/ethnic persecution sexual assault/abuse terrorism & torture traumatic grief	diagnosis dissociation general psychopathology measure development memory

Reference Citation for This Review

van der Kolk, B. A.. & Fisler, R. Psychometric review of Traumatic Memory Inventory (1996). In B. H. Stamm (Ed.). *Measurement of stress, trauma, and adaptation*. Lutherville, MD: Sidran Press.

Measure Authors

Bessel A. van der Kolk, M.D., & Rita Fisler, M.A.

Measure Contact Name

Jennifer Burbridge, M.A.
          Joji Suzuki, B.A.
Address: 227 Babcock Street
          Brookline, MA 02146 USA
Phone: 617.731.3200 x136
Fax: 617.731.4917
E-mail: joji@channel1.com
          us003263@pop3.interramp.com

TRAUMATIC MEMORY INVENTORY

Patient name_____ Patient ID# _____
Interviewer_____ Date of interview___/___/___
DES Score_____ PDEQ Score _____

PART I: TRAUMATIC MEMORY

I. INTRODUCTION

1) Age_____
2) Sex ___Male ___Female

Indicate age(s) of trauma(s) on the timeline below

BIRTH——NOW

Type of trauma(s)

__Sexual abuse/assault   __Injured/killed someone
__Physical abuse/assault   __Combat
__Accident   __Imprisonment/torture
__Witness death   __Emotional abuse
__Natural disaster   __Death of child
__Being injured (as the trauma)   __Other (Specify)

3) Which trauma has had the greatest effect on your life?_____
_____

☞ **Focus on the memories for this trauma for the entire interview.**

4) _____ Age of onset of trauma

5) _____ Total duration of trauma (put X for one-time event)

6) If interpersonal violence is involved, relationship to perpetrator

__1) father   __8) family "friend"
__2) stepfather/mother's boyfriend   __9) teacher or priest
__3) grandfather   __10) stranger
__4) brother   __11) spouse
__5) other male relative   __12) acquaintance
__6) mother   __13) other (Specify_____
__7) other female relative   _____)

_____Total number of perpetrators

II. HISTORY OF MEMORY (write narrative of memory here and on the opposite blank page; be sure to include the information necessary to answer the following questions):

7) Have you always known that this trauma happened to you?
(Was there a time that you had no recollection that these things ever happened to you?)

0	1		2	3
no recollection at times		<---->		always known what had happened

☞   **If answer is 3, skip to question #10**

8) How have you remembered the event(s) over time ?
___1) always had memories, but did not think of events as trauma
___2) always had some memories, but details were filled in later
___3) had period of complete amnesia, now have clear memories
___4) had complete amnesia, filled in some blanks, but missing pieces remain
___5) have fragments of memories, but no coherent picture of what happened
___6) have no clear memories, but feelings, or other evidence makes me believe that I was traumatized

9) Under what circumstances did forgotten memories come up ?
___1) related to anniversary
___2) related to emotions having to do with the trauma (such as intimacy, trust, power, fear, anger)
___3) related to sensory reminders (eg sounds, sights, smells, etc)
___4) retrieved in talking therapy
___5) retrieved in altered state of consciousness (hypnosis, meditation, drugs)
___6) spontaneous (no awareness of precipitants)
___7) other (specify)_____

III. Awareness of Memories

10) How have you remembered the event(s)?

Initially

When you first became aware of what had happened, how was the memory registered in your mind? **(Listen for patient's report first, then probe for specific details, ie What did you see?)**

___ (X) As visual images (What did you see?)_____

___ (X) As physical sensations (kinesthetic) (What did you feel?)_____

___ (X) As smells (Olfactory) (What did you smell?)_____

___ (X) As sounds (Auditory) (What did you hear?)_____

___ (X) As intense emotions (Affective) (How did you feel?)_____

___ (X) All of them together (Did you see, feel, smell, and hear at the same time?)_____

___ (X) As a story (Narrative) (Were you capable of telling other people what had happened?)_____

Peak

When you were most haunted by the memories, how was the memory registered in your mind? (**Listen for patient's report first, then probe for specific details, ie What did you see?**)

___ (X) As visual images (What did you see?)_____
_____
_____

___ (X) As physical sensations (kinesthetic) (What did you feel?)_____
_____
_____

___ (X) As smells (Olfactory) (What did you smell?)_____
_____
_____

___ (X) As sounds (Auditory) (What did you hear?)_____
_____
_____

___ (X) As intense emotions (Affective) (How did you feel?)_____
_____
_____

___ (X) All of them together (Did you see, feel, smell, and hear at the same time?)_____
_____
_____

___ (X) As a story (Narrative) (Were you capable of telling other people what had happened?)_____
_____
_____

Currently

When the event(s) come(s) to mind, how do you remember it? (**Listen for patient's report first, then probe for specific details, ie What do you see?**)

___ (X) As visual images (What do you see?)_____
_____
_____

___ (X) As physical sensations (kinesthetic) (What do you feel?)_____
_____
_____

___ (X) As smells (Olfactory) (What do you smell?)_____
_____
_____

___ (X) As sounds (Auditory) (What do you hear?)_____
_____
_____

___ (X) As intense emotions (Affective) (How do you feel?)_____
_____
_____

___ (X) All of them together (Do you see, feel, smell, and hear at the same time?)_____
_____
_____

___ (X) As a story (Narrative) (Are you capable of telling other people what had happened?)_____
_____
_____

How long did it take before you could talk to someone else about what had happened in a coherent fashion ?

___ immediately   ___ les than a day
___ less than a week   ___ less than a month
___ I still cannot tell the whole story of what happened

How long did it take before you could talk to someone else about what had happened without being interrupted by intense feelings or sensations related to the event ?

___ immediately   ___ les than a day
___ less than a week   ___ less than a month
___ I still cannot tell the whole story of what happened without getting intense feelings or sensations

11) FLASHBACKS

A. Do you have flashbacks in which the event(s) comes back as if it were happening all over again (while you are awake) ?

___1) yes, currently
___2) used to, no longer
___3) no

☞ skip to 12 if no flashbacks at all

B. If yes, does the entire event come back, or only parts of it (ie. just the smell, sound or the hand of the perpetrator)?

___1) entire trauma
___2) fragments
___3) both

☞ Complete next question only if the flashbacks are fragments of the trauma

C. If fragments, does the event come back as (check all that apply):

___1) Visual (as images)
___2) Tactile/kinesthetic (physical sensations)
___3) Olfactory (smells)
___4) Auditory (sounds)
___5) Affective (emotions)
___6) All of them together
___7) As a story (narrative)

Compare the modalities from Question #10 (Initially/Peak/Current) with the modalities of the flashback. If different, explain the discrepancies._____
_____
_____
_____
_____
_____

12) How often do memories (flashbacks, nightmares, unwanted memories, etc) of the trauma come to mind without your wanting them to?

A ___0) never
___1) daily
___2) 2-4/wk
___3) weekly
___4) monthly
___5) less than once a month

B. Longest intrusion free period
  __1) more than a week
  __2) more than a month
  __3) more than a year

13) CURRENT TRIGGERS
What sort of things trigger memories of the event ?

  __1) anniversaries
  __2) being upset with people
  __3) people being upset with me
  __4) other emotions
  __5) sensory reminders (such as sounds, sights, smells)
  __6) being touched in certain ways
  __7) in talking therapy
  __8) relived in altered state of consciousness (hypnosis, mediation, drugs)
  __9) getting off alcohol or drugs
  __10) spontaneous (no awareness of precipitants)
  __11) other (specify) _____
  __12) nothing triggers memories

14) NIGHTMARES

Do you have nightmares about the trauma ?

  __1) yes , currently
  __2) used to, but have not had them in 3 months
  __3) no

If yes, are they :
  __1) Dreamlike (bizarre, illogical)
   2) Lifelike: exact representations of some aspect of the trauma- no admixture of other elements
    __a) replay of entire trauma
    __b) fragments (sights, smells, feelings, etc)
  __3) Combination of dreamlike and lifelike

15) If you have both nightmares and flashbacks, do they have the same content?

  __1) same
  __2) different
  __3) do not have both

If answer is 2, how are they different?_____
_____

IV. CONTROL AND MASTERY
16) What do you do to control the intrusive memories ?

	in past (X)	currently (X)
1) eating	—	—
2) talking with people	—	—
3) alcohol or drugs (which ones)_____	—	—
4) work, keeping busy	—	—
5) cleaning	—	—
6) religion	—	—
7) being with friends	—	—
8) music	—	—
9) therapy (what sort)_____	—	—
10) self harm (how)_____	—	—
11) sex	—	—
12) sleeping	—	—
13) television	—	—
14) other _____	—	—
15) nothing helps to control the memories	—	—

17) Interviewer

A On the basis of subject's narrative rate for:

___1) Significant functional impairment in effort to avoid re-exposure
___2) Avoids exposure, but no significant effects on occupational or interpersonal functioning
___3) Find self in situations reminiscent of trauma, but unaware of setting it up
___4) Attracted to trauma-related feelings, thoughts or actions.

B. On the basis of subject's narrative, rate cohesiveness of narrative:

       0   1   2   3
Least cohesive <---> Most Cohesive

IV. ACCURACY AND CONFIRMATION

Use this scale for question #18 through #19

       0   1   2   3
    Not at all <---> Completely

18) Do you think that your perceptions of the event(s) have changed over time (ie the role in the trauma or the extent of the trauma)?

                    0 1 2 3

If yes, in what way ?_____
_____
_____

19) How sure are you that your memories are accurate in regards to:

a) time	0 1 2 3
b) place	0 1 2 3
c) person	0 1 2 3
d) events	0 1 2 3

20) Have you ever checked out what you remember with others ?

___1) Not tried to confirm

___2) Disconfirmed by others only

___3) No confirmation, but no alternative versions are offered by other potential witnesses
(what _____
_____)

___4) Others who knew subject at time of trauma support subject and BELIEVE it is true

___5) Clear confirmatory evidence
(what _____
_____)

___6) Adult trauma; No delayed memories, issue of confirmation not relevant

___7) Other _____
_____
_____

Interviewer's comments about reliability of information

_____
_____
_____
_____
_____
_____

PART II: NON-TRAUMATIC MEMORY

Now I would like you to remember another event in your life that made a deep impression on you, but that was not traumatic. For example, the birth of a child, an illness, wedding, a vacation, graduation, a particularly important relationship, an accomplishment in school or at work. Please tell me what event you'd like to pick, and how old you were when it happened.

Event

_____

_____

_____

_____

_____Age at the time of experience

1) _____Total duration of event in months (put X for one-time event)

Use this scale for questions #2 through #3
0   <---->   3
no / not at all   yes / completely

2) Have you been continuously aware that this event has happened to you?

0 1 2 3

3) Have there been times that you put it out of your mind and were surprised that it came up?

0 1 2 3

4) How do you remember the event(s)?

Initially: **When you first became aware of what had happened, how was the memory registered in your mind?**

Peak: **When you were most haunted by the memories, how was the memory registered in your mind?**

Currently: **When the experience comes to mind now, how do you remember it?**

	Initially (X)	Peak (X)	Currently (X)
1. As visual images (what did/do you see?)	—	—	—
2. As physical sensations (kinesthetic) (what did/do you feel?)	—	—	—
3. As smells (Olfactory) (what did/do you smell?)	—	—	—
4. As sounds (Auditory) (what did/do you hear?)	—	—	—
5. As intense emotions(Affective) (how did/do you feel?)	—	—	—
6. All of them together (did/do you see, feel, smell, and hear at the same time?)	—	—	—
7. As a story(narrative) (were/are you capable of telling other people what had happened?)	—	—	—

How long did it take before you could tell it as a coherent story to someone?

___ immediately   ___ less than a day
___ less than a week   ___ less than a month
___ I still cannot tell the whole story of what happened

How long did it take you before you were able to talk about what had happened, without being interrupted by intense feelings or sensations related to the event ?

___ immediately   ___ less than a day
___ less than a week   ___ less than a month
___ I still cannot tell the whole story of what happened without getting intense feelings or sensations

5) Have you always known that this event happened to you?
(Was there a time that you had no recollection that these things ever happened to you?)

0	1		2	3
no recollection at times		<---->		always known what had happened

☞ **If answer is 3, skip to question #8**

6) How have you remembered the experience over time?

__1) always knew what happened, and think about it with the same emotional intensity as I do now
__2) always knew it, but but details have changed over time
__3) had period of complete amnesia, now have clear memories
__4) had complete amnesia, filled in some blanks, but missing pieces remain
__5) have fragments of memories, but no coherent picture of what happened
__6) have no clear memories, but feelings, or other evidence makes me believe it happened.

7) Under what circumstances do memories of this event come up ?

__1) anniversaries
__2) being upset with people
__3) people being upset with me
__4) other emotions
__5) sensory reminders (such as sounds, sights, smells, etc)
__6) being touched in certain ways
__7) in talking therapy
__8) relived in altered state of consciousness (hypnosis, mediation, drugs)
__9) getting off alcohol or drugs
__10) spontaneous (no awareness of precipitants)
__11) other (specify) _____
__12) None

8) How often do memories of the experience come to mind without your wanting them to ?

A.__1) daily
__2) 2-4/wk
__3) weekly
__4) monthly
__5) less than once a month

B. Longest period that you have not thought about this event.
__1) more than a week
__2) more than a month
__3) more than a year

9) A. Are there times that the experience comes back as if it were happening again, while you are awake ?

   __1) yes
   __2) no

B. If yes, does the entire experience come back, or only parts of it?

   __1) entire experience
   __2) fragments

   ☞ **If entire experience, skip to question #10**

C. If fragments, does the experience come back as:
   __1) Visual (as images)
   __2) Tactile/kinesthetic (physical sensations)
   __3) Olfactory (smells)
   __4) Auditory (sounds)
   __5) Affective (emotions)
   __6) All of them together
   __7) As a story (narrative)

10) Do you have dreams about the experience ?

   __a) yes
   __b) no

If yes, are they

   __1) Dreamlike (bizarre, illogical)
   2) Lifelike exact representations of some aspect experience - no admixture of other elements
    __a) replay of entire experience
    __b) fragments (sights, smells, feelings, etc)
   __3) Combination

11) If you have both dreams and intense waking re-experiences, do they have the same content ?
   __1) same
   __2) different
   __3) not both

  Use this scale for questions #12 through #14
    0 1 2 3
   Not at all <---> Completely

12) Do you think that your perceptions of the trauma have changed over time ?

               0 1 2 3
If yes, in what way?_____
_____

13) How accurate do you believe your memories are in regards to:

1) time	0 1 2 3
2) place	0 1 2 3
3) person	0 1 2 3
4) events	0 1 2 3

14) Have you ever found that what you remember about this experience is quite different from what other people remember ?

0 1 2 3

What do you make of that ?_____
_____
_____

==

15) We now have come to the end of our interview, please tell me what it was like for you ?

16) What lessons do you feel you have learned that would help other people who have gone through experiences similar to yours ?

Summary and interviewer's comments (Including whether subject was capable of telling non-traumatic story which remained uncontamined by previous telling of traumatic experience- comment on this in detail).

TMI Score Sheet   Date of interview____/____/_____

Patient Name_____ ID Number_____ (id) Ag
e_____ (age) Interviewer_____

Traumatic Memory

Gender (0=male   1=female)   0 1 (gender)

Age of onset of trauma _____ (ageons)
Duration of trauma (in years; _____ (durat)
99=less than one year, 0=one time event)

PDEQ Score   _____ (pdeq)
DES Score   _____ (des)

Type of trauma (0=no   1=yes)
        Sexual abuse/assault   0 1 (type1)
        Physical abuse 0 1 (type2)
        Accident   0 1 (type3)
        Witness death   0 1 (type4)
        Natural disaster   0 1 (type5)
        Being injured   0 1 (type6)
        Injure/kill other   0 1 (type7)
        Combat 0 1 (type8)
        Imprison/torture   0 1 (type9)
        Emotional abuse 0 1 (type10)
        Death of Child 0 1 (type11)
        Other(Specify_____   0 1 (type12)
        _____)

If abuse, w/in family (0=no 1=yes 2=no abuse)
            0 1 2 (famil)

Childhood trauma (0=no 1=yes) Childhood is age<14
            0 1 (child)

Number of perpetrator(s)   _____ (perp)

Amnesia (0=total amnesia   3=no amnesia)
            0 1 2 3 (knew)

How memories came up(0=no 1=yes 2=no amnesia)
        Anniversary   0 1 2 (memup1)
        Emotions   0 1 2 (memup2)
        Sensory 0 1 2 (memup3)
        Therapy 0 1 2 (memup4)
        Altered states 0 1 2 (memup5)
        Spontaneous   0 1 2 (memup6)

```
Other(Specify_____    0   1   2   (memup7)
             _____)

Sensory modalities (0=no   1=yes)
         Initially        Peak       Currently
Visually       0   1 (init1)   0   1 (peak1)    0   1 (curr1)
Tactile 0   1 (init2)    0   1 (peak2)    0   1 (curr2)
Olfactory      0   1 (init3)   0   1 (peak3)    0   1 (curr3)
Auditory       0   1 (init4)   0   1 (peak4)    0   1 (curr4)
Affective      0   1 (init5)   0   1 (peak5)    0   1 (curr5)
All together   0   1 (init6)   0   1 (peak6)    0   1 (curr6)
Narrative      0   1 (init7)   0   1 (peak7)    0   1 (curr7)

Flashbacks(1=yes  2=used to   3=no)
           1   2   3   (flash1)

Form of flashback  (0=no flashback    1=entire trauma
2=fragments   3=both)
           0   1   2   3   (flash2)

Modalities of flashback  (0=no    1=yes    2=no flashback)
        Visual  0   1   2 (flash3)
        Tactile 0   1   2 (flash4)
        Olfactory      0   1   2 (flash5)
        Auditory       0   1   2 (flash6)
        Affective      0   1   2 (flash7)
        All together   0   1   2 (flash8)
        Narrative      0   1   2 (flash9)

Frequency of intrusion  (0= no intrusions   1=daily
2=2-4/wk  3=weekly  4=monthly  5=less than 1/month)
           0   1   2   3   4   5(intrus)
Triggers  (0=no    1=yes)
        Anniversaries  0   1  (trigg1)
        Upset with others    0   1  (trigg2)
        Others upset w/ me   0   1  (trigg3)
        Other emotions 0   1  (trigg4)
        Sensory reminders    0   1  (trigg5)
        Being touched  0   1  (trigg6)
        Therapy 0   1  (trigg7)
        Altered states 0   1  (trigg8)
        Off EtOH/drugs 0   1  (trigg9)
        Spontaneous    0   1  (trigg10)
        Other(Specify_____   0   1  (trigg11)
        _____)
        None     0   1  (trigg12)

Nightmares (1=yes  2=not in 3 months   3=none)
           1   2   3   (night1)

Form of nightmare  (0=no nightmare 1=dreamlike
```

2=lifelike & entire trauma 3=lifelike & fragments
4=both)
                    0 1 2 3 4(night2)

Content of nightmare compared to flashbacks (0=don't
have both 1=same 2=different)
                    0 1 2 (nigth3)

Avoidance (0=no   1=yes)
        Eating 0 1 (avoid1)
        Talking w/ others   0 1 (avoid2)
        EtOH/drugs   0 1 (avoid3)
        Keeping busy   0 1 (avoid4)
        Cleaning   0 1 (avoid5)
        Religion   0 1 (avoid6)
        Being with friends   0 1 (avoid7)
        Music   0 1 (avoid8)
        Therapy 0 1 (avoid9)
        Self-harm   0 1 (avoid10)
        Sex   0 1 (avoid11)
        Sleeping   0 1 (avoid12)
        Television   0 1 (avoid13)
        Other(Specify_____ 0 1 (avoid14)
        _____)
        None   0 1 (avoid15)

Perception of the trauma changing over time (Scale 0-3:
0=not at all   3=definitely)
                    0 1 2 3 (change)

Confirmation of trauma (0=no 1=yes 2=not relevant)
                    0 1 2 (cnfrm)

Degree of narrative (Scale 0-3: 0=no narrative
3=coherent narrative)
                    0 1 2 3 (narr)

Non-traumatic memory

Age of onset of experience   _____ (age2)

Amnesia (0=no   1=yes) 0 1 (amnesia)

Modalities of non-traumatic memory (0=no   1=yes)
        Visual 0 1 (prisen1)
        Tactile 0 1 (prisen2)
        Olfactory   0 1 (prisen3)
        Auditory   0 1 (prisen4)
        Affective   0 1 (prisen5)
        All together   0 1 (prisen6)
        Narrative   0 1 (prisen7)

Comments

_____

_____

_____

_____

TMI Scoresheet 2/96

van der Kolk

Traumatic Stress Schedule (TSS)
National Center for PTSD Review

Type of Population
Adults

Cost
Unknown

Copyright
Contact Fran Norris, Ph.D.

Languages
English

What It Measures
Assesses retrospectively recalled traumatic stress exposure.

Measure Content Survey, Procedure, or Process
Structured interview to assess retrospectively recalled traumatic stress exposure. Scores for Rape, Sexual assault, Physical assault, Death of family/close friend, Crime victimization, Motor vehicle accident involving injury, injury or property damage due to disaster, Witness to or threatened with natural disaster, Terrifying/shocking experience, Major life change, 5 PTSD symptoms.

Theoretical Orientation Summary
empirical

Time Estimate

Administration	Scoring
10–30 minutes	10 minutes

Equipment Needed

Paper & Pencil	Computer	Basic Psychophysiological	Specialized Equipment
X			

Psychometric Maturity

Under Construction	Basic Properties Intact	Mature
X	qualitative	

Psychometric Properties Summary
unknown

Particular Sensitivity

Age	Change over Time	Culture / Ethnicity	Gender	Geography / Climate	Sexual Orientation	Socioeconomic Status	Urban / Rural
?	?	?	?	?	?	?	?

Estimate of Number of In-Process Studies

unknown

Unpublished References

unknown

Published References

Norris, F. (1990). Screening for traumatic stress. *Journal of Applied Social Psychology, 20*, 1704–1718.

General Comments

Key Words

Population	Stressor	Topic
adults	any	measure development research

Reference Citation for This Review

Ford, J. (1996). Psychometric review of Traumatic Stress Schedule (TSS). In B. H. Stamm (Ed.). *Measurement of stress, trauma, and adaptation*. Lutherville, MD: Sidran Press.

Reviewer Contact Name

Julian Ford, Ph.D.
Address: National Center for PTSD (116-D)
                    VA Medical Center
                    White River Junction, VT 05009 USA
Phone: 802.296.5132
Fax: 802.296.5135
E-mail: Julian.Ford@Dartmouth.Edu

Measure Contact Name

Fran Norris, Ph.D.
Address: Dept. of Psychology
                    Georgia State University,
                    University Plaza, Atlanta GA 30303 USA
Phone:
Fax:
E-mail:

TSI Autonomy and Connection Scales

Type of Population

Adults

Cost

Free

Copyright

Laurie Anne Pearlman, Ph.D., Traumatic Stress Institute

Languages

English, Chinese, Spanish, Russian

What It Measures

The complete TSI Belief Scale, from which the TSI Autonomy and Connection Scales (TSI A & C) are drawn, is intended to measure disruptions in beliefs about self and others which arise from psychological trauma or from vicarious exposure to trauma material through psychotherapy or other helping relationships. The A & C scales pertain to the Experience of Autonomy of Connection

Measure Content Survey, Procedure, or Process

The A & C scales assess disruptions in cognitive schemas, or beliefs about self and others, in two areas, roughly corresponding to the concepts of self and others, which may be impacted by trauma (McCann, Sakheim, & Abrahamson, 1988). The scale consists of 35 items. The subject uses a 6-point Likert Scale to endorse the degree to which s/he agrees with each statement. The instrument yields two subscale scores, one for the structure of the Experience of Connection and one for the Experience of Autonomy (a higher score indicating more disruption).

Theoretical Orientation Summary

The TSI A & C Scale is based in Constructivist Self Development Theory (CSDT; McCann & Pearlman, 1990b, Pearlman & Saakvitne, 1995a, 1995b). The theory draws upon and integrates self psychology, object relations, interpersonal and social cognition theories.

Time Estimate

Administration	Scoring
10–15 minutes	10–15 minutes

Equipment Needed

Paper & Pencil	Computer	Basic Psychophysiological	Specialized Equipment
X			

Psychometric Maturity

Under Construction	Basic Properties Intact	Mature
	X	

Psychometric Properties Summary

Multigroup factorial invariance analyses conducted by Stamm and colleagues yielded the two factors that form the two scales. Structural Reliabilities (stability) as measured by the Tucker's Coefficient of Congruence were at or above .95 for Experience of Connection scale and at or above .71 for the Experience of Autonomy scale (Pearlman, Mac Ian, Mas, Stamm, & Bieber, 1992; Stamm, Bieber, & Pearlman, 1991). In the context of CSDT, we conceptualize these factors as representing aspects of the individual's frame of reference, roughly corresponding to the experience of identity (self) and world view (other). No structural differences have been identified across males and females. Previous studies have used the TSI A & C scales to address schema disruption and parental style (Sandberg & Stamm, 1992) and schema disruption and the effect of being the emotional support provider for the victim of physical or sexual assault (Varra & Stamm, 1992).

Particular Sensitivity

Age	Change over Time	Culture / Ethnicity	Gender	Geography / Climate	Sexual Orientation	Socioeconomic Status	Urban / Rural
?	?	?	?	?	?	?	?

Estimate of Number of In-Process Studies

Unpublished References

Pearlman, L. A., & Mac Ian, P. S. (manuscript in preparation). The TSI Belief Scale: Data from four criterion groups

Pearlman, L. A., Mac Ian, P., Mas, K., Stamm, B. H., & Bieber, S. (October, 1992). Understanding disrupted schemas: The relation among theory, psychotherapy, and research. Presented at the Eighth Annual Meeting of The International Society for Traumatic Stress Studies. Los Angeles, CA.

Sandberg, C. T., & Stamm, B. H. (1992). Adult Schema disruption and early destructive parenting. Presented at the Eighth Annual Meeting of The International Society for Traumatic Stress Studies. Los Angeles, CA.

Stamm, B. H., Bieber, S. L., & Pearlman, L. A. (October, 1991). A preliminary report on scale construction and generalizability of the TSI Belief Scale. Paper presented at the annual meeting of the International Society for Traumatic Stress Studies. Washington, DC.

Varra, E. M., & Stamm, B. H. (1992). Vicarious traumatization: Emotional support providers of sexual and physical assault victims. Presented at the Eighth Annual Meeting of the International Society for Traumatic Stress Studies. Los Angeles, CA.

Published References

McCann, I. L., & Pearlman, L. A. (1990b). *Psychological trauma and the adult survivor: Theory, therapy, and transformation.* New York: Brunner/Mazel.

McCann, I. L., Sakheim, D. K., & Abrahamson, D. J. (1988). Trauma and victimization: A model of psychological adaptation. *The Counseling Psychologist, 16* (4), 531–594.

Pearlman, L. A., & Saakvitne, K. W. (1995a). *Trauma and the therapist: Countertransference and vicarious traumatization in psychotherapy with incest survivors.* New York: W.W. Norton.

Pearlman, L. A., & Saakvitne, K. W. (1995b). Constructivist self development theory approach to treating therapists with vicarious traumatization and secondary traumatic stress disorders. In C.R. Figley (Ed.), *Compassion fatigue: Coping with secondary traumatic stress disorder in those who treat the traumatized.* New York: Brunner/Mazel.

General Comments

We ask that all who use the instrument agree to share their raw data with us to further our validation efforts. Those who wish to use the Belief Scale will receive scoring instructions after signing a Data Share Agreement. As they become available, new revisions are sent to all who have a data sharing agreement on file. To obtain copies of the TSI Belief Scale, scoring instructions, reliability information, and normative data, contact The Traumatic Stress Institute, 22 Morgan Farms Drive, South Windsor, CT 06074, 203.644.2541. Please enclose a self-addressed stamped envelope.

Key Words

Population	Stressor	Topic
adults	any	assessment research

Reference Citation for This Review

Stamm, B. H., & Pearlman, L. A. (1996). Psychometric review of TSI Autonomy & Connection Scales. In B. H. Stamm (Ed.). Measurement of stress, trauma and adaptation. Lutherville, MD: Sidran Press.

Measure Contact Name

B. Hudnall Stamm, Ph.D.

Address   Traumatic Stress Research Group
                PO Box 531
                Hanover, NH 03755 USA

Phone/Voice Mail:

Fax:

E-mail: b.hudnall.stamm@dartmouth.edu

Measure Contact Name

Laurie Anne Pearlman, Ph.D.

Address: The Traumatic Stress Institute
                22 Morgan Farms Drive
                South Windsor, CT 06074

Phone: 203.644.2541

Fax: 203.644.6891

E-mail: lap.tsi@aol.com

TSI Belief Scale, Revision L

Type of Population
Adults

Cost
Free

Copyright
Laurie Anne Pearlman, Ph.D. Traumatic Stress Institute

Languages
English, Chinese, Spanish, Russian

What It Measures
The TSI Belief Scale is intended to measure disruptions in beliefs about self and others that arise from psychological trauma or from vicarious exposure to trauma material through psychotherapy or other helping relationships. The scale is intended to provide a quick (15 minute) screening instrument for clinicians questioning the possibility of a trauma history in their clients, as well as indicating specific psychological need areas requiring attention in the psychotherapy process (McCann & Pearlman, 1990a). It is also intended, in conjunction with other measures, to diagnose the existence of vicarious trauma in helpers (McCann & Pearlman, 1990b; Pearlman & Saakvitue, 1995a, 1995b).

Measure Content Survey, Procedure, or Process
The TSI Belief Scale assesses disruptions in cognitive schemas, or beliefs about self and others, in five psychological need areas which are impacted by trauma (Pearlman & Saakvitue, in press). The scale consists of 80 items. The subject uses a 6-point Likert Scale to endorse the degree to which s/he agrees with each statement. Scores obtained include a total score (a higher score indicating more disruption) and 10 subscale scores (average scores) indicating relative disruptions of the five need/schema areas: safety, trust, esteem, intimacy, and control.

Theoretical Orientation Summary
The TSI Belief Scale is based in Constructivist Self Development Theory (CSDT; McCann & Pearlman, 1990a; Pearlman & Saakvitne, 1995a, 1995b). The theory draws upon and integrates self psychology, object relations, interpersonal and social cognition theories.

Time Estimate

Administration	Scoring
15–20 minutes	5–10 minutes

Equipment Needed

Paper & Pencil	Computer	Basic Psychophysiological	Specialized Equipment
X			

Psychometric Maturity

Under Construction	Basic Properties Intact	Mature
	X	

Psychometric Properties Summary

The overall reliability (Cronbach's alpha) of the total Belief Scale (revision L) is .98. The subscale reliabilities range from .77 (other-control) to .91 (self-esteem). The scale has reliably discriminated among survivors of childhood sexual abuse, and other trauma in a psychiatric population (Mas & Pearlman, manuscript in preparation). Other studies have found significant differences (more disruptions) in trauma survivors vs. non-survivors (Pearlman & Mac Ian, manuscript in preparation). No consistent sex differences have been found in studies to date. Additional work with the scale is being conducted by researchers across the country. Multigroup Factorial Invariance analyses conducted by Stamm and colleagues have yielded two factors which are stable across populations. (Pearlman, Mac Ian, Mas, Stamm, & Bieber, 1992; Stamm, Bieber, & Pearlman, 1991). These factors have been tentatively named "experience of autonomy" and "experience of connection." In the context of CSDT, we conceptualize these factors as representing aspects of the individual's frame of reference, roughly corresponding to the experience of identity (self) and world view (other).

Particular Sensitivity

Age	Change over Time	Culture / Ethnicity	Gender	Geography / Climate	Sexual Orientation	Socioeconomic Status	Urban / Rural
?	?	?	?	?	?	?	?

Estimate of Number of In-Process Studies

Unpublished References

Mas, K., & Pearlman, L. A. (manuscript in preparation). Disrupted schemata in adult survivors of childhood sexual abuse.

Pearlman, L. A., & Mac Ian, P. S. (manuscript in preparation). The TSI Belief Scale: Data from five criterion groups.

Pearlman, L. A., Mac Ian, P., Mas, K., Stamm, B. H., & Bieber, S. (October 1992). Understanding disrupted schemas: The relation among theory, psychotherapy, and research. Presented at the annual meeting of the International Society for Traumatic Stress Studies. Los Angeles, CA.

Stamm, B. H., Bieber, S. L., & Pearlman, L. A. (October 1991). A preliminary report on scale construction and generalizability of the TSI Belief Scale. Paper presented at the annual meeting of the International Society for Traumatic Stress Studies. Washington, DC.

Published References

McCann, I. L., & Pearlman, L. A. (1990a). *Psychological trauma and the adult survivor: Theory, therapy, and transformation*. New York: Brunner/Mazel.

McCann, I. L., & Pearlman, L. A. (1990b). Vicarious traumatization: A framework for understanding the psychological impact of working with victims. *Journal of Traumatic Stress, 3*, 131–150.

McCann, I. L., Sakheim, D. K., & Abrahamson, D. J. (1988). Trauma and victimization: A model of psychological adaptation. *The Counseling Psychologist, 16*, (4), 531–594.

Pearlman, L. A., & Saakvitne, K. W. (1995a). *Trauma and the therapist: Countertransference and vicarious traumatization in psychotherapy with incest survivors*. New York: W.W. Norton.

Pearlman, L. A., & Saakvitne, K. W. (1995b). Constructivist self development theory approach to treating therapists with vicarious traumatization and secondary traumatic stress disorders. In C. R. Figley (Ed.). *Compassion fatigue: Coping with secondary traumatic stress disorder in those who treat the traumatized*. New York: Brunner/Mazel.

General Comments

We ask that all who use the instrument agree to share their raw data with us to further our validation efforts. Those who wish to use the Belief Scale will receive scoring instructions after signing a Data Share Agreement. As they become available, new revisions are sent to all who have a data sharing agreement on file. To obtain copies of the TSI Belief Scale, scoring instructions, reliability information, and normative data, contact The Traumatic Stress Institute, 22 Morgan Farms Drive, South Windsor, CT 06074, 203.644.2541. Please enclose a self-addressed stamped envelope.

Key Words

Population	Stressor	Topic
adults	any	assessment treatment

Reference Citation for This Review

Pearlman, L. A. (1996). Psychometric review of TSI Belief Scale, Revision-L. In B. H. Stamm (Ed.). *Measurement of stress, trauma, and adaptation*. Lutherville, MD: Sidran Press.

Measure Contact Name

Laurie Anne Pearlman, Ph.D.

Address: The Traumatic Stress Institute
                 22 Morgan Farms Drive
                 South Windsor, CT 06074 USA
Phone: 203.644.2541
Fax: 203.644.6891
E-mail: lap.tsi@aol.com

TSI Belief Scale Revision L Sample Items

Self-Safety: the need to feel one is reasonably invulnerable to harm inflicted by self or others.

    1. I generally feel safe from danger.

    4. I find myself worrying a lot about myself.

    15. I believe I can protect myself if my thoughts become self-destructive.

Other Safety: the need to feel that valued others are reasonably protected from harm inflicted—by oneself or others.

    9. I'm reasonably comfortable about the safety of those I care about.

    19. Sometimes I think I'm concerned about the safety of others than they are.

    40. I worry a lot about the safety of loved ones.

Self-trust: The belief that one can trust one's judgments

    44. I feel uncertain about my ability to make decisions.

    70. I have sound judgment.

    74. I feel confident in my decision-making ability.

Other-trust: the belief that one can rely upon others.

    47. I can depend on my friends to be there when I need them.

    64. Most people don't keep the promises they make.

    66. Trusting other people is generally not very smart.

Self-esteem: the belief that one is valuable and worthy of respect.

    27. I deserve to have good things happen to me.

    32. I am basically a good person.

    34. Bad things happen to me because I'm bad.

Other-esteem: the belief that others are valuable and worthy of respect.

    31. This world is filled with emotionally disturbed people.

    50. Most people are basically good at heart.

    56. I don't have a lot of respect for the people closest to me.

Self-intimacy: the belief that time spent alone is enjoyable.

    35. Some of my happiest experiences involve other people.

    36. There are many people to whom I feel close and connected.

    39. I often feel cut off and distant from other people.

Self-control: the need to be in charge of one's own feelings and behaviors.

    65. Strong people don't need to ask for others' help.

    68. I feel bad about myself when I need others' help.

    80. When someone suggests I relax, I feel anxious.

Other-control: The need to manage interpersonal situations.

    24. I don't have much control in relationships.

    25. I am often involved in conflicts with other people.

    55. I often feel helpless in my relationships with others.

TSI Life Event Questionnaire (LEQ)
Long form—Revision 1; Short form—Revision 3

Type of Population

General adult population

Cost

The short form of the LEQ is available at no charge. The long form is available for $2.00.

Copyright

Laurie Anne Pearlman, Ph.D., Traumatic Stress Institute

Languages

English

What It Measures

The LEQ short form provides a way of identifying individuals with childhood sexual, nonsexual, and adult trauma histories. The long form provides extensive information about the subject's trauma history, including age at the time of abuse, allowing for the exploration of developmental issues. The LEQ short form is intended as a screening instrument to alert the therapist to the existence of specific traumatic life events in the client's history. The long form provides a detailed review of the client's lifetime trauma history, informing the therapist of events which otherwise may not be revealed in the course of therapy and allowing the client to review his/her entire trauma history at once. Both forms also provide an opportunity for the client to indicate level of distress related to the incidents at the time they occurred and now.

Measure Content Survey, Procedure, or Process

The long form LEQ consists of 204 potentially traumatic or stressful life events, including sexual trauma, war trauma, loss of significant others, and so forth. The short form consists of 18 potentially traumatic life events.

Theoretical Orientation Summary

The measure is based in a constructivist perspective (Constructivist Self Development Theory, McCann & Pearlman, 1990). For this reason, in addition to inquiring about specific events experienced, it attempts to assess in a very general way the individual's response (amount of distress) to those events. Because the theory is developmental, the questionnaire also asks the individual's age at the time the event took place.

Time Estimate

Administration	Scoring
5-45 minutes depending on form	5–10 minutes

Equipment Needed

Paper & Pencil	Computer	Basic Psychophysiological	Specialized Equipment
X			

Psychometric Maturity

Under Construction	Basic Properties Intact	Mature
	X	

Psychometric Properties Summary

Particular Sensitivity

Age	Change over Time	Culture / Ethnicity	Gender	Geography / Climate	Sexual Orientation	Socioeconomic Status	Urban / Rural
?	?	?	?	?	?	?	?

Estimate of Number of In-Process Studies
Unknown

Unpublished References
Unknown

Published References
Mac Ian, P.S., & Pearlman, L.A. (1992). Development and use of the TSI Life Event Questionnaire. *Treating Abuse Today: The International News Journal of Abuse, Survivorship and Therapy, 2* (1), 9–11.

General Comments
To obtain the LEQ short form, send a self-addressed, stamped envelope to the Traumatic Stress Institute, 22 Morgan Farms Drive, CT 06074. To obtain the long form, please enclose a check for $2.00 payable to CAAP.

Key Words

Population	Stressor	Topic
adults clinical research	any	assessment

Reference Citation for This Review
Pearlman, L. A. (1996). Psychometric review of TSI Life Event Questionnaire (LEQ). In B. H. Stamm (Ed.). *Measurement of stress, trauma, and adaptation.* Lutherville, MD: Sidran Press.

Measure Contact Name
Laurie Anne Pearlman, Ph. D.
Address: The Traumatic Stress Institute
               22 Morgan Farms Drive
               South Windsor, CT 06074 USA
Phone: 203.644.2541
Fax: 203.644.6891
E-mail: lap.tsi@aol.com

Subject # _____ Sex (circle one): M F Your age _____ Date _____

This is a list of potentially stressful events which sometimes occur in people's lives. We want to know which of these events you have experienced or believe you have experienced and how distressing each one is for you. Sometimes people have strong feelings or have great difficulty remembering such stressful events. If at any time you feel too uncomfortable to continue filling out this questionnaire, feel free to stop and talk with your therapist about your thoughts and feelings in your next session. If you choose to complete the questionnaire, we ask for the following information. For each event you believe you experienced, we would like four pieces of information: (1) your age(s) when the event occurred, (2) how often this event occurred, (3) how distressing it was for you when it happened, and (4) how distressing it is for you now when you think about the experience. In the first column after the item, write your AGE(S) (or age range e.g., 5–12) when it happened. In the next column put a number for HOW OFTEN this event occurred or circle "many times" if this event occurred on numerous occasions. In the last columns, using the scale below indicated how much DISTRESS you feel related to each event.

1	2	3	4	5	6
not at all distressing	slightly distressing	moderately distressing	quite distressing	very distressing	extremely distressing

		Your Age(s)	How Often (# or circle)	Distress Then	Distress Now
A.	**AFFECTED BY WAR, MILITARY, OR HOLOCAUST**				
A1.	stationed overseas during a war	_____	___or many times	_____	_____
A2.	served in military	_____	___or many times	_____	_____
A3.	fired a weapon or were fired upon in combat	_____	___or many times	_____	_____
A4.	felt responsible for death of US military personnel	_____	___or many times	_____	_____
A5.	felt responsible for death of enemy military personnel or civilian	_____	___or many times	_____	_____
A6.	wounded in combat	_____	___or many times	_____	_____
A7.	involved in an attack in which others were seriously injured or killed	_____	___or many times	_____	_____
A8.	discharged dishonorably or because of emotional problems	_____	___or many times	_____	_____
A9.	participated in torture, rape, mutilation, or other atrocities	_____	___or many times	_____	_____
A10.	observed torture, rape, mutilation, or other atrocities	_____	___or many times	_____	_____
A11.	prisoner of war or missing in action	_____	___or many times	_____	_____
A12.	had a parent/loved one wo was a victim of torture, holocaust, and/or mass killing	_____	___or many times	_____	_____
A13.	you were a victim of torture, holocaust, and/or mass killing	_____	___or many times	_____	_____
A14.	parent was killed, missing in action, or victim of war	_____	___or many times	_____	_____
A15.	parent was prisoner of war or in an internment camp	_____	___or many times	_____	_____
A16.	parent/loved one was away due to declared or undeclared war	_____	___or many times	_____	_____
A17.	lost a parent in concentration or refugee camp	_____	___or many times		

B. EXPERIENCED A NATURAL OR HUMAN-INDUCED DISASTER (e.g., fire, airplane crash, acts of terrorism)

B1. experienced a large-scale or serious human-induced disaster _____ ___or many times _____ _____

B2. involved in a serious accident _____ ___or many times _____ _____

B3. involved in a serious accident in which others suffered serious physical injury _____ ___or many times _____ _____

B4. saw dead or dying people (other than a parent/ caretaker, child or spouse) as a result of a disaster or serious accident _____ ___or many times _____ _____

B5. lost home due to disaster _____ ___or many times _____ _____

C. EXPERIENCED PHYSICAL OR EMOTIONAL LOSS OF A SIGNIFICANT OTHER

Parent/Caretaker

C1. had a parent who as a child was put in foster care, orphanage, government school or detention farm/home _____ ___or many times _____ _____

C2. parent died through suicide, murder, or accident _____ ___or many times _____ _____

C3. lost a parent through separation or divorce _____ ___or many times _____ _____

C4. parent died as a result of substance abuse _____ ___or many times _____ _____

C5. parent was institutionalized (e.g., hospital or prison _____ ___or many times _____ _____

C6. parent was absent due to illness _____ ___or many times _____ _____

C7. parent died due to illness _____ ___or many times _____ _____

C8. lost parent in a natural disaster sucha as earthquake, hurricane or tornado _____ ___or many times _____ _____

C9. lost parent in a human-induced disaster _____ ___or many times _____ _____

Your Child   **CHILD'S AGES(S)**

C10. lost a child through death (suicide, murder or accident) _____ _____ ___or many times _____ _____

C11. lost a child through war _____ _____ ___or many times _____ _____

C12. lost a child as a result of substance abuse _____ _____ ___or many times _____ _____

C13. lost a child through institutionalization (hospital or prison) _____ _____ ___or many times _____ _____

C14. lost a child through death due to illness _____ _____ ___or many times _____ _____

C15. lost a child in a natural disaster such as hurricane, earthquake, etc. _____ _____ ___or many times _____ _____

C16. lost a child in a human-induced disaster such as fire, airplane crash _____ _____ ___or many times _____ _____

C17. lost a child in an accident in which you were driving _____ _____ ___or many times _____ _____

C18. lost a child through custody dispute _____ _____ ___or many times _____ _____

C19. lost a child as a result of kidnapping _____ _____ ___or many times _____ _____

C20. lost a child as a result of an abortion _____ _____ ___or many times _____ _____

C21. lost a child as a result of miscarriage _____ _____ ___or many times _____ _____

C22. unable to have children _____ ___or many times _____ _____

Spouse/Significant other (family members or love ones)

C23. lost a spouse/significant other through death (suicide, murder or accident) _____ ___or many times _____ _____

C24. lost a spouse/significant other through war _____ ___or many times _____ _____
C25. lost a spouse/significant other as a result of substance abuse _____ ___or many times _____ _____
C26. lost a spouse/significant other through institutionalization (hospital or prison) _____ ___or many times _____ _____
C27. lost a spouse/significant other through to death due to illness _____ ___or many times _____ _____
C28. lost a spouse/significant other in a natural disaster such as hurricane, earthquake, etc. _____ ___or many times _____ _____
C29. lost a spouse/significant other in a human-induced disaster such as fire, airplane crash _____ ___or many times _____ _____
C30. lost a spouse/significant other in an accident in which you were driving _____ ___or many times _____ _____
C31. lost a spouse/significant other as a result of kidnapping _____ ___or many times _____ _____
C32. lost a spouse/significant other as a result of a abortion _____ ___or many times _____ _____
C33. lost a spouse/significant other as a result of a miscarriage _____ ___or many times _____ _____
C34. lost a spouse/significant other as a result of infertility _____ ___or many times _____ _____
C35. spouse or significant other was unfaithful _____ ___or many times _____ _____

D. EXPOSED TO LIFE-THREATENING ILLNESS
D1. you were diagnosed with a life-threatening illness _____ ___or many times _____ _____
D2. a close family member was diagnosed with a life-threatening illness _____ ___or many times _____ _____

E. OBSERVED DOMESTIC VIOLENCE, NEGLECT PHYSICAL, OR EMOTIONAL ABUSE (ETC.)
E1. parent/caretaker physically violent with a family member or loved one _____ ___or many times _____ _____
E2. caretaker verbally abusive with a family member or loved one _____ ___or many times _____ _____
E3. sibling or other family member put in foster care or removed from the home because of neglect or abuse _____ ___or many times _____ _____
E4. caretaker used an object to hit a family member or loved one _____ ___or many times _____ _____
E5. caretaker burned or bruised a family member or loved one _____ ___or many times _____ _____
E6. saw a caretaker inflict injury that required medical attention (e.g., cast, stitches) which wasn't given _____ ___or many times _____ _____
E7. saw a caretaker inflict injury that required medical attention which was given _____ ___or many times _____ _____
E8. saw a caretaker participate in abuse of animals _____ ___or many times _____ _____
E9. saw a caretaker participate in murder of another human _____ ___or many times _____ _____
E10. saw a caretaker participate in ritualistic activities (e.g., killing animals and/or use of blood) _____ ___or many times _____ _____
E11. observed people dying or dead as a result of abuse _____ ___or many times _____ _____

E12. saw or heard parent/caretaker threaten to kill another family member or loved one with a weapon _____ ___or many times _____ _____

E13. saw or heard a parent/caretaker threaten to kill himself or herself with a weapon _____ ___or many times _____ _____

E14. saw caretaker try to kill a family member or loved one by shooting, stabbing, strangling _____ ___or many times _____ _____

E15. saw your spouse or partner hit, kicked, or thrown down by a family member or loved one _____ ___or many times _____ _____

E16. saw your spouse or partner hit, kick or throw another family member or loved one _____ ___or many times _____ _____

E17. loved one or parent/caretaker was institutionalized against their will by your parent/caretaker _____ ___or many times _____ _____

E18. loved one/parent/caretaker was the victim of a crime _____ ___or many times _____ _____

F. EXPERIENCED DOMESTIC VIOLENCE, NEGLECT

F1. you were removed from your home because of parental abuse/neglect _____ ___or many times _____ _____

F2. ignored by caretaker or partner _____ ___or many times _____ _____

F3. told you were stupid _____ ___or many times _____ _____

F4. ridiculed if you showed your feelings _____ ___or many times _____ _____

F5. special belongings (e.g., toys, blanket, pet) were taken away _____ ___or many times _____ _____

F6. made to wait for spankings or beatings _____ ___or many times _____ _____

F7. hit (spanked) with an object by parent/caretaker _____ ___or many times _____ _____

F8. not fed of punished by withholding food _____ ___or many times _____ _____

F9. adult urinated or defecated in front of you _____ ___or many times _____ _____

F10. adult urinated or defecated on you _____ ___or many times _____ _____

F11. adult spit on you _____ ___or many times _____ _____

F12. hit with a fist, kicked, or thrown down stairs or against a wall by a parent/caretaker or spouse/partner _____ ___or many times _____ _____

F13. punished in inhumane ways (e.g., tied or locked up) _____ ___or many times _____ _____

F14. burned or bruised by parent/caretaker or spouse/partner _____ ___or many times _____ _____

F15. required but did not get medical attention (e.g., stitches or cast) for wounds (broken bones, gashes) inflicted by caretaker or partner _____ ___or many times _____ _____

F16. required and received medical attention for wounds inflicted by caretaker or partner _____ ___or many times _____ _____

F17. told by caretaker or partner that you were crazy _____ ___or many times _____ _____

F18. threatened by caretaker/partner that he/she would "put you away" _____ ___or many times _____ _____

F19. institutionalized/hospitalized against your will by caretaker or partner _____ ___or many times _____ _____

F20. punished when you were found masturbating _____ ___or many times _____ _____

F21. told you were hurting or killing parent or caretaker if you disobeyed or disagreed _____ ___or many times _____ _____

F22. you were given enemas that felt punishing _____ ___or many times _____ _____

F23. threatened by caretaker or partner that he/she would kill you _____ ___or many times _____ _____

F24. forced to participate in abuse and killing of
animals   _____   ___or many times _____   _____
F25. forced to participate in abuse and killing of
humans   _____   ___or many times _____   _____
F26. attempted suicide   _____   ___or many times _____   _____
F27. inflicted injury upon yourself   _____   ___or many times _____   _____
F28. emotionally abused by caretaker or partner   _____   ___or many times _____   _____
F29. parent/caretaker threatened to abandon you   _____   ___or many times _____   _____
F30. parent/caretaker abandoned you   _____   ___or many times _____   _____
F31. felt unwanted as a child   _____   ___or many times _____   _____

G. OBSERVED SEXUAL ABUSE or RAPE

G1. observed adult masturbating or with an erection   _____   ___or many times _____   _____
G2. observed or heard adults engaging in sexual
activity   _____   ___or many times _____   _____
G3. observed sexual activity between and adult
and child   _____   ___or many times _____   _____
G4. observed genitals, breast, or buttocks during
direct or subtle invitation to engage in sexual
activity   _____   ___or many times _____   _____
G5. saw or heard a family member or loved forced
to have sex   _____   ___or many times _____   _____
G6. observed rape of parent or sibling   _____   ___or many times _____   _____
G7. observed rape of a non-family member   _____   ___or many times _____   _____
G8. observed rape of parent or sibling by two or
more assailants   _____   ___or many times _____   _____
G9. observed the rape of a non-family member by
two or more assailants   _____   ___or many times _____   _____
G10. someone else you care about was the victim of
a rape   _____   ___or many times _____   _____
G11. adult or older family member walked around
the house in his/her underwear   _____   ___or many times _____   _____

H. EXPERIENCED SEXUAL CONTACT AS A CHILD (under 18) WITH SOMEONE AT LEAST 5 YEARS OLDER THAN YOU

H1. felt sexual threat from family members/s or
loved one   _____   Who
_____   ___or many times _____   _____
H2. slept with adult/caretaker/family member   _____   Who
_____   ___or many times _____   _____
H3. slept with an adult who was nude   _____   Who
_____   ___or many times _____   _____
H4. family member exposed his/her genitals   _____   Who
_____   ___or many times _____   _____
H5. non-family member exposed his/her genitals   _____   Who
_____   ___or many times _____   _____
H6. non-family member touched, kissed, hugged, or
caressed you in a sexual way   _____   Who
_____   ___or many times _____   _____
H7. family member or loved one touched, kissed,
hugged, or caressed you in a sexual way   _____   Who
_____   ___or many times _____   _____

H8.   someone showed you sexually explicit movies
      or pictures or someone wanted to take nude or
      sexual movies or pictures of you   _____   Who
                                                          _____ ___or many times _____   _____

H9.   someone made you or tried to make you watch
      sexual activity   _____   Who
                                                          _____ ___or many times _____   _____

H10. someone talked to you about sexual things
      that you found disturbing   _____   Who
                                                          _____ ___or many times _____   _____

H11. engaged in sexual activity with a family member
      or relative   _____   Who
                                                          _____ ___or many times _____   _____

H12. engaged in sexual activity with a non-family
      member   _____   Who
                                                          _____ ___or many times _____   _____

H13. engaged in sexual activity against your wishes   _____   Who
                                                          _____ ___or many times _____   _____

H14. as a child, sought sexual activity with an adult
      or older child   _____   Who
                                                          _____ ___or many times _____   _____

H15. engaged in sexual activity which included
      vaginal intercourse   _____   Who
                                                          _____ ___or many times _____   _____

H16. engaged in sexual activity which included anal
      intercourse   _____   Who
                                                          _____ ___or many times _____   _____

H17. engaged in sexual activity which included oral sex _____   Who
                                                          _____ ___or many times _____   _____

H18. forced to have sex with an animal   _____   Who
                                                          _____ ___or many times _____   _____

H19. forced to have groups sex   _____   Who
                                                          _____ ___or many times _____   _____

H20. raped with an object   _____   Who
                                                          _____ ___or many times _____   _____

H21. engaged in sexual activity and were told it was
      your fault   _____   Who
                                                          _____ ___or many times _____   _____

H22. became aroused by unwanted sexual activity   _____   Who
                                                          _____ ___or many times _____   _____

H23. someone tried to engage you in unwanted sexual
      activity but it did not take place or was not   _____   Who
      completed
H24. persons watched while you were being sexually   _____ ___or many times _____   _____
      abused   _____   Who

                                                          _____ ___or many times _____   _____

I.   **EXPERIENCED SEXUAL ABUSE AS
      AN ADULT**
      Rape
I1.   someone tried to engage you in unwanted sexual
      activity as an adult but it did not take place/was
      not completed   _____   ___or many times _____   _____

I2. raped by someone you knew, such as a partner or date _____ ___or many times _____ _____

I3. raped by a stranger _____ ___or many times _____ _____

I4. experienced a rape by 2 or more assailants _____ ___or many times _____ _____

I5. kidnapped by a rapist _____ ___or many times _____ _____

I6. victim of physical or verbal assault by rapist _____ ___or many times _____ _____

I7. suffered physical injuries as a result of the rape _____ ___or many times _____ _____

I8. forced by the rapist to have oral sex _____ ___or many times _____ _____

I9. forced by the rapist to have vaginal intercourse _____ ___or many times _____ _____

I10. forced by the rapist to have anal sex _____ ___or many times _____ _____

I11. threatened with death during the rape _____ ___or many times _____ _____

I12. assaulted with a weapon as part of the rape _____ ___or many times _____ _____

Psychotherapist

I13. felt sexual threat or invitation from therapist _____ ___or many times _____ _____

I14. therapist wanted to meet you outside therapy _____ ___or many times _____ _____

I15. therapist tried to engage you in sexual activity that did not take place _____ ___or many times _____ _____

I16. therapist kissed, hugged, or caressed you in a sexual way _____ ___or many times _____ _____

I17. engaged in sexual activity with your therapist _____ ___or many times _____ _____

I18. therapist ended your therapy after engaging in sexual activity _____ ___or many times _____ _____

I19. you left therapy because of sexual advances made by your therapist _____ ___or many times _____ _____

I20. you left therapy because of sexual activity with your therapist _____ ___or many times _____ _____

I21. therapist ended your therapy in order to have sexual relationship with you _____ ___or many times _____ _____

I22. you filed charges because of sexual advances made by your therapist _____ ___or many times _____ _____

Clergy (e.g.priest/nun, minister, rabbi)

I23. felt sexual threat or invitation from your clergy _____ ___or many times _____ _____

I24. clergy tried to engage you in activity that did not take place _____ ___or many times _____ _____

I25. clergy kissed, hugged, or caressed you in a sexual way _____ ___or many times _____ _____

I26. you engaged in sexual activity with clergy _____ ___or many times _____ _____

I27. you left setting because of sexual advances made by clergy _____ ___or many times _____ _____

I28. you left setting because of sexual activity with clergy _____ ___or many times _____ _____

I29. lost a position because you would not engage in sexual activity with your clergy _____ ___or many times _____ _____

I30. lost a position because you engaged in sexual activity with your clergy _____ ___or many times _____ _____

I31. filed charges because of advances/harassment by your clergy _____ ___or many times _____ _____

Medical care provider (e.g., doctor,nurse,technician)

I32. felt sexual threat or invitation from your provider _____ ___or many times _____ _____

I33. provider examined you in a way that felt sexual _____ ___or many times _____ _____

I34. provider tried to engage you in sexual activity
that did not take place _____ ___or many times _____ _____

I35. provider kissed, hugged, or caressed you in a
sexual way _____ ___or many times _____ _____

I36. engaged in sexual activity with provider _____ ___or many times

I37. left provider's care because of sexual advances
made by your provider _____ ___or many times

I38. left provider's care because of sexual activity
with your provider _____ ___or many times

I39. provider terminated care because you would
not engage in sexual activity _____ ___or many times

I40. provider terminated care because sexual activity
took place _____ ___or many times

I41. you filed charges because of advances or
harassment by your provider _____ ___or many times

Supervisor (e.g., employer, teacher)

I42. supervisor tried to engage you in sexual activity
that did not take place _____ ___or many times _____ _____

I43. supervisor kissed, hugged or caressed you in a
sexual way _____ ___or many times _____ _____

I44. engaged in sexual activity with supervisor _____ ___or many times _____ _____

I45. you left setting because of sexual advances made
by your supervisor _____ ___or many times _____ _____

I46. you left setting because of sexual activity with
your supervisor _____ ___or many times

I47. lost your position because you would not engage
in sexual activity with your supervisor _____ ___or many times

I48. lost your position because you engaged in sexual
activity with your supervisor _____ ___or many timesI.

I49. filed charges because of advances or harassment
by your supervisor _____ ___or many times

**J. EXPERIENCED JOB LOSS OR
UNEMPLOYMENT** _____ ___or many times

K. INVOLVED IN LITIGATION
K1. you filed suit (other than mentioned previously _____ ___or many times
K2. you had suit filed against you _____ ___or many times

**L. OBSERVED CRIMINAL ACTIVITY OTHER
THAN RAPE SUCH AS A MURDER,
ASSAULT, OR MUGGING** _____ ___or many times

**M. EXPERIENCED CRIMINAL ACTIVITY
OTHER THAN RAPE**
1 harmed psychologically or emotionally through
criminal activity such as mugging or robbery _____ ___or many times
1 harmed physically as a result of mugging or
robbery, etc _____ ___or many times

N. FELT RESPONSIBLE FOR THE SERIOUS
INJURY OR DEATH OF ANOTHER PERSON
IN A NON WAR RELATED SITUATION   _____   ___or many times

O. EXPERIENCED CRIMINAL ACTIVITY
OTHER THAN RAPE

O1. in a paid or volunteer work situation, you heard
about physically and/or emotionally abusive
events or experiences of others   _____   ___or many times

O2. in a non-work related situation, you heard about
physically and/or emotionally abusive events or
experiences of others   _____   ___or many times

P. OTHER TRAUMA (Please specify)

_____   _____   ___or many times

Q1. HAVE YOU DEALT WITH THESE ISSUES
IN THERAPY?   YES___ NO___

Q2. WAS IT HELPFUL?_____

1	2	3	4	5	6
not at all helpful	slightly helpful	somewhat helpful	quite helpful	very helpful	extremely helpful

R. HOW DISTRESSING WAS THIS QUESTIONNAIRE TO FILL OUT?

6 Extremely distressing
5 Very distressing
4 Quite distressing
3 Somewhat distressing
2 Slightly distressing
1 Not at all distressing

PLEASE USE TS SPACE FOR ANY COMMENTS YOU WOULD LIKE TO MAKE

_____

_____

**THANK YOU FOR COMPLETING THE QUESTIONAIRRE. WE WOULD LIKE TO ENCOURAGE YOU TO
TALK TO YOUR THERAPIST ABOUT ANY THOUGHTS OR FEELINGS YOU MAY HAVE RELATED TO
THE QUESTIONNAIRE.**

ID#_____   Age_____   Sex (circle one)   M   F   Date_____

TSI Life Event Questionnaire (Short Form)
Revision 3 (3/95)

We would like to know which of the following types of events you may have experienced. *BEFORE EACH CATEGORY PLEASE WRITE:*

(Y) YES to indicate you have experienced such an event,
(NS) NOT SURE to indicate you think it is possible that you have, or
(N) NO to indicate you have not experienced such an event.

In the space **AFTER** the item, write your **AGE(S)** when the event occurred.

**YOUR
AGE(S)**

_____ 1. Experienced war, military, or holocaust.   _____

_____ 2. Experienced a natural or human–induced disaster (e.g., fire).   _____

_____ 3. Experienced physical or emotional loss of a significant other.   _____

_____ 4. Exposed to life–threatening illness.   _____

_____ 5. Experienced life–threatening illness.   _____

_____ 6. Observed domestic violence, neglect or physical abuse.   _____

_____ 7. Observed emotional abuse of significant other.   _____

_____ 8. Experienced domestic violence, neglect, or physical abuse as a child.   _____

_____ 9. Experienced domestic violence, neglect, or physical abuse as an adult.   _____

_____10. Experienced emotional abuse.   _____

_____11. Observed sexual abuse or rape.   _____

_____12. Experienced sexual contact before age 18 with someone in your family
          who was at least 5 years older   _____

_____13. Experienced sexual contact before age 18 with someone other
          than a family member, who was at least 5 years older.   _____

_____14. Observed criminal activity other than rape such as a murder, assault,
          assault, or mugging.   _____

_____15. Experienced criminal activity other than rape.   _____

_____16. Felt responsible for the serious injury or death of another person in
          a non–war–related situation.   _____

_____17. Heard about physically and/or emotionally abusive or traumatic
          events or experiences of others you care about.   _____

_____18. Experienced rape or other sexual assault at age 18 or older.   _____

_____19. Other trauma (please specify)_____   _____

War-Zone Related PTSD Scale of the SCL-90-R
(WZ-PTSD Scale)

Type of Population
Adults with War-Zone (combat) related PTSD

Cost
Need to purchase the SCL-90-R.

Copyright

Languages
English

What It Measures
Continuous measure of PTSD symptomatology, with cutoff scores predictive of PTSD diagnosis.

Measure Content Survey, Procedure, or Process
Consists of 25 SCL-90-R items found to discriminate combat veterans with and without PTSD. The Brief Symptom Inventory (BSI), A 55-item version of the SCL-90-R, contains 20 of the WZ-PTSD scale items.

Theoretical Orientation Summary
Empirical, psychometric approach.

Time Estimate

Administration	Scoring
10–15 minutes	10–15 minutes

Equipment Needed

Paper & Pencil	Computer	Basic Psychophysiological	Specialized Equipment
X			

Psychometric Maturity

Under Construction	Basic Properties Intact	Mature
	X	

Psychometric Properties Summary
In a sample of 202 combat veterans the WZ-PTSD scale had very high internal consistency (.97) and item-total correlations ranged from .67 to .83. For the prediction of a PTSD diagnosis based on the SCID or the CAPS, the optimal cutoff for the WZ-PTSD scale was 1.3, yielding a sensitivity of .90, a specificity of .65, an efficiency of .82, and a kappa of .58. In this sample, only the Mississippi Scale had greater diagnostic utility. In a cross-validation sample of 101 combat veterans the optimal cutoff score for the WZ-PTSD scale was again 1.3, with a sensitivity of .87, a specificity of .72, an efficiency of .81, and a kappa of .59. In the cross-validation sample the WZ-PTSD scale had the highest diagnostic utility of all of the measures considered.

Particular Sensitivity

Age	Change over Time	Culture / Ethnicity	Gender	Geography / Climate	Sexual Orientation	Socioeconomic Status	Urban / Rural
?	?	?	?	?	?	?	?

Estimate of Number of In-Process Studies

Unpublished References

Weathers, F. W., Litz, B. T., Herman, D. S., Keane, T. M., Steinberg, H. R., Huska, J. A., & Kraemer, H. C. The utility of the SCL-90-R for the diagnosis of war-zone related PTSD. Manuscript submitted for publication.

Published References

Keane, T. M., Malloy, P. F., & Fairbank, J. A. (1984). Empirical development of an MMPI subscale for the assessment of combat-related post-traumatic stress disorder. *Journal of Consulting and Clinical Psychology, 52,* 888–891.

Koretzky, M. B., & Peck, A. H. (1990). Validation and cross-validation of the PTSD subscale of the MMPI with civilian trauma victims. *Journal of Clinical Psychology, 46,* 296–300.

Lyons, J. A., & Keane, T. M. (1992). Keane PTSD scale: MMPI and MMPI-2 update. *Journal of Traumatic Stress, 5,* 111–117.

Watson, C. G., Kucala, T., & Manifold, V. (1986). A cross-validation of the Keane and Penk MMPI scales as measures of post-traumatic stress disorder. *Journal of Clinical Psychology, 42,* 727–732.

Key Words

Population	Stressor	Topic
adults soldiers veterans	combat	assessment diagnosis

Reference Citation for This Review

Weathers, F. W. (1996). Psychometric review of War-Zone Related PTSD Scale of the SCL-90-R (WZ-PTSD Scale). B. H. Stamm (Ed.). *Measurement of stress, trauma, and adaptation.* Lutherville, MD: Sidran Press.

Measure Contact Name

Frank W. Weathers, Ph.D.
Address: National Center for PTSD (116B-2)
                   Boston DVA Medical Center
                   Boston, MA 02130 USA
Phone: 617.232.9500 x4130/4136
Fax: 617.278.4501
E-mail: Weathers.Frank_W@Boston.VA.GOV

West Haven Secondary Trauma Scale (WHSTS)
National Center for PTSD Review

Type of Population
Adult Veterans

Cost
Available from the author at no charge.

Copyright

Languages
English

What It Measures
Secondary trauma following warzone trauma exposure.

Measure Content Survey, Procedure, or Process
This questionnaire assesses secondary trauma following warzone exposure, particularly traumatic experiences associated with homecoming. Scales are available for Secondary Trauma Exposure and for Social Support.

Theoretical Orientation Summary

Time Estimate

Administration	Scoring
10 minutes	5 minutes

Equipment Needed

Paper & Pencil	Computer	Basic Psychophysiological	Specialized Equipment
X			

Psychometric Maturity

Under Construction	Basic Properties Intact	Mature
X		

Psychometric Properties Summary
Reliability Retest (Unspecified Interval) r=.90 (24 veterans)

Validity Predictive (Correlates more strongly [.27-.32 vs.-.17-.07] with CAPS and Mississippi PTSD Scale than Combat Exposure Scale)

Normative Data available on 95 Vietnam veterans in inpatient PTSD treatment

Particular Sensitivity

Age	Change over Time	Culture / Ethnicity	Gender	Geography / Climate	Sexual Orientation	Socioeconomic Status	Urban / Rural
?	?	?	?	?	?	?	?

Estimate of Number of In-Process Studies

unknown

Unpublished References

Lubin, H., & Johnson, D. (1994). Measuring the trauma of return: The West Haven Secondary Trauma Scale (WHSTS). Presented at the Annual Convention of the International Society for Traumatic Stress Studies. Chicago, IL.

Published References

unknown

General Comments

Key Words

Population	Stressor	Topic
adult veterans	civilian post-war trauma	research secondary traumatic stress

Reference Citation for This Review

Ford, J. (1996). Psychometric review of West Have Secondary Trauma Scale (WHSTS). In B. H. Stamm (Ed.). *Measurement of stress, trauma, and adaptation.* Lutherville, MD: Sidran Press.

Reviewer Contact Name

Julian Ford, Ph.D.

Address: National Center for PTSD (116-D)
VA Medical Center
White River Junction, VT 05009 USA
Phone: 802.296.5132
Fax: 802.296.5135
E-mail: Julian.Ford@Dartmouth.Edu

Measure Contact Name

David Read Johnson, Ph.D.,

Address: National Center for PTSD Clinical
Neuroscience Division
VA Medical Center (116-A)
950 Campbell Ave
West Haven, CT 05616 USA
Phone: 203.932.5711 ext. 4454
Fax: 203.937.3481
E-mail:

The When Bad Things Happen Scale

Type of Population

Children and adolescents with at least a third grade reading level. Possibly younger if the child is assisted. An audio tape recording (with a woman's voice) is available.

Cost

Free to all of those who agree to share the raw data they collect in order to help establish the scale's psychometric properties.

Copyright

The self-report questionnaire is copyrighted.

Languages

A Hebrew version of the first revision of the WBTH scale (which is in its third revision) is available. It has been used to study children's reactions to the Gulf War in Israel.

What It Measures

All *DSM-IV* symptoms of PTSD, additional PTSD symptoms as manifested in children, and associated symptoms (anxiety, sadness, omen formation, survivor guilt, guilt/self-blame, fantasy denial, self-destructive behavior, dissociative responses, antisocial behavior, risk-taking behavior, and changed eating habits). Each symptom is assessed by two or more questions. The scale allows diagnoses to be made, and it allows an overall severity score to be computed.

Measure Content Survey, Procedure, or Process

95 questions about frequency of experiencing PTSD symptoms. The child checks "Never," "Some," or "Lots."

Theoretical Orientation Summary

Time Estimate

Administration	Scoring
10–20 minutes	5–15 minutes

Equipment Needed

Paper & Pencil	Computer	Basic Psychophysiological	Specialized Equipment
X			

Psychometric Maturity

Under Construction	Basic Properties Intact	Mature
X		

Psychometric Properties Summary

Yet to be established. However, when 15 adolescents in a children's psychiatric ward were administered The When Bad Things Happen (WBTH) Scale and a self-report form of the Pynoos et al. Childhood PTSD-Reaction Index (CPTSD-RI), the two scales correlated .84 (Moller-Thau & Fletcher, 1995). When PTSD diagnosis was made using the CPTSD-RI when a child scored in the Moderate, Severe, or Very Severe PTSD ranges, the WBTH scale agreed that 10 children had PTSD and three did not, but the WBTH scale indicated that two children had PTSD that the

CPTSD-RI said did not. The kappa statistic for this level of agreement is .67, which is indicative of good agreement (Moller-Thau & Fletcher, 1995).

Particular Sensitivity

Age	Change over Time	Culture / Ethnicity	Gender	Geography / Climate	Sexual Orientation	Socioeconomic Status	Urban / Rural
X	?	?	?	?	?	?	?

Estimate of Number of In-Process Studies

4. One of these is a national effort to gather data for validation for the interview and other related interviews and scales. If you are interested in joining this effort, please contact Ken Fletcher at the addresses and telephones below.

Unpublished References

Moller-Thau, D., & Fletcher, K. E. (1995). Diagnosing childhood PTSD with two self-report measures: The childhood PTSD Reaction Index and The When Bad Things Happen Scale. Yeshiva University and University of Massachusetts Medical Center. Unpublished manuscript.

Published References

General Comments

This scale is intended for both clinical and research use. The intent is to eventually pare down the items during the norming process. This scale can be administered to nontraumatized comparison groups as well, as long as a stressor is provided (either the same stressor as the exposed group or the most stressful event that the nontraumatized child has been exposed to). This scale is one of a set. See also "Childhood PTSD Interview," "Childhood PTSD Interview—Parent Form," and the "Parent Report of the Child's Reaction to Stress." IBM-compatible data entry programs are available from the author for all of these scales. The data entry programs run in the data entry creation program distributed (for free from other users or academic computer departments or for $50 from the Center for Disease Control or the World Health Organization). EPI INFO programs allow data bases to be created which can be analyzed on a basic level within EPI INFO itself and by other statistical programs (such as SPSS, SAS, and Systat) or by databases and spreadsheets that will read dBase file formats.

Key Words

Population	Stressor	Topic
adolescents children	any	assessment diagnosis research

Reference Citation for This Review

Fletcher, K. E. (1996). Psychometric review of The When Bad Things Happen Scale. In B. H. Stamm (Ed.). *Measurement of stress, trauma, and adaptation*. Lutherville, MD: Sidran Press.

Measure Contact Name

Kenneth E. Fletcher, Ph.D.

Address:	University of Massachusetts Medical Center
	Psychiatry Dept.
	55 Lake Avenue North
	Worcester, MA 01655-0001 USA
Phone:	508.856.3329
Fax:	508.856.6426
E-Mail:	FLETCHER@UMASSMED.UMMED.EDU

When Bad Things Happen Sample Items

- Was the bad thing scary?
- Do you think about the bad thing now even when you do not want to?
- Do you daydream about the bad thing?
- Do you try to push away thoughts about the bad thing and think about other things?
- Do you sometimes feel like you can not feel anything?
- Like you are a robot?
- Or like you are made out of stone?
- Are you on the look out for something bad to happen?
- Since the bad thing happened, do you think you can tell the future?
- Do you like doing unsafe things since the bad thing?
- Like doing crazy things that might get you or someone else hurt?

Women's War-Time Stressor Scale

Type of Population

Women who have served in military or civilization capacities in a war zone or during war time.

Cost

Free

Copyright

Languages

English

What It Measures

The scale is a self-report measure of various stressors experienced during war time.

Measure Content Survey, Procedure, or Process

While instruments have effectively measured war zone stress in males, the stressors specific to women in a war zone have not been fully addressed. This scale encompasses potential stressors related to the quality of care provided or observed, significant interpersonal difficulties/discriminatory experiences as a woman and/or minority, exposure to severe physical and environmental stressors (including threat to life), and the catastrophic exposure to end-of-life events, that is, situations specifically involving the dying and the dead.

Theoretical Orientation Summary

Cognitive behavioral

Time Estimate

Administration	Scoring
NA	NA

Equipment Needed

Paper & Pencil	Computer	Basic Psychophysiological	Specialized Equipment
X			

Psychometric Maturity

Under Construction	Basic Properties Intact	Mature
	X	

Psychometric Properties Summary

The original WWSS has sound psychometric properties with subsets of women who served in the Vietnam era. Data suggest that wartime exposure has multiple components in a female population. Vocational role, physical context, and social milieu all emerged as significant aspects of wartime participation. Analysis of psychometric data also confirmed the link between total wartime exposure and both self-reported symptoms of PTSD and general psychological distress.

Particular Sensitivity

Age	Change over Time	Culture / Ethnicity	Gender	Geography / Climate	Sexual Orientation	Socioeconomic Status	Urban / Rural
?	?	?	X	?	?	?	?

Estimate of Number of In-Process Studies
Unknown

Unpublished References
Unknown

Published References
Wolfe, J., & Brown, P. J. (1993). Development of a War-Time Stressor Scale for Women. *Psychological Assessment: A Journal of Consulting and Clinical Psychology, 5* (3), 330–335.

Key Words

Population	Stressor	Topic
adult women	war zone experience	assessment diagnosis research

Reference Citation for This Review
Wolf, J. (1996). Psychometric review of Woman's War-Time Stressors Scale. B. H. Stamm (Ed.). *Measurement of stress, trauma, and adaptation.* Lutherville, MD: Sidran Press

Measure Contact Name
Jessica Wolfe, Ph.D.

Address: VA Medical Center
                 National Center for PTSD
                 Women's Health Science Division (116B-3)
                 150 S. Huntington Ave.
                 Boston, MA 02130 USA

Phone: 617.232.9500 x4129, x4145
Fax: 617.278.4515

World Assumptions Scale

Type of Population
   Adults; any

Cost
   Free

Copyright

Languages
   English

What It Measures
   Three fundamental assumptions that generally go unquestioned and unchallenged: benevolence of the world (personal and impersonal), meaningfulness of the world, and self-worth.

Measure Content Survey, Procedure, or Process
   This is a 32-item questionnaire with three subscales that measure assumptions about the benevolence of the world, the meaningfulness of the world, and self-worth. Respondents use 6-point Likert scales to indicate the extent of their agreement or disagreement with each statement. Higher scores indicate greater belief in the three assumptions; lower scores indicate more shattering of assumptions (Janoff-Bulman, 1992).

Theoretical Orientation Summary
   The instrument is based on a theoretical perspective that views trauma in terms of the shattering of fundamental assumptions (Janoff-Bulman, 1992).

Time Estimate

Administration	Scoring
5–10 minutes	5–10 minutes

Equipment Needed

Paper & Pencil	Computer	Basic Psychophysiological	Specialized Equipment
X			

Psychometric Maturity

Under Construction	Basic Properties Intact	Mature
		X

Psychometric Properties Summary
   Reliabilities for the three subscales are .87 for benevolence of the world, .76 for meaningfulness of the world, and .80 for self-worth.

Particular Sensitivity

Age	Change over Time	Culture / Ethnicity	Gender	Geography / Climate	Sexual Orientation	Socioeconomic Status	Urban / Rural
?	X	?	X	?	?	?	?

Estimate of Number of In-Process Studies

Unknown

Unpublished References

Unknown

Published References

For a major review, see Janoff-Bulman, R. (1992). *Shattered assumptions: Towards a new psychology of trauma.* New York: The Free Press.

General Comments

The WAS is not restricted to use with trauma populations.

Key Words

Population	Stressor	Topic
adult	any	assessment research

Reference Citation for This Review

Janoff-Bulman, R. (1996). Psychometric review of World Assumption Scale. In B. H. Stamm (Ed.). *Measurement of stress, trauma, and adaptation.* Lutherville, MD: Sidran Press.

Measure Contact Name

Ronnie Janoff-Bulman, Ph.D.

Address: Department of Psychology
             University of Massachusetts
             Amherst, MA 01003 USA
Phone: 413.545.0264
Fax:
E-mail: JANBUL@PSYCH.UMASS.EDU

World Assumptions Scale

1Using the scale below, please select the number that indicates how much you agree or disagree with each statement. Please answer honestly. Thanks.

1.	2.	3.	4.	5.	6.
strong disagree	moderately disagree	slightly disagree	slightly agree	moderately agree	strongly agree

1. _____ Misfortune is least likely to strike worthy, decent people.
2. _____ People are naturally unfriendly and unkind.*
3. _____ Bad events are distributed to people at random.*
4. _____ Human nature is basically good.
5. _____ The good things that happen in this world far outnumber the bad.
6. _____ The course of our lives is largely determined by chance.*
7. _____ Generally, people deserve what they get in this world.
8. _____ I often think I am no good at all.*
9. _____ There is more good than evil in the world.
10. _____ I am basically a lucky person.
11. _____ People's misfortunes result from mistakes they have made.
12. _____ People don't really care what happens to the next person.*
13. _____ I usually behave in ways that are likely to maximize good results for me.
14. _____ People will experience good fortune if they themselves are good.
15. _____ Life is too full of uncertainties that are determined by chance.*
16. _____ When I think about it, I consider myself very lucky.
17. _____ I almost always make an effort to prevent bad things from happening to me.
18. _____ I have a low opinion of myself.*
19. _____ By and large, good people get what they deserve in this world.
20. _____ Through our actions we can prevent bad things from happening to us.
21. _____ Looking at my life, I realize that chance events have worked out well for me.
22. _____ If people took preventive actions, most misfortune could be avoided.
23. _____ I take the actions necessary to protect myself against misfortune.
24. _____ In general, life is mostly a gamble.*
25. _____ The world is a good place.
26. _____ People are basically kind and helpful.
27. _____ I usually behave so as to bring about the greatest good for me.
28. _____ I am very satisfied with the kind of person I am.
29. _____ When bad things happen, it is typically because people have not taken the necessary actions to protect themselves.
30. _____ If you look closely enough, you will see that the world is full of goodness.
31. _____ I have reason to be ashamed of my personal character.*
32. _____ I am luckier than most people.

* reverse score

Scoring

Reverse score the asterisked statements and then sum the responses for each of the three subscales, as indicated below.

Benevolence of the World: items 2+4+5+9+12+25+26+30

Meaningfulness of the World: items 1+3+6+7+11+14+15+19+20+22+24+29

Self-Worth: items 8+10+13+16+17+18+21+23+27+28+31+32

This instrument, by Ronnie Janoff-Bulman, may be reproduced without charge and freely distributed, as long as no funds are exchanged.

World View Survey

Type of Population
Children and adolescents 12 or older, and adults.

Cost
Free to all of those who agree to share the raw data they collect in order to help establish the scale's psychometric properties.

Copyright

Languages
English

What It Measures
Beliefs that may be affected by exposure to traumatic stressors.

Measure Content Survey, Procedure, or Process
75 self-report statements about current beliefs, with 4-point agree/disagree rating scales. Mention of exposure to specific stressor is not made. Five a priori scales of beliefs can be formed: 1) assumption of safety, security, and enjoyability of the world; 2) assumption of the predictability, orderliness, justness, understandability, certainty, and controllability of the world; 3) assumption of self-worth and sense of empowerment; 4) assumption of the (trust)worthiness of others; and 5) possible positive beliefs that may result from exposure to stress. An audio tape recording (in a woman's voice) is available.

Theoretical Orientation Summary
Similar to Janoff-Bulman's (1992) notion of shattered assumptions.

Time Estimate

Administration	Scoring
15–20 minutes	10–15 minutes

Equipment Needed

Paper & Pencil	Computer	Basic Psychophysiological	Specialized Equipment
X			

Psychometric Maturity

Under Construction	Basic Properties Intact	Mature
X		

Psychometric Properties Summary
None so far

Particular Sensitivity

Age	Change over Time	Culture / Ethnicity	Gender	Geography / Climate	Sexual Orientation	Socioeconomic Status	Urban / Rural
?	?	?	?	?	?	?	?

Estimate of Number of In-Process Studies

2

Unpublished References

Unknown

Published References

Janoff-Bulman, R. (1992). *Shattered assumptions: Toward a new psychology of trauma.* New York: The Free Press.

General Comments

Not restricted to use with trauma populations. An IBM-compatible data entry program is available from the author for this scale. The data entry program runs in the data entry creation program distributed (for free from other users or academic computer departments or for $50 from the Center for Disease Control or the World Health Organization). EPI INFO programs allow data bases to be created which can be analyzed on a basic level within EPI INFO itself and by other statistical programs (such as SPSS, SAS, and Systat) or by databases and spreadsheets that will read dBase file formats.

Key Words

Population	Stressor	Topic
adolescents adults	any	measure development research

Reference Citation for This Review

Fletcher, K.E. (1996). Psychometric review of World View Survey. In B. H. Stamm (Ed.). *Measurement of stress, trauma, and adaptation.* Lutherville, MD: Sidran Press.

Measure Contact Name

Kenneth E. Fletcher, Ph.D.
Address: University of Massachusetts Medical Center
                   Psychiatry Dept.
                   55 Lake Avenue North
                   Worcester, MA 01655-0001 USA
Phone: 508-856-3329
Fax: 508-856-6426
E-mail: FLETCHER@UMASSMED.UMMED.EDU

World View Survey Sample Items

- You can never know what to expect next in life.
- The world is a dangerous place to live.
- Life is mostly *un*fair.
- When bad things happen to you, it is mostly your own fault.
- Nowadays I feel like every new day I am alive is a gift.
- I am a jinx.
- There really isn't much to be afraid of in life.
- Sometimes I feel ugly all over.
- I have strong religious beliefs.
- I feel cut off from people these days.
- I feel like I have control over my life.
- Life is confusing.
- I do not deserve all the bad things that have happened to me in my life.